CW00546448

China Insights

This book series collects and presents cutting-edge studies on various issues that have emerged during the process of China's social and economic transformation, and promotes a comprehensive understanding of the economic, political, cultural and religious aspects of contemporary China. It brings together academic endeavors by contemporary Chinese researchers in various social science and related fields that record, interpret and analyze social phenomena that are unique to Chinese society, its reforms and rapid transition. This series offers a key English-language resource for researchers and students in China studies and related subjects, as well as for general interest readers looking to better grasp today's China. The book series is a cooperation project between Springer and China Social Science Press of China.

More information about this series at http://www.springer.com/series/13591

Lin Li

The Chinese Road
of the Rule of Law

CHINA SOCIAL SCIENCES PRESS

Lin Li
Institute of Law
Chinese Academy of Social Sciences
Beijing
China

Translated by Xiaoqing Bi, CASS Law Institute, Beijing, China

Published with financial support of the Innovation Program of the Chinese Academy of Social Sciences.

ISSN 2363-7579 ISSN 2363-7587 (electronic)
China Insights
ISBN 978-981-10-8964-0 ISBN 978-981-10-8965-7 (eBook)
https://doi.org/10.1007/978-981-10-8965-7

Jointly published with China Social Sciences Press

The printed edition is not for sale in China Mainland. Customers from China Mainland please order the print book from: China Social Sciences Press.

Library of Congress Control Number: 2018935880

Printed on acid-free paper

This Springer imprint is published by the registered company Springer Nature Singapore Pte Ltd.
part of Springer Nature
The registered company address is: 152 Beach Road, #21-01/04 Gateway East, Singapore 189721, Singapore

Series Foreword

Since the Opium War, modern China has come under attack and been bullied for its backwardness; this cultural circumstance has given many Chinese people a psychological inferiority complex, as China has lagged behind other countries technologically, institutionally, and culturally. Efforts to change the situation in which Western countries were strong but China was weak and to revitalize China needed to start with cultural criticism and culture renovation. Therefore, the Chinese people turned their eyes to the outside world and learned from Japan, Europe, the USA, and even Soviet Russia. We have always been overwhelmed by stress and anxiety and have had a burning desire to reverse the state of being bullied as a result of underdevelopment, poverty, and weakness and to catch up with and surpass the Western powers. In pursuing the more than one-hundred-year-old dream of building a powerful country and reviving China, we have focused on understanding and learning from others, but seldom, if ever, have others learned from and understood us. This has not greatly changed in the course of modernization since China's reform and opening up in 1978. The translation and introduction of many Western works in the 1980s and 1990s is a very good example. This is the history of the Chinese people's understanding of the relationship between China and the rest of the world since the beginning of modern times.

At the same time, in pursuing the dream of turning China into a powerful country and rejuvenating it through material (technological) criticism, institutional criticism, and cultural criticism, the Chinese people have struggled to find a path that would make the country prosperous and the people strong while preventing the country from being ruined and the race from being destroyed. This path first represents a thought, a banner, and a soul. The key issue has been what kind of thought, banner, and soul can save the country, making it prosperous and the people strong. For more than one hundred years, the Chinese people have constantly carried out experiments and attempts amidst humiliation, failure, and anxiety. They have experienced failure in adopting advanced Western technology and thought on the basis of safeguarding China's feudal system and practicing a constitutional monarchy after the collapse of the Western capitalist political path and a great setback in worldwide socialism in the early 1990s. The Chinese people ultimately embarked on a path toward a successful revolution with national independence and liberation; in particular, they have adopted a path leading to the socialist modernization of China—a road toward socialism with Chinese characteristics—by combining the theoretical logic of scientific socialism with the historical logic of China's social development. After more than 30 years of reform and opening up, China's socialist market economy has rapidly developed; tremendous achievements have been made in economic, political, cultural, and social constructions; comprehensive national strength, cultural soft power, and international influence have substantially improved; and a great success has been achieved in socialism with Chinese characteristics. Although the latter project has not yet become full-fledged, its systems and institutions have basically taken shape. After more than one hundred years of pursuing dreams, China is rising among the nations of the world with a greater degree of confidence in the path it has chosen, the theory it has adopted, and the institutions it has created.

Meanwhile, we should be aware that given the long-standing cognition and cultural psychology of learning from Western countries; we seldom take the initiative in showcasing ourselves—historical China and current China in reality—to the world, though China has emerged as a great world power. Due to a deeply rooted view that "Western countries are strong and China is weak," developed through Western-Chinese cultural exchanges, Western people and nations seldom have a sense of Chinese history or the current developments in China, let alone an understanding of China's developmental path and such in-depth issues as the scientificity and effectiveness of China's theory and institutions or their unique value for and contributions to human civilization. As self-recognition is not displayed, the "China Collapse Theory," "China Threat Theory," "China State Capitalism," and other so-called theories coined by certain people with ulterior motives and differing political views have been widely spread.

During our development, based on "crossing the river by feeling the stones," we have paid attention to learning from Western countries, understanding the world and learning to know ourselves through Western experience and discourse but have neglected self-recognition and efforts to let others know us. When we strive to become part of the world in a more tolerant and friendly way, we are not objectively, truly understood. Therefore, we should describe the path to the success of socialism with Chinese characteristics, tell Chinese stories, disseminate Chinese experiences, use international expressions to show a real China to the world, and help people around the world realize that the Western manner of modernization is not the endpoint of human historical evolution and that socialism with Chinese characteristics is also a valuable treasure of human thought. This is undoubtedly a very important task for an academic cultural researcher with a sense of justice and responsibility.

In this connection, the Chinese Academy of Social Sciences organized its top-notch experts and scholars and several external experts to write the China Insights series. This series not only provides an overview of China's path, theories, and institutions but also objectively describes China's current development in the areas of political institutions, human rights, the rule of law, the economic system, finance, social governance, social security, population policies, values, religious faith, ethnic policies, rural issues, urbanization, industrialization, ecology, ancient civilization, literature, art, etc., thus depicting China in a way that helps readers visualize these topics.

We hope that this series will help domestic readers more correctly understand the course of the more than 100 years of China's modernization and more rationally look at current difficulties, enhance the urgency for and national confidence in comprehensively intensifying reform, build a consensus on reform and development and gather strength in this regard, as well as deepen foreign readers' understanding of China, thus fostering a better international environment for China's development.

Beijing, China   Zhao Jianying
January 2014

Contents

Chapter 1
Introduction: The Road and Theory of Socialist Rule of Law with Chinese Characteristics

The Decision of the CPC Central Committee concerning Several Major Issues in Comprehensively Advancing Governance by Law, adopted at the Fourth Plenary Session of the Eighteenth CPC Central Committee (hereinafter referred to as the Decision), has for the first time in history made an overall strategic arrangement in the form of the highest-level political document of the ruling party for the construction of the system of socialist rule of law with Chinese characteristics and a socialist state under the rule of law, for promoting and safeguarding the construction of socialism with Chinese characteristics, for modernizing the system and capacity of state governance, and for deepening in an all-round way various reforms under new situation by comprehensively advancing governance by law and strengthening the construction of the rule of law, thereby providing important institutional and legal safeguards for building China into a moderately well-off society in an all-round way and for realizing the Chinese dream of rejuvenating the Chinese nation. The Decision expounds the CPC's political idea and strategic thinking of ruling the country by law and draws a grand blueprint of construction of socialist state under the rule of law. As a programmatic document on comprehensive advancement of ruling the country by law, it is of profound realistic and historical significance.

1.1 Taking the Road of Socialist Rule of Law with Chinese Characteristics

The road of socialist rule of law with Chinese characteristics is the concentrated embodiment of the achievements and experiences, as well as the only correct road, of the construction of socialist rule of law in China. At its very beginning, the Decision unequivocally makes the important assertion that China must adhere to the road and construct the system of socialist rule of law with Chinese characteristics and build itself into a socialist country under the rule of law, thereby clarifying the connotation,

L. Li, *The Chinese Road of the Rule of Law*, China Insights,
https://doi.org/10.1007/978-981-10-8965-7_1

defining the nature, and pointing out the direction of the work of comprehensively advancing governance by law.

The question of road is the most basic question because road determines the fate and the future. The socialist road with Chinese characteristics is the product of the combination of the basic principles of scientific socialism and the actual situation and characteristics of the times in China, the basic achievements made by the CPC and the Chinese people in the long-term practice, and a correct road that is deeply rooted in the Chinese soil, reflects the will of the Chinese people, and adapts to the demands of the progress of China and development of times. The socialist road with Chinese characteristics means that China should, under the leadership of the CPC, proceed from the basic national situations, take economic construction as the center, adhere to the Four Cardinal Principles and to the reform and opening up, liberate and develop social productive forces, construct socialist market economy, socialist democratic politics, advanced socialist culture, socialist harmonious society, and socialist ecological civilization, promote the comprehensive development of the human being, gradually realize the common prosperity of the whole people, and built itself into a prosperous, democratic, civilized, harmonious and modernized socialist country. The road of socialist rule of law with Chinese characteristics is an indispensable and important component of the road of socialism with Chinese characteristics and the basis of comprehensive advancement of governance by law and construction a socialist state under the rule of law.

The road of socialist rule of law with Chinese characteristics is a choice made by history and the Chinese people, as well as an inevitable demand of social development in China. China is an ancient country with a history over 5000 years. The traditional Chinese legal system is a long-standing, well-established and unique legal system in the world. Ancient China had made great contributions to the legal civilization of mankind. After the Opium War in 1840, China was gradually reduced to a semi-colonial and semi-feudal society. To change the suffering fate of the state and the nation, some people with lofty ideals tried to transplant the western political system and the rule of law model into China. In an important speech given in commemoration of the 60th anniversary of the establishment of the National People's Congress, Party Secretary-General Xi Jinping pointed out that, after the Revolution of 1911, China had tried many different political systems, such as constitutional monarchy, restoration of the monarchy system, parliamentary system, multi-party system, and presidential system, and various political forces and their representatives had entered into political arena one after another, but none of them had found the correct solution to China's problem: China remained a poor and weak country rent by disunity and tyrannized and exploited by imperialist powers and Chinese people were still living in misery and humiliation. Facts have proved that the democratic revolution led by bourgeois revolutionists and various plans of copying western model of political system had all failed to complete the historical mission of national salvation and combating imperialism and feudalism, or to achieve political and social stability, let along to provide institutional safeguard for national prosperity and people's happiness. Under the leadership of the CPC, Chinese people were finally able to overturn the "three big mountains", realize democracy, gain control of state political power, become the masters of the country, and after revolution, construction, reform and development, gradually embark on the road of developing socialist democracy and constructing a socialist country under the rule of law.

The road of socialist rule of law with Chinese characteristics is the road of development of the rule of law taken by the CPC on the basis of long-term practice of constructing socialist democracy and the rule of law since the establishment of the New China, especially the practice of comprehensively implementing the basic strategy of ruling the country by law, speeding up the theoretical research, practical exploration and institutional innovation on the construction of a socialist country under the rule of law, continuously deepening the understanding of socialism with Chinese characteristics, of socialist democratic politics with Chinese characteristics and of the policy of comprehensively advancing the rule of law and constructing a socialist state under the rule of law since the Fifteenth Party Congress. It is the correct road chosen by the CPC by proceeding from the national conditions and the realities in China, taking the construction of a moderately well-off society in an all-round way and realizing the great rejuvenation of the Chinese nation as its strategic objectives, summarizing the practical experience of construction of socialist rule of law in China, drawing on the beneficial results of development of the rule of law civilization in other countries, and absorbing the nutrients from the essence of the traditional Chinese legal culture; it is a historical achievement made by the CPC over a long period of time, especially since the Third Plenary Session of the Eleventh CPC Central Committee, by summarizing the successful experiences and profound lessons in the construction of socialist rule of law, namely, in order to safeguard people's democracy, the CPC must strengthen the rule of law, institutionalize democracy and bring it under the law, take ruling the country by law as its basic strategy of state governance, and actively construct socialist rule of law. The road of socialist rule of law with Chinese characteristics is the product of the unity of history and reality and the combination of theory and practice. It has its own space-time orientation and epoch characteristics in the following four coordinates of historical position.

Firstly, compared with the rule of law mode and road of western capitalist countries such as UK, France, Germany and US, which are of capitalist nature, the rule of law mode and road in China is of socialist nature. These two roads or modes of rule of law are of totally different natures and should never be confused with each other and China should never copy the rule of law mode of western capitalist countries. Practice has shown that "blindly copying the political systems of other countries would never work, even ruin the future of the nation because foreign political systems are not compatible with the national conditions in China and blindly copying them is like trying to draw a tiger, only to end up with the likeness of a dog." Adhering to the socialist nature and the socialist road of rule of law is a basic premise of comprehensively advancing the rule of law and constructing a socialist state under the rule of law. This is an issue of position, principle and direction that allows of no doubt and cannot be discussed. It is also an essential requirement of the construction of socialist rule of law with Chinese characteristics.

Secondly, compared with the rule of law mode and the rule of law road of the former Soviet Union and former socialist countries in Eastern Europe and contemporary socialist countries like Vietnam and Cuba, the rule of law road taken by China is a socialist road of rule of law with "Chinese characteristics". The historical gene of the Chinese nation, the historical and cultural traditions, and the current reality and social conditions in China have determined that China must take the road of socialist rule of law with Chinese characteristics and that it can only draw on, but never copy or clone, the mode and road of the rule of law in the Soviet Union, Vietnam and other socialist countries.

Thirdly, compared with the ideal socialist society expounded and described by classic Marxist writers, China is currently at the primary stage of socialism and will remain at this stage for a long period of time. Therefore, "the construction of the rule of law in China at the current stage still has many problems and cannot meet the demand of the development of various causes and undertakings of the Party and the state, the expectations of the people, and the objective of the modernization of the state governance system and governance capacity. The main manifestations of these problems are the followings: some laws and regulations have failed to reflect objective laws and the will of the people, lack pertinence and operability and there is a prominent tendency of departmentalization, scrambling for power and shirking responsibilities in the legislative work; the phenomena of non-compliance with law, slack enforcement of law, failure to bring lawbreakers to justice, detachment of powers and responsibilities in the law enforcement system, duplicate law enforcement, selective law enforcement, irregular, lax, non-transparent, and uncivilized, unfair, and corrupt enforcement of law and administration of justice are still prevalent and have caused great concern among the general public; some members of society lack the awareness of respecting the law, trusting the law, observing the law, applying the law and upholding their rights in accordance with the law; some state personnel, especially leading cadres, lack the consciousness of and the capacity for acting in accordance with law and the phenomena of knowingly violating the law, replacing the law by personal views, suppressing the law with power, and bending the law for personal gain still exist." All these problems, which are inevitable at the primary stage of socialism, contravene the principles of socialist rule of law, harm the people's interests, and impede the development of the Party and the state. Therefore no effort should be spared in solving these problems in the process of advancement of the rule of law in China.

Fourthly, compared to the traditional legal culture and legal system in Chinese history, the road of the rule of law taken by China today is a modern road of the rule of law. It is a mode of rule of law that adheres to openness, inclusiveness, and disciplinary innovation, and represents advanced productive force, advanced production relations and advanced culture. It is the result of long-term development, improvement and endogenous evolution on the basis of Chinese historical and cultural traditions and economic and social development and of drawing on the beneficial results of the rule of law civilization of all mankind. Therefore, the road of socialist rule of law with Chinese characteristics carries forward the fine tradition of traditional Chinese legal system and traditional Chinese legal culture by making the past serve the present and bringing forth the new through the old while at the same time adapts foreign things for Chinese use and advances with the times, thereby bringing state governance under the rule of law in the process of promoting the modernization of state governance and building China into a strong modern socialist power in the process of peaceful rise of the Chinese nation.

Adhering to the road of socialist rule of law with Chinese characteristics means adhering to the CPC's leadership, to the system of socialism with Chinese characteristics, and to the theory of socialist rule of law with Chinese characteristics. The road, theoretical system and institutions of socialism with Chinese characteristics are the bases of comprehensive advancement of the rule of law in China. The CPC's leadership is the most essential characteristic of socialism with Chinese characteristics and the most basic guarantee of socialist rule of law. The socialist system with Chinese characteristics is the fundamental institutional basis of the system of socialist rule of law with Chinese characteristics and the basic institutional guarantee of comprehensive advancement of governance by law. The theory of socialist rule of law with Chinese characteristics is the theoretical guidance and support of the system of socialist rule of law with Chinese characteristics and the guideline of comprehensive advancement of governance by law in China.

The above three aspects are in essence the core elements of the road of socialist rule of law with Chinese characteristics that determines and guarantees the institutional attributes and direction of development of the system of socialist rule of law with Chinese characteristics.

The CPC's leadership is the premise, the key and the guarantee of adhering to the road of socialist rule of law with Chinese characteristics. The Decision points out that adhering to the CPC's leadership is a basic demand of socialist rule of law, the foundation and lifeline of the CPC and the state that has a direct bearing on the interest and welfare of the people of all nationalities in the whole country, and an element inherent in the comprehensive advancement of the rule of law in China. The CPC's leadership is consistent with socialist rule of law. The socialist rule of law must adhere to the CPC's leadership and the CPC's leadership must rely on socialist rule of law. Only under the CPC's leadership can the rule of law be implemented, the people become the masters of the country, and the state and social life be brought under the rule of law in an orderly way. Implementing the CPC's leadership in the whole process and all aspects of governance by law is one of the basic experiences of construction of socialist rule of law in China. The CPC must use the rule of law thinking and rule of law method to promote governance by constitution and governance by law, and make sure that itself is able to lead the legislation, ensure the enforcement of law, support administration of justice, and take the lead in observing the law. Advancing governance by law in an all-round way will never weaken the CPC's leadership, but, on the contrary, will reinforce the ruling basis, strengthen the ruling authority, enhance the ruling capacity, and raise the ruling level of the CPC.

Adhering to the road of socialist rule of law with Chinese characteristics means adhering to the system of socialism with Chinese characteristics, which consists of the basic political system of people's congresses, the system of multi-party cooperation and political consultation led by the CPC, the system of regional national autonomy, the system of community level self-governance, the socialist legal system, the basic economic system of taking public ownership as the mainstay of the economy and allowing diverse forms of ownership to develop side by side, and various economic, political, cultural and social systems as well as various concrete institutions built on the above-mentioned basic politic and legal systems. Adhering to the road of socialist rule of law with Chinese characteristics relies on the system of socialism with Chinese characteristics as its fundamental institutional basis. The comprehensive advancement of governance by law and the construction of the system of socialist rule of law with Chinese characteristics and of a socialist state under the rule of law relies on the system of socialism with Chinese characteristics as its basic institutional safeguard. Without this institutional basis and fundamental institutional safeguard, the comprehensive advancement of governance by law will be like a tree without roots, the construction of socialist rule of law will become water without a source, the system of socialist rule of law will become a castle in the air, and the development of socialist rule of law with Chinese characteristics will inevitably go down the wrong path.

In order to unswervingly follow the road of socialist rule of law with Chinese characteristics, China must take the theory of socialist rule of law with Chinese characteristics as its theoretical and practical guidance and support. The theory of socialist rule of law with Chinese characteristic is the product of combination of universal principles of Marxism, the Marxist theories of state and law and the practice of construction of socialist rule of law with Chinese characteristics, an important component of the theoretical system of socialism with Chinese characteristics, the epitome of the spirit, the culture, the consciousness, the idea, the core values, as well as the theoretical system of socialist rule of law, and the theoretical basis and practical guidance of comprehensive advancement of governance by law and construction of a socialist state under the rule of law. The core of the theory of socialist rule of law with Chinese characteristics is to take Marxism-Leninism, Mao Zedong Thought, Deng Xiaoping Theory, the important "Three Represents" Thought, and the Scientific Outlook on Development as the guidance, implement in a deep-going way the spirit of a series of important speeches given by Party Secretary General Xi Jinping's, adhere to the organic unity of upholding CPC's leadership, the people being masters of the country, and ruling the country by law, unswervingly march the road of socialist rule of law with Chinese characteristics, and firmly uphold the authority of the Constitution and laws, the people's rights and interests, social justice, national security and social stability, so as to provide powerful rule of law guarantees for the realization of the "Two Centuries" struggle objectives and the Chinese dream of the great rejuvenation of the Chinese nation.

In order to unswervingly adhere to the road of socialist rule of law with Chinese characteristics, China must advance in an all-round way the general objective of ruling the country by law, construct the system of socialist rule of law with Chinese characteristics, and build China into a socialist state under the rule of law. As the Decision clearly points out, this general objective requires that "the Chinese people, under the leadership of the Chinese Communist Party, persist in the system of socialism with Chinese characteristics, implement the theory of socialist rule of law with Chinese characteristics, shape a perfect system of legal norms, a highly effective system for the implementation of the rule of law, a strict system for rule of law supervision, and a powerful system of rule of law guarantees, develop a sound system of intra-Party regulations, simultaneously advance governance by law, exercise of the ruling power by law and administration by law, persist in the unified construction of a law-based country, a law-based government and a law-based society, realize scientific legislation, strict law enforcement, fair administration of justice, and observance of law by the entire population, and promote the modernization of the state governance system and governing ability."

This general objective has the following significances: firstly, it announces to the world that China will unswervingly take the road of the socialist rule of law with Chinese characteristics, which is the concentrated embodiment of the achievements and experiences of the construction of socialist rule of law and the only correct road of constructing a socialist state under the rule of law. The CPC must send a correct and clear message to the whole society on the question of what road the rule of law China should take. Secondly, it clearly pinpoints the key link in comprehensive advancement of governance by law in China, which involves many aspects of work. In the practical work, there must be a key link that can be used to grasp the overall situation and propel the work in various fields. This key link is the construction of socialist system of the rule of law with Chinese characteristics. The work in all fields of governance by law must be planned and carried out around this key link.

Thirdly, constructing the system of socialist rule of law with Chinese characteristics and building a socialist state under the rule of law is a necessary requirement of the modernization of the system and ability of state governance as well as of comprehensive deepening of the reform. It is conducive to promoting the modernization of the system and ability of state governance, to advancing in an all-round way various aspects of the work of ruling the country by law within the framework of deepening the reform in an all-round way, and to the continuous deepening of the reform on the track of the rule of law.

1.2 Adhering to the Theory of Socialist Rule of Law with Chinese Characteristics

The theory of socialist rule of law with Chinese characteristics, which is a scientific theoretical system based on the road and the system of socialist rule of law with Chinese characteristics and the practice of advancing governance by law in an all-round way in China, consists of following main components:

First, the system of theories and thoughts on the values of socialist rule of law with Chinese characteristics, which involves the categories and contents of political philosophy, philosophy of law, and the theoretical system of socialism with Chinese characteristics and consists of following five parts: (1) Marxist theories of the state and law, including Marxist outlooks on the state, political parties, democracy, law, the rule of law, human rights, equality, justice and power, as well as Marxist legal thinking; (2) The spirit, consciousness, ideas, values, and principles of socialist rule of law, the socialist principle of constitutionalism,[1] the thought, ideology, culture, and doctrine of the socialist rule of law, etc.; (3) the systems of theory, discipline and curriculum of socialist law science with Chinese characteristics; (4) the rule of law attitude, mentality, preference, feeling, perception, standpoint, and believe of citizens and civil servants; and (5) theories on the general principles, values, functions, doctrines, methodologies, and knowledge of the rule of law.

Second, the theoretical system of institutional norms of socialist rule of law with Chinese characteristics, which involves such categories and contents as basic institutions, legal norms, procedure, and structure of the rule of law and mainly consists of the following four parts: (1) Theories on state constitution and constitutionalism, such as those on the fundamental political system provided for in the Constitution (the people's congress system) and other basic political systems (the system of regional national autonomy, the system of multiparty cooperation and consultation under the leadership of the CPC, the system of democratic self-governance at the grassroots, and the system of special administrative regions), those on basic economic, social, and cultural systems in China, the system of socialist democratic election, the system of human rights protection, the legislative system, and the socialist legal system with Chinese characteristics; (2) theories on the system of socialist rule of law with Chinese characteristics, such as the system of supervision over the implementation of the constitution, the system of laws and administrative regulations, the system of the implementation, supervision and safeguarding of the rule of law, and the system of intra-Party regulations; (3) theories on the law-based government with Chinese characteristics, administration by law and administrative law enforcement system, judicial power, judicial system, judicial procedure, legal supervision system, the system of fair administration of justice, and the system of exercising the ruling power by law; (4) basic theories on the general system, institutions, procedures, rules, norms and framework of the rule of law.

Third, theories on the actual operation of the socialist rule of law with Chinese characteristics, which involve such categories and content as the application of the rule of law theory, the rule of law behavior, the rule of law practice and the operation of the legal system and mainly consist of the following five parts: (1) Theories on various links in the construction of the rule of law, including scientific legislation, strict law enforcement, judicial fairness and respect for the law by the entire population; (2) theories on various aspects of implementation of the rule of law, such as ruling the

---

[1] The principle of constitutionalism mainly includes the following principles: the principle of popular sovereignty, according to which people are the masters of the country; the principle of the rule of law, namely the supremacy of the Constitution and laws; the principle of human rights, namely respecting and safeguarding human rights; the ruling principle, namely the principle of democratic politics and scientific and law-based exercise of the ruling power; the principle of fair, efficient and clean administration of justice; and the principle of supervision over power. The principle of the rule of law mainly has the following content: the universality, the openness, the definiteness, the stability, and the predictability of the rule of law; the non-retroactivity of law; the equality before the law; *nullum crimen sine lege*; the organic unity of the Party's leadership, the people being masters of the country and ruling the country by law; combing the rule of law with the rule of virtue; and proceeding from the national conditions whiling learning from and drawing on the positive results of development of the rule of law civilization of mankind.

country by law, administration by law, exercising the ruling power by law, running the armed forces by law, and acting by law; (3) theories on various fields of development of the rule of law, including those on a state under the rule of law, government under the rule of law, society under the rule of law, economy under the rule of law, rule of law politics, and rule of law culture; (4) theories on running the Party in accordance with regulations and exercising ruling power by law, including those on the requirements that the ruling party acts within the scope of the Constitution and laws, exercises leadership over the legislation, ensures the enforcement of law, supports administration of justice and takes the lead in observing the law; and (5) basic theories on the general patterns, characteristics, mechanisms, behaviors and modes of the operation of the rule of law.

Fourth, theories on relations of socialist rule of law with Chinese characteristics, which involve such phenomena and contents as the external relations affecting the existence and development of the rule of law, the coexistence of and interaction between the rule of law and various factors and mainly consist the following seven kinds of relations: (1) relations between the socialist rule of law with Chinese characteristics and the road, theory and system of socialism with Chinese characteristics, the deepening of reform in an all-round way, the building of a moderately well-off society in an all-round way, and the Chinese dream of the great rejuvenation of the Chinese nation; (2) relations between the socialist rule of law with Chinese characteristics and the market economy, democratic politics, harmonious society, advanced culture, and ecological civilization; (3) relations between the socialist rule of law with Chinese characteristics and morality, discipline, policy, intra-Party regulations, customs, village regulations and agreements, social norms on self-governance and other social norms; (4) relations between the socialist rule of law with Chinese characteristics and democracy, freedom, human rights, equality, justice, security, order, dignity, harmony, authority, peace, and happiness; (5) relations between the socialist rule of law with Chinese characteristics and promotion of development, upholding of stability, establishment of order, and resolution of conflicts and disputes; (6) relations between the socialist rule of law with Chinese characteristics and political parties, religion, ruling the country by virtue, running the Party in accordance with regulations, modernization of state governance, and good law and good governance; and (7) relations between the socialist rule of law with Chinese characteristics and the rule of law civilization of mankind, western legal theories, traditional Chinese legal system, theories of international governance, and the advancement of the global rule of law.

The main features of the socialist rule of law with Chinese characteristics are determined by its nature, road and theory. The rule of law is a symbol of the progress of human civilization. The socialist rule of law with Chinese characteristics is a unique and exotic flower in the garden of the rule of law civilization of mankind, a theoretical, institutional and practical system of socialist rule of law that is compatible with the actual situation in China, has Chinese characteristics, and embodies the objective law of social development. The socialist rule of law with Chinese characteristics is a huge system that consist of content at the following three levels: at the first level are theoretical value and spiritual culture of socialist rule of law with Chinese characteristics, including the values of socialist rule of law, the spirit, consciousness, theory, belief and culture of the rule of law, and the authority of the constitution and laws—which constitute the spiritual support and theoretical basis of socialist rule of law with Chinese characteristics; at the second level are the institutional and operation systems of the socialist rule of law with Chinese characteristics, including a complete system of legal norms, a highly efficient implementation system, a strict supervision system, a powerful safeguarding system, a sound intra-Party regulations system—which constitute the legal institutional support and operational mechanism of the socialist rule of law with Chinese characteristics; at the third level are the behaviors, activities and practical operation of the socialist rule of law with Chinese characteristics, including scientific legislation, strict enforcement of law, fair administration of justice, and observance of law by the entire population, the principle that laws must be observed and strictly enforced, and lawbreakers must be prosecuted, and the principles of exercising the ruling power by law, administration by law, acting by law, resolution of disputes by law—which constitute the practical bases and ways of realization of the socialist rule of law with Chinese characteristics.

Under the precondition of adhering to the socialist rule of law with Chinese characteristics and on the basis of proceeding from the national conditions and taking the road of socialist rule of law with Chinese characteristics, China must also pay attention to drawing on and absorbing the useful foreign experiences of construction of the rule of law and the achievements made by all mankind in the development of the rule of law civilization, conform to the trend of the times, and continuously enrich and improve the civilization of socialist rule of law with Chinese characteristics. The socialist rule of law with Chinese characteristics has strong inclusiveness and openness as well as unique cultural characteristics. China should respect the rule of law principles of human political civilization (such as the principle that the government can do nothing except those specifically authorized by law whereas citizens can do anything except those specifically prohibited by law, the principle of *nullum crimen sine lege*, the principle of administration by law, the principle of judicial fairness, and the principle that administration of justice is the last line of defense for social justice), carry out research on the relevant principles of the rule of law (such as the principle of equality of everyone before the law, the principle of non-retroactivity of law, and the principle of the normativity, openness, predictability and justiciability of law), and draw on the rule of law procedures of other countries (such as administrative, criminal, and civil procedures, legislative voting procedure, and administrative decision-making procedure). In a word, "China should adopt an all-inclusive attitude towards the colorful world, study with an open mind the good things in other countries, digest and absorb them and transform them into our own while at the same time maintaining independence and keeping the initiative in our own hands and never indiscriminately copy foreign ideas and institutions. In advancing governance by law, China should "borrow useful experiences of the rule of law from foreign countries, but never blindly copy foreign rule of law ideas and modes". This is a basic stance and attitude that China must take in adhering to the theory and taking the road of socialist rule of law with Chinese characteristics.

In adhering to the theory and taking the road of socialist rule of law with Chinese characteristics, we must continuously enhance our theoretical self-confidence in the theory of socialist rule of law with Chinese characteristics, our path self-confidence in the road of socialist rule of law with Chinese characteristics, our institutional self-confidence in the system of socialist constitution with Chinese characteristics and the system of socialist rule of law with Chinese characteristics, and our practical self-confidence in the great exploration of advancing governance by law in an all-round way and constructing a socialist state under the rule of law, so as to make new contributions to the construction of the rule of law, to the building of China into a moderately well-off society in an all-round way, and to the realization of the Chinese dream of the great rejuvenating the Chinese nation.

Chapter 2
The Historical Process of Constructing Socialist Rule of Law with Chinese Characteristics

2.1 The Historical Process of Constructing Socialist Rule of Law with Chinese Characteristics

The socialist rule of law with Chinese characteristics was established through the total destruction of the old legal system of the Kuomintang Regime and the adoption of the Soviet mode of socialist legal system in accordance with the Marxist theory of state and law and in light of the action situation of the New-Democratic Revolution in China. After the establishment of the People's Republic of China (PRC) in 1949, the construction of the socialist rule of law with Chinese characteristics has undergone two stages of development—which can be further divided into six periods—along with the tortuous political, economic, social and cultural developments in China.

2.1.1 Construction of the Legal System During the Period Between the Founding of the New China and the Beginning of the Reform and Opening up

2.1.1.1 Laying the Cornerstone of the Legal System of the New China: Between the Establishment of the PRC in October 1949 and the Promulgation of the Constitution in September 1954

The period between the establishment of the PRC in October 1949 and the promulgation of the Constitution in September 1954 was the foundation-laying period of the socialist legal system in China. In the early years of the New China, the legal system mainly served the purposes of upholding the new-born political power, consolidating the proletarian dictatorship, and suppressing class enemies. In February 1949, on the eve of the establishment of the New China, the Central Committee of the Communist Party of China (CPC) promulgated the Instructions to Abolish the Six Codes of the

© China Social Sciences Press and Springer Nature Singapore Pte Ltd. 2018
L. Li, *The Chinese Road of the Rule of Law*, China Insights,
https://doi.org/10.1007/978-981-10-8965-7_2

Kuomintang Regime and Establish the Judicial Principles of Liberated Areas, which announced that: "Under the people's democratic dictatorship, the Six Codes of the Kuomintang Regime should be abolished. The people's judicial work should take the new people's laws, rather than the Six Codes, as its basis." This provision removed the obstacles to and laid the foundation for the complete abolition of the false legal system of the Kuomintang Regime, including the Six Codes and the corresponding legislative, law enforcement and judicial systems, the establishment of the legitimacy of the political system of the People's Republic of China, and the construction of the system of law and the corresponding legislative, law enforcement and judicial systems of the New China. Mr. Zhang Youyu once pointed out that: "We were absolutely right to abolish the Six Codes of the Kuomintang Regime soon after the Liberation because they represented the legal system of the Kuomintang Regime. Without abolishing this legal system, we would not be able to establish our own revolutionary legal system."

In September 1949, the Common Program of the Chinese People's Political Consultative Conference, which served as an interim constitution at that time, and the Organic Law of the Central People's Government were adopted at first plenary session of the Chinese People's Political Consultative Conference. Article 17 of the Common Program provided that: "All laws, decrees and judicial systems of the Kuomintang reactionary government which oppress the people shall be abolished. Laws and decrees protecting the people shall be enacted and the people's judicial system shall be established." These two constitutional laws and other related laws had laid the foundation of the system of law in the early years of the New China.

To meet the needs of political struggle and construction of the legal system in the early years of the New China, the state established a "pluralistic legislative system" for this period of political transition. Under this system, the Chinese People's Political Consultative Conference was responsible for adopting basic state laws; the Central People's Government was responsible for adopting and interpreting state laws and decrees and supervising over their implementation; the Government Administration Council had the power to promulgate resolutions and orders and supervise over their implementation, to abolish or revise the resolutions and orders adopted by various ministries, commissions, bureaus and councils under it and by local governments at various levels that contravened state laws, decrees or the resolutions and orders adopted by the Government Administration Council, and to submit bills to the Central People's Government; people's government councils of greater administrative areas, provinces, cities, and counties had the power to adopt decrees, regulations, and separate regulations in accordance with general principles of organic law of local governments; and organs of self-government of regional national autonomous areas had the power to adopt separate regulations. Such a legislative system had raised the legislative efficiency and markedly speeded up the legislative work at both the central and the local levels, as evidenced by the following laws and regulations adopted in China during this period of time: (1) those establishing organs of state power, such as Common Program of Chinese People's Political Consultative Conference; Organic Law of Chinese People's Political Consultative Conference; Organic Law of the Central People's Government; General Principles of Organic Regulations for

Conferences of People's Representatives from Various Circles; General Principles of Organic Regulations for People's Government Councils of Greater Administrative Areas; General Principles of Organic Regulations for the Government Administration Council of the Central People's Government and Its Subordinate Organs; Provisional Organic Regulations for People's Courts; Provisional Organic Regulations for the Supreme People's Procuratorate of the Central People's Government; General Principles of Organic Regulations for Conferences of People's Representatives from Various Circles of Provinces; General Principles of Organic Regulations for Conferences of People's Representatives from Various Circles of Cities; and General Principles of Organic Regulations for Conferences of People's Representatives from Various Circles of Counties; (2) those aimed at suppressing bandits and counterrevolutionaries, consolidating political power, and upholding social order, such as Regulations on Punishing Counter-Revolutionaries; Provisional Measures for the Control of Counter-Revolutionaries; Regulations on Public Security in Cities; and Regulations on Public Security in Rural Areas; (3) those aimed at restoring the national economy, maintaining economic order and punishing corruption, such as National Guidelines on the Implementation of the Tax Law; Decision on the Unification of Financial and Economic Work; Regulations on the Punishment of the Crime of Interfering with National Currency; Interim Measures for the Prohibition of Carrying State Currency into or out of the Country; Interim Measures for Providing Relief to Unemployed Workers; Regulations on Labor Insurance: Interim Regulations on Private Enterprises; Regulations on the Punishment of Corruption; Measures for Dealing with the Problems of Corruption and Waste and Overcoming Bureaucratism; and Provisional Customs Law; (4) those on land reform and social democratic reform, such as Land Reform Law; Decision on the Identification of Class Status in Rural Areas; Measures for Dealing with Land Properties of Overseas Chinese in the Land Reform; and Marriage Law.

The judicial system of the New China was established along with the establishment of the new-born people's political power. On 1 October 1949 the Central People's Government Council appointed at its first meeting Mr. Shen Junru as the President of the Supreme People's Court and Mr. Luo Ronghuan as the Procurator-General of the Supreme People's Procuratorate of the Central People's Government. On 22 October of the same year, the inaugural meetings of the Supreme People's Court and the Supreme People's Procuratorate of the Central People's Government were held in Beijing, at which Mr. Shen Junru and Mr. Luo Ronghuan formally took office as the President of the Supreme People's Court and the Procurator-General of the Supreme people's Procuratorate of the Central People's Government, respectively. In 1951, the Central People's Government promulgated the Provisional Organic Regulations for People's Courts, Provisional Organic Regulations for the Supreme People's Procuratorate of the Central People's Government, and General Principles of Organic Regulations for Local People's Procuratorates at Various Levels, which provided for the structures, the functions and the powers of people's courts and people's procuratorates at various levels, thereby laying the foundation for the construction from top to bottom of the organizational systems of people courts and people's procuratorates at various levels.

The election at the grassroots level began in March 1953 and was successfully completed in May 1954. By August 1954, local people's congresses had been established in all administrative areas at or above the county level: "Apart from Taiwan, which had not yet been liberated, Chinese people had already established their own organs of political power in 25 provinces, in Inner Mongolia Autonomous Region, in Tibetan Area, in Changdu Area, in the three municipalities directly under the Central Government, and in 2216 counties and county-level administrative areas, 163 cities, 821 municipal districts, and 224,660 townships. Moreover, organs of self-government had also been established in 65 national autonomous areas at or above the county level."[1] In the first five years of the New China, the Chinese people had made great achievements in the construction of people's democratic political power, which had enabled them to become the masters of their own country, to exercise their rights as masters of the country, and to administer state affairs.

2.1.1.2 The Establishment of the Legal System with Chinese Characteristics: Between the Promulgation of the 1954 Constitution and the Start of the "Anti-rightist Movement" in 1957

The period between 1954 and 1957 was the formative period of the socialist legal system in China, in which the first socialist constitution was adopted. In early 1953, the Central People's Government Council decided to establish the Drafting Committee for the Constitution of the People's Republic of China. The Committee was chaired by Mao Zedong and consisted of 32 other members, including Zhu De and Soong Ching-ling. On September 15, 1954, the Draft Constitution was adopted by the First National People's Congress (NPC) at its first session, thereby providing a constitutional basis for the establishment and development of the socialist legal system and marking the formal establishment of the legal system of the New China.

Around the time of the drafting of the 1954 Constitution, Mao Zedong once said that "Just as an organization needs a charter, a state needs a constitution as its fundamental law. After the adoption of the Draft Constitution, everyone in the country must implement it. Especially state personnel, including all of you in this room (referring to the participants of the 22nd Meeting of the Central People's Government Council), must take the lead in implementing it. Anyone who fails to do so violates the Constitution."

During this period, the emphasis of the Party's work had been shifted from class struggle to economic construction. In 1956, Liu Shaoqi pointed out in the Political Report given at the Eighth National Congress of the CPC that: "Currently, one of the urgent tasks in our work is to systematically adopt laws, so as to strengthen our legal system"; "the tempest of revolution is over. New relations of production have already been established. Our task now is to ensure the smooth development of social

---

[1]Lou (1955).

productive forces. As a result, the method of socialist revolution must also change accordingly. A complete legal system is therefore necessary."

(1) Carrying out legislative work. The 1954 Constitution clearly provided that the NPC was the only organ that have state legislative power (The Resolution of the Second Session of the First National People's Congress Authorizing Its Standing Committee to Formulate Separate Regulations, adopted in July 1955, gives the Standing Committee of the National People's Congress the legislative power), thereby establishing a centralized and unified system of legislative power. Statistics show that, between 1954 and 1957, the total number of laws adopted by the NPC and its Standing Committee, laws and administrative regulations adopted by the State Council, and important normative documents adopted by various ministries and commissions under the State Council had reached 731.[2] These laws, administrative regulations and normative documents had enriched the system of law and provided the basis and safeguard for bringing the economic, political and social constructions in the early years of the New China into the orbit of law. Meanwhile, the drafting of some important basic laws, such as the criminal law, the civil law, and the criminal procedure law, had also been speeded up. By 1957, the 22nd draft of the Criminal Law had been completed and distributed among deputies to the NPC for their opinions; the main part of the drafting work of the Civil Law had been completed and the draft law had been sent to relevant units for their opinions; and the drafting of the Criminal Procedure Law had also begun and the first draft was completed in June 1957.

(2) Establishing the judicial system. The Organic Law of People's Courts and the Organic Law of People's Procuratorates were re-drafted at the first session of the First NPC. The new Organic Law of People's Courts changed the court organizational system in China from the original three-level system (consisting of people's courts at the county and provincial levels and the Supreme People's Court) to the four-level system (consisting of people's courts at the grassroots, intermediate and provincial levels and the Supreme People's Court), established various special people's courts, such as military courts, railway transport courts, water transport courts, and forest affairs courts, and implemented a trial system whereby the second instance is final. The Supreme People's Court is the highest adjudicative organ in the country, responsible for supervising over the trial work of local people's courts and special people's courts at various levels. Judicial committees were set up in people's courts at various levels to be responsible for summarizing trial experiences, discussing major or difficult cases, and dealing with other trial related issues.

The Organic Law of People's Procuratorates changed the leadership system of procuratorial organs from the past "dual leadership" system (namely a people's procuratorate works under the leadership of the procuratorate at the next higher level and the people's government council at the same level) into a "vertical leadership system (namely a local procuratorate or special procuratorate works under the leader-

---

[2]Including the Organic Regulations of the Urban Residents Committees, Regulations on Residence Registration, Model Articles of Association for Agricultural Producers' Cooperatives, Regulations on Arrest and Detention, and Regulations of the People's Republic of China on Administrative Penalties for Public Security.

ship of people procuratorate at the next higher level and all people's procuratorates work under the unified leadership of the Supreme People's Procuratorate). People's procuratorates in the whole country were divided into four levels. A procuratorial committee under the leadership of the chief procurator was set up within each procratorate. People's procuratorates are state legal supervision organs, responsible for general legal supervision, supervision over criminal investigation, trial supervision and supervision over prison administration.

Some basic principles and systems of judicial work had been established. They include: the system whereby the public security organs, procuratorates and courts divide their functions, each taking responsibility for its own work, and coordinate their efforts and check each other; the principle of equality before the law; the people's assessor system; the system of open trial; the defense system; the collegial penal system; the withdrawal system; the trial system whereby the second instance is final; the system of review of death sentences; and the trial supervision system. These systems are still important bases of the judicial system in China even today.

Strengthening the construction of the public security system. The public security forces in the early years of the New China were made up of members of the military forces. After the promulgation of the 1954 Constitution, ordinary polices force was separated from the armed police forces to be mainly responsible for the maintenance of social order. In 1957, the NPC Standing Committee adopted the Regulations on People's Police, which clearly provided for the nature, tasks, functions and powers of people's police, thereby putting the construction of the police force on the right track.

Establishment of the reform-through-labor system. During this period of time, the government promulgated the Regulations on Reform through Labor and the Interim Measures for the Release upon Completion of a Sentence and Employment Placement of Persons subject to Reform through Labor. These two sets of regulations established the reform through labor system in China and contained concrete provisions on the guiding principles, policies, and method of reform through labor, and the employment placement of persons who had been released after reform through labor. Meanwhile, the State Council had also adopted the Decision on Issues concerning Reeducation through Labor, which provided for the scope of application and concrete method of reeducation through labor.

(3) Promoting disciplinary inspection and legislative work. In accordance with the organic laws of the State Council, local people's congresses, and the standing committees of local people's congresses, the Ministry of Supervision was set up under the State Council and supervision organs were established under the people's councils and commissions of provinces, municipalities directly under the Central Government, and cities divided into districts; when necessary, supervision organs of a prefectural commission or provincial commission could send special supervision groups, which were under direct leadership of the sending organs, to counties or cities not divided into districts. In November 1955, the State Council promulgated the General Organic Regulations of the Ministry of Supervision, which contained concrete provisions on the system of supervision, thereby putting the state supervision work on the track of law and proper procedure.

In November 1954, the establishment of the Legislative Affairs Bureau under the State Council was approved at the second meeting of the Standing Committee of the First NPC. The State Council promulgated the General Organic Regulations of the Legislative Affairs Bureau under the State Council, which contained special provisions on the tasks, internal organs, institutional structure, rules of procedure and meeting system of the Bureau.

Meanwhile, the lawyer's system and notary system had also been established. By June 1957, a total of 19 lawyer's associations and 817 legal consultation offices had been established throughout the country, with over 2500 full-time lawyers and over 300 part-time lawyers; by the end of 1957, notary public offices had been set up in 51 cities throughout the country, the business of notarization were accepted by the courts of over 1200 cities and counties; there were near 1000 full-time notaries throughout the country, who had performed over 290,000 notarial acts. A preliminary state arbitration system had been established and the Interim Provisions on the Arbitration Procedure of China International Economic and Trade Arbitration Commission were adopted, which contained detailed provisions on the scope of arbitration, the appointment of arbitrators, arbitration organizations, and enforcement of arbitration awards.

(4) Establishing and developing legal education. Legal education began by the training of cadres. In November 1949, Chaoyang University was transformed into China University of Political Science and Law—the first university in New China specialized in the training of judicial personnel. In 1950, Renmin University of China was established. The Law Faculty of this university became the first faculty in New China that provides formal undergraduate legal education. By 1957, the number of law schools and law faculties in colleges and universities throughout the country had reached ten, with 8245 students. During the first eight years the New China, a total of 13,090 undergraduate students and 263 graduate students had graduated from various law schools and faculties.

2.1.1.3 Setbacks in the Construction of Socialist Legal System with Chinese Characteristics: Between the Start of the "Anti-rightist Movement" and the End of the "Cultural Revolution"

The period between 1957 and 1976 was a period of setbacks in the history of the People's Republic of China as well as in the construction of the legal system with Chinese characteristics. The "Leftist" mistakes, especially the "Cultural Revolution", had severely damaged the people's congress system and seriously impeded the work of the Party and the state and the construction of socialist democracy and legal system, thereby leaving a profound lesson for China.

In the second half of 1957, there was a fundamental change in Mao Zedong's attitude towards the rule of law. At an enlarged meeting of the Political Bureau of CPC Central Committee, held in Beidaihe in August 1958, Mao said that: "Although the law is something that cannot be discarded altogether, we have our own way of dealing with cases. I prefer Judge Ma Xiwu's method of mainly relying on mediation, and carrying out investigations and studies and making judgment on site…Since the Great Leap Forward, people have been so busy with production, free airing of views, great debates and big-character posters that they have no time for committing crimes. We cannot fight such crimes as theft without relying on the masses of people. We should not use the law to rule the majority of people, but should help them to develop a good habit. The army is not ruled by the military law, but by the conference of 1400 military officers (namely the expanded meeting of the Central Military Commission of the CPC). The Civil Law and the Criminal Law have so many provisions that nobody can remember all of them. Even I cannot remember the content of the Constitution, which was drafted with my own participation…90% of the rules and regulations are made by various government departments and bureaus. We run the country basically not by following these rules and regulations, but by making resolutions and holding meetings, four times a year. We don't rely on the Civil Law or the Criminal Law to maintain social order. The National People's Congress and the State Council may adopt laws and regulations, but we still rely on our own ways. Liu Shaoqi once asked: do we want the rule of law or the rule of man? It seems that in reality we reply on the rule of man. Law can only be taken as reference in our work."[3]

From then on, the construction of the socialist legal system in China had gradually gone into retrogression, the evidences of which are the followings:

Firstly, the basic principles of socialist legal system, such as the principles that everyone is equal before the law, that the public security organs, procuratorates and courts divide their functions, each taking responsibility for its own work, and coordinate their efforts and check each other, that courts try cases independently in accordance with law, that procuratorates exercise general power of legal supervision independently and in accordance with law, and that the defendant has the right to defense, were denounced;

Secondly, the legislative work was gradually grinding to a halt: the number of normative documents adopted by the NPC and its Standing Committee and the State Council had decreased from 143 in 1958 to only 14 in 1965. Between 1958 and 1966, not only no new legislation had been initiated, but the drafting of such basic laws as the criminal law, the criminal procedure law, the civil law and the civil procedure law had also come to a stop.

Thirdly, some legal institutions had been abolished. In 1959 the Ministry of Justice, the Ministry of Supervision, and the Legislative Affairs Bureau of the State Council were abolished; the lawyer's team and the notary's team were disbanded; the judicial system whereby the public security organs, procuratorates and courts divide their functions, each taking responsibility for its own work, and coordinate their efforts and check each other was abolished and replaced by the system whereby public security organs, procuratorates and courts work together in one office.

Fourthly, beginning from 1957, sabotaging the legal system, violating citizens' rights, and arbitrarily arresting people had become increasingly common practices.

During the unprecedented ten-year "Cultural Revolution", almost all the democratic and legal institutions established in New China had been totally destroyed

---

[3]General Office of the Standing Committee of the National People's Congress (1991).

and the socialist legal system severely undermined; all activities of the NPC and its Standing Committee had ceased and the Central Cultural Revolution Group had became the de facto highest organ of power in China. People all over the country were "kicking aside Party committees and governments to make revolution", lawful government organs were replaced by revolutionary committees; citizen's rights were seriously violated; and there were no legal guarantee of the life and property of the individual. During the "Cultural Revolution", countless people, from the state president to ordinary citizens, had been denounced and struggled against, confiscated of their properties, imprisoned, even beaten to death. Public security organs, procuratorates and courts had been "totally smashed": people's procuratorates were formally abolished; the Ministry of Public Security and the Supreme People's Court were actually in a state of paralysis.

2.1.2   Construction of the Rule of Law with Chinese Characteristics Since the Reform and Opening up

The construction of the rule of law with Chinese characteristics since the reform and opening up has undergone four stages of development.

2.1.2.1   Restoration and Reconstruction of the Rule of Law: Between the End of the "Cultural Revolution" (1976) and the Promulgation of the 1982 Constitution (December 1982)

With the end of the "Cultural Revolution" in 1976, the CPC and the government began to bring order out of chaos. On December 13, 1978, Deng Xiaoping made an important speech entitled "Emancipate the Mind, Seek Truth from Facts and Unite as One in Looking to the Future" at the closing ceremony of a working conference of the CPC Central Committee. In the speech, he pointed out that, to ensure people's democracy, we must strengthen our legal system. Democracy has to be institutionalized and written into law, so as to make sure that institutions and laws do not change whenever the leadership changes, or whenever the leaders change their views or shift the focus of their attention. In December 18, 1978, the Third Plenary Session of the Eleventh CPC Central Committee was held. At this meeting, the Chinese leadership emancipated its mind, summarized the historical experiences and lessons, especially the historical lesson of the "Cultural Revolution". This meeting raised the construction of democracy and the legal system to a new height and became a milestone in the history of the development of the rule of law in China. The participants of the meeting unanimously held that, in order to safeguard people's democracy, it is necessary to strengthen the socialist legal system, institutionalize democracy and bring it into the orbit of law, so as to enable it to have stability, continuity and great authority and ensure that there are laws to go by, the laws are observed and strictly enforced, and lawbreakers are prosecuted. The legislative work should become an important item in the agenda of the NPC and its Standing Committee. Procuratorial and judicial organs should keep their independence and be faithful to law and institutions, to the interest of the people, and to facts and truth, and ensure that people are equal before their own law and no one has the privilege above the law.

In September 1979, the CPC Central Committee issued the Instruction on Resolutely Ensuring the Effective Implementation of the Criminal Law and the Criminal Procedure Law [CPC Central Committee Doc. No. 64 (1979)], which pointed out the special significance of the promulgation of the Criminal Law and Criminal Procedure Law to the strengthening of the socialist rule of law. Whether these laws can be strictly implemented is an important indicator of whether China can implement the socialist rule of law. The Instruction criticized the long existing tendencies of neglecting the legal system, putting policy above the law, putting personal views above the law, and suppressing law with power and made specific demands on how Party committees should lead the judicial work: firstly, to deal with cases in strictly accordance with the Criminal Law and Criminal procedure Law, and firmly change and correct all the ideologies and practices inconsistent with the two laws. Leaders of Party committees at various levels may not substitute law with their own personal opinions and impose them on others. Secondly, the Party's leadership over judicial work should be mainly limited to leadership by guidelines and policies. The most important aspect of strengthening Party leadership is to effectively ensure the independent exercise of procuratorial power by people's procuratorates and the exercise of adjudicative power by people's courts without interference from any administrative organ, organization or individual. Thirdly, to rapidly improve judicial organs at various levels and build a strong contingent of judicial workers. Fourthly, to carry out publicity of law in an extensive and deep-going way, so as to make preparations for the formal implementation of the Criminal Law and the Criminal procedure Law. Fifthly, Party organizations at various levels, leading cadres and all Party members should take the lead in abiding by the law. China must adhere to the principle of equality before the law, never allow any citizen to be free from the application of the law or have privileges above the law, and abolish the system of examination and approval of the trial of cases by Party committees at various levels. Document No. 64 of the CPC Central Committee is considered an important symbol of the new stage of construction of the socialist legal system in China.

While continuously strengthening legislative work, China was also restoring and reconstructing other components of the socialist legal system.

On September 9, 1979, the CPC Central Committee issued an instruction emphasizing that "it is necessary to strengthen the Party's leadership over judicial work, and truly ensure that judicial organs exercise their functions and powers provided for by the Constitution and laws and that the CPC's leadership over judicial work is main leadership through documents and policies."[4] Meanwhile, the CPC Central Committee also gave instruction "to quickly construct judicial organs at various levels and make efforts to build up a strong contingent of judicial workers". Under the

---

[4]He and Lu (1993).

leadership of the CPC, a socialist judicial system with Chinese characteristics had been gradually perfected.

The Organic Law of People's Courts was supplemented and revised at the Twelfth Session of the Fifth NPC in 1979 and at the second meeting of the Standing Committee of the Sixth NPC in 1983. The two amendments further improved organization of the court system.

The Constitution of the People's Republic of China adopted at the First Session of the Fifth NPC in March 1978 re-established people's procuratorate system in Article 43; the Supreme People's Procuratorate officially began its operation on June 1 of the same year; and, in accordance with the relevant provisions of the Constitution, the NPC adopted the Organic Law of People's Procratorates on July 1, 1979.

Public security, judicial administration and national security organs had also been restored or reconstructed. On June 15, 1979, the Political and Legislative Affairs Group of the CPC Central Committee submitted to the Central Committee the Suggestions on the Restoration of Judicial Organs. On September 13, 1979, the Standing Committee of the Fifth NPC, on the basis of sufficient preparation, decided at its eleventh meeting to reconstruct the Ministry of Justice, "so as to meet the need of the construction of the socialist rule of law and strengthen the work of judicial administration".[5] After the reestablishment of the Ministry of Justice, local departments (bureau) of justice at various levels had also been established one after another and judicial administration work resumed.

The Criminal Procedure Law and Organic Law of People's Courts, promulgated in July 1979, specifically provide that a criminal defendant may retain a lawyer as his defender. In early 1979, the Government of Hulan County of Heilongjiang Province began to assign lawyers to carry out criminal defense work. Soon afterwards, seven cities and counties in the country, including Beijing, Shanghai, the cities of Daqing and Harbin in Heilongjiang Province, and Bishan County in Sichuan Province, had restored lawyers' organizations and resumed some parts of lawyer's work; by October 1980, lawyer's associations had been established in the three provinces of Henan, Shaanxi and Shandong; preparatory committees or preparatory leading groups for lawyer's association were established in 17 provinces and municipalities, including Beijing, Tianjin, Shanghai, Liaoning Province, Heilongjiang Province, Jiangsu Province and Gansu Province; and a total of 381 legal consultation offices with over 3000 full-time lawyers had been established throughout the country. In August 1980, the Interim Regulations of the People's Republic of China on Lawyers was adopted at the Fifteenth Session of the Fifth NPC.[6]

In January 1980, the Political and Legal Affairs Commission of the CPC Central Committee was restored.

In July 1982, China Law Society was established. Legal research and education institutions smashed during the "Cultural Revolution" had been quickly restored and begun to develop. Major journals and newspapers in the field of law, such as Studies

---

[5]Editorial Committee for Contemporary China Pictorial (1995).

[6]See Han (1998).

in Law, Democracy and Legal System, and China Legal News had been restored or created.

In June 1983, the State Council proposed at the First Session of the Sixth NPC to establish the Ministry of National Security, with a view to strengthening its leadership over national security work. On July 1, 1983, the inaugural meeting of the Ministry of National Security was held. The Ministry was established through the merger of the Investigation Department of CPC Central Committee, Political Protection Bureau of the Ministry of Public Security, some units of United Front Work Department of CPC Central Committee, and some units of State Administration of Science, Technology and Industry for National Defense. Another important indicator of the beginning of the construction of the rule of law in China in the new era was the historical trial of the two "counterrevolutionary cliques", namely "Lin Biao's Counter-Revolutionary Clique" and "Jiang Qing's Counter-Revolutionary Clique". Between the end of 1980 and beginning of 1983, the core members of the two "counterrevolutionary cliques" in local governments and the military had also been tried. These trials were of great significance to the construction of the rule of law in China: it put an end to the "Cultural Revolution"—a period of lawlessness in Chinese history and brought the country on the road towards the rule of law.

By the end of 1982, the large-scale work of redressing unjust, false and erroneous cases had been basically completed. According to incomplete statistics, during this period of time, over 30 major unjust, false and erroneous cases had been redressed with the approval of the CPC Central Committee; in the whole country, about three million cadres who had been victims of unjust, false and erroneous cases had been rehabilitated; 470,000 CPC members who had been expelled from the Party as a result of being implicated in unjust, false and erroneous cases had their Party membership restored; tens of millions of innocent cadres and ordinary citizens who had been implicated in these cases had their names cleared; and 530,000 so-called "rightists" had been rehabilitated.[7]

2.1.2.2   The Development of the Rule of Law: From the Promulgation of the 1982 Constitution to the Opening of the Fourteenth Party Congress in 1992

The Third Plenary Session of the Eleventh CPC Central Committee removed the ideological obstacles to the construction of the rule of law in the new era and made the comprehensive revision of the Constitution the first priority. In September 1980, the Committee on the Revision of the Constitution, chaired by Ye Jianying, was established by the NPC. On December 4, 1982, the new Constitution was adopted at the Fifth Session of the Fifth NPC on the basis of democratic discussion. The 1982 Constitution consisted of a Preamble and four chapters, with a total of 138 articles. It retained the basic principles of the 1954 Constitution and embodied many important new reforms and developments in light of the needs of socialist construction in the

---

[7]You et al. (1993).

new era. For example, the Constitution established in the Preamble and Article 5 the principle of the socialist rule of law and provided for the basic status of the Constitution and constitutional safeguarding system, so as to uphold the unity and dignity of the rule of law. The Constitution also strengthened the construction of the executive body of the highest organ of state power by expanding the functions and powers of the Standing Committee of the NPC; strengthened the construction of local organs of state power by establishing standing committees under the local people's congresses at or above the county level and giving them the task of ensuring the implementation of the Constitution and laws in their respective administrative areas. People's congresses of provinces, autonomous regions and municipalities directly under the Central Government have the functions and powers of adopting local regulations and supervising the work of government, the people's courts and the people's procuratorate at the same level. The Constitution contained new and clearer provisions on the fundamental rights of citizens and strengthened measures for their safeguarding. Moreover, the 1982 Constitution also embodied many other reforms in the area of construction of state political power and state systems.

The 1982 Constitution was an important milestone in the development of the rule of law in New China and greatly safeguarded and promoted the construction of the rule of law in the new era.

Article 31 of the 1982 Constitution provided that: "The state may establish special administrative regions when necessary. The systems to be instituted in special administrative regions shall be prescribed by law enacted by the National People's Congress in the light of the specific conditions." In December 1984, the Chinese and British governments signed a Joint Declaration on Hong Kong, which confirms that the government of the People's Republic of China would resume the exercise of sovereignty over Hong Kong on July 1, 1997, thereby realizing a century-old dream of Chinese people.[8] On April 10, 1985, the Sino-British Joint Declaration on Hong Kong was formally approved and the Drafting Committee for the Basic Law of Hong Kong Special Administrative Region was established at the Third Session of the Sixth NPC. On April 4, 1990, the Basic Law of Hong Kong Special Administrative Region was adopted at the Third Session of the Seventh NPC. On April 13, 1987, China and Portugal signed the Joint Declaration on Macao, which put the drafting of the Basic Law of Macao Special Administration Region on the agenda of the NPC. On April 13, 1988, the Seventh NPC adopted at its First Session the Decision to Establish the Drafting Committee for the Basic Law of Macao Special Administration Region. On March 31, 1993, the Basic Law of Macao Special Administration Region was adopted at the First Session of the Eighth NPC. The promulgation of the two basic laws was an important event in the state life as well as in the construction of the rule in China. By establishing the principle of "one state, two systems" in the form of basic law, it represents an innovation in China's legislative history; it established the fundament system in Hong Kong and Macao after their return to China, thereby providing important legal safeguard for the economic development and political stability in the two special administrative regions.

---

[8]Editorial Department for Law Yearbook of China (1987).

In February 1988, the CPC Central Committee made a formal proposal to revise the Constitution, so as to recognize the legitimacy of private sector of the economy and of the lawful transfer of the land. This was because there was a serious deficiency in the economic system established by Article 6 of the 1982 Constitution, which provided that: "The basis of the socialist economic system of the People's Republic of China is socialist public ownership of the means of production, namely, ownership by the whole people and collective ownership by the working people. The system of socialist public ownership supersedes the system of exploitation of man by man; it applies the principle of 'from each according to his ability, to each according to his work.'" This means that only ownership by the whole people and collective ownership by the working people were lawful and that the Constitution recognized the legitimacy of only the public sector of the economy. In April 1988, the Seventh NPC deliberated and adopted at its first session the Amendment to the Constitution, which provides that: "The state permits the private sector of the economy to exist and develop within the limits prescribed by law" and that: "The right to the use of land may be transferred according to law." Later, in May 1990, the State Council issued by Order No. 55 the Interim Regulations Concerning the Assignment and Transfer of the Right to the Use of the State-owned Land in the Urban Areas, which provide for the concrete rules on the trading of the right to the use of the land.

In November 1985, the Standing Committee of the Sixth NPC adopted at its thirteenth meeting the Resolution on Acquainting Citizens with Basic Knowledge of Law, which greatly promoted the work of popularization of law, and markedly raised the people's consciousness of the law and the rule of law.

During this period of time, the NPC and its Standing Committee had put the emphasis of their legislative work on the economic field and adopted the Law on Economic Contract, the Statistics Law, the Law on Environmental Protection (for Trial Implementation), Marine Environment Protection Law, Water Pollution Prevention and Control Law, Food Hygiene Law (for Trial Implementation), and Maritime Traffic Safety Law, and approved the Regulations on the Requisition of Land by the State for Construction. Meanwhile, to meet the needs of opening up to the outside world and introduction of foreign capital and technologies, China had also adopted the Law on Chinese-Foreign Equity Joint Ventures, the Income Tax Law on Chinese-foreign Equity Joint Ventures, the Individual Income Tax Law, the Trademark Law, and the Patent Law, and approved the Regulations on Special Economic Zones in Guangdong Province. By then, China had already adopted some basic laws in the economic field, but these laws were still unable to meet the actual needs. It was therefore necessary to adopt more laws in the economic field, especially in the field of foreign economic cooperation, so as to ensure the smooth progress of the opening up and economic reform.[9] In 1993, Mr. Peng Chong, the then vice chairman of the NPC, pointed out in his summarization of the legislative work of the Seventh NPC that, during the previous five years, the NPC and its Standing Committee adopted a total of 87 decisions on legal issues, including the Amendment to the Constitution, 59 laws, and 27 decisions on other legal issues.

---

[9]See Chen (1985).

The 1988 Constitutional Amendment, by confirming the status of the private sector of the economy and allowing the transfer of the right to the use of land, has played a positive role in promoting the reform, opening up and economic construction. During the years that followed, the Standing Committee of the NPC had always taken the adoption of laws in the fields of economic construction, reform and opening up as the emphasis of its legislative work and had adopted 21 laws in the economic fields, and revised many important laws, including the Civil Procedure Law (for Trial Implementation), the Land Administration Law, the Law on Chinese-Foreign Equity Joint Ventures, the Environmental Protection Law, the Patent Law, and the Trademark Law.[10]

2.1.2.3   Constructing the Socialist Rule of Law in the Field of the Market Economy and Implementing the Basic Strategy of Ruling the Country by Law: From the Fourteenth CPC Party Congress in 1992 to the Eighteenth CPC Party Congress in 2012

Two events in the period between 1992 and 1997 will go down in history: the first one was the establishment of the socialist market economy and the construction of a primary legal system of socialist market economy; and the second one was the establishment of the basic strategy of constructing a socialist state under the rule of law and the reaching of an initial consensus among all Party members and Chinese people on the concept of the rule of law. It was the first time in the history of exploration of the socialist road that the market economy was combined with the socialist system and the principles of people being the master of their own country and adhering to the Party's leadership were combined with the principle of ruling the country by law. This opened up a new path for the development of the theory and practice of socialism with Chinese characteristics.

The Report of the Fourteenth CPC Party Congress pointed out that the objective of the economic reform in China is to establish and improve the socialist market economic system on the basis of adhering to the principle of taking public ownership and distribution according to work as the main body and other economic sectors and modes of distribution as the supplements, so as to establish the general reform objective of constructing a socialist market economic system. Accordingly, China should pay high attention to the construction of the rule of law, strengthen the legislative work, establish and improve the legal system of socialist market economy, especially it should speed up the adoption of laws and regulations urgently needed in the construction of the socialist economic system, such as those safeguarding reform and opening up, strengthening macro economic management, and regulating micro economic behaviors.

In 1993, with the deepening of reform and opening up, the revision of the Constitution once again became an urgent task. In March 1993, the Eighth NPC adopted at its first session a new amendment to the Constitution, which points out that China is at

---

[10]Peng (1993).

the primary stage of socialism and institutionalizes in the form of basic law theories of socialism with Chinese characteristics, the reform and opening up, and socialist market economy. This is conducive to attracting foreign capital and advanced technologies and promoting the development of the productive forces in China. Confirming the constitutional status of socialist market economy means China had began the large-scale adoption of laws and regulations in the economic field on the basis of the Constitution, thereby completely bringing the market-oriented reform into the legal system with the Constitution as its core. Practice has proved that the two amendments to the Constitution have played important role in promoting and safeguarding the reform, opening up and modernization in China. It has been proved by practice that the two amendments to the Constitution in 1988 and 1993 have played an important promotional and safeguarding role in the reform, opening up and modernization construction in China. To uphold the authority and stability of the Constitution, starting from 1988, China began to adopt the method of deliberation on and promulgation of "Constitutional amendments". Such amendments are promulgated as appendices to the main body of the Constitution.

In November 1993, the Fourteenth CPC Central Committee put forward for the first time the basic framework of socialist market economy at its Third Plenary Session: "to establish a modern corporate system adapted to the needs of the market economy, with clearly established ownership, well defined power and responsibility, separation of enterprises from administration, and scientific management", thereby promoting the reform of the SOEs towards the rationalization of the property rights relationships of enterprises and construction of a modern corporate system. This reform provided China with the tools for the realization of the two major tasks of economic reform in China, namely separation of enterprises from administration and transformation of enterprise management mechanism, which is dependent on a whole of system of law compatible with modern corporate system comprising of company law, securities law, financial law, bankrupt law, and unemployment benefit law. One of the important components of the framework of socialist market economic system is the legal system of socialist market economy.

In 1996, the Eighth NPC adopted at its fourth session the Ninth Five-year Plan for National Economic and Social Development and Long-range Objectives to 2010, which for the first time provided for the objective of "ruling the country by law and building a socialist state under the rule of law" in a document that has the effect of state law. Meanwhile, there had been an upsurge of explorations on the strategy of ruling the country by law in the law circle throughout the country and the concepts of "the legal system" and "the rule of law" (in Chinese language, the two terms have the same pronunciation: "*fazhi*") had become hot topics at that time."[11]

---

[11]"The rule of law" and the "legal system" are two different concepts and a distinction must be made between them both in theory and in practice. The main differences between the two concepts are the followings:

Firstly, "the rule of law" is a dynamic concept, meaning "regulation by law" or "governance by law" and indicating the condition, mode, degree, and process of the operation of law, whereas legal system is a static concept referring to "the system of law", "laws and institutions", or "laws and the system of law", namely the condition, mode and form of the existence of laws or the system of law.

At the Fifteenth Party Congress in 1997, the CPC established ruling the country by law (or in accordance with law) as the basic strategy of state governance and the construction of a socialist state under the rule of law as the objective of development of democratic politics. Ruling the country by law is the basic strategy by which the Party leads the Chinese people in governing state affairs, an objective requirement of

---

Secondly, the two concepts have different cultural deposits. The concept of the rule of law emerged in ancient Greece and Rome and gradually matured during the period of bourgeois revolution in modern history. After thousands of years of historical development, now its content and form have been basically recognized by most cultures. For example, the many ideas relating to the rule of law, such as the authority of law, transparency, popular sovereignty, safeguarding of human rights, and check and balance of power, have more or less been integrated into the legal culture of different countries. The expression and understanding of the concept of the rule of law have been established by usage in the international community, whereas the concept of "legal system" does not have such a profound historical and cultural deposit. In China, the cultural deposit of the "legal system" is in the final analysis only a kind of "kingly system". Replacing the concept of "the rule of law" with that of "legal system" is neither compatible with the original cultural intention of the "the rule of law", nor conducive to the communication and exchange between China and the international community.

Thirdly, the two concepts have different connotations. Currently, although the concrete meaning of "the rule of law" used by the jurists and politicians may vary from country to country, it is mainly a concept opposite to "the rule of man", with a relatively consistent and definite connotation. In contrast, the concept of "legal system" has no prescriptive connotation, and is often used in a more arbitrary way. Any country has its own legal system in any given period of time, but not necessarily implements the rule of law. Therefore, both a slavery society and a feudal society could establish its own legal system. Generally speaking, the established meaning of the concept "legal system" is "system of law" whereas the concept "the rule of law" is a common legal cultural heritage of mankind, rather than a patent of the bourgeoisie.

Fourthly, the two concepts have different significance of existence. The rule of law is a concept opposite to the rule of man. As such, it has clear-cut characteristics and functions of opposing and resisting the rule of man and ensuring lasting political stability. In contrast, "legal system" is a neutral concept relative to economic system, political system, and cultural system. There is no difference between ancient and contemporary or between Chinese and foreign concepts of "legal system". In a general sense, the concept has no time feature. It does not clearly express a stance against the rule of man and it is possible to have a "legal system under the rule of man". For example, the Nazi Regime in Hitler's Germany and the Apartheid Regime in South Africa had both implemented their policies through a legal system.

Fifthly, the two concepts are established on different bases. The concept of the rule of law, as an inevitable result of the development of modern commodity (market) economy and democratic politics, has been accepted by many countries and become a strategy of state governance. That is to say that the rule of law must take the market economy and democratic politics as its basis. It is a method of ruling the country that exists on the basis of market economy and under the democratic political system. Therefore, "the market economy is an economy under the rule of law" and the rule of law takes the market economy as its basis of existence and development. There will be no rule of law without the market economy, and vice versa. A legal system can be built on any form of economic basis that has existed since the emergence of law in human history, whereas the rule of law is inherent linked to democratic politics: the latter is the necessary basis and precondition for the emergence, existence and development of the former and the former is the basic mode and forceful safeguard of the existence and maintenance of the latter. Therefore, in a certain sense, it can be said that: "democratic politics is the politics under the rule of law", but there is no necessary linkage between democratic politics and legal system, which can also be linked to oligarchy, monarchy and fascism.

the development of socialist market economy, an important symbol of social progress, and an important safeguard for the long-term stability of the country.

In March 1999, a new constitutional amendment was adopted at the second session of the Ninth NPC. This amendment enshrines into the Constitution the guiding status of Deng Xiaoping's Theory, the basic economic system and distribution system at the current stage of social development, and the important role of the non-public sector of the economy and makes the ruling the country by law a basic constitutional principle. China is a country with a very long feudal history and lacks the tradition of democracy and the rule of law. The establishment of the basic strategy of ruling the country by law and the transition from the rule of man to the establishment of the legal system and then to implementation of the rule of law marked an important historical breakthrough in the construction of socialist rule of law with Chinese characteristics.

In 2002, the Report of the Sixteenth CPC National Congress pointed out that the key to the development of socialist democracy is to organically combine the principle of adhering to the Party's leadership with the principle of people being the masters of the country (popular sovereignty) and the principle of ruling the country by law. The Party's leadership is the basic guarantee for popular sovereignty and ruling the country by law, popular sovereignty is the essential requirement of socialist democratic politics, and ruling the country by law is the basic strategy by which the Party leads the people to govern the country. "The organic combination of the three principles" is the essential characteristic of socialist political civilization and the political orientation that China must adhere to in developing socialist democratic politics and building a socialist state under the rule of law. The report stressed the need to reform and improve the CPC's leadership mode and ruling mode. The Party's leadership mainly refers to political, ideological and organizational leadership, namely leading the country and society by adopting major policies, putting forward legislative proposals, recommending important cadres, carrying out ideological publicity, giving full play to the role of Party organizations and Party members, and adhering to the principle of ruling the country by law. The report pointed out that it is necessary to implement judicial reform, improve the institutional setup, division of functions and powers, and management of judicial organs in accordance with the requirements of judicial fairness and strictly implement the law, further develop a sound judicial system featuring clearly specified powers and responsibilities, mutual coordination and restraint and highly efficient operation. In 2004, a new amendment to the Constitution was adopted at the Second Session of the Tenth NPC. This constitutional amendment revised and improved many important systems provided for in the Constitution in accordance with the "people first" idea and the principle of human rights protection. Especially, by enshrining into the Constitution the important thought of the "Three Represents" and the principles of respecting human rights and safeguarding lawful private property, it once again confirms in the form of basic law the major developments and innovations of the theory and practice of reform and opening up.

At its Seventeenth National Congress in 2007, the CPC made strategic arrangements for the construction of the socialist rule of law with Chinese characteristics, put forward the general task of implementing in a comprehensive way the basic policy of ruling the country by law and speeding up the construction of a socialist state under the rule of law. This general task requires the Party and the Government to adhere to the scientific and democratic law-making, and improve the socialist system of law with Chinese characteristics; to strengthen the implementation of the Constitution and laws, adhere to the principle of equality of all citizens before the law, uphold social justice and the unity, the dignity and the authority of the socialist rule of law; to implement administration by law, deepen judicial reform, build up the rank of legal workers; carry out publicity of the rule of law in a deep-going way and promote the spirit of the rule of law; and to respect and safeguard human rights.

In March 2011, Mr. Wu Bangguo, the Chairman of the NPC Standing Committee, declared in the Work Report of the NPC Standing Committee at the Fourth Session of the Eleventh NPC that a socialist system of law with Chinese characteristics had already taken form. This system is based on the national conditions of China and adapted to the needs of reform, opening up and socialist modernization, embodies in a concentrated way the will of the Party and the will of the people, takes the Constitution as the key, other constitutional laws and the civil law, the commercial law and other branch laws as the backbone, and consists of different levels of legal norms, including laws, administrative regulations, and local regulations. The socialist legal system with Chinese characteristics is the legal basis for preserving the true color of the socialism with Chinese characteristics and the legal embodiment of the innovative practice of the socialism with Chinese characteristics, as well as the legal safeguard for the prosperity of socialism with Chinese characteristics. The formation on schedule of the Chinese legal system marked the realization in general of the objective of ensuring that there is laws to go by in the political, economic and social life of the country, and a big step forward in the legislative work of the construction of socialist rule of law with Chinese characteristics.

2.1.2.4 A Historical New Starting Point of the Rule of Law in China: Construction of Socialist Rule of Law with Chinese Characteristics Since the Eighteenth CPC National Congress

If it can be said that the strategic decision to construction democracy and the rule of law made at the Third Plenary Session of the Eleventh CPC Central Committee had brought the "first spring" of construction of socialist rule of law with Chinese characteristics since the reform and opening up, the series of major decisions and strategic arrangements made by the CPC since the Eighteenth Party Congress, such as those on implementing in a comprehensive way the rule by law, speeding up the construction of a "law-based China", and the modernization of state governance, are bringing the "second spring" of construction of socialist rule of law with Chinese characteristics.

The Report of the Eighteenth Party Congress clearly states that the basic tasks of China in the construction of the socialist rule of law with Chinese characteristics at the new historical starting point is to implement the rule by law in a comprehensive way and speed up the construction of a socialist state under the rule of law.

The speech made by Party Secretary-General Xi Jinping at the Conference held in Commemoration of the Thirtieth Anniversary of the Promulgation of the Current Constitution on December 4, 2012 further stressed that ruling the country by law is first and foremost ruling the country by the Constitution and highlighted the importance of implementing the Constitution and laws. As such, the speech played a significant programmatic and guiding role in the construction of the rule of law in China.

On February 23, 2013, the Political Bureau of the CPC Central Committee held the fourth collective study on implementing the policy of ruling the country by law, presided by Party Secretary-General Xi Jinping. In the study session, Xi emphasized that the objective of building a moderately prosperous society in a comprehensive way has raised higher demand for China with respect to ruling the country by law. The CPC must implement in an all-round way the spirit of the Eighteenth Party Congress, take Deng Xiaoping Theory, the important thought of "Three Represents" and Scientific Outlook on Development as its guidance, comprehensively promote scientific legislation, strict law enforcement, fair administration of justice, and observance of law by the whole population, simultaneously advance rule by law, governance by law, and administration by law, and the integrative construction of a law-based state, a law-based government, and a law-based society, and continuously break new ground for ruling the country by law.

Since the Eighteenth Party Congress, the CPC has put forward the follow new ideas and new concepts about constructing the rule of law and ruling the country by law:

- Comprehensively promoting the rule by law and speeding up the construction of a socialist state under the rule of law;
- Taking ruling the country by law as the basic strategy and the rule of law as the basic mode of state governance;
- Paying more attention to the role played by the rule of law in state and social governance;
- The "new sixteen-character guideline": scientific legislation, strict law enforcement, fair administration of justice, and observance of law by the whole population (the original "sixteen characters guideline" is: "there must be laws to go by, the laws must be observed and strictly enforced, and lawbreakers must be prosecuted");
- Striving to improve the capacity of leading cadres for applying the thinking and the method of the rule of law;
- The objectives of building a well-off society in an all-round way and constructing the rule of law: implementing in an all-round way the basic strategy of ruling the country by law, basically completing the construction of a law-based government, continuously improving public trust in the administration of justice, genuinely respecting and safeguarding human rights, and bringing all work of the state under the rule of law;
- Ruling the country by law is first and foremost ruling the country by the Constitution, exercising state power by law is first and foremost exercising state power

by the Constitution, and the life and the authority of the Constitution lies in its implementation;

- Exercising state power by law plays a major role in promoting ruling the country by law;
- Adhering to the simultaneous promotion of ruling the country by law, exercising state power by law, and administration by law and to the integrative construction of a law-based state, a law-based government and a law-based society;
- Creating a rule-of-law environment in which people are unwilling, unable, and afraid to break the law, no one has the privilege above the Constitution and laws, and it is absolutely prohibited to substitute law by personal views, suppress law with power, or bend the law for personal gains; and
- The rule of law being listed as one of the core socialist values (prosperity, democracy, civility, harmony, freedom, equality, justice, the rule of law, patriotism, dedication, integrity and friendship).

At the Third Plenary Session of the Eighteenth Central Committee, the CPC put forward new demands and new tasks for China in the construction of the rule of law, namely upholding the authority of the Constitution and laws, deepening the reform of administrative law enforcement, ensuring the independent and fair exercise of judicial and procuratorial powers, further developing the mechanism for the operation of judicial power, and improving the system of judicial protection of human rights.

Especially the Decision of Third Plenary Session of the Eighteenth Central Committee has set the following 17 tasks for the reform of the political and legal work: (1) reforming the judicial administration system, unifying the management of staffs, funds and properties of courts and procuratorates below the provincial level; (2) exploring ways to establish a judicial jurisdiction system that is appropriately separated from the administrative divisions to ensure that the state laws are enforced properly and uniformly; (3) establishing a judicial personnel management system fitting their professional characteristics, improving the system for unified recruitment, orderly exchange and level-by-level promotion of judges, procurators and the police, improving the classified management system of legal personnel, and guaranteeing the job security of judges, procurators and the police; (4) optimizing the distribution of judicial functions and powers, improving the system of judicial power division, coordination, checks and balances, and strengthening and standardizing the legal and social supervision over judicial activities; (5) reforming the judicial committee system, improving the responsibility system of handling cases by the presiding judge and the collegiate bench, by which the judges hand down verdicts and the collegiate bench is responsible for carrying them out; (6) clarifying the functions of courts at all levels, and standardizing their supervision through the judicial hierarchy; (7) promoting openness of trial, making the procuratorial work more transparent, and recording and keeping all court files and increasing the persuasiveness of legal instruments and pressing ahead with the publication of court ruling documents that have come into effect; (8) strictly regulating the procedures of sentence commutation, release on parole and medical parole, and enhancing the supervision system; (9) extensively implementing the people's assessor system and people's supervisor system to expand channels for the people to participate in legal affairs; (10) further standardizing the legal procedures for sealing up, sequestering, freezing and confiscating properties involved in a legal case; (11) improving the mechanism for preventing and correcting wrong cases and the accountability system, prohibiting the practices of extorting a confession by torture, corporal punishment and maltreatment, and strictly implementing rules on the exclusion of illegal evidences; (12) gradually reducing the number of charges that could lead to the death penalty; (13) abolishing the reeducation-through-labor system, improving laws for the punishment and rectification of unlawful and criminal acts, and perfecting the community correction system; (14) improving the national judicial relief and legal aid system; (15) improving the mechanism for protecting lawyers' rights to practice while punishing illegal practice, strengthening professional ethics and giving full play to the important role of lawyers in safeguarding the legitimate rights and interests of citizens and legal persons in accordance with the law; (16) strengthening the application and protection of intellectual property rights (IPR), improving the technological innovation incentive mechanism, and exploring ways to set up IPR courts; (17) reforming the system for handling complaints in the form of letters and visits, implementing an online system for handling complaints in the form of letters and visits, and improving the mechanism to resolve the people's appeals on the spot and in a timely manner.

In order to implement judicial reform in an active and steady way, the Leading Group for Comprehensively Deepening the Reform of the CPC Central Committee adopted the Opinions on Deepening the Judicial and Reforms and Plan for the Division of Work in the Implementation of Reform, Framework Opinions on Several Issues Concerning Pilot Reform of the Judicial System, and Work Program of Pilot Judicial Reform in Shanghai Municipality, which further provided for the objectives and principles of judicial reform as well as the roadmap and timetable for the implementation of the reform, thereby providing the policy guidance for overcoming the difficulties in the orderly implementation of the pilot reform, and indicating that the judicial reform in China had entered into a new stage of combining top-level design with practical exploration and advancing on the whole with breakthrough at key points.

At the Fourth Plenary Meeting of the Eighteenth CPC Central Committee, held on October 20–23, 2014, the issue of construction of the socialist rule of law with Chinese characteristics was discussed and the Decision on Several Major Issues concerning Comprehensively Advancing Governance in accordance with Law (hereinafter referred to as the Decision) was adopted. This was the first time in the 160-year history of International Communist Movement, 90-year history of the CPC, 60-year history of the People's Republic of China and 30-year history of reform and opening up in China for a ruling political party of the proletariat to convene a plenary meeting to make a decision on the issue of the rule of law. The Decision was an important milestone marking the historical step taken by China to transform itself from a big power with a sound legal system to a big power under the rule of law, and a new historical starting point and new stage in ruling the country by law and constructing the rule of law in China.

Ruling the country by law is the essential requirement of and an important safeguard for the implementation of the strategy of adhering to and developing socialism with Chinese characteristics as well as an inevitable requirement of the modernization of state governance system and the governance capacity and is of great importance to the exercise of political power by the ruling Party, to the well-being of the people, and to the long-term stability of the country. In order to build a moderately prosperous society in an all-round way, realize the Chinese dream of the great rejuvenation of Chinese nation, deepen the reform in a comprehensive way, further improve and develop the system of socialism with Chinese characteristics, and improve the governance capacity of the Party, China must implement the strategy of ruling the country by law in an all-round way. Currently China is at the primary stage of socialism, the decisive stage in the construction of a moderately prosperous society in an all-round way, and a critical stage and a deep water zone of reform. At this stage, the international situation is complicated and changing constantly and the CPC is faced with unprecedented heavy tasks of carrying out reform, promoting development and maintaining stability and unprecedented number of conflicts, risks and challenges. As a result, the strategy of ruling the country by law is playing an increasingly prominent and important role in the work of Party and the state. Faced with the new situation and new tasks, the CPC needs to take into overall consideration of domestic and international situations and give fuller play to the guiding and regulating role of the rule of law, so that China will be able to seize the important strategic opportunity of development, make an overall arrangement of social forces, balance social interests, adjust social relations, regulate social conducts, keep society both vibrant and orderly during the profound changes, achieve economic growth, good governance, a flourishing culture, social justice, and a healthy ecology, and attain its strategic goal of peaceful development.

The Decision, consisting of 17,000 Chinese characters and containing over 180 reform measures, is a programmatic document on comprehensively advancing governance by law at a new historical starting point. It consists of the following seven parts, which provides for in detail the great significance, guiding ideology, overall objectives, basic principles, and general tasks of comprehensive advancement of ruling the country by law:

Part One: Introduction—Adhering to the Road of Socialist Rule of Law with Chinese Characteristics and Establishing a Socialist System of the Rule of Law with Chinese Characteristics

Firstly, it clearly puts forward the guiding ideology of comprehensive advancement of ruling the country by law: to comprehensive advance ruling the country by law, China must implement the spirit of the 18th Party Congress and the 3rd Plenum of the 18th Party Congress, hold high the magnificent banner of Socialism with Chinese characteristics, take Marxism-Leninism, Mao Zedong Thought, Deng Xiaoping Theory, the important "Three Represents" thought, and the Scientific Outlook on Development as guidance, implement in a deep-going way the spirit of the series of important speeches by General Secretary Xi Jinping, adhere to the organic unity of the leadership of the Party, the people being masters of the country, and ruling the country according to the law, unwaveringly march the road of socialist rule of law with Chinese characteristics, firmly uphold the authority of the Constitution and the laws, protect the people's rights and interests according to the law, uphold social fairness and justice, protect national security and stability, and provide powerful rule of law guarantees for the realization of the "Two Centuries" struggle objectives and the Chinese dream of the great rejuvenation of the Chinese nation.

Secondly, it clearly puts forward the general objective of comprehensive advancement of ruling the country by law, including: constructing a socialist system of the rule of law with Chinese characteristics and a socialist country under the rule of law, namely, adhering to the leadership of the CPC and to the socialist system with Chinese characteristics, implementing the theory of socialist rule of law with Chinese characteristics, shaping a perfect system of legal norms, a highly effective system to implement the rule of law, a strict system of rule of law supervision, a powerful system of rule of law guarantees, and a well-established system of intra-Party regulations, persisting in simultaneous advancement of ruling the country by law, governance by law and administration by law and in the unified construction of a law-based country, a law-based government and a law-based society, realizing scientific legislation, strict law enforcement, judicial fairness and respect for the law among the entire population, and advancing the modernization of the state governance system and governance capacity.

Thirdly, it clearly puts forward the five basic principles that must be adhered to in the advancement of ruling the country by law: the leadership of the CPC, the people being the masters of the country, the equality of everyone before the law, the combination of ruling the country by law with ruling the country by virtue, and proceeding from the reality in China.

Part Two: Perfecting a Socialist Legal System with Chinese Characteristics, with the Constitution as Its Core, and Strengthening the Implementation of the Constitution

First, ideological innovation and basic thinking: laws are important tools to rule the country and good laws are the precondition for good governance. To construct a socialist legal system with Chinese characteristics, China must persist in giving priority to legislation, giving full play to the guiding and driving role of legislation, and grasp the crucial matter of raising the quality of legislation; strictly abide by the ideas of putting people first and legislating for the sake of the people; implement the socialist core value system; ensure that every piece of legislation conforms to the spirit of the law, reflects the popular will and is endorsed by the people; let the principles of fairness, justice and transparency penetrate into the entire process of legislation; perfect legislative systems and mechanisms, pay equal attention to legislation, revision, abolition and interpretation and strengthen the timeliness, systematicness, focus and effectiveness of laws and regulations.

Second, improving constitutional implementation and supervision system, including: improving the constitutional supervision system of the National People's Congress and its Standing Committee and completing procedural mechanisms for constitutional interpretation; strengthening the systems for record keeping and review, and building the relevant capacities, so as to bring all normative documents into the scope of recording and review; designating the 4th of December of each year as the National Constitution Day; and establishing a constitutional oath system to require all state personnel elected or appointed by the National People's Congress and its Standing Committee to openly swear a constitutional oath when taking office.

Third, improving the legislative system. (1) Improving procedures for Party poli-cymaking concerning major issues in legislative work. All legislations involve adjust-ment of major structures or major policies must be reported to the CPC Central Committee for discussion and decision. The CPC Central Committee puts forward suggestions on constitutional revision to the National People's Congress, and con-stitutional revision is conducted according to the procedure determined in the Con-stitution. Major questions relating to the formulation and revision of laws are to be reported to the CPC Central Committee by the Party Group of the NPC Standing Committee. Increasing the proportion of full-time committee members with expe-rience in the rule of law practice and establishing and completing legislative expert consultant systems for special committees and work committees. (2) Completing structures and mechanisms for people's congresses with legislative power to lead legislative work, give full play to the dominant role of people's congresses and their standing committees in legislative work; establishing a system whereby the drafting of laws that are comprehensive in nature, affect the overall picture, or are funda-mental or important in other ways is organized by the relevant special committee of the NPC and the Legislative Affairs Commission of the NPC Standing Com-mittee, with the participation of relevant government departments. Strengthen the proportion of full-time committee members with experience in rule of law practice. Establish and complete legislative expert consultant systems with special commit-tees and work committees. (3) Strengthening and improving the construction of the government legislative system, completing procedures for the formulation of admin-istrative regulations and rules and mechanisms for the participation by the general public in government legislation. The drafting of important administrative manage-ment laws and regulations is to be organized by government legal affairs bodies. (4) Clearly establishing the boundaries of legislative powers and effectively preventing through institutions, mechanisms and work procedures the legalization of depart-mental interests and local protectionism; strengthening the legal interpretation work, timely clarifying the meanings of legal provisions and the legal basis for applying them; and clarifying the limits and scope of local legislation, giving local legislative powers to cities divided into districts in accordance with the law.

Fourth, promoting scientific legislation and democratic legislation in a deep-going way: (1) completing systems of soliciting opinions from deputies to people's con-gresses in the drafting of laws, regulations and rules, perfecting systems of collecting and demonstrating legislative projects, completing channels and methods for people from all walks of society to orderly participate in law-making activities lead by leg-islative bodies, and exploring ways of entrusting third parties with drawing up laws and regulations drafts; (2) improving mechanisms for the communication between legislative organs and the general public, broadening channels for citizens' orderly participation in legislation, completing mechanisms for the open solicitation of opinions on draft laws, regulations and rules and mechanisms for feedback on the extent to which the public opinions are adopted in the drafting of laws and regulations; (3) improving procedures for voting on legal drafts and allowing important provisions to be voted on individually.

Fifth, strengthening the legislation in key areas: guaranteeing citizens' rights in accordance with the law, accelerating the perfection of legal systems embodying equality of rights, opportunities and rules, protecting citizens' personal rights, property rights, basic political rights and rights in all other areas against infringement, guaranteeing that citizens' economic, cultural, social and all other rights are implemented, bringing the protection of citizens' rights under the rule of law, enhancing the consciousness of respecting and protecting human rights among the general public, and completing channels and methods that provide remedy for the infringement of citizens' rights.

Sixth, establishing linkages between legislation and reform policymaking, ensuring that major reforms have a legal basis and that legislation actively adapts to the needs of reform and economic and social development and that what have been proven effective in practice be timely upgraded into law, that where practical conditions are not yet mature and trials are necessary, these must be authorized according to statutory procedure, and that laws and regulations that are incompatible with the needs of reform are timely revised or abolished.

Part Three: Advancing Administration by Law in a Deep-Going Way and Accelerating the Construction of a Law-Based Government

First, innovation of ideas and basic thinking: the vitality and the authority of the law lie in its implementation. Governments at all levels must persist in conducting their work on the track of the rule of law and under the Party's leadership, innovate the law enforcement systems, perfect law enforcement procedures, advance comprehensive law enforcement, strictly define law enforcement responsibilities, establish an authoritative and efficient system of administration by law with unified duties and powers, accelerate the construction of a law-based government with scientific functions, statutory powers and responsibilities, which strictly enforces the law enforcement and is open and just, clean and effective, law-abiding and honest.

Second, comprehensively performing administrative functions according to the law: (1) perfecting legal systems of administrative organization and administrative procedure, advancing the adoption of statutes on the organization, functions, powers, procedures and responsibilities of administrative organs, prohibiting administrative organs from establishing powers outside of the law, or making decision to impinge on the lawful rights and interests of citizens, legal persons or other organizations, or to increase their duties without a basis in law and regulations, and implementing a governmental power list system; (2) propelling the standardization and legalization of governmental duties and responsibilities at all levels, perfecting legal systems of duties and responsibilities of government at different levels, especially those of the central and local governments, strengthening the central government's responsibilities of macro-level management and institutional construction and its necessary law enforcement powers, strengthening the duties of provincial governments to comprehensively plan and move forward the equalization of basic regional public services, and strengthening the implementation duties of city and county governments.

Third, completing mechanisms for policymaking according to the law: (1) establishing mechanisms within administrative bodies for the review of the lawfulness of major policy decisions, whereby policy decision that has not been reviewed or is determined to be unlawful in the review may not be submitted for deliberation; (2) implementing government legal advisor system and ensuring that legal advisors play a positive role in the formulation of major administrative policy decisions and in the implementation of the system of administration by law; (3) establishing mechanisms for the investigation and tracing of life-long responsibility for major policy decisions, whereby the legal liability of the administrative head, other leading personnel bearing responsibility and corresponding responsible personnel will be strictly investigated in cases where grave mistakes in policymaking or a long-term delay in the making of policies that should have been made in a timely manner have resulted in major damage or deleterious influences.

Fourth, deepening the reform of the administrative law enforcement system. (1) advancing comprehensive law enforcement, substantially reducing the categories of government law enforcement teams at both city and county levels, focusing on carrying out comprehensive law enforcement in the fields of food and drug safety, industrial and commercial quality inspection, public hygiene, production safety, culture and tourism, resources and the environment, agriculture, forestry and water conservation, traffic and transportation, urban and rural construction, fisheries and other such areas. cross-departmental comprehensive law enforcement may be practiced in areas that meet the relevant conditions; (2) perfecting administrative law enforcement at both the city and county government levels, and strengthening unified leadership and coordination; rationalizing the system of coercive administrative law enforcement and urban management law enforcement system; (3) strictly implementing the system whereby only administrative law enforcement personnel holding qualification certificates are allowed to work on relevant posts, the system of qualification of administrative law enforcement personnel, the system of separating the imposition of fines from the collection of fines, and the system of separating income from expenses; (4) improving linkage mechanisms between administrative law enforcement and criminal justice, perfecting case transfer standards and procedures, establishing systems for the share of information, notification of case details and transfer of cases between administrative law enforcement, public security, procuratorial and adjudicative organs, and realizing seamless linkages between administrative punishment and criminal punishment.

Fifth, persisting in strict, standardized, fair and civilized law enforcement. (1) perfecting law enforcement procedures and establishing systems for the recording of entire law enforcement process; clearly define concrete operational procedure, focusing on standardizing administrative licensing, administrative punishment, administrative enforcement, administrative appropriation, administrative fees collection, administrative inspection and other such administrative law enforcement acts; strictly implementing the legal examination and verification system for major law enforcement decisions; (2) establishing and completing basic standard systems for administrative discretion, strengthening the informatization construction and information sharing in administrative law enforcement, and raising the levels of efficiency and standardization of law enforcement; (3) implementing in an all-round way the system of responsibilities for administrative law enforcement, strengthening supervision over law enforcement and punishing and controlling corruption in law enforcement.

Sixth, strengthening the constraint on and supervision over administrative powers: (1) taking the strengthening of the constraint on internal government power as the focus point for strengthening constraint on administrative power; perfecting departmental-level internal government supervision and special internal supervision, improving supervision by higher-level bodies over lower-level bodies, establishing regularized supervision systems; and perfecting rectification mechanism and accountability mechanism; (2) perfecting the auditing system to ensure that auditing supervision powers are exercised independently and in accordance with the law; strengthening leadership of higher-level auditing bodies over lower-level auditing bodies; exploring the uniform management of the human, financial and material resources of local auditing bodies below the provincial level; and advancing the construction of professionalized auditing.

Seventh, comprehensively advancing openness in government affairs: (1) advancing open policymaking, open implementation, open management, open services and open results; focusing on moving forward with the disclosure of government information relating to finances and budgetary affairs, public resource allocation, approval and implementation of major construction programs, public interest undertaking construction and other such areas; and implementing the system of public announcement of administrative law enforcement and the informatization of government affairs.

Part Four: Guaranteeing Judicial Fairness and Raising Judicial Credibility

First, innovation of ideas and basic thinking: fairness is the lifeline of the rule of law. Judicial fairness plays an important role as the guidance in the realization of social justice, and judicial unfairness has a fatally damaging effect on social justice. China must improve the judicial administration system and the mechanisms for the operation of judicial power, standardize judicial conduct, strengthen supervision over judicial activities, and strive to enable the people to feel fairness and justice in every judicial case.

Second, improving systems for ensuring the independent and impartial exercise of adjudicative and procuratorial powers in accordance with law: (1) establishing a system for recording, reporting, and investigating the responsibility of leading cadres for interfering in judicial activities or meddling with the handling of cases; (2) establishing and improving mechanisms for ensuring that administrative organs appear in court to respond to litigation, support courts in accepting administrative cases, and respect and enforce effective court judgments; improving legal provisions on punishing the acts of obstructing judicial organs from lawfully performing their duties, refusing to enforce effective judgments and decisions, showing contempt for the authority of the court and other such violations and crimes; (3) establishing and improving mechanisms for the protection of judicial personnel performing their statutory duties.

Third, optimizing the configuration of judicial functions and powers: (1) establishing and improving institutional systems in which the public security organs, procuratorates, judicial organs and judicial administrative organs each perform it own functions, while at the same time coordinate with each other and check and balance each other; (2) improving the judicial system, promoting pilot projects on institutional reforms aimed at separating the adjudicative power from the enforcement power; improving systems for the enforcement of criminal penalties, unifying criminal enforcement systems; reforming systems for the management of personnel and finances of judicial organs, exploring and implementing a system of separation between the judicial administrative power and adjudicative or procuratorial powers in courts and procuratorates; (3) establishing circuit court divisions under the Supreme People's Court, exploring ways of establishing trans-regional people's courts and people's procuratorates to handle cross regional cases; (4) reforming the system of acceptance of cases by the court, transforming the case filing review system into a case filing registration system, and ensure that all cases that should be accepted by the people's courts are filed and dealt with; (5) improving appeals systems, with the trial of the first instance focusing on the determination of facts and application of law, the trial of the second instance focusing on the resolution of disputes over fact and law, second-instance judgments being final, and retrials focusing on rectifying errors in accordance with law and upholding the authority of judgments. If procuratorial organs, in the course of performing their duties, find out that administrative organs have performed their duties unlawfully or not performed their duties, they should supervise and urge such administrative organs to make corrections; and exploring the establishment of systems for the initiation of public interest lawsuits by procuratorates; (6) defining the internal competence of judicial organs at all levels and completing the internal supervision and restraint mechanisms of judicial organs; prohibiting internal personnel of judicial organs from interfering in case currently being handled by other personnel in violation of the relevant provisions; establishing mechanisms for the recording and investigation of responsibilities for the interference by internal personnel of judicial organs in the handling of cases; improving case handling responsibility systems for presiding judges, collegial panels, head procurators and leading investigators, and implementing a system of accountability of the person handling the cases.

Fourth, promoting strict administration of justice: (1) strengthening and standardizing judicial interpretation and case guidance, and unifying standards on the application of law; (2) advancing trial-centered reform of the litigation system; (3) clarifying the work duties, work flow and work standards of all types of judicial personnel, and implementing a system of lifetime responsibility for case-handling quality and a wrongful case accountability system.

Fifth, ensuring the masses participation in the judiciary: (1) improving the people's assessors system, gradually implementing a system whereby people's assessors no longer hear issues relating to the application of law and only hear issues relating to the determination of fact; building open, dynamic, transparent, and convenient sunshine judicial mechanisms; and establishing an integrated online open inquiry system for effective legal documents.

Sixth, strengthening the judicial protection of human rights: (1) improving the systems implementing the principle of legally prescribed punishment for a specified crime, the principle of exclusion of unlawfully obtained evidence, and other legal principles; (2) effectively overcoming difficulties in enforcement of judgments, adopting a law on compulsory enforcement of judgments and standardizing judicial procedures for sealing, seizing, freezing and disposing of assets involved in cases; (3) implementing systems for the conclusion of trials and termination of legal proceedings, separating litigation from petitions, and guaranteeing parties' lawful right to appeal.

Seventh, strengthening the supervision over judicial activities: (1) improving the people's supervisor system, standardize media reporting of cases to prevent public opinion from influencing judicial fairness; (2) standardizing the contacts and interactions between judicial personnel and parties to the case, lawyers, people with special interests in the case and intermediary organizations in accordance with law; (3) resolutely abolishing all kinds of unwritten rules, absolutely prohibiting the practices of showing mercy outside the law, or dealing with cases under the influence of connections, favors or money.

Part Five: Strengthening the Rule of Law Consciousness of the Whole People and Promoting the Construction of a Society Under the Rule of Law

First, innovation of ideas and basic thinking: the authority of the law comes from the people's genuine acceptance of and belief in the law. The people depend on the law to guarantee their rights and interests, whereas the law depends on the people to uphold its authority. We must carry forward the spirit of socialist rule of law, build a socialist culture of the rule of law, enhance the enthusiasm and initiative of the entire society to vigorously enforce the rule of law, create a social atmosphere in which abiding by the law is honorable and violating the law is disgraceful, make the whole body of the people become faithful upholders, conscientious observers and firm protectors of socialist rule of law.

Second, promoting the rule of law consciousness among the general public: (1) guiding the people to consciously abide by the law, consult the law when encountering problems, and rely on the law to solve their problems; perfecting the systems whereby state personnel study the law and use the law in their daily work; making the Constitution and the laws a subject of study of central groups of Party committees (Party groups), and a mandatory course in Party schools, administrative academies, cadre academies and socialist academies; incorporating the education on the rule of law into the national educational system, starting rule-of-law education at an early age, and setting up class on the knowledge of the rule of law in primary and secondary schools; (2) completing legal popularization, publicity and education mechanisms; integrating the education on the rule of law into spiritual civilization construction, launching mass rule-of-law cultural activities, completing the system of public interest popularization of law by mass media, strengthening the use of new media and new technologies in the popularization of law, and improving the effectiveness of popularization of law; (3) strengthening the construction of social honesty, completing law compliance credit records of citizens and organizations, perfecting commendation mechanisms for abiding by the law and punitive mechanisms for violating the law and breaking promises, make respect for the law and abiding by the law into a common pursuit and conscious act of the whole people; (4) strengthening the construction of citizens' morality, carrying forward China's excellent traditional culture, giving full play to the role of the rule of law in resolving prominent problems in the area of morality.

Third, advancing governance by law at multiple levels and in multiple areas: (1) adhering to systematic governance, governance in accordance with law, comprehensive governance, and governance at the source, and raising the rule of law level of social governance; (2) giving full play to the positive role of people's organizations and social organizations in the construction of a law-based society; (2) giving full play to the role of social organizations in guiding and regulating the behavior of their members, and safeguarding their rights and interests; (3) appropriately dealing with social problems involving ethnicity, religion and other such factors in accordance with law, and promoting harmony in ethnic and religious relationships.

Fourth, building a complete legal service system: moving forward with the construction of a public legal service system covering urban and rural residents, improving the legal aid system; developing the legal services industry, including lawyer's services, notaries public services, etc., and completing the unified judicial testimony management system.

Fifth, completing mechanisms for upholding rights and mediating disputes in accordance with law: (1) strengthening the authoritative position of law in safeguarding the interests of the masses and resolving social contradictions; (2) bringing petitioning by letters and visits onto track of the rule of law, ensuring that those who make reasonable and lawful claims can get reasonable and lawful results in accordance with legal provisions and procedures; (3) improving mechanisms for preventing and resolving social contradictions and disputes, improving pluralized dispute resolution mechanisms; improving the joint work systems for people's mediation, administrative mediation and judicial mediation; and improving the arbitration system and the administrative adjudication system; (4) advancing comprehensive treatment of public security, and improving and implementing the leadership responsibility systems.

Part Six: Strengthening the Construction of Rule-of-Law Work Teams

First, innovation of ideas and basic thinking: To comprehensively advancing ruling the country by the law, we must forcefully raise the ideological and political quality, professional abilities and levels of professional ethics of rule-of-law work teams, strive to build a team of socialist rule-of-law work who are loyal to the Party, to the country, to the people, and to the law, and provide powerful organizational and talent guarantees to accelerate the construction of a socialist country under the rule of law.

Second, building high-quality specialized rule of law teams: (1) putting ideological and political construction first, and opening up channels for the circulation of cadres and talent between legislative, law enforcement, judicial, and other organs; (2) advancing the regularization, specialization and professionalization of special rule of law teams, and raising their professional quality and specialization levels; perfecting access systems, improving national uniform qualification and examination systems, and establishing uniform pre-appointment training systems for legal professionals; establishing systems to recruit legislative workers, judges and procurators from among lawyers and legal scholars and experts who meet the requirements, opening up channels for transferred military cadres who meet the conditions to join specialized rule of law teams, establish standardized and convenient mechanisms for recruiting talents from among graduates from colleges of political science and law; (3) establishing systems for the level-by-level selection of judges and prosecutors.

Third, strengthening the construction of legal service teams: (1) improving the professional quality of the lawyer's teams and perfecting mechanisms for professional guarantees. (2) Party and government bodies and public organizations at all levels should appoint publicly employed lawyers, and enterprises may appoint corporate lawyers; (3) developing teams of notary public, grassroots legal service worker and people's mediators and promoting the construction of teams of legal service volunteers.

Fourth, innovating mechanisms for fostering talents in the field of the rule of law: (1) persisting in using Marxist legal thinking and the theory of socialist rule of law with Chinese characteristics to occupy the legal education and legal research battlefield in tertiary education and research bodies in all directions, strengthening research on basic legal theory, constructing complete theory systems, disciplinary systems and course systems of socialist law science with Chinese characteristics, organizing the compilation and the comprehensive use of national uniform core legal textbooks, and bringing them into the mandatory scope of the judicial examination; enabling the theory of socialist rule of law with Chinese characteristics to enter textbooks, classrooms and people minds, and fostering rule-of-law talents and reserve forces who are well acquainted with and adhere to the system of socialist rule of law with Chinese characteristics; and building up teams of foreign-oriented rule-of-law talents who thoroughly understand international legal rules and are good at dealing with foreign-oriented legal affairs; (2) improving two-way interaction and personnel exchange mechanisms between political-legal departments of the government and legal-education institutions and legal research bodies, focusing on forging teams of high-level legal scholars and experts and building teams of high-quality academic leaders, backbone teachers and full and part-time teachers.

Part Seven: Strengthening and Improving the Party's Leadership in the Comprehensive Advancement of Ruling the Country by Law

First, innovation of ideas and basic thinking: The Party's leadership is the most fundamental guarantee for comprehensively advancing ruling the country by law and accelerating the construction of a socialist country under the rule of law. We must strengthen and improve Party leadership over the rule-of-law work, and let Party leadership penetrate into the entire process of comprehensively advancing ruling the country by law.

Second, persisting in the exercise of the ruling power by law. Exercising the ruling law by law is the key to ruling the country by law: (1) leading cadres at all levels must cherish the law with a heart of reverence, keep firmly in mind that the legal red line may be exceeded and that the legal baseline may not be touched. They must take the lead in abiding by the law and handle affairs in accordance with law, not exercise their power in violation of the law, substitute the law with their personal views, use their power to suppress the law, or bend the law for the benefit of their relatives and friends; (2) completing systems and work mechanisms for ruling the country by law under the leadership of the Party, perfecting working mechanisms and procedures for guaranteeing that the Party determines the principles and policies on and makes arrangements for ruling the country by law; perfecting mechanisms for Party committees to make policy decisions according to the law, giving full play to the advantages of both policies and laws, and promoting the interrelation and interaction between Party policies and state laws; Party committees must regularly listen to work reports of political-legal bodies and take the lead in promoting judicial fairness and upholding the authority of the law; principle responsible persons in the Party and the government must perform their duty as the primary responsible persons for the construction the rule of law; (3) Party organizations and Party members and cadres in people's congresses, governments, consultative conferences, trial bodies and prosecutorial bodies must firmly implement the Party's theories, lines, principles and policies, and policy decisions and arrangements of Party committees; (4) political-legal commissions, which are the organizational form in which Party committees lead political-legal work, must be maintained for the long run.

Third, strengthening the construction of intra-Party regulatory systems: (1) improving internal Party systems and mechanisms for formulating regulations; strengthening internal mechanisms for the recording, review and interpretation of intra-Party regulations; forming complete supporting systems for intra-regulations; paying attention to linking and coordinating intra-Party regulations with state laws, and raising the capacity for implementing intra-Party regulations; (2) intra-Party regulations and Party disciplines are stricter than state laws. Party organizations at all levels and all Party members and cadres must not only take the lead in abiding by state laws, but also put strict demands on themselves according to the even higher standards of intra-Party regulations and Party disciplines; (3) opposing and overcoming formalism, bureaucratism, hedonism and extravagant tendencies in accordance with Party disciplines and state laws, and developing strict and long-term mechanisms to ensure that any corrupt act or corrupt element is firmly punished according to Party disciplines and the law.

Fourth, enhancing the rule of law thinking of Party members and cadres, and their ability to handle affairs according to the law. Making achievements in the construction of the rule of law an important criterion for measuring the work achievements of leading cadres at all levels, and bringing it into the career achievement assessment indicator system for government officials; making the ability to abide by the law and conduct affairs according to the law an important criterion for evaluating cadres; when appointing cadres with identical conditions, giving priority to those with good accomplishments in the construction of the rule of law and having a strong ability to conduct affairs according to the law.

Fifth, bringing grassroots governance under the rule of law: strengthening the construction of grassroots rule of law bodies and grassroots rule of law teams, establishing rule of law work mechanisms for moving the centre of gravity and forces downward, improving grassroots infrastructure and equipment, and advancing the mechanisms for encouraging rule of law cadres to carry out activities at the grassroots units.

Sixth, implementing in a deep-going way the policy of ruling the army strictly in accordance with law: the Party's absolute leadership over the army is a core and fundamental requirement of ruling the army according to the law. (1) innovatively developing the theory and practice of ruling the army in accordance with law, building and perfecting military rule of law systems with Chinese characteristics, and raising the rule-of-law level of national defence and military construction; (2) persisting in vigorously and prudently advancing national defence and military reform along the track of the rule of law, deepening reform of military leadership and command structures, force composition, policy structures and other aspects, and accelerating the perfection and development of a socialist military system with Chinese characteristics; (3) establishing military regulatory systems that are adapted to the construction of a modern military and operational requirements, strictly standardizing the powers and procedures to formulate military regulations and institutions, and bringing all military normative documents into the scope of review; (4) reinforcing the implementation strength of military regulations, clearly establishing law enforcement responsibilities, improving law enforcement systems, completing law enforcement supervision mechanisms, strictly investigating responsibilities, and promoting the effective implementation of the policy of ruling the army according to the law; (5) completing the system of military legislative work and establishing and perfecting legislative bodies in leading organs; establishing a military advisor system in leading organs at all levels and perfecting legal consultation guarantee systems for major policy decisions and military actions; and reforming military discipline inspection and supervision systems; (6) enhancing the rule of law consciousness and rule of law qualities of officers and soldiers, improving military legal talent training mechanisms; and strengthening research on the theory of military rule of law.

Seventh, guaranteeing the practice of "one country, two systems" in accordance with law and advancing the unity of the motherland and protecting the rights and interests of Hong Kong, Macau and Taiwan compatriots in accordance with law.

Eighth, strengthening foreign-related legal work: perfecting foreign-related legal and regulatory systems, promoting the construction of new system of open economy; actively participating in the formulation of international norms, strengthening China's discourse power and influence in international legal affairs, and using legal methods to safeguard China sovereignty, security and development interests; strengthening foreign-related legal services, deepening international judicial cooperation, perfecting China's judicial assistance systems, and expanding the coverage of international judicial assistance; and strengthening international cooperation on anti-corruption, actively participating in international cooperation concerning law enforcement security, and jointly fight against violent and terrorist forces, ethnic separatist forces, religious extremist forces, drug smuggling and cross-border organized crime.

2.2   Historical Achievements Made by China in the Construction of the Socialist Rule of Law with Chinese Characteristics

The rule of law is the indicator of a certain historical stage of development of political civilization. As the crystallization of human wisdom, it is aspired and pursued by people of all countries. The CPC has attached great importance to the construction of the rule of law and, in the great practice of leading Chinese people in winning the victories of socialist revolution, construction, and reform and in the process of continuously developing socialist democratic politics with Chinese characteristics, has summarized both the positive and the negative experiences of constructing the socialist rule of law, established the rule of law as the basic strategy and method of ruling the country and managing state affairs, used the rule-of-law thinking and method to actively promote theoretical innovation, institutional reform, and practical development of socialist rule of law, and made historical achievements that have attracted worldwide attention in all the main areas of construction of the rule of law.

2.2.1   Establishment of Ruling the Country by Law as a Basic Strategy of State Governance

The establishment of the PRC ushered in a new era of construction of the rule of law in China. However, in the late 1950s, especially during the ten-year "Cultural Revolution", the socialist legal system in China had been severely sabotaged. Since the Third Plenary Session of the Eleventh Central Committee, the CPC has learnt a lesson from the bitter experience of the "Cultural Revolution" and made the important decision to shift the emphasis of its work to socialist modernization and to implement the policy of reform and opening up, and clearly pointed out that, without democracy, there will be no socialism or socialist modernization. To build a modernized socialist state and safeguard people's democracy, China must strengthen the socialist legal system, institutionalize democracy and bring it into the scope of law, so as to ensure the stability, continuity and authority of such system and law, and prevent them from being changed with the change of the view or the focus of attention of state leaders, and ensure that there are laws to go by, the laws are observed and strictly enforced, and those who violate the law are investigated for responsibilities. Developing socialist democracy and improving socialist legal system has become a basic policy adhered to by the CPC and promoted the historical transition from "the rule of man" to "the rule of law" in China. At the Third Plenary Session of its Eleventh Central Committee, the CPC made a decision to establish a socialist market economy, to pay high attention to the construction of the legal system and to establish and perfect the legal system of socialist market economy. At its Fifteenth National Congress, the CPC established, for the first time in history, the rule of law as its basic strategy for leading the people in administering state affairs, and the construction of a socialist country under the rule of law as the objective of development of democratic politics, thereby realizing the fundamental transition from the construction of "the legal system" to the construction of "the rule of law" and marking a new beginning of the construction of socialist rule of law with Chinese characteristics. At its Sixteenth National Congress, the CPC clearly pointed out that, in order to develop democratic political system with Chinese characteristics, China must adhere to organic unity of the Party's leadership, the principle of people being the master of the country and the strategy of ruling the country by law, thereby further pointing out the correct direction and the path of development of the rule of law and construction of socialist rule of law in China. At its seventeenth and eighteenth national congresses, the CPC continued to hold high the banner of socialist rule of law and implemented the basic strategy of ruling the country by law through the promotion of scientific legislation, strict law enforcement, fair administration of justice, and observance of law by the whole people.

Ruling the country by law means that the Chinese people, under the leadership of the CPC, manage political, economic, cultural and social affairs of the state through various channels and in various forms in accordance with the provisions of the law, ensure that various kinds of work of the state are carried out in accordance with law, and gradually realize the institutionalization of socialist democracy and bring it under the rule of law. It also means implementing democracy and the rule of law and opposing dictatorship and the rule of man, controlling power and public officials in accordance with law, respecting and safeguarding human rights, and enhancing people's well-being.

Ruling the country by law means to adhere to the principles of the supremacy of people's sovereignty and the supremacy of the Constitution and laws, respecting and safeguarding human rights, exercising the ruling power in accordance with law, promoting democratic and scientific legislation, administration by law, and fair administration of justice, and supervising, checking and balancing public power. Under the current constitutional framework and rule-of-law context, ruling the country by law has the following six basic elements: (1) the leading core of ruling the country by law is the CPC. The CPC's leadership is a necessary requirement and a basic guarantee of the comprehensive implementation of the strategy of ruling the country by law; (2) the subjects of ruling the country by law are the broad masses of people, rather than public officials, leading cadres or government organs. Ruling the country by law is by no means governing the people by law and under no circumstance may the people be treated as the objects of governance by law; (3) the objects of ruling the country by law are behaviors and acts of state organs and state personnel, namely various kinds of work of managing political, social, economic and cultural affairs of the country on behalf of the people, with governance and management as their main content. Since public power without supervision and restraint will inevitably become corrupt, the key to ruling the country by law is to control and regulate power and public officials in accordance with law, prevent the abuse of public power and corruption while at the same time ensure that public power is truly exercised in the service of the people; (4) the basis of ruling the country by law are the Constitution and laws, which embody the unity of the propositions of the CPC and the will of the whole people. Ruling the country by law means the rule of good law, namely laws that embody justice and fairness, the propositions of the CPC, and the common will of the whole people, and therefore are conducive to economic and social development and to the promotion of people's welfare; (5) the methods of ruling the country by law include management, control, and the necessary rewards and punishments; (6) the purposes of ruling the country by law is to ensure that various kinds of work of the Party and the government are carried out in accordance with law, realize the institutionalization of socialist democracy and bring it under the rule of law, so as to ensure that such institutions and laws are not changed with the change of the view or the focus of attention of state leaders, that citizens' human rights and fundamental freedoms are truly protected by law, and that public powers of state organs are under strict regulation by the law, and to build China into a prosperous, democratic, and civilized socialist state under the rule of law. Developing socialist democracy and building socialist rule of law, and comprehensively advancing the strategy of ruling the country by law is not only the inevitable choice made by history and the people, but also a necessary requirement that China must meet in order to comprehensively deepen the reform and modernize state governance, promote sustainable economic development, uphold social justice, and realize the Chinese dream of great rejuvenation of the Chinese nation.

2.2.2   Establishing the Rule of Law as the Basic Method of State Governance

The rule of law is a concept with rich cultural connotation and realistic political meaning. At the conceptual level, it mainly refers to the theories, thoughts, values, consciousness and doctrines of ruling and managing the state; at the institutional level, it mainly refers to various principles established or formed on the basis of law and the summarization of legal systems, procedures and norms; at the operational level, it mainly refers to the process and the conditions of realization of legal order and law. The CPC has established the rule of law as the basic mode of state governance. This means, on the one hand, that the ruling party has completely negated the rule of man, authoritarianism, dictatorship, and other modes of state governance that are incompatible with people's democracy and socialist system and unswervingly taken the road of socialist rule of law with Chinese characteristics, and, on the other hand, that the ruling party, in the process of ruling the country, must combine the rule of law with the rule of virtue, the rule-of-law method and thinking with political thinking and political method, administrative thinking and administrative method, and market thinking and economic methods, and realize state governance through comprehensive methods and system engineering. However, among all these methods, the rule of law is the most fundamental method and path dependence.

The CPC stated at its Eighteenth National Congress that the rule of law is a basic mode of state governance. Party Secretary General Xi Jinping pointed out that the CPC must attach more importance to giving full play to the important role of the rule of law in state and social governance. This embodies a new understanding of the objective laws of socialist revolution, construction and reform and of the CPC's leadership and its ruling principles and a new demand on the CPC to comprehensively advance the rule of law. The CPC, after long period of carrying out revolution, construction and reform, has undergone two major transformation: first, the transformation from a party leading the people to seize state power to a party that has been leading the people to hold state power and rule the country for a long period of time; and secondly, the transformation from a party leading the people to carry out state construction under the conditions of external blockade and implementation of the planned economy to a party leading in the people to carry out state construction under the condition of opening up to the outside world and developing socialist market economy. The leadership position and the core role played by the CPC as the ruling party demand that the CPC must, on the one hand, adhere to democratic ruling, scientific ruling, and ruling in accordance with law, continuously improve the capacity for and the level of ruling, put forward and apply correct principles, policies, and strategies, lead the adoption and implementation of the Constitution and laws, adopt scientific leadership system and method, mobilize and organize the people to administer state and social affairs, manage economic and cultural undertakings and effectively run the Party, the country and the armies; and, on the other hand, transform the mode of state governance from one that mainly relies on campaigns and administrative means to one that mainly relies on the Constitution and laws, and from one that mainly relies on political and policy methods to one that mainly relies on the rule-of-law method and the strategy of ruling the country by law.

Deng Xiaoping once pointed out that, in the future, the role of Party committees is primarily to ensure the effectiveness of law. Before legislation, we can only rely on policies in our work; after legislation, we must resolutely carry out our work in accordance with law.[12] The CPC pointed out at its Fourth Plenary Session of Sixteenth Central Committee that exercising the ruling power in accordance with law is a basic ruling mode of the Party under the new historical condition. Ruling by law means to adhere to the principle of rule of law and construction of a socialist state under the rule of law, exercise leadership over the legislative work, take the lead in abiding by the law, ensure the enforcement of laws, make continuous effort to bring economic, political, cultural, and social life under the rule of law, and use the idea, system and procedure of the rule of law to ensure the effective administration of the state affairs by the people under the Party's leadership.

Establishing the rule of law as the basic mode of state governance is the result of the new summarization by the CPC of its practice and experience in revolution,

---

[12]Literature Research Office of the CPC Central Committee (1998).

construction and reform and a new idea developed by CPC for the construction of socialist rule of law, the promotion of ruling the country by law, and exercise of state power in accordance with law. It has the following main requirements: firstly, the CPC must uphold the organic unity of principles of adhering the Party's leadership, people being masters of the country and ruling the county in accordance with law. This is the intrinsic requirement and substantive characteristic of developing a democratic political system with Chinese characteristics and building a socialist state under the rule of law. Secondly, the Party leads the people in adopting and implementing the Constitution and laws. The Party itself must act within the scope of the Constitution and laws, so as to truly be able to lead the legislation, ensure law enforcement, support administration of justice, and take the lead in abiding by laws. These are the basic content and main task of exercising ruling power in accordance with the Constitution and laws. Thirdly, the Party must adhere to the principle of equality before the Constitution and laws. All organizations and individuals must act within the scope the Constitution and laws, take the Constitution and laws as their code of conduct, exercise their power or rights in accordance with the Constitution and laws. They are not allowed to have privileges above the Constitution and laws, and absolutely prohibited from replacing the law with their personal views, suppressing law with power, or bending the law for personal gains. This is the basic principle and bottom line of adhering to socialist rule of law. Fourthly, the Party must play the central leading role in commanding the whole situation, coordinating the efforts of all quarters, and adhering to basic strategy of ruling the country by law and the basic mode of exercising the ruling power in accordance with law. It must be good at turning its propositions into the will of the state through legal procedures, enabling candidates recommended by Party organizations to become leaders of organs of state power, and exercising the leadership over the country and society through organs of state power, support organs of state power, administrative organs, adjudicative organs, and procuratorial organs to carry out their work independent of and in coordination with each other. This is the general requirement and basic method of ruling the country by law. Fifthly, Party organizations at all levels and all Party members should take the lead in implementing the rule of law, continuously raise their capacity for and the level of exercising the ruling power in accordance with law, promote the institutionalization of various governance activities, and bring such activities under the rule of law. Leading cadres at all levels should improve their capacity for applying the rule-of-law thinking and method to deepen the reform, promote development, resolve conflicts, and uphold stability, so as to create a good rule-of-law environment in which people handle affairs in accordance with law, seek legal advice when encountering difficulties, and rely on law to solve their problems and conflicts, and advance various kinds of work on the track of the rule of law. This is a basic quality and governing ability that all Party organizations and leading cadres should possess under the new situation of advancing the rule of law in a comprehensive way.

Regulating and safeguarding the ruling behaviors and intra-Party activities of the ruling party is the necessary requirement of the organic unity of the Party's leadership and ruling the country by law and the substantive characteristic of the socialist democratic political system with Chinese characteristics. In the process of leading the Chinese people to implement the basic state policy of ruling the country by law, leading the making of law, ensuring the enforcement of law, and taking the lead in abiding by law, the ruling party has been more and more conscientiously adhering the principles of ruling by the Constitution and laws, acting within the scope of the Constitution and laws, strengthening the construction of the system of intra-Party regulations and institutions, and bringing the Party regulations into the orbit of ruling of law. In May 2013, the first intra-Party "Legislation Law" in the history of the CPC—Regulations on the Adoption of Intra-Party Regulations—was promulgated, together with the support procedural norms—Provisions of the CPC on the Recordation of Intra-Party Regulations and Normative Documents. In August of the same year, the CPC Central Committee promulgated the Decision on the Abolition and Announcement of Invalidation of Some Intra-Party Regulations and Normative Documents. In accordance with this decision, among the intra-Party regulations and normative documents promulgated since 1978, 300 have been abolished and announced invalid; 467 remain valid, but 42 of them will be revised. At the end of 2013, the CPC Central Committee promulgated the Outline of the Five-year Plan for the Adoption of Intra-Party Regulations (2013–2017). The above-mentioned measures have greatly strengthened and standardized the construction of the system of intra-Party regulations and institutions and safeguarded and propelled the implementation by the CPC of the principle of running the Party in accordance with regulations and the principle of ruling the country by law.

2.2.3 Adhering to the People First Principle and Respecting and Safeguarding Human Rights

Human rights are the rights every person is entitled to as a human being. They include not only individual rights, but also collective rights, and not only civil and political rights, but also economic, social and cultural rights. Since China is still a developing country, it should give priority to people's right of existence and right to development. The key to the promotion of human rights is to ensure that all members of society enjoy on an equal basis the right to participation and the right to development.

Adhering to the people first principle and respecting and safeguarding human rights is the primary function of socialist rule of law and an important part of the task of advancing ruling the country by law in a comprehensive way. China attaches great importance to respecting and safeguarding human rights and, in the process of exploring the socialist road with Chinese characteristics, abides by universal principles of human rights while, at the same time, opened up a new path of development of human rights with Chinese characteristics by proceeding from the basic national conditions. The 1982 Constitution gives more prominence to the safeguarding of the fundamental rights of citizens by moving the provisions on "Fundamental Rights and Duties of Citizens" from Chapter Three to Chapter Two and increasing the number of provisions in this chapter from a dozen or so to over 20. In 1991, the Chinese government promulgated the first white paper on human rights; in 1997, the principle of "respecting and safeguarding human rights" was written into the report of the Fifteenth Party Congress; in 2004, the principle that "the state respects and safeguards human rights" was enshrined into the Constitution, thereby providing a sound constitutional basis for the development of human rights course in China and embodying an important characteristic of the socialist rule of law with Chinese characteristics.

China is a country of statutory law. In order to fully safeguard human rights, it is necessary for China not only to enshrine human rights into the Constitution, but also to adopt legislative, law enforcement and judicial measures for the effective implementation of civil, political, economic, social and cultural rights. In China, safeguarding human rights through state legislation mainly means to incorporate the content and demands of human rights into the Constitution, laws and regulations, make them a part of state legal safeguarding system and targets of constitutional protection, thereby providing the basic premises and important basis for the realization of human rights. Safeguarding human rights through administrative law enforcement means that administrative organs of various types and at various levels conscientiously perform their administrative functions, act in strict in accordance with law, faithfully implement laws and regulations, so as to realize various human rights provided for in the Constitution, laws, and regulations, and enable each citizen to enjoy the concrete socialist human rights. The judicial safeguarding of human rights is an indispensable remedy and the last line of defense of human rights and has a unique and important position and role in the human rights safeguarding system in China.

The Chinese government must ensure that all citizens enjoy extensive rights, protect the personal rights, property rights, basic political rights and other rights of citizens, promote the implementation of the economic, cultural, and social rights, uphold the basic interests of the broad masses of people, and safeguard people's aspiration for and pursuit of a good life.

To respect and safeguard human rights and ensure all citizens enjoy extensive rights in accordance with law, China not only provides for fundamental rights and freedoms of citizens in the Constitution, but also provides for concrete rights of citizens and measures for their protection in laws and regulations; not only safeguards citizens' substantive rights through substantive laws, but also safeguard citizens' procedural rights through procedural laws; and Chinese citizens not only enjoy domestic human rights provided for by the Constitution and laws, but also enjoy extensive international human rights through international human rights conventions ratified by China.

According to the Constitution, Chinese citizens enjoy extensive personal rights, political rights, economic and property rights, labor rights and social rights, cultural and educational rights, and rights of special subjects. Between 1978 and 2011, China had adopted close to 160 laws and regulations relating to the protection of human rights, including the followings: first, those protecting economic, social and cultural rights, such as the Labor Law, the Employment Promotion Law, the Labor Contract Law, the Law on Production Safety, the Law on the Prevention and Control of Occupational Diseases, the Trade Union Law, the Law on Compulsory Education, the Regulations on the Paid Leaves of Employees, and the Provisions on the Prohibition of Child Labor; second, those protecting the civil and political rights of citizens, such as the General Principles of Civil Law, the Criminal Law, the State Compensation Law, the Law on the Protection of Consumer Rights and Interests, the Inheritance Law, the Property Law, the Tort Law, and the Marriage Law; third, those protecting the rights of special groups, including the Marriage Law, the Law on the Protection of Women's Rights and Interests, the Law on the Protection of Minors, the Law on the Protection of Rights and Interest of the Elderly, the Law on the Protection of Disabled Persons, the Health Law, and the Special Provisions on Labor Protection for Female Employees; fourth, those protecting human rights in the judicial field, including the Criminal Procedure Law, the Prison Law, the Civil Procedure Law, the Administrative Procedure Law, the State Compensation Law, and the Lawyer's Law; and fifth, those protecting citizens' right to environment, such as the Environmental Protection Law and the Law on the Prevention and Treatment of Water Pollution.

China actively ratifies international human rights treaties and safeguards the extensive rights of citizens in accordance with international human rights law. Today, China has already ratified 27 international human rights treaties, including the International Covenant on Economic, Social and Cultural Rights. Moreover, China has also recognized the 14 ILO conventions ratified by the Kuomintang Government (1930–1947) and signed the International Covenant on Civil and Political Rights in October 1998.

To better implement the Constitution and laws and promote the development of the human rights cause, the Chinese government promulgated the National Human Rights Action Plan (2009–2010) in April 2009. This was the first national action plan adopted by China that takes human rights as its theme—a historical breakthrough and a milestone in the development of human rights cause in China. In June 2012, on the basis of successful implementation of the first human rights action plan and the summarization of related experiences, the Chinese government issued the Human Rights Action Plan (2012–2015), which contained tasks, road map and timetable for the phased realization of the objective of full respect and safeguarding of human rights.

The Decision on Some Major Issues Concerning Comprehensively Deepening the Reform, adopted at the Third Plenary Session of the 18th CPC Central Committee, laid out plans for the improvement of judicial protection of human rights in the process of advancing the rule of law and deepening the judicial reform by further standardizing the judicial procedures for the seal up, seizure, freeze and disposal of property involved in a case, improving mechanisms for the prevention and rectification of, and investigation into the responsibilities for, misjudged cases, gradually reducing the application of the death penalty, abolishing the system rehabilitation-through-labor, and improving the system of community rectification, the legal aid system, and the lawyer's system. These plans have provided guidance for the continuous improvement of the system of judicial protection of human rights in China.

2.2.4   The Formation on Schedule of the Socialist Legal System with Chinese Characteristics

Developing a socialist legal system and ensuring that there is law to go by is a key task of China in the construction of the rule of law as well as a fundamental objective of its legislative work in the new era.

In 1982, the Report of the Fifth Session of the Fifth NPC clearly pointed out that: "In its legislative work, China must take its actual national condition as the starting point and, in accordance with socialist legal principles, gradually establish an independent legal system with Chinese characteristics."

In 1987, the CPC announced to the world at its Thirteenth National Congress that "The socialist democracy and legal system are gradually constructed and a socialist legal system with the Constitution as its basis is beginning to take shape in China."

In March 1988, the Seventh NPC pointed out at its First Session that: "In the past five years, China has made major progresses in legislative work and enabled the people to have laws to go by in the basic aspects of their political, economic and social lives. A socialist legal system with the Constitution as its basis has taken form."

In 1993, in order to deepen the economic reform and establish the market economic system, the CPC Central Committee pointed out in the Decision on Issues concerning the Establishment of socialist Market Economic System that: "The objectives of the construction of the legal system are: speeding up legislation in the economic field, further improving civil, commercial and criminal laws and laws on state organs and administration, and basically establishing a legal system compatible with the socialist market economy by the end of this century."

It took China thirteen years (from 1997 to 2010) to realize the above objectives. This process can be roughly divided into three stages:

The period of the Ninth NPC (1998–2003) was the stage of "initial formation of the socialist legal system with Chinese characteristics". The so-called "initial formation" refers to the initial formation of a legal system that takes the Constitution as its basis, the civil law, criminal law, economic law, administrative law, procedure laws, and other basic laws as its core, and laws, administrative regulations and local regulations at various levels as its content. In March 2003, Mr. Li Peng, the Chairman of the NPC Standing Committee, pointed out in the report summarizing the work of the NPC Standing Committee in the previous five years that: "After unremitting efforts made by this NPC on the basis of the work carried out by previous NPCs, the construction of various branches of law that constitute the system of law with Chinese characteristics has been basically completed, with main laws adopted in each branch. A socialist system of law with Chinese characteristic, with the Constitution as its core, and the basic laws adopted by the NPC and its Standing Committee, administrative regulations adopted by the State Council, and local regulations adopted by local people's congresses as its main content, has taken initial shape."

During the Tenth NPC (2003–2008), "the socialist system of law with Chinese characteristics had basically taken form". This means that, on the basis of a system of law that had "taken initial shape", the adoption and revision of laws that serve as the support to other laws, those that are urgently needed in practice and those for which conditions are ripe for their adoption or revision in each branch law have been completed.

During the Eleventh NPC (2008–2013), "a socialist system of law with Chinese characteristics had taken form". This means that the construction of various branches of law that cover all aspects social relations have been completed, the basic and key laws in each branch have been adopted, the corresponding administrative and local regulations have been relatively complete, and the internal structure of the system has become scientific, harmonious and unified.

The socialist system of law with Chinese characteristics takes the Constitution as the commander, laws as its backbone, and administrative regulations and local regulations as its important components. It is an organic unity consists of the Constitution and other constitutional laws, civil laws, commercial laws, administrative laws, economic laws, social laws, criminal laws, litigation laws and non-litigious procedure laws.

After the establishment of the PRC, especially since the reform and opening up, the Chinese people, under the leadership of the CPC, have made unremitting efforts in the formulation and adoption of constitution and laws. Today, China has adopted 243 effective laws, over 720 administrative regulations, more than 9200 local regulations, and over 780 regulations on the exercise of regional national autonomy and separate regulations. Together, they form a socialist system of law with Chinese characteristics that is based on the actual conditions in China, adapted to the needs of reform and opening up and socialist modernization, embodies in a concentrated way the will of the Party and the will of the people, takes the Constitution as its commander, and constitutional law, civil law, commercial law, economic law, administrative law and other branch laws as its backbone, and consists of different levels of legal norms, including laws, administrative regulations, and local regulations, thereby enabling Chinese people to have laws to go by in economic, political, social, cultural and ecological construction and in all other aspects of social life.

Currently the system of law with Chinese characteristics consists of seven branches of law at three different levels. The Constitution is the basic of the country, occupies a commanding position and has the highest authority and legal effect in the whole system. The adoption of all laws, administrative regulations, and local regulations must take the Constitution as the basis, follow the basic constitutional principles and may not contravene the Constitution.

The system of law with Chinese characteristics has three levels: at the first level are laws, including basic laws and ordinary laws, which are adopted and interpreted by the NPC and its Standing Committee; at the second level are administrative regulations adopted by the State Council in accordance with the Constitution and laws; and at the third level are local regulations. They mainly include: those adopted by people's congresses of provinces, autonomous regions, and municipalities directly under the Central Government and their standing committees; those adopted by the people's congresses of larger cities and their standing committees, which must be reported to the standing committees of provinces and autonomous regions for approval before they can be implemented; the people's congresses of the national autonomous areas have the power to formulate regulations on the exercise of autonomy and separate regulations; they may make adaptations to laws and administrative regulations on the basis of the characteristics of the local nationality (nationalities), but such adaptations may not contradict the basis principles of the laws and administrative regulations and no adaptation may be made to the provisions of the Constitution and the Law on Regional National Autonomy or to the provisions in other laws and administrative regulations specially formulated to govern the national autonomous areas. The people's congresses of the provinces and cities where special economic zones are located or their standing committees may, upon authorization by decision of the National People's Congress, formulate regulations and enforce them within the special economic zones.

Currently the system of law with Chinese characteristics consists of the following seven branches laws: (1) constitutional laws, which refer to the totality of legal norms that support the Constitution and directly safeguard the implementation of the Constitution and the operation of state political power. By the end of August 2011, China had adopted the Constitution and 38 constitutional laws and a number of relevant administrative regulations and local regulations. (2) Civil and commercial laws. Civil laws are the legal norms adjusting property and personal relations between equal subjects, such as those between citizens, between legal persons, and between citizens and legal persons; commercial laws are legal norms adjusting relations between commercial subjects. By the end of August 2011, China had adopted 33 civil and commercial laws and a large number of administrative regulations and local regulations regulating commercial activities. (3) Administrative laws are legal norms regulating the relationship between administrative organs and persons subjected to administration. By the end of August 2011, China had adopted 79 administrative laws and a large number of administrative regulations and local regulations regulating administrative powers. (4) Economic laws are legal norms that regulate the social-economic relations resulting from the state intervention in, or administration or regulation of economic activities for the overall interest of society. By the end of August 2011, China had adopted 60 economic laws and a large number of administrative regulations and local regulations in this area. (5) Social laws are legal norms governing labor relations, social security, social welfare and the protection of the rights and interests of special groups. By the end of August 2011, China had adopted 18 laws and a large number of administrative regulations and local regulations in this respect. (6) Criminal laws are legal norms regulating crimes and their punishments. By the end of August 2011, China had adopted the Criminal Law, eight amendments to the Criminal Law, a number of decisions on the punishment of fraudulent purchase of foreign exchange, illegal transfer of foreign exchange to the overseas and illegal trade in foreign exchange, and nine legal interpretations of provisions of the Criminal Law. (7) Litigious and non-litigious procedure laws are legal norms regulating the litigious activities and non-litigious activities aimed at resolving social disputes. Currently, China has already adopted many litigious and non-litigious procedure laws, such as the Criminal Procedure Law, the Civil Procedure Law, the Administrative Procedure Law, the Special Maritime Procedure Law, the Arbitration Law, the People's Mediation Law, the Notary Law, and the Extradition Law.

The socialist system of law with Chinese characteristics is the rule of law basis of keeping the true color of socialism with Chinese characteristics, the rule of law embodiment of the creative practice of socialism with Chinese characteristics, and the rule of law guarantee of the prosperity of socialism with Chinese characteristics. Its formation is an important milestone in the construction of the rule of law in China, embodies the great achievements of the reform and opening up, and socialist modernization, and therefore has great realistic significance and profound historical significance. In order to advance ruling the country by law in a comprehensive way, China should continuously strengthen the legislative work, promote democratic and scientific law-making, improve the quality of legislation, and continuously develop the socialist system of law with Chinese characteristics.

2.2.5   Steadily Advancing the Construction of a Law-Based Government

Administration by law is an important link in ruling the country by law and the construction of a law-based government is an important component of the construction of the rule of law in China. To construct a law-based government means to adhere to administration by law and build governments at all levels into lawful, limited, standardized, law-abiding, and accountable governments. At its Fifteenth National Congress held in 1997, the CPC put forward the basic strategy of ruling the country by law, which requires that all government organs must abide by the principle of administration by law. To implement this basic strategy and advance administration by law, the State Council issued the Decision on Advancing Administration by Law in a Comprehensive Way in 1999. The Working Rules of the State Council, revised in 2003, formally establish administration by law as one of the three basic principles of government work and clearly provide that the core of administration by law is the regulation of administrative power. In 2004, the State Council promulgated the Program for Comprehensively Promoting Administration by Law, which established the objective of constructing a law-based government. In 2010, the State Council promulgated the Opinions on Strengthening the Construction of a Government Ruled by Law, which made comprehensive arrangement and raise overall demand on the construction of a law-based government with respect to emphasizing the importance, urgency and general requirements of construction of a law-based government, enhancing the consciousness of and capacity for administration by law of administrative personnel, especially leading cadres, strengthening and improving institutional construction, adhering to lawful, scientific, and democratic decision-making, comprehensively improving the transparency of government affairs, strengthening administrative supervision and accountability, resolving social conflicts and disputes in accordance with law, and strengthening organization, leadership, supervision and inspection. At its Eighteenth National Congress, the CPC stressed that China must "advance administrative by law, and make sure that law enforcement is strict, standardized, fair and civilized". At the Third Plenary Session of its Eighteenth Central Committee, the CPC further pointed out that, to advance the construction of the rule of law, China must adhere to the simultaneous advancement of ruling the country by law, exercising the ruling power by law, and administration by law and to the unified construction of a law-based country, a law-based government, and a law-based society. It must deepen the reform of the administrative law enforcement system, integrate law enforcement subjects, realize relative centralization of law enforcement power, promote comprehensive law enforcement, concentrate efforts on the solution of the problems of overlapping of powers and duplicate law enforcement, and establish an authoritative and high-efficient administrative law enforcement system that integrates power and responsibility; reduce the levels of administrative law enforcement, strengthen grassroots law enforcement in such key areas as food and drug administration, production safety, environmental protection, labor protection, and seas and islands management; and rationalize the system and improve the quality of urban management law enforcement and service; improve administrative law enforcement procedure, regulate law enforcement discretional power, strengthen the supervision over administrative law enforcement, implement in a comprehensive way the administrative law enforcement accountability system and the system of guarantee of law enforcement expenditures by state finance, so as to ensure strict, standardized, fair and civilized law enforcement.

Since the reform and opening up, especially since the Fifteenth Party Congress, China has been carrying out in a deep-going way the work of administration by law and steadily advancing the construction of a law-based government, and made major achievements in this respect.

In the area of administrative legislation, between 1979 and September 2014, the State Council had submitted near 200 bills of law to the NPC and its Standing Committee for deliberation and adopted more than 720 administrative regulations; the various ministries and commissions under the State Council and local governments with legislative power had adopted over 26,000 ministerial rules and local regulations. In 1989, China promulgated the Administrative Procedure Law, which allows courts to review the legality of concrete administrative acts. Since then, the number of cases of administrative litigation has been increasing steadily. "Lawsuit brought by citizens against government organs" has become a litigation system parallel to criminal and civil litigation systems. The 1994 State Compensation Law for the first time in Chinese history makes it clear that if an administrative organ or its functionaries, in exercising their administrative functions and powers, commit any act infringing upon the right of the person of a citizen, the victim shall have the right to compensation, thereby providing legal basis for the accountability of the government and the safeguarding of human rights. The 1996 Law on Administrative Penalty standardizes the power and the procedure of imposition of administrative penalty, thereby establishing the rules on and the system of administrative penalty. The 1999 Law on Administrative Reconsideration provides that a citizen, legal person or any other organization who considers that his or its lawful rights and interests have been infringed upon by a specific administrative act of an administrative organ may applies for administrative reconsideration to an administrative organ at the next higher level. The 2003 Administrative License Law clearly provides for the establishment and the scope of administrative license and standardizes the government act of administrative licensing, thereby advancing the reform of the administrative licensing system. Through administrative legislation, China has constructed a system of basic laws in the three areas of administrative organization, administrative act and administrative remedy, and adopted administrative laws and regulations in the fields national defense, foreign affairs, customs, personnel management, civil affairs, overseas Chinese affairs, public security, safety, education, science and technology, culture, sports, tourism, urban management, environmental protection, medicine and health, and food safety. Together, these laws and administrative regulations form a relatively complete administrative law system and embody such ideas as rule of administrative law and regulating and restricting administrative power. Administrative power comes from the people and should serve the people. Therefore, it is necessary to strengthen the restriction on and supervision over administrative power, so as to ensure that it is exercised by the people and for the people.

In 1999, the State Council held a meeting on advancing administration by law in a comprehensive way and adopted the Decision on Advancing Administration by Law in a Comprehensive Way, which concretizes the various requirements of administration by law. In March 2004, the State Council promulgated the Program for Comprehensively Promoting Administration by Law, which made overall arrangement for administration by law and construction of a law-based government. The Program contains the following specific requirements on administrative law enforcement: lawful administration, reasonable administration, due process, high efficiency, convenience for the people, honesty and trustworthiness, and integration of power and responsibility. It requires the government to adopt measures to rationalize administrative law enforcement system, speed up the construction of administrative procedure, and regulate administrative law enforcement behavior. More specifically, these measures include: deepening the establishment of an administrative law enforcement system with well-defined powers and responsibilities, standardized law enforcement conduct, effective supervision, and strong safeguards; exercising power and performing duties in strict accordance with legal procedures; improving the system of review of administrative law enforcement case files; establishing the system of the qualifications of subjects of administrative law enforcement and implement the system of accountability for administrative law enforcement; and strengthening the work of sorting out and supervising the issuance of red-heading documents. During the 30 years since the reform and opening up, especially during the past five years, there has been a rapid development of administrative reconsideration and administrative litigation, which is continuously pushing forward the construction of a clean, honest, and efficient government under the rule of law. Administrative reconsideration and administrative litigation are important mechanisms that provide legal remedies for administrative acts and rectify administrative mistakes. According to the Program, in order to construct a law-based government, China must press ahead with the reform of administrative system, improve the quality of institutional construction, rationalize the law enforcement system, and raise the legal quality of law enforcement personnel—which is also the direction and road of construction of a law-based government in China.

In the process of construction of a law-based government, the government has strengthened the supervision over such abstract administrative acts as the adoption of administrative regulations, rules and other normative documents. On January 15, 2008, the State Council adopted the Decision on Abolishing Some Administrative Regulations, which carried out a comprehensive screening of the 655 administrative regulations adopted before the end of 2006, abolished 49 administrative regulations whose major contents have been replaced by new laws or administrative regulations, and announced invalid 43 administrative regulations that had actually become invalid due to the expiration of their application period or the disappearance of their adjustment objects. On the basis of strengthening the work of recordation and examination of administrative rules and regulations, the State Council further improved the system of three-level recordation and review of administrative rules, regulations and normative documents at four levels of government (at the provincial, municipal, county and township levels), so as to promote administration by law at all local levels. Between March 2003 and the end of 2007, the State Council had reviewed 8402 local regulations, regulations on the exercise of autonomy, separate regulations, rules and regulations of local governments, and ministerial rules and regulations submitted to the State Council for the record and dealt with problematic 323 rules and regulations. The State Council has adopted the Regulations on the Implementation of the Administrative Reconsideration Law, actively explored the reform of the administrative reconsideration system, and strengthened the capacity building for administrative reconsideration personnel at all levels; and since the implementation of the Administrative Reconsideration Law, over 80,000 administrative disputes have been resolved through administrative reconsideration procedure each year.

2.2.6 Continuously Improving the Judicial System

The CPC attaches high importance to the reform and improvement of the judicial system. At its Fifteenth National Congress, it clearly put forward the reform task of " pressing ahead with judicial reform and ensuring through institutional building the independent exercise of adjudicative and procuratorial powers by judicial organs". The CPC continued to make new arrangements for the reform of the judicial system at its sixteenth, seventeenth and eighteenth national congresses. Judicial reform, as an important component of political reform in China, has undergone the process of gradual advancement and continuous deepening. Since the 1990s, China has implemented the judicial reform that takes enhancing the court's functions, increasing the openness of trial, strengthening defense by the lawyer, and building up professional contingents of judges and procurators as its main content. In 2004, China launched a large scale judicial reform with unified planning, arrangement and implementation. In accordance with the requirements of fair administration of justice and strict law enforcement, the reform proceeded from the prominent problems on which the people had expressed strong concerns and the key links that affect judicial fairness, took the rules and characteristics of administration of justice as the starting points, and further improved the organizational setup, division of functions and powers, and the management system of judicial organs, so as to build a highly efficient judicial system with clear definition of powers and responsibilities and with different components cooperating with and checking and balancing each other. In 2008, China launched a new round of judicial reform, which proceeds from the judicial demands of the people, takes the upholding of the people's common interests as its basis, the promotion of social harmony as its main line, and the strengthening of the supervision over and check and balance of power as its emphases, focuses on the key links that affect judicial fairness and restrict judicial capacity, aims at overcoming institutional and systematic obstacles, and put forward concrete reform tasks of optimizing the allocation of judicial functions and powers, implementing the criminal policy of tempering justice with mercy, building up the judicial contingent and strengthening the safeguarding of judicial funds. Through several rounds of reform, the judicial system in China has been improved continuously and won the acceptance and support by the general public.

First, optimizing the allocation of functions and powers of judicial organs and promoting fair and clean administration of justice. Reforming and improving the system of enforcement of civil and administrative judgments, establishing a unified system of administration, separation of powers, and check and balance, so as to effectively solve the problem of difficulties in enforcement of judgments; comprehensively implementing the reform whereby the power of arrest in cases of duty crimes is "moved to the procuratorate at the next high level", strengthening the supervision by higher-level procuratorates over lower-level procuratorates, and preventing wrongful arrest and the practice of "substituting investigation with arrest"; exploring the system of guiding cases, establishing a unified criterion on adjudication as a visible fair "reference system", and reducing the phenomenon of "different sentencings for similar cases"; strengthening legal supervision by procuratorial organs over the filing, investigation, and trial of criminal cases, the administration of places of custody, the commutation of criminal punishment, and other links of enforcement, so as to make legal supervision more effective; rationalizing the relationship between higher- and lower-level courts, reforming the trial committee system and the collegial panel system, guaranteeing the independence of trial and judicial fairness; increasing the openness of adjudicative affairs, procuratorial affairs, police affairs, and prison affairs, implementing the system of disclosure of information about the acceptance and filing of cases, the bases of law enforcement, and the process and the result of handling of cases, so as to ensure that judicial power is exercised under the sun; the people's assessor's system has been continuously improved, the people's supervisor's system has been constructed in a comprehensive way, and the reform of system of commutation of sentence and the system of parole committee has been progressing through continuous exploration; the public have been allowed to participate in administration of justice and supervisors are also subjected to supervision; strengthening democratic supervision and completing and improving the mechanism for the democratic supervision over judicial work by non-CPC personages; the mechanism for the expression of the will of netizens and the mechanism for the survey of public opinions have been gradually established, the people's right to know, right to participation, right of expression and right of supervision have been further guaranteed...Through a combination of many different reform measures, China has improved its judicial system, increased judicial openness, strengthened legal supervision and democratic supervision, raised the level of transparency of judicial activities, put under effective control such problems as irregular law enforcement, nonfeasance, and arbitrary law enforcement, promoted strict, fair, civilized and clean law enforcement, and enhanced the public trust in judicial organs.

Second, implementing the criminal policy of tempering justice with mercy and promoting social harmony and stability. Through the revision of the Criminal Law, Criminal Procedure Law and other important laws, China has adjusted the constitutive elements and statutory sentencing of some crimes of serious endangering social order, improved the structure of criminal punishment, raised the ability to punish serious crimes and strengthened the judicial protection of human rights; adopted the rules on the exclusion of illegal evidence, established the system of recording and videotaping the whole process of interrogation of criminal suspects, and implemented the lawyer's rights to meet his client, to consult the case file, and to carry out investigation and collect evidence and the lawful rights and interests of criminal suspects and defendants; implemented the death penalty policy of "kill less and cautiously", reduced the crimes punishable by death, and strictly restricted the application of the death penalty. The Eighth Amendment to the Criminal Law, promulgated in 2011, abolishes the death penalty for 13 economic and other non-violent crimes, which consisted 19.1% of all capital crimes in China, provides that the death penalty shall generally not be given to a person attaining the age of 75 at the time of trial, and establishes the system of restrictions on commutation of sentence for those sentenced to death with a reprieve, thereby providing legal basis and institutional conditions for the gradual reduction of application of the death penalty. On October 27, 2014, the Draft of the Ninth Amendment to the Criminal Law was submitted to the Standing Committee of the NPC for deliberation. The Draft Amendment proposed the abolition of the death penalty for nine more crimes, including the crime of smuggling weapons and ammunition, the crime of smuggling nuclear materials, the crime of smuggling counterfeit currencies, the crime of counterfeiting currencies, the crime of fraudulent fund-raising, the crime of organizing prostitution, the crime of forcing others into prostitution, the crime of interference with the exercise of military duty, and the crime of fabricating rumors to mislead people and shake the confidence of the army in wartime. China has also made efforts in exploring the establishment criminal reconciliation system, striving to repair the social relations damaged by crimes, and reducing social antagonism, improving the community correction system, helping criminals to actively integrate themselves into society, and reducing recidivism. By June 2012, 1.054 million people had been sentenced to community correction and 587,000 had completed community correction in the whole country. The recidivism among those undergoing community correction was around 0.2%. China has improved the mechanism of lenient treatment for juvenile delinquents, and established the conditional non-prosecution system and the system of safekeeping of criminal records, so as to help minors who have committed minor crimes to reintegrate themselves into society, and enhance social harmony. By July 2011, a total of 2331 juvenile courts had been establishment throughout the country and between 2002 and 2011, the recidivism among juvenile delinquents had been kept between 1 and 2%.

Third, improving the system of management of the law enforcement and judicial personnel and the quality of law enforcement and judicial work: implementing unified national judicial examination system, and bringing junior judges, junior procurators, lawyers, and notaries public into the scope of national judicial examination system. Between 2002 and the end of 2011, near 500,000 people in the whole country had passed the national judicial examination and acquired legal professional qualifications. A system of police law enforcement qualification grade examination was established. In 2011, a total of 1.73 million police took part in the first law enforcement qualification examination. Among them, 1.69 million passed the examination. Through the deepening of the reform of the law enforcement personnel recruitment system, colleges of political science and law throughout the country had enrolled a total of 65,000 new students, who had been employed by grassroots law enforcement units after graduation. This had greatly improved the quality of law enforcement personnel at the grassroots level. The reform of national judicial examination system has greatly increased the reserve of legal personnel in central and western regions and ethnic minority areas and alleviated the shortage of judges and procurators at the grassroots level. By overcoming the special difficulties faced by judges, procurators, police and judicial administrative personnel, the government has stabilized the contingent of grassroots law enforcement and judicial personnel. Meanwhile, law enforcement and judicial organs have been continuously improving the occupational training system, actively innovating the ideas, means and methods of occupational training, and adapting the training to the requirements of law enforcement practice. During the past five years, 1.5 million judges, 750,000 procurators, and 6 million police in the whole country have received occupational training, which greatly enhanced their law enforcement and judicial capacity and their capacity for serving the people.

Through the improvement of the lawyer's system, China has established the professional status of lawyers as the legal workers of socialism with Chinese characteristics, effectively safeguarded the practicing right of lawyers, and promoted the healthy development of the lawyer's profession. By the end of 2011, China had 18,200 law firms with 215,000 lawyers; in 2011, the number of enterprises and institutions that had hired lawyers as legal counsels was 392,000, 24.6% more than that of 2008; the number of cases handled by lawyers was 2.315 million, 17.7% more than that of 2008; the number of non-litigation cases handled by lawyers was 625,000, 17% more than that of 2008; and the number of legal aid cases was 845,000, 54.5% more than that of 2008.

Fourth, overcoming the financial and equipment difficulties faced by law enforcement and judicial organs, so as to guarantee their performance of functions in accordance with law. In the new round of judicial reform, the government has put forward the reform plan that changes the fund guarantee system from the current system of "bearing and administrating funds at different levels" into a system of "clear responsibilities, classified burdens, separation of income from expenditure, and blanket guarantee", strengthened the guarantee by central and provincial finances, and established the mechanism for the normal growth of public expenditure. The state has also adopted standards on the infrastructure construction and guiding standard on the equipment for judicial organs, so as to improve office and case-handling conditions, raise the informatization and technicalization levels of judicial organs, and provide a solid material guarantee for the enhancement of judicial capacity; and increased the investment in the construction of infrastructure and facilities of law enforcement and judicial organs by adhering to the principle of "downward shift of focus of work, safeguards and investment" and giving priority to the construction of facilities in and provision of equipment to grassroots law enforcement and judicial organs. These reform measures have effectively overcome the long-existing difficulties of shortage of staff and fund and backwardness of equipment, greatly enhanced the fighting capacity of grassroots law enforcement and judicial organs, as well as the morale of law enforcement and judicial personnel. Since 2010, the number of fugitives captured by grassroots police stations has consisted 40% of the total number of fugitives captured by public security organs in the whole country; the number of police response by grassroots police stations has consisted 70% of the total number of police response by public security organs in the whole country; between 2009 and September 2012, the number of approval of arrest and public prosecution by grassroots procuratorates had consisted 95% of the total number of approval of arrest and public prosecution by procuratorial organs in the whole country; Between 2009 and September 2012, the number of various types of cases tried and judgments enforced by grassroots courts had consisted 89.28% of the total number of cases tried and judgments enforced by all the courts in the whole country; during the Eleventh Five-year Plan period, judicial offices in the whole country participated in the mediation of 3.6 million disputes, and assisted the government in dealing with 3.134 million social conflicts.

2.2.7 Markedly Enhancing the Consciousness of the Rule of Law Among All Members of Society

Popularizing legal knowledge and establishing the idea of the rule of law among all citizens, cultivating the social atmosphere of studying the law, respecting the law, and abiding by the law, and creating a good environment of the rule of law in which people are not willing, not able, and not dare to violate the law, and rely on law to do business, deal with their problems, and solve their conflicts are the basic conditions and important signs of the success of the construction of the rule of law in China. Since the opening up and reform, the rule of law, has been not only profoundly changing the Chinese society, but also transforming the mind of Chinese people. Ideas such as democracy, the rule of law, freedom, human rights, fairness and justice have been subtly influencing people's values and integrating themselves into people's daily life. The rule-of-law consciousness of the whole society has been markedly enhanced.

Beginning from 1985, the Chinese government has adopted six decisions on carrying out popularization of law among all citizens and implemented six consecutive five-year plans on the popularization of law. During the period of "first five-year plan" for the campaign of popularization of law, more than 700 million citizens had studied primary knowledge of law; during the "second five-year plan" period, programs for the popularization of law had been made for people in 96 different industries to study over 200 laws and regulations in their respective industries; during the "third five-year plan" period, a campaign of governance by law had been carried out in 30 provinces, autonomous regions and municipalities directly under the Central Government, covering 95% of the prefecture-level cities, 87% of the counties (districts and cities), and 75% of the grassroots unites in the whole country; during the "fourth five-year plan" period, over 850 million citizens had received various forms of education on the rule of law; during the "fifth five-year" period, 24,600 provincial- and ministerial-level leading cadres and 415,300 prefecture-level leading cadres attended lectures on the legal system, which had further improved the consciousness and ability of leading cadres at various levels to exercise state power and make decisions in accordance with law. Currently, China is implementing in a comprehensive way the "Sixth Five-year Plan" (2011–2015), which is widely popularizing various laws and regulations of the socialist system of law with Chinese characteristics, further improving the level of law-based social governance, and playing an important role in promoting the rule of law and speeding up the construction of a socialist state under the rule of law.

The popularization of law is targeted at all citizens but its main focus is on public servants. As far as ordinary citizens are concerned, the popularization of law is aimed at not only enabling each of them to know the law and abide by the law, but more importantly, also enabling them to use the law as weapon to uphold their lawful rights and interests. As far as civil servants are concerned, it is aimed at helping them to firmly establish the idea of the rule of law, and conscientiously deal with public affairs in accordance with law; as far as the whole society is concerned, it is aimed at promoting the spirit of the rule of law, nurturing the culture of the rule of law, and creating a good social atmosphere of the rule of law. During the period of "Fifth Five-year Plan of Popularization of Law", the government had strengthened the training, examination and assessment of civil servants on the legal knowledge relating to their job responsibilities; over 42 million civil servants had participated in various kinds of training, 27 million civil servants had taken part in examinations and assessments, and over 98% of civil servants had met the requirement of taking part in the study of the law each year; over 33,500 training courses on the knowledge of law had been held for enterprise management personnel, with more than 2.9 million participants; over 51,300 lectures and symposiums had been held, with more than 6.2 million participants; legal training had also been provided to over 12 million members of Party committees and villagers committees in rural areas and over 156 million rural migrant workers in cities, which had greatly enhanced the legal consciousness of the rural population.

China attaches great importance to the combination of popularization of legal knowledge and governance by law and has carried out extensive campaigns of "ruling the province (city, county, township and village) by law" and constructing a province (city, or district) under the rule of law, so as to integrate the construction of the rule of law into the daily work of each local government, each government organ, and each unit, as well as into the daily life of each citizens, raise the general level of the rule of law of all members of society, and combine the study of law with the use of law. By the end of 2010, the campaign of construction of local governments under the rule of law had been comprehensively carried out in 26 provinces (autonomous regions and municipalities directly the Central Government), 241 cities (prefectures and leagues), and 1856 counties (cities and districts) in the whole country; leading groups on the popularization of law, headed by the main leaders of Party committees and governments, had been set up throughout the country; a work mechanism for the popularization of law, led by Party committees, supervised by people's congresses, and implemented by governments had been established and continuously improved; and similar groups had also been set up in each government departments and in each industries to strengthen the leadership over the work of popularization of law in their respective departments and industries.

Since 1994, the Politburo of CPC Central Committee has organized over 100 lectures or collective study sessions on the legal system. Among them, near 30 were on the construction of the rule of law or on issues related to the rule of law. These lectures and collective study sessions have played a very good demonstrative role in promoting legal knowledge and raising the consciousness of the rule of law among all members of society, especially civil servants. A series of studies on the rule of law have been organized for members of the NPC Standing Committee, the Executive Meeting of the State Council, and the Standing Committee of the CPPCC National Committee. Collective study of law for members of Party organizations and state organs at various levels has become institutionalized.

Besides, China has also made remarkable achievements in areas of legal service, legal education, legal research, training of legal personnel, and building up a contingent of legal workers.

2.3   Basic Experience of Construction of Socialist Rule of Law with Chinese Characteristics

In the past 60 years, China has gone through a tortuous road, made remarkable achievements, and gained precious experiences in the construction of socialist rule of law with Chinese characteristics.

2.3.1 Always Adhering to the Leadership of the CPC Over the Construction of the Rule of Law

Adhering to CPC's leadership over the construction of the rule of law is a scientific summarization of the 60 years of experience in the construction of the rule of law in China, an intrinsic requirement of and basic guarantee for the reform and the development of the socialist rule of law with Chinese characteristics, and the most substantive characteristic of and most fundamental guarantee for the socialist rule of law with Chinese characteristics. Today, the CPC's central task, the environment in which it operates, and the structure of its membership are very different from those in the revolutionary years and the early years of the PRC. These differences objectively demand the strengthening and improvement of the Party's leadership and the organic unity of the Party's leadership over the country and the rule of law. In order to exercise the leadership over the construction of the rule of law, the CPC must improve its leadership and ruling capacity and methods. It should be able to transform the main method of state and social administration from one that mainly relies on orders and administrative means to one that mainly relies on democratic and the rule of law method. The Party's leadership is mainly political, ideological and organizational leadership, exercised through adopting major polices, putting forward legislative proposals, recommending important cadres, carrying out ideological publicity, and ensuring that the Party always play a core leadership role in controlling the overall situation and coordinating the efforts of all quarters in the construction of the rule of law. The report of the Fourth Plenary Session of the Eighteenth CPC Central Committee pointed out that: "A basic experience of the construction of socialist rule of law in China is to implement the Party's leadership in the whole process and all aspects of ruling the country by law." The Party must exercise leadership over legislation, ensure law enforcement, take the lead in abiding by law, act within the scope the Constitution and laws, and exercise the ruling power in accordance with the Constitution and law; "and further strengthen the unified leadership over, make overall arrangement and coordination of the comprehensive advancement of ruling the country by law, and promote the interconnection and interaction between Party polices and state laws while at the same time giving full play to their respective advantages".

2.3.2 Always Adhering to the Road of Socialist Democracy and Rule of Law with Chinese Characteristics

Another basic experience gained by the CPC in the construction of the rule of law in China is to proceed from the reality in China, take the historical and current national conditions in China as the starting point, and adhere to the road of development of socialist rule of law with Chinese characteristics. Several thousand years of political history of mankind has repeatedly demonstrated a truth: the legal system a country implements and the road of development of democracy and the rule of law it takes must be compatible with the national conditions of that country. The socialist rule of law in China is deeply rooted in the vast fertile soil on which the Chinese nation has survived and developed for thousands of years, comes from the great practice carried out by the CPC and Chinese people of struggling for national independence, liberation, and prosperity, and is a legal system adapted to the national conditions and the requirement of social progress in China. Compared with the capitalist rule of law, the rule of law in China is a socialist rule of law; compared with the ideas of state and legal system of the ideal socialism envisaged by Karl Marx and Friedrich Engels, it is the rule of law at the primary stage of socialism; compared with the socialist rule of law of the former Soviet Union and East European countries in the past, and those of Viet Nam, North Korea and Cuba in the present day, it is a socialist rule of law with Chinese characteristics; and compared with the traditional legal system and legal culture in Chinese history, it is a modernized socialist rule of law with its basic characteristics of political nature, particularity, periodicity, and modernity. Adhering to the construction and development of socialist rule of law with Chinese characteristics is the inevitable result of historical and social development and a common choice made by the Chinese people and Chinese nation. China should actively draw on the positive experience of development of the rule of law culture of mankind, but never take the western road of development of the rule of law.

2.3.3 Always Attaching High Importance to the Strategic Position and the Role of the Rule of Law in the Modernization Construction

The rule of law, as the achievement of political civilization created by mankind, is playing an increasingly important role in the economic and social development. The construction of the rule of law in China had met with many setbacks during the first 30 years of the PRC, especially during the "Cultural Revolution", mainly because of the lack of correct understanding of the important position of the construction of the rule of law in state construction. After the Third Plenary Session of the Eleventh CPC Central Committee, the Party and the government have attached high importance to the construction of the rule of law. At its Fifteenth National Congress, the CPC established the rule of law as the basic strategy of state governance and set the historical task of "ruling the country by law and constructing a socialist state under the rule of law". Ruling the country by law is one of the basic tasks of socialist modernization, an important content of the construction of socialist democratic politics, and an important guarantee for the realization the goals of socialist modernization construction.

Comprehensively advancing the rule of law at the new historical starting point is an essential requirement of and important guarantee for the development of socialism with Chinese characteristics, an inevitable precondition for the modernization of state governance system and capacity and, therefore, is of great importance to the governance and rejuvenation of the Chinese nation, to the happiness and well-being of the Chinese people, and to the lasting political stability of the country. It is a basic precondition for the solution of a series of major problems faced by the Party and the state in their development, for the liberation and enhancement of social vitality, and for the promotion of social fairness and justice, the maintenance of social harmony and stability, and the guarantee of lasting political stability of the country; an inevitable precondition for the construction in a comprehensive way of a moderately prosperous society and the realization of the Chinese dream of great rejuvenation of Chinese nation, the deepening of the reform in a comprehensive way, the perfection of the socialist system with Chinese characteristics, and enhancement of the Party's ruling level and ruling capacity. Especially, China must give full play to the leading and regulatory role of the rule of law, so as to take into better consideration of domestic and international situations, seize important strategic opportunities, coordinate social forces, adjust social relations, regulate social behaviors, keep Chinese society vigorous and orderly in the process of profound transformation, achieve economic development, political uprightness, cultural prosperity, and ecological soundness, and realize the strategic goal of peaceful development.

2.3.4   Strengthening the Construction of the Rule of Law Culture and Enhancing the People's Consciousness of the Socialist Rule of Law

Because of the influence of the remnants of the legal consciousness and tradition of feudal society and the "ultra-left" ideological trend emerged after the establishment of the PRC, the Chinese people's consciousness of the rule of law is still low. "Law cannot be implemented by itself." The people are the subjects of social activities. The construction of a sound socialist rule of law cannot succeed without the enhancement of the people's legal consciousness. Therefore, it is necessary to transform the people's ideas from that of the rule of man to that of the rule of law, from that of legal nihilism to that of the faith in the rule of law, from that of obligation-centralism to that of combination of rights and obligations, carry out in a deep-going way the publicity of and education on the legal system, carry forward the spirit of socialist rule of law, establish the ideology of socialist rule of law, and enhance the people's consciousness of studying the law, respecting the law, abiding by the law, and applying the law; improve the capacity of leading cadres for applying the rule of law thinking and method to deepen the reform, promote development, resolve conflicts, and maintain stability; and strengthen the implementation of the Constitution and laws, uphold the unity, dignity and authority of the socialist legal system, and create a rule of law environment in which people are unwilling, unable and afraid to violate the law.

2.3.5 Always Adhering to Coordinated Development of the Rule of Law, the Economy and Society and Using the Rule of Law to Guide and Guarantee the Smooth Implementation of Various Reforms

The rule of law is a regulator of social relations and a distributor of social interests. The construction of the rule of law must be coordinated with economic and social development. The state should not only adapt itself to the need of economic and social development, adopt, revise, abolish and interpret laws in due time and promote the reform of the legal system, but also guide, regulate, and promote economic and social development, create a good rule of law environment for socialist economic, political, social, cultural and ecological constructions, and lay sound rule of law foundation for the solution of conflicts and disputes, fight against crimes, maintenance of stability, and realization of social fairness and justice.

The correct handling of the relationship between the reform and the rule of law is both a necessary precondition for the success of the reform and opening up and an important mission to be accomplished by China in the construction of the rule of law. The CPC put forward the basic strategy of "closely integrating reform decision-making with legislative decision-making" as early as in beginning of the 1990s, and the NPC also put forward the legislative principle of "closely combining legislative decision-making with reform decision-making" so as to provide a good rule of law safeguard for the reform, opening up, and economic and social development. Against the historical background of constructing the rule of law in China, "all major reforms must be based on law. In the whole process of reform, China must attach high importance to applying the rule of law thinking and method, give full play to the leading and promotional role of the rule of law, strengthen the coordination between relevant legislative works, and ensure that the reform is carried out on the track of the rule of law." Ensuring that "all major reforms are based on law" is both a socialist rule of law outlook on reform and a guiding ideology and basic principle that must be adhered to in order to correctly handle the relationship between the reform and the rule of law.

2.3.6 Always Adhering to the "People First" Principle and to the Principle of Respecting and Safeguarding Human Rights

The socialist nature of people's democracy means that upholding the long-term and basic interest of the people is a historical mission of socialist rule of law and that respecting and safeguarding human rights is a necessary precondition for making people the master of the country, for upholding people's interest, and for constructing a socialist state under the rule of law. The report of the Seventeenth National Congress of CPC clearly pointed out that the CPC must "respect and safeguard human rights and guarantee in accordance with law that all members of society enjoy on an equal basis the right of participation and the right to development." The Decision of the Third Plenary Session of the Eighteenth CPC Central Committee stressed the need for respecting and safeguarding human right, further strengthening the system of judicial protection of human rights, further standardizing the judicial procedures of seal up, seizure, freezing and disposition of properties involved in cases; improving mechanisms for preventing, rectifying and investigating the responsibilities for miscarriage of justice, strictly prohibiting the practice of extorting a confession by torture and maltreatment of prisoners and detainees, and strictly implementing the rules on the exclusion of illegally obtained evidence; and gradually reducing the number of capital crimes in the Criminal Law…All these announcements and provisions have not only pointed out the direction of development of the rule of law and the reform of the judicial system in China, but also provided action plans and guidance for the construction of human rights system in China. Only by adhering to the "people first" ideology and truly respecting and safeguarding human rights, can the Chinese government mobilize the people to the maximum extent, give full play to their social creativity, and realize social harmony.

2.3.7   Always Adhering to the Organic Unity of the Party's Leadership, the People Being Masters of the Country and Ruling the Country by Law

The key to developing socialist democratic politics, deepening the political reform, improving the socialist legal system, advancing the rule of law in a comprehensive way and speeding up the construction of a socialist state under the rule of law is to unswervingly adhere to the organic unity of the Party's leadership, the people being masters of the country and ruling the country by law. The report of the Eighteenth CPC National Congress pointed out that the CPC must ensure the organic unity of the leadership of the Party, the people being masters of the country and ruling the country by law, so as to guarantee the fundamental position of the people as masters of the country, enhance the vitality of the Party and the country, keep the people fully motivated, expand socialist democracy, accelerate the building of a socialist country based on the rule of law, and promote socialist political progress. The Decision of the Fourth Plenary Session of the Eighteenth CPC National Congress pointed out that the CPC must adhere to the Party's leadership over legislation, ensure law enforcement, support judicial work, take the lead in abiding by the law, unite the basic strategy of ruling the country by law with the basic method of exercising ruling power in accordance with the law, unite the Party's general responsibility for the overall situation and for coordinating people's congresses, governments, consultative conferences, trial bodies and prosecutorial bodies in carrying out their duties and conducting their work in accordance with the law and their charters, unite the formulation and implementation of the Constitution and laws by the people under the leadership of the Party with the adherence to the principle that the Party must act within the scope of the Constitution and laws, be good at turning the Party's propositions into the will of the state through legal procedures, and be good at ensuring that the candidates recommended by Party organizations become leaders of state political bodies through legal procedures, be good at implementing the Party's leadership over the country and society through state political bodies, and be good at utilizing democratic centralist principle to safeguard the authority of the CPC Central Committee and the unity of the entire Party and the entire country.

References

Chen P (1985) Work report of the Standing Committee of the Sixth National People's Congress of the People's Republic of China

Editorial Committee for Contemporary China Pictorial (1995) Judicial administration work in contemporary China. Contemporary China Publishing House, Beijing, p 57

Editorial Department for Law Yearbook of China (1987) Law Yearbook of China. Law Press China, Beijing, p 522

General Office of the Standing Committee of the National People's Congress (ed) (1991) Forty years construction of the National People's Congress System. China Democracy and Legal System Press, Beijing, p 102

Han Y (ed) (1998) General history of the legal system of the People's Republic of China, Part II. Party School of CPC Central Committee Press, Beijing, pp 794–795

He L, Lu M (eds) (1993) The trial work in contemporary China, Part. I. Contemporary China Publishing House, Beijing, p 155

Literature Research Office of the CPC Central Committee (1998) A chronicle of Deng Xiaoping's thought. Central Party Literature Press, Beijing, p 122

Lou B (1955) Basic knowledge of the Constitution of the People's Republic of China. New Knowledge Press, Beijing, p 32

Peng C (1993) Work report of the Standing Committee of the Eighth National People's Congress of the People's Republic of China

You L et al (eds) (1993) A Comprehensive History of the People's Republic of China, vol 4. Red Flag Publishing House, Beijing, p 42

Chapter 3
Formation and Improvement of the Socialist Legal System with Chinese Characteristics

The advancement of the rule of law and the construction of a state under the rule of law can be realized only through a series of methods and approaches, including values established by law, institutions designed by law, conducts regulated by law, and orders constructed by law. Therefore, having laws to go by and having good laws and good governance are the basic precondition of implementing the rule of law, as well as the basic requirement of bringing social values under the rule of law in China. The legal system refers to the totality of all legal norms in a country. It embodies in a concentrated way the systematization and integration of the principle of "having laws to go by" and an advanced legal form of construction a harmonious society by means of the entirety of all the current legal norms in a country. In China, the formation of the legal system with Chinese characteristics is an important precondition of and a basic legal safeguard for comprehensive advancement of ruling the country by law and the construction of a country under the rule of law.

3.1 Legal Systems and Their Classification

What is a legal system? Is it constructed artificially by legislators or formed naturally in historical development? What standards and principles can be applied in the construction, deconstruction or classification of the legal system in a country? What are the coordination and development of legal system? Chinese scholars carried out a large-scale debate on the above questions in the first half of the 1980s.[1] The debate has undoubtedly played an important role in promoting the construction of the legal system, especially the legislative work in China. However, after the basic strategy of state governance and objective of political development of "ruling the country by

---

[1] See Zhang et al. (1984). The book contains over 30 theses that carried out comprehensive explorations on the legal system and the system of law science in China. It deepened the research in legal theory and promoted the construction of the legal system in China in the 1980s. The book still has a profound influence even today.

© China Social Sciences Press and Springer Nature Singapore Pte Ltd. 2018
L. Li, *The Chinese Road of the Rule of Law*, China Insights,
https://doi.org/10.1007/978-981-10-8965-7_3

law and constructing a socialist state under the rule of law" and the historical task of "formation of a socialist legal system with Chinese characteristics by the year 2010" were put forward, the theoretical support and institutional design generated from the above-mentioned debate for the coordinated development of the legal system are apparently no longer able to meet today's need of construction of a legal system based on the socialist market economy.

3.1.1 The Understanding of the Legal System by Western Countries

As we all know, western legal theories, especially those of continental law countries (such as France, Germany, Italy, Spain and other continental European countries and countries that have been the former colonies of France, Spain, the Netherlands, and Portugal, such as Algeria, Ethiopia, and some Central and South American countries) usually use the concept of "legal system" in two senses.

In the first sense, legal system has the same meaning as genealogy of law. In English legal literature, "genealogy of law" is also referred to as "legal family", "legal group", and "legal system". To avoid confusions in terminology, especially to avoid the use of the polysemous term "legal system", some western comparative law scholars use the term "legal tradition" instead. However, generally speaking, western scholars usually treat "legal genealogy" and "legal system" as the same concept in the study of systems of law in the world.

In the view of western comparative law scholars, the genealogies of law (legal systems) in the world are diversified. For example, in the book Panorama of the World's Legal Systems, (Washington Law Books Company, 1928), American legal scholar John Henry Wigmore divided the legal systems in the world in ancient times into 16 different systems: Egyptian legal system, Mesopotamian legal system (Babylonian or Cuneiform legal system), Hebrew legal system, Chinese legal system, Indian legal system, Greek legal system, Roman legal system, Japanese legal system, Islamic legal system, Celtic legal system, Slavic legal system, Germanic legal system, Maritime legal system, Cannon legal system, Continental legal system and Anglo-American legal system. In his 1971 book Introduction to Comparative Law, German comparative law scholar Konrad Zweigert supported the idea of dividing the legal systems in the world into seven categories, namely the French legal system, the Germanic legal system, the Scandinavian legal system, the English Legal system, the Russian legal system, the Islamic legal system and the Indian legal system. However, Zweigert held that the legal systems in some countries, such as Greece, South Africa, Israel, the Philippines, and the PRC, are "hybrid" legal systems, and "it is difficult to put these legal systems into any particular category." Especially, people often find out that many components in a given legal system bear the characteristics of its own "parent law" or another "parent law". Under this circumstance, it is not possible to put a whole legal system into a specific legal family, but only possible to categorize the laws in a certain field, such family law, inheritance law, or commercial law.[2] In the book Major Legal Systems in the World Today, the famous French comparative law scholar René David mainly discussed issues relating to families of law; J. H. Wigmore discussed the diversity of legal families in the world in his book A Panorama of the World's Legal Systems; and J. D. M. Derrett mainly introduced the seven families of law in the world in his book An Introduction to Legal Systems. He wrote that: "We can put similar families of law together to form a 'system' by ignoring the minor differences between them, just as we do with religions (Christianity, Islam, Hindu, etc.), and languages (Romance languages, Slavic languages, Semitic languages, and languages of the Nile Valley)." David held that: "Dividing laws into systems and simplifying them into a few types is conducive to the introduction and understanding of the laws of the countries in the contemporary world." In a certain sense, Zweigert equaled legal system with legal family and believed that factors that are crucial for the constitution of a legal system include: "(1) historical background and development of a legal order, (2) its predominant and characteristic mode of thought in legal matters, (3) especially distinctive institutions, (4) the kind of legal sources it acknowledges and the way it handles them, and (5) its ideology."[3] In a legal system, which consists of such factors as legal traditions and historical sources of law, the overall arrangement and the construction of various laws are formed in a long process of historical development. During the initial formation of laws, there were not many theories on the "legal system". The formation of legal systems had been mainly driven by practical needs. Therefore, after the historical sources and composition of each legal system have been clearly described by western comparative law works, a profile of the "legal system" has naturally emerged.

Legal system in the second sense refers to the dichotomy between public law and private law. The concepts of public law and private law were first put forward by Domitius Ulpianus in ancient Rome. He held that public law adjust political relations and objectives to be realized by the state whereas private law adjusts the relationship between individual citizens and determines the conditions and limits of individual interests.[4] This dichotomy between public and private laws is still in use even today. Modern theories on the criteria of division between public and private laws include: the interest theory, the application theory, the subject theory, the power theory, the behavior theory and the rights relations theory. Later there has also been a "trend towards the convergence of public and private laws in theory and practice", namely some public laws begin to show characteristics of private law and *vice versa*.[5]

On the basis of the dichotomy between public and private laws, contemporary jurists have developed "economic law" and "social law", which are in between public and private laws, thus dividing the legal system into four parts. Similarly, some jurists have constructed the "Five-law System", consisting of the civil law, commercial law, civil procedure law, criminal procedure law and criminal law, and the "Six-law

---

[2]Zweigert (1992, pp. 139, 141).

[3]Ibid., 131.

[4]Bonfante (1992, p. 9).

[5]See Li (2000, pp. 116–117).

System", consisting of constitutional law, civil law, criminal law, administrative law, civil procedure law and criminal procedure law, by taking the dichotomy between the public and private law as the basic premise.

Although the criteria used by different theories for the division of a legal system into private and public law are different, they are all based on the same basic cognitive premise, namely the recognition of the different natures of economic-social relations and the law as a manifestation and a means of adjustment of such relations. And they are all based on the recognition of the private sector and the economic relations of the system of private ownership.

In common law countries, such as the UK (with the exception of Scotland), the US (with the exception of the State of Louisiana), and former colonies and vessel states of the British Empire, including India, Pakistan, Singapore, Burma, Canada (with the exception of Quebec), Australia, New Zealand, and Malaysia, the legal system is divided not into public and private laws, but into common law and equity law. In terms of the classification of law, common laws and equity laws lack systematicness and strict criteria. Most of them have developed from various forms of litigation dating back to the Middle Ages. For example, in the common law system there is no independent civil law or commercial law. The relevant contents of these two laws are dispersed in property law, tort law, contract law, trust law, and law of negotiable instrument.[6]

3.1.2 Discussions on the Legal System in the Soviet Union

Scholars in the former Soviet Union followed the political principles and political logic established by their revolutionary mentor Lenin in 1922, namely: "We do not recognize any 'private law'. In our opinion, everything in the economic field belongs to the scope of public law, rather than to the scope of private law…we not only expand the scope of the state's intervention in 'private law' and the state's power to abolish 'private' contracts, but also apply our revolutionary legal consciousness to the 'legal relationship between citizens'", thereby negating the premise and the standard of the division between public law and private law.[7] Meanwhile, to demonstrate the fundamental differences between socialist legal system and western capitalist legal theories and adapt to the nature of the economic basis of the ideal socialist public ownership, the Soviet scholars took a new approach and "tried to find a 'unique' standard to divide the legal system into branch laws".[8] This strong political will and practical need triggered theoretical debates over legal system among Soviet scholars.

"During the first such debate in 1938–1940, they came to the conclusion that the basis of division of laws into branches is the substantive standard, namely the particularities of the relations or objectives adjusted by law. In accordance with

---

[6]Wu and Zongling (1987, p. 216).

[7]Lenin (1959, p. 587).

[8]Lazarev (1999, p. 161).

this standard, they divided the legal system into ten branches of law: state law, administrative law, labor law, land law, Kolkhoz Law, budget law, family law, civil law, criminal law and procedure law."[9]

In the mid 1950s, there was a new development in the debate over legal system in Soviet Union: an additional standard—the mode of legal adjustment—was put forward as a supplement to the main standard on the objects adjusted by law. Actually this standard was proposed by a Soviet legal scholar during the debate in the 1930s, but had not been accepted until then.

In the second debate over the legal system in the Soviet Union in 1956, most scholars held that the division that takes the objects adjusted by law as the only standard is inadequate and almost unanimously agreed to take objects adjusted by law and the mode of adjustment as the unified basis of the division of branches of law.[10]

This standard was confirmed in the 1981 debate.

In the third debate held in 1982, principles and objectives of law and a series of other factors were listed as addition criteria for the division of branches of law. Soviet scholars' reaction to the increasing number of branch laws and constituent factors of the legal system was unanimous: the system of law should be built on an integrated multi-level basis. For example, Alexeyev held that the Soviet legal system can be divided into three groups of branch laws: (1) specialized (basic) branches of law, including state law, administrative law, civil law, criminal law and procedure law; (2) other basic branches of law, including labor law, land law, Kolkhoz law, family law, financial law, and social security law; (3) second-level comprehensive branches of law, including the law of the sea, banking law, economic law, insurance law and law on the protection of natural environment.

By the mid 1990s, some Russian scholars gradually revised the Soviet view on the legal system by not only recognizing the dichotomy between public law and private law, but also giving a relatively novel definition to the legal system: "The legal system refers to all the legal norms that are divided into branches of law (constitutional law, administrative law, civil law, criminal law, etc.) and legal institutions (institutions of election, institution of property, the institution of self-defense, etc.) according to the objects adjusted by all legal norms (the nature and complexity of the relations adjusted) and the methods of adjustment (method of direct stipulation, method of permission, and other methods)."[11] Apparently, Russian scholars had already made a breakthrough from the narrow definition of the legal system that took the objects and methods of adjustment as its content and expanded the concept by bringing legal institutions into its scope. Of course, the definition of the legal system put forward by Chinese scholars in the 1980s also mentioned "legal institutions" as a constitutive element of the legal system. However, they hardly mentioned this concept in their

---

[9]Ibid.

[10]Wu and Ren (1984).

[11]Lazarev (1999, pp. 38–39).

works, giving people the impression that there is no connection between legal system and legal institutions.[12]

It is a historical fact that Russia has inherited, reformed and innovated the legal tradition of the Soviet Union. The socialist China has borrowed the "Soviet legal science", including its theory on legal system, from its "Big Brother". Russia has made and is still making breakthroughs in some fields of the Soviet legal science. Should China also reexamine its own system of legal theory with a scientific and down-to-earth attitude? The answer is of course yes.

3.1.3 China's Understanding of the Legal System

From the point of view of the task and objective of construction of socialist legal system under the new situation in China, the theoretical preparation for the construction of the legal system by the academic circle is obviously insufficient and it is imperative to strengthen the research and exploration in this field.

For example, whether the legal system is artificially constructed or naturally formed is a quite controversial question. In the book The Story of Law, American Lawyer John Maxy Zane, while commenting on the Greek philosopher Plato, used vivid language to explain the difficulties in the formation of a good legal system. He wrote that: "It takes the accumulated errors, mistakes, and concentrated effort of many ages to make a good law, and yet a philosopher or a legislator assumes that he can dash off a full system in a few hours. Locke, with far more knowledge than Plato, attempted a system of laws for a little American colony. The result was a farrago of impracticable nonsense. Bentham, the great lawgiver, was so deluded that he thought that he knew all the law in the world. He concocted a constitution which he professed would suit the Khedive of Egypt, the wild Indian rabble of a newly freed South American republic, a state of the United States, and every other political society. Many philosophers have thought with Plato that God and nature had designed them for lawgivers, but doubtless they have all been mistaken."[13]

In the past, the Chinese law circle had a narrow understanding of the concept of "legal system", holding that "legal system normally refers to the organically unified whole consisting of all the current legal norms in a country grouped into different branches of law."[14] Even today, the Chinese law circle has not yet broke away from this understanding of the legal system. What is the socialist legal system with Chinese characteristics? In the lecture "The Legislative System, Legal System and Legislative Principles in China", given to the Standing Committee of the Tenth NPC on April 25, 2003, the lecturer answered this question: the so-called legal system refers to the totality of the legal norms in a country, which are grouped into several branches of law in accordance with certain principles and requirements and in

---

[12]Editorial Department for Law Teaching Materials (1982, p. 268).

[13]Zane (2002, p. 138).

[14]Encyclopedia of China Publishing House (1984, p. 84).

light of the objects and methods of adjustment by different legal norms, and together form an organically unified whole. "With regard to the division of branches of law, the Standing Committee of the Ninth NPC organized special studies and reached a consensus: it is appropriate to divide the legal system in China into the following seven branches of law[15]": the constitution and other constitutional laws; civil and commercial laws; administrative laws; economic laws; social laws; criminal laws; and litigious and non-litigious procedure laws. The above understanding of the legal system by Chinese scholars mainly comes from the traditional Soviet theory on the legal system, which emerged and developed under specific historical conditions and backgrounds.

Apparently, the significance of the division of the legal system into branches of law in socialist countries represented by the former Soviet Union is more political than academic or practical. Its primary purpose is to answer the question of whether the legal system is socialist or capitalist in nature; constructing the state legal system in according to legal science or tradition is only of secondary importance, because only this theory and method of classification can replace the classification standard of the dichotomy between public law and private law, which takes the recognition of private ownership as its basis of legitimacy, and manifest the public ownership and socialist nature of this new type of legal system as a more advanced system than the capitalist legal system.

Since a legal system can be constructed without using the above-mentioned method of division of branch laws and, for the past thousands of years, the majority of the countries in the world have not used this method of division without affecting the formation, existence and development of their legal systems, it can be concluded that there are many different approaches to constructing the legal system and the division of branches of law is only one of them. This actually raised the question of the necessity of using the method of division of branches of law to construct the legal system. The necessity for this method of construction of the legal system would be greatly reduced if it is based only on ideological and political reasons, or if the legal system is constructed at the advanced stage of socialism at which, according to classic Marxist writers, the productive force is highly developed and private ownership system and exploitation have already been eliminated.

Actually these two criteria division have not been sufficiently explained and are theoretically untenable in many respects. For example, by taking objects of legal adjustment as the criterion, we have categorized administrative laws as a branch of law. Then why can't we use the same criterion to categorize legislative laws or laws on judicial administration as a branch law? Criminal laws have been categorized as a branch law by taking the method of legal adjustment as the criterion. So why can not the laws on rewards be categorized into a branch law by using the same criterion? Besides, there are other criteria for the categorization of branches of law. For example, China has adopted a large number of laws adjusting various subjects of legal relations, such as the civil servant law, the people's police law, the judge's law, and the law on procurators. So why cannot we categorize these laws into an

---

[15] See Yang (2003).

independent branch law by taking the subjects of legal relations as the criterion? For another example, according the existing criterion, international law is divided into public international law, private international law and international criminal law. So why cannot domestic laws be divided according to the same criterion? Apparently, social relations adjusted by law as the criteria used in the division of branches of law have not been unified in practice and this has inevitably affected the scientificity of the legal system constructed on such criteria. In essence, the criteria for the division of branches of law are determined by the actual political, economic, and social needs of a country. There is no absolute or unchangeable criterion for the division of branches of law and it is wrong to copy the criteria of other countries without taking into consideration the actual domestic conditions (Table 3.1).

The Chinese scholars' view on the legal system actually only stresses the classification of the current legal norms into branches of law and their integrality, while ignoring the basic fact that a legal system itself is a parent system made up of several subsystems. This raises an important question: what is the purpose of identifying a legal system and its components: to divide and deconstruct it or to synthesize and construct it? Of course there is no absolute boundary between deconstruction and construction. In a certain sense, there is no construction without deconstruction; and deconstruction would lose its value of existence without construction. However, as far as the legal system is concerned, construction should be the purpose, and deconstruction is only the means to serve the purpose of constructing the legal system. The reduction (deconstruction) of a law into a category of social relations adjusted by law or a category of means of adjustment is not what the legislators want, but only a rational cognitive tool abstracted by legal theory and used by legislators to realize their legislative purpose. The use of this means by the legislators is often unselfconscious. And because it is only one of the means, but not the only means for the realization

Table 3.1 Chart II-1

	Soviet Union	Russia	PRC	Before PRC
1.	State law	Constitution	Constitution and constitutional laws	Constitution
2.	Administrative law	Administrative law	Administrative law	Administrative law
3.	Labor law	Social law	Social law	
4.	Land law	Economic law	Economic law	
5.	kolkhoz law	Military law		
6.	Budget law			
7.	Family law			
8.	Civil law	Civil and commercial law	Civil and commercial law	Civil law
9.	Criminal law	Criminal law	Criminal law	Criminal law
10.	Litigation law	Litigation and non-litigation procedure law	Litigation and non-litigation procedure law	Civil procedure law and criminal procedure law

of legislative purpose, legislators can also use other means to realize their purposes, and make a large number of laws even without resorting to this particular means. Carl Marx once wrote that: "Both political legislation and citizen's legislation are merely the manifestations and the recordings of the demands of economic relations. "[16] In this sense, legislators can not and should not create laws in accordance with the requirement of "legal system". Hayek also clearly pointed out that: "The idea that all law is, can be, and ought to be, the product of the free invention of a legislator, is actually false, an erroneous product of that constructivist rationalism."[17] When legal scholars were still debating the categorization of laws on the protection of the disabled, minors, the elderly, women, and consumers, namely whether to decide the categorization of these laws in the legal system according to the subjects, the objects or the mode of adjustment, these laws had already been made by the legislators and their existence is reasonable, necessary and independent of the will of scholars, regardless of which branch of law scholars put them in. As far as the construction of legal system is concerned, "practice" is always the mother and "demand" is always the father. Legal system is created by practice and demand rather than the other way round. Therefore, a legal system can be understood only by taking the actual need for the construction of legal system and the actual condition of the legal system as the starting point and carrying out rational induction, summarization and analysis.

It is not important which branch of law a piece of legislation should be put in before or after it is made because branches of law are also created by people in light of actual need. The ancient Chinese did not distinguish between the criminal and civil laws and integrated all laws into one code, while the ancient Romans made a distinction between public and private laws. Both systems were reasonable at their times and whatever cognitive method is used to judge them, they had played their due roles in the society on which they depended for their existence and demonstrated their value of existence, whether as an institution or as a culture. As far as legislators are concerned, their purpose of using the branch law thinking to determine the position of a law in the legal system before its adoption is no more than ensuring the categorization of the objects adjusted by law or the consistency of the method of legal adjustment. In reality, however, such considerations must be subject to the actual need of legislation and follow the procedural and technical requirements of legislation. For example, when the Chinese legislators were formulating the basic laws of Hong Kong and Macao SARs, they must first consider how to implement the policy of "one country, two systems" and the corresponding legislative techniques. And when they formulated the Legislation Law and the Supervision Law, they did not take the categorization of the constitutional law as the starting point of their legislative plan or legislative motion. The legislators' consideration of the categorization of law is of little importance to the legislation. How to use branch law thinking to find the position of a law in the legal system after it is adopted is actually a question of in which "container" a legislative product should be stored after it is produced: if a place can be found for it in an existing "containers" created according to the theory on the division of branch

---

[16]Marx and Engels (1958, pp. 121–122).

[17]von Hayek (2000, p. 115).

laws, then put it in that place; if not, a new container could be created for it without causing any damage to the unity and integrity of the existing legal system. The unity and integrity of a legal system is upheld mainly through legislative procedures and techniques, especially an effective constitutional review system, rather than relying on a logic theory on the legal system. Society and social relations are developing and changing continuously, the elaboration and diversity of the division of labor in society is an inevitable trend of development in the process of modernization. This will inevitably lead to great changes in legal relations and the overcrowding of the existing "containers" in the legal system. Therefore, it is necessary to understand and analyze the construction of legal system from a developing and open perspective.

3.2 The Historical Process and Great Significance of the Formation of the Socialist Legal System with Chinese Characteristics

3.2.1 The Historical Process of the Formation of the Socialist Legal System with Chinese Characteristics

The CPC has always attached great importance to the legislative work. As early as during the period of New Democratic Revolution, the CPC had often tried to strengthen the outcomes of revolution and establish and uphold the people's democratic revolutionary political power through legislation whenever conditions permitted. Before the establishment of the Chinese Soviet Republic, the CPC had adopted local Soviet organic laws and outlines of the organic laws of revolutionary committees in various revolutionary bases under its leadership, such as the Interim Organic Law of the Soviet of Jiangxi Province, adopted in November 1927, the Organic Law of Soviet Political Power of Western Fujian Province, adopted in August 1929, the Interim Organic Law of Xinjiang Soviet, adopted in March 1930, and the Interim Organic Program of the Soviet of Hubei-Henan-Anhui Border Region, adopted in July 1931. After its establishment in Ruijin City, Jiangxi Province, the Chinese Soviet Republic adopted a series laws, including the Outline of the Constitution of the Chinese Soviet Republic, the Soviet Organic Law, Detail Rules on Election, Organic Program of the Committee on the Improvement of Women's Life, Regulations on the Punishment of Counterrevolutionaries, Regulations on Marriage, Marriage Law, Land Law, Labor Law, and Interim Tax Regulations, thereby establishing a prototype of new revolutionary legal system with the Outline of the Constitution of the Chinese Soviet Republic as its basis.

During the period of War of Resistance against Japanese Aggression, the CPC adopted the Administrative Program of the Government of Shanxi-Hebei-Shandong-Henan Border Areas, the Administrative Program of the Government of Shanxi-Chahar-Hebei Border Area, the Administrative Program of the Government of Shaanxi-Gansu-Ningxia Border Areas, the Administrative Program for the Strengthening and Construction of Northwest Shanxi Province, the War-time Administrative Program of Shandong Province, the Regulations of Shandong Province on the safeguarding of Human Rights, Interim Regulations of Shanxi-Hebei-Shandong-Henan Border Areas on Safeguarding People's Rights, Regulations of Shaanxi-Gansu-Ningxia Border Areas on Safeguarding Human and Property Rights, Rules for the Implementation of Regulations of Bohai District on the Protection of Human Rights, Regulations of Central Jiangsu Province on the Safeguarding of Human Rights, Regulations on the Punishment of Traitors during the Period of War of Resistance against Japanese Invasion, Regulations on the Punishment of Thieves and Bandits during the Period of War of Resistance against Japanese Invasion, Regulations on the Punishment of Embezzlements, Regulations on the Prohibition of Opium and Other Narcotic Drugs, Regulations on the Punishment of Violations of Financial Ordinances, Land Regulations of Shaanxi-Gansu-Ningxia Border Areas, Regulations of Shaanxi-Gansu-Ningxia Border Areas on Land Tenancy, Regulations of Shaanxi-Gansu-Ningxia Border Areas on Land Right, Draft Regulations of Shaanxi-Gansu-Ningxia Border Areas on Labor Protection, Interim Regulations of Shanxi-Hebei-Shandong-Henan Border Areas on Labor Protection, Marriage Regulations of Shaanxi-Gansu-Ningxia Border Areas, Regulations of Shaanxi-Gansu-Ningxia Border Areas on Inheritance, Regulations of Shaanxi-Gansu-Ningxia Border Areas on the Handling of Divorce Cases Involving Relatives of Anti-Japan Soldiers, Organic Regulations of the Higher Court of Shaanxi-Gansu-Ningxia Border Areas, Interim Regulations on Litigation by Soldiers and Civilians in Shaanxi-Gansu-Ningxia Border Areas, Draft Organic Regulations of County Judicial Departments of Shaanxi-Gansu-Ningxia Border Areas, Interim Measures of Shanxi-Chahar-Hebei Border Area for the Implementation of the Assessors' System, and Measures of Northwest Shanxi Province for the Implementation of the Circuit Trial System. Statistics show that the CPC had promulgated 51 pieces of rules, regulations, detailed rules for implementation, measures and instructions on election, and 56 laws, rules, regulations, and instructions on organizations and standing orders,[18] thereby further developing the new revolutionary legal system created by the CPC in the previous period of time.

During the period of the War of Liberation, the people's political powers in liberated areas continued to attach importance to the legislative work. According to incomplete statistics, during this period, communist governments in liberated areas had adopted the Outline of Administrative Program of the Administrative Committee of Shanxi-Chahar-Hebei Border Areas, Administrative Program of Temporary Administrative Committee of Jiangsu-Anhui Border Areas, Constitutional Principles of Shanxi-Chahar-Hebei Border Areas, Common Administrative Program of Democratic Governments of Various Provinces (Special Cities) in Northeast China, and Administrative Policies of the People's Government of East China, and other constitutional laws, eight regulations and instructions on election, 19 organic rules and regulations, and many other laws, regulations, and ordinances in the fields of land law, marriage law, and criminal law, thereby accumulating important legisla-

---

[18]See Han and Zhaoru (1981).

tive experiences and creating legal conditions for the establishment of socialist legal system in the New China.

On February 28, 1949, on the eve of the establishment of the PRC, the CPC Central Committee issued the Instruction on Abolishing the Six Codes of the Kuomintang Regime and Establishing the Judicial Principles of the Liberated Areas, which pointed out that: "Under the political power of people's democratic dictatorship with the worker-peasant alliance led by the proletariat as its main body, people's courts should no longer take the Six Codes of the Kuomintang Regime, but should take the people's new laws, as the basis of judicial work. Before the systematic promulgation of new people's laws, the policies of the CPC and various programs, laws, regulations and resolutions that have already been promulgated by people's governments should be taken as the basis of judicial work. Under the current situation when the system of people's laws is still incomplete, judicial organs should abide by the following principle in carrying out their work: if there are relevant provisions in the existing programs, laws, orders, regulations and resolutions, such provisions shall be taken as the basis of judicial work; if no such provisions exist, new democratic policies should be taken as the basis of judicial work." The attitude of the CPC, as a revolutionary party, towards the old laws was best explained in this Instruction: "During the period of War of Resistance against Japanese Invasion, we had used certain provisions of the laws of Kuomintang Regime that were beneficial to the protection of people's interests in various bases under our control. In areas under Kuomintang's reactionary rule, we also frequently use some beneficiary provisions in reactionary laws to protect and struggle for the interests of the people and expose the true nature of reactionary laws. This course of action was undoubtedly correct. However, such a temporary tactical move should not be interpreted as our basic recognition of Kuomintang's reactionary laws or basic adoption of Kuomintang's old reactionary laws under the new democratic political power." A revolutionary party must negate the old laws and the old legal system. To do otherwise is equal to admitting the illegality of its own revolution and of the political power it has established after the revolution. Before the opening of the first National People's Congress, the Common Program of the Chinese People's Political Consultative Conference, which served as a temporary constitution at that time, provided in Article 17 that: "All laws, decrees and judicial systems of the Kuomintang reactionary government which oppress the people shall be abolished. Laws and decrees protecting the people shall be enacted and the people's judicial system shall be established." Dong Biwu once pointed out that: "When we establish a new political power, we naturally must adopt new laws, degrees, rules, regulations and institutions. After smashing the old legal system, we must establish a new legal system. Otherwise we are anarchists. How can we uphold the new order without laws, degrees, rules, regulations and institutions?"[19]

In 1954, Dong Biwu announced at the first meeting of the First National People's Congress that: "Now the country has entered into a period of planned construction. Our constitution has already been promulgated. In the future, it is not only possible, but also necessary to gradually establish a relatively complete system of laws, so

---

[19]Biwu (1985, p. 218).

as to effectively safeguard the state construction and protect people's democratic rights."[20]

"Why should we raise the issue of legislation? Because our legislative work, especially the legislation aimed at protecting economic construction, has lagged behind the objective demands. In the future, we must concentrate our efforts on the legislative work if we want to have laws to go by in our work."[21]

In order to strengthen the legislation and provide legal basis and legitimacy[22] to the newly established people's democratic political power as soon as possible, the newly established government of the PRC adopted the decentralized legislative mode before the promulgation of the Constitution. Under this mode, all people's governments at or above the county level had legislative power and manage part or all the affairs within their respective administrative areas by exercising their legislative function and power in accordance with law.[23] This legislative mode had greatly improved the legislative efficiency and speeded up the legislation at both the central and local levels. Statistics show that, between 1950 and 1953, a total of 435 pieces of legislation had been made at the central level, averaging 109 per year. Although there is no comprehensive and detailed statistics on local legislation in this period of time, but we can get a general picture by looking at the legislation in Zhejiang Province, Inner Mongolia Autonomous Region and Shanghai Municipality: Zhejiang Province

---

[20] Editorial Group for Collected Legal Works of Biwu (2001, p. 235).

[21] Ibid., p. 166.

[22] French scholar Jean-Marc Coicoud gives the following definition to legitimacy: "Legitimacy is the assessment of the relationship between the ruler and the ruled, the process in which the political power and those obeying it prove their own legality, and the recognition of the ruling power." The first requirement of legitimacy is the consent of the ruled; the second requirement is the recognition of the ruling power by social values and society; and the third requirement is the recognition of the ruling power and its values by the law. When explaining why legitimacy also applies to China, he points out: Firstly, political legitimacy is a political question of great concern to Chinese people. The Chinese government should not and cannot ignore such questions as how the people assess the behavior of their government and what, in the opinion of the Chinese people, are or should be the duties of the government? Secondly, the profound transformation China is currently undergoing and, especially, the profoundness of the transformations that China has experiences since it was forced to open up to the western countries in the 19th century have given legitimacy a special significance. Thirdly, Deng Xiaoping's economic reform has brought China into a transitional period and affected every aspect of social life, including the legitimacy of the political system, in China. It is without any doubt that the economic growth and its profound impact on Chinese society is the source of legitimacy of the political power in China. See Coicoud (2002, pp. 1–7).

[23] According to the General Principles of Organic Regulations for People's Governments of Provinces, Cities, and Counties, promulgated by the Government administrative Council on January 6, 1950, people's governments at the provincial level had the power to formulate interim decrees and regulations on the administrative affairs of their respective provinces, which should be reported to the Government Administrative Council for approval or for the record. People's governments of municipalities directly under the Central Government, of municipalities directly under greater administrative areas, or of municipalities directly provincial governments had the power to formulate interim regulations on administrative affairs of their respective municipalities and report them to governments at the next higher level for approval or for the record; people's governments at the county level had the power to formulate separate regulations on administrative affairs of their respective counties and report them to provincial governments for approval or for the record.

had adopted 653 pieces of interim decrees and separate regulations between 1950 and 1953, averaging 163 per year; Inner Mongolia had adopted 368 pieces of various regulations and normative documents, with an annual average of 73.6; Shanghai had adopted 799 pieces of interim decrees and regulations and separate regulations between 1950 and September 1954, with an annual average of 159.[24]

In September 1954, the First NPC adopted at its first meeting the first constitution of the PRC, which comprehensively provided for the basic state system in China and changed the system whereby the legislative power is shared by the central and local governments to a centralized legislative system.

According to the 1954 Constitution, the NPC is the highest organ of state power in China, as well as the only legislative authority in the country. Its legislative functions and powers include: revising the Constitution, adopting laws, and supervising the implementation of the Constitution. Later, in the revisions of the Constitution in 1975 and 1978, the provision that "The NPC is the only legislative authority in the country." was deleted.

The Standing Committee of the NPC is a permanent acting body of the NPC. The 1954 Constitution provided that the Standing Committee of the NPC has the following legislative functions and powers: to interpret the laws; to adopt decrees; to annul decisions and orders of the State Council that contravene the Constitution, laws or decrees; to revise or annul inappropriate decisions issued by the government authorities of provinces, autonomous regions, and municipalities directly under the central authority; and to decide on the ratification or abrogation of treaties concluded with foreign states.

In 1955, the First NPC adopted at its second session the Resolution Authorizing the Standing Committee of the National People's Congress to Adopt Separate Administrative Regulations, which expanded the scope of organs exercising the state legislative power so that it covers the NPC Standing Committee. The reason for this resolution was that: "With the progress of socialist construction and socialist reform, the state urgently needs to adopt various laws to satisfy the needs of state construction and state work. During the period when the NPC is not in session, there will inevitably be some laws of partial nature that urgently need to be adopted and implemented. Therefore…it is necessary to authorize the Standing Committee of the NPC to adopt, in a timely manner, laws of partial nature, namely separate regulations, in accordance with the spirit of the Constitution and in light of the actual need."[25] At its first session held in 1959, the Second NPC further authorized the NPC Standing Committee to revise the provisions in the current laws that are no longer applicable in light of the development of the situation and the actual need of work. The 1954 Constitution provided that the State Council had the following administrative legislative competences: to formulate administrative measures, issue decisions and orders in accordance with the Constitution, laws and decrees; to review the situation of implementation of the decisions and order issued by the State Council; to submit

---

[24]See Wu et al. (1984, pp. 36, 241).

[25]Secretariat of the Second Session of the First National People's Congress of the People's Republic of China (ed) (1955, p. 995).

bills to the NPC or its Standing Committee; to revise or annul inappropriate orders and directives issued by ministers or by heads of commissions; and to revise or annul inappropriate decisions and orders issued by local administrative organs of state.

In 1956, Liu Shaoqi pointed out in the Political Report to the Eighth National Congress of the CPC: "Currently one of the urgent tasks in state work is to start systematical construction of a relatively complete system of law and to strengthen the legal system"; "the period of stormy revolution has passed and new relations of production have been established; the emphasis of our task has shifted to ensuring the smooth development of social productive forces. Therefore the method of socialist revolution must also be changed and a complete legal system needs to be constructed."

To establish a complete legal system, it is necessary to strengthen legislation. However, the 1954 Constitution provided for a centralized legislative mode,[26] in which the legislative power was concentrated at the central level.[27] This legislative mode had, in a certain sense, impeded the development of the legal system in China. According to statistics, between 1954 and 1979, a total of 1115 pieces of legislation, including various opinions, measures, orders, resolutions, decisions, notices, reports, and official replies, had been adopted at the central level, with an annual average of 59; since there was no local legislative power, the number of local legislation was zero during this period of time.[28] The centralized legislative system ensured in a powerful way the unified leadership of the central authorities over various undertakings in the country while at the same time significantly affected the local initiatives and impeded the comprehensive development of socialist legal system in China.

During the "Cultural Revolution", class struggle was taken as the guiding principle and the country was in a state of lawlessness. The state legislative work was suspended, public security organs, procuratorates and courts were smashed, the basic rights of the broad masses of cadres and ordinary citizens brutally trumped upon, and socialist democracy and legal system seriously sabotaged.

Learning a bitter historical lesson from the "Cultural Revolution", the CPC pointed out at the Third Plenary Session of its Eleventh Central Committee that, in order to develop socialist democracy, it is necessary to strengthen socialist legal system, institutionalize democracy and bring it into the orbit of law, and establish the basic policy of developing socialist democracy and strengthening socialist legal system in the process of modernization. Strengthening the socialist legal system means that

---

[26]The 1954 Constitution provided that the NPC is the only legislative authority in the country that has the power to revise the Constitution and adopt laws. In 1955, the First NPC adopted at its second session the Resolution Authorizing the Standing Committee of the National People's Congress to Adopt Separate Administrative Regulations, which expanded the scope of organs exercising the state legislative power so that it covers the NPC Standing Committee. The reason for this resolution was that: "With the progress of socialist construction and socialist reform, the state urgently needs to adopt various laws to satisfy the needs of state construction and state work. During the period when the NPC is not in session, there will inevitably be some laws of partial nature that urgently need to be adopted and implemented. Therefore…it is necessary to authorize the Standing Committee of the NPC to adopt, in a timely manner, laws of partial nature, namely separate regulations, in accordance with the spirit of the Constitution and in light of the actual need."

[27]Mao (1977, p. 276).

[28]See Wu et al. (1984, p. 241).

there must be laws to go by, the laws must be observed and strictly enforced, and lawbreakers must be prosecute. The CPC also demanded at the Third Plenary Session that: "We must ensure that there are laws to go by. From now on, the legislative work should become an important agenda of the NPC and its Standing Committee." Ensuring that there are laws to go by had become the primary task of legal construction in the new era. In 1980, Deng Xiaoping further stressed that: "We should continue to develop socialist democracy and improve the socialist legal system. This is a basic, consistent policy that has been implemented by the Central Committee ever since its Third Plenary Session, and there must be no wavering in its enforcement in future. There are still inadequacies in our democratic system, so it is necessary to draw up a whole series of laws, decrees and regulations to institutionalize democracy and give it legal sanction."[29]

Building a socialist legal system and ensuring that there are laws to go by is a long-term task of China in the construction of socialist rule of law as well as a basic objective of the legislative work in the new historical period. In the article entitled "Emancipate the Mind, Seek Truth from Facts and Unite as One in Looking to the Future", published in 1978, Deng Xiaoping wrote that: "The trouble now is that our legal system is incomplete, with many laws yet to be enacted… So we must concentrate on enacting criminal and civil codes, procedural laws and other necessary laws concerning factories, people's communes, forests, grasslands and environmental protection, as well as labour laws and a law on investment by foreigners. These laws should be discussed and adopted through democratic procedures. All this will ensure that there are laws to go by…The relations between one enterprise and another, between enterprises and the state, between enterprises and individuals, and so on should also be defined by law, and many of the contradictions between them should be resolved by law. There is a lot of legislative work to do, and we don't have enough trained people. Therefore, legal provisions will have to be less than perfect to start with, then be gradually improved upon. Some laws and statutes can be tried out in particular localities and later enacted nationally after the experience has been evaluated and improvements have been made. Individual legal provisions can be revised or supplemented one at a time, as necessary; there is no need to wait for a comprehensive revision of an entire body of law. In short, it is better to have some laws than none, and better to have them sooner than later."[30] These ideas confirmed to the reality at that time, had become a guideline of legislative work in China for a period of time after 1978, and played an important guiding role in speeding up the legislation and timely resolving the problem of "having no law to go by".

The most obvious sign of the beginning of the construction of legal system in the new era was the large-scale legislation in 1979. In July 1979, the Fifth NPC adopted at its second session the Criminal Law, the Criminal Procedure Law, the organic laws of local people's congresses and local people's governments at various levels, laws on the election of the NPC and local people's congresses at various levels,

---

[29]Deng (1975–1982).

[30]Deng Xiaoping, "Emancipate the Mind, Seek Truth from Facts and Unite as One in Looking to the Future", in *ibid*., pp. 146–147.

organic law of the people's courts, organic law of people's procuratorates, and law on Chinese-foreign joint ventures. "This was the first time in the Chinese socialist legislative history that so many important laws had been adopted in one session of the NPC".[31] Deng Xiaoping pointed out during this session of the NPC that: "At this session of the National People's Congress, we formulated seven laws...This was a necessary precondition for creating a political situation of stability and unity. Following this session, we shall formulate a series of laws. We lack many necessary civil laws. We also need to enact many laws governing economic development, such as those pertaining to factories. The laws that we have made are too few. We need about one hundred of laws which we do not presently have. Therefore, we have much work to do and this is just the beginning."[32]

In 1982, the Standing Committee of the Fifth NPC pointed out in its work report to the Fifth Session that: "We must carry out the legislative work by taking the actual conditions in China as the starting point, and gradually establish an independent legal system with Chinese characteristics in accordance with socialist legal principles."

In 1987 the CPC announced in the report to its Thirteenth National Congress: "the socialist democracy and legal system are gradually constructed and a socialist system of law with the Constitution as the basis is gradually taking shape in China" while at the same time pointing out that "China is at the primary stage of socialism. It must take the public ownership system as the main body and vigorously develop planned commodity economy, speed up the construction of socialist market system and a complete system of economic laws and regulations, adopt as soon as possible policies and laws on the private sector of the economy, and protect the lawful rights and interests of private enterprises. In conclusion, the construction of the legal system must run through the entire process of the reform and we must ensure that there are laws to go by, the laws are observed and strictly enforced, and lawbreakers are prosecuted in every aspect of the political, economic, and social life of the country."

In March 1988, the Seventh NPC pointed out at its First Session that: "In the past five year, we have made major progresses in the legislative work... Now there are laws to go by in the basic aspects of the political, economic, and social life of the country. A socialist legal system with the Constitution as its basis has already taken form." Mr. Li Peichuan pointed out in the book Theory and Practice of Socialist Legislation in China that the period between 1978 and 1990 was "a period of large-scale legislation in China, in which a multilevel socialist legal system with Chinese characteristics and with the Constitution as the core had gradually established on a desolate, almost empty basis...the adoption of these laws, administrative regulations, local regulations, and administrative rules has enabled China to basically have laws to go by in the political, economic, and social life of the county."[33]

After Deng Xiaoping's speeches given during an inspection tour to Southern provinces in 1992, the CPC, in order deepen economic reform and establish a socialist market economic system, adopted in 1993 the Decision on Several Issues con-

---

[31] Wu et al. (1984), p. 64.

[32] Deng (1975–1982, pp. 146–147).

[33] Li (1991, p. 356).

cerning the Establishment of Socialist Market Economic System, which "set the following goals of legal construction in China: speeding up economic legislation, further improving civil, commercial and criminal laws and laws on state organs and administrative management, and establishing a primary legal system adapted to the socialist market economy by the end of this century." In 1993, the Eighth NPC adopted at its first session an amendment to the Constitution, which includes into the Constitution such contents as "China is currently at the primary stage of socialist", "developing a theory of socialism with Chinese characteristics", and "adhering to the policy of reform and opening up" and specifically provides that "The state practices socialist market economy", and "strengthens economic legislation and improves macro-regulation and control." This amendment provides constitutional basis for the establishment and development of there socialist market economy and therefore is of great significance. "The establishment of a socialist market economic system must be safeguarded by a relatively complete legal system. Currently China has not yet adopted the laws that are urgently needed for regulating the behaviors of subjects of market economy, upholding market economic order and improving macro-regulation and control. Therefore, China should speed up the legislative work without delay."[34]

In 1994, the Standing Committee of the Eighth NPC announced at its second meeting that: "In accordance with requirements of the Constitution, the Standing Committee will take economic legislation as its primary task and strive to establish the basic framework of the legal system of socialist market economy within its term of office."

In 1995, the NPC Standing Committee "continued to place the legislative work high on its agenda, speeded up the economic legislation, and took an important step toward the establishment of the framework of socialist market economic legal system."

In 1996, the Standing Committee of the Eighth NPC pointed out at its fourth meeting that, during the previous year, the Committee had "taken an important step towards the development of the legal system of socialist market economy, and provided legal safeguard for the smooth progress of reform, opening up and modernization construction."

In 1997, the Standing Committee of the Eighth NPC pointed out in the work report to its fifth meeting that the Committee "has been pushing ahead with legislation and taken an important step towards the development of the legal system of socialist market economy, which has already taken initial shape…"

In 1997, the Report of the Fifteenth CPC National Congress, while establishing the basic policy of ruling the country by law, specifically set the legislative goal in the process of constructing a socialist state under the rule of law, namely "the formation of a socialist legal system with Chinese characteristics by the year 2010".

In 1998, the Standing Committee of the Ninth NPC pointed out in the summarization of its legislative work that, in the previous five years, it had "not only increased number, but also improved the quality of laws, thereby laying a foundation for the formation of a socialist legal system with Chinese characteristics. In the future, the

---

[34]Peng (1993).

Committee will continue to strengthen the legislative work in accordance with the goals and tasks set at the Fifteenth CPC National Congress, put the economic legislative work high on agenda, improve the quality of legislation, and strive to build a socialist legal system with Chinese characteristics."

We can see from the above that, with the continuous deepening of economic and social reforms and development of socialist democracy and rule of law, our understanding of the legal system has also been deepening continuously—from "establishment of an independent legal system with Chinese characteristics" to "initial formation of a socialist legal system"; from "the formation of the framework of a legal system of socialist market economy" to "the establishment of a legal system of socialist market economy", from "the establishment of a socialist legal system" to "the formation of a socialist legal system with Chinese characteristics", and from "initial formation", to "basic formation" and to "formation"—all these changes have reflected the continuous deepening of the state's understandings of the legislative work, the legal system, and the process of the formation of a socialist legal system with Chinese characteristics.

It took China 13 years—from 1997 to 2010—to form a socialist legal system with Chinese characteristics. This process can be divided into the following three stages:

(1) The period of the Ninth NPC: "the initial formation of a socialist legal system with Chinese characteristics";
(2) The period of the Tenth NPC: "the basic formation of a socialist legal system with Chinese characteristics";
(3) The period between the Eleventh NPC and 2010: "the formation of a socialist legal system with Chinese characteristics".

In March 2003, the Standing Committee of the Tenth NPC pointed out in the work report at its first meeting that, on the basis of the work done by the previous NPCs, and after unremitting efforts made by this NPC, the various branches of law that constitute the socialist legal system with Chinese characteristics had already been complete,[35] and the main laws in each branch of law had already been adopted. With the adoption of these laws by the NPC and its Standing Committee, together with administrative regulations adopted by the State Council and local regulations by local adopted by various people's congresses, a socialist legal system with Chinese characteristics with the Constitution as its core had taken initial shape. The Tenth NPC and its Standing Committee had set the goal of their legislative work in the

---

[35] In China, the branch law classification system is the core of the construction of the legal system, whereas in western countries, the so-called legal system is mainly concerned with the division between public and private laws and its derivatives. When we take the establishment of branches of law as the objective of division of legal system, the first problem we will encounter is: what is the significance of dividing the legal system into branch laws? Namely, will deconstructing the legal system without using the concept of "branch laws" affect the construction of the legal system? Or, in other words, whether it is true that in countries not using the branch law classification system, the legal system cannot be regarded as a "system"? The answer is of course negative. Neither common law countries nor civil law countries have adopted branch law classification system. However, this does not affect the existence and normal operation of the legal system or the implementation of the rule of law in these countries.

next five years as: "the basic formation of a socialist legal system with Chinese characteristics".

In 2007, the report to the Seventeenth Party Congress announced that a socialist legal system with Chinese characteristics has basically taken form.

In March 2008, Mr. Wu Bangguo, Chairman of the Standing Committee of the Eleventh NPC, pointed out at the first meeting of the Committee that the socialist legal system with Chinese characteristics is a unified whole that takes the Constitution as its core and laws as its backbone, consists of seven branches of law (the Constitution and other constitutional laws, civil and commercial laws, administrative laws, economic laws, social laws, criminal laws, and laws on contentious non-contentious proceedings) and three levels of legal norms (laws, administrative regulations and local regulations).

2010 was the final year of the formation of the socialist legal system with Chinese characteristics. The highest organ of state power in China formally announced that the socialist legal system with Chinese characteristics had already formed. This is an important indication of the comprehensive implementation of the strategy of ruling the country by law and a major achievement in the construction of the rule of law in China.

On March 10, 2011, the Chairman of the Standing Committee of the NPC, Mr. Wu Bangguo, announced at the Fourth Session of the Eleventh NPC that, by the end of 2010, China had already adopted 236 valid laws, over 690 administrative regulations and more than 8600 local regulations. Today, the construction of various branches of law that cover all aspects of social relations have been completed...a socialist legal system with Chinese characteristics that is based on national conditions, adapted to the needs of reform, opening up, and socialist modernization construction, embodies in a concentrated way the will of the Party and the will of the people, takes the Constitution as the key link, constitutional laws, civil laws and commercial laws and other branches of laws as the main body, and consists of different levels of legal norms, including laws, administrative regulations, and local regulations, has taken form, thus providing legal basis for the construction of economic, political, cultural, social and ecological civilizations in China and marking the completion on schedule of the legislative goal of establishing a socialist legal system with Chinese characteristics by the year 2010.

3.2.2 Criteria of the Formation of a Legal System with Chinese Characteristics

The famous British Jurisprudent Joseph Raz maintained in the book the Authority of Law that, from the point of view of analytical jurisprudence, a complete theory on legal system should include the answers to the following four questions:

First, the question of existence, namely "what is the criteria on the existence of a legal system"? A theory of legal system should be able to provide some criteria for distinguishing between existing legal systems and those that have already ceased to exist or those that have never existed;

Second, "the question of characteristics (and the related question of membership)", namely the question of what criteria should be used for deciding which legal system a law belongs to. We can deduce from membership the criteria on characteristics and answer the question of which laws constitute a legal system.

Third, the question of structure, namely whether all legal systems or certain kind of legal system have a common structure, whether laws belonging to the same legal system have certain recurring patterns of relationship, and exactly what constitute important differences between legal systems?

Fourth, the question of content, namely whether there are laws that exist in one form or another in all or certain kinds of legal system? Whether there are some contents that are indispensable to all legal systems or some important content that can be used to distinguish between important types of law?[36]

Although the above arguments were put forward by Professor Laz from the perspective of analytical jurisprudence and do not touch upon the value and the actual operation of the legal system, they do provide us with some useful ideological resources: A legal system is not formed naturally or spontaneously, but is constructed by legislators (sovereign); it is not merely a division of branch laws or construction of a system, but also a system consisting of many subordinate systems and elements; and the criteria of the constitution of a legal system are diversified and multi-angled.

Based on the national conditions in China and taking into consideration historical factors and current situation of construction of the rule of law, this author maintains that the formation of the socialist legal system with Chinese characteristics must meet the following criteria:

First, the criteria of the constitution of legal system. In the socialist legal system with Chinese characteristics, which takes the Constitution as the core and laws as the main body, various branch laws, including the Constitution and constitution-related laws, civil and commercial laws, administrative laws, economic laws, social laws, criminal laws, laws on contentious non-contentious proceedings, legal norms at different levels, including laws, administrative regulations, local regulations, and regulations on the exercise of autonomy (separate regulations), and different types of laws, including law codes and separate laws, revised laws and original laws, special laws and general laws, procedural laws and substantive laws, interpretation laws and original laws, local laws and central laws, international laws and domestic laws, must form a unified organic whole, with coordinated and harmonious relationships between upper- and lower-level laws and between laws at the same level.

Second, quantitative criteria of the legal system. Up to now, more than 230 effective laws have been adopted by the NPC and its Standing Committee, over 600 effective administrative regulations adopted by the State Council, more than 7000 local regulations adopted by local people's congresses and their standing committees, and near 700 regulations on the exercise of autonomy and separate regulations adopted by regional national autonomous areas. The construction of various branches

---

[36]Raz (2003, pp. 2–3).

of law that constitute the socialist legal system with Chinese characteristics have been completed and the basic, primary, and backbone laws in each branch of law have been adopted. The large amount of legislative achievements made by China since the establishment of the PRC, especially since the reform and opening up, have created the necessary conditions and laid a sound foundation for the completion on schedule of the construction of the socialist legal system with Chinese characteristics.

Third, criteria of the scope of adjustment of legal system. The construction of the socialist legal system with Chinese characteristics means all aspects of the economic, political, cultural, social, and international relations, including the relations between the state and the citizen, between the central and local governments, between local governments, between citizens, between citizens and mass organizations, between political parties, between various ethnic groups, between various organizations, between rights and obligations, between power and responsibility, between the man and the nature, and between individuals and society, must be put into the scope of regulation by law and that there must be laws to go by in all the main aspects the political, economic, social and cultural life of the country.

Fourth, the internal technical criteria of the legal system. The socialist legal system with Chinese characteristics should be a complete system of laws without any omission of important legislation or any "decorative legislation". It should be reasonable in structure, scientific in style and layout, standardized in language, strict in logic, and consistent, coordinated and orderly in content. Various kinds of laws should dovetail and coordinate with each other both in spirit and in principles, both in form and in content, both in norm and in text, and both in part and in whole, so as to constitute an integrated organic entity. Meanwhile, best efforts should be made to minimize the gaps, contradictions, conflicts, loopholes, repetitions, and defects in the legal system and eliminate in time backward and conflicting laws in the system.

Fifth, the value effect criteria of the legal system. The socialist legal system with Chinese characteristics is the transformation into law of value principles as well as the systematization of codes of conduct. The laws that all citizens, legal persons and mass organizations are required to abide by and the ruling party, legislative, administrative and judicial organs and armed forces are required to implement must be good laws that are compatible with the national conditions in China and the will of Chinese people, embody fairness, justice, and public order and social morals, the principles of social development, and progress of human civilization. In the legal system, laws of different categories, at different levels and in different forms should all play their due roles in social life, so as to safeguard human rights and realize the legislative objectives through good law and good governance.

3.2.3   The Great Significance of the Formation of the Socialist Legal System with Chinese Characteristics

The formation on schedule of the socialist legal system with Chinese characteristics is a great achievement of socialist construction, a major result of the legalization of the basic policies adopted by the CPC since the reform and opening up, and an important indicator of comprehensive advancement of rule of law in China, and therefore is of great significance.

3.2.3.1   The Formation of the Socialist Legal System with Chinese Characteristics Is a Great Achievement of Socialist Construction

The main social function of legislation in a modern state is to realize the legal adjustment of social relations, the legal distribution of social interests, the legal regulation of social order, and the legal confirmation of the results of social construction. The role played by law in social progress is self-evident. The 1804 French Civil Code was adopted under the sponsorship of Napoleon, and later named the Napoleonic Code. When summing up his own life before his death in 1821, Napoleon remarked that: "My real glory is not the 40 battles I won—for my defeat at Waterloo will destroy the memory of those victories. …What nothing will destroy, what will live forever, is my Civil Code."[37] Mao Zedong pointed out that: "As far as the constitutional governments the world has so far known are concerned, whether in Britain, France, the United States or the Soviet Union, a body of basic laws, that is, a constitution, has generally been promulgated after a successful revolution to give recognition to the actual establishment of democracy."[38] China is a statutory law country and the socialist legal system is the total sum of all the current laws in the country, the comprehensive result of the state legislation in all aspects, at all levels, and in all fields. Its primary political value and social function is to confirm and protect in the form of will of the state and legal norms the results of socialist construction and reform. The 1954 Constitution, as the first socialist constitution adopted by the PRC, "reinforced the results of people's revolution and the new political and economic victories won by Chinese people since the establishment of the PRC, reflected the basic demand of the state during the period of transition and the common wish of the broad masses of people to construct a socialist society", and confirmed the fact that the Chinese people, who had been oppressed for thousands of years, had become the masters of the country. The 1982 Constitution "confirmed in the form of law the results of the

---

[37] The Code Napoleon (The French Civil Code) (1979), "The Translators' Preface", p. 3. France urgently needed to adopt a civil code after the Revolution. One of the important reasons being that, "after the success of the revolution, it was necessary to abolish the old laws and promulgate new laws, namely to reinforce the victory of the Bourgeois Revolution, and lay a legal foundation for the development of capitalism through the adoption of statutory laws".

[38] Mao (1964, p. 693).

struggle by Chinese people of all nationalities, and laid down the fundamental system and tasks of the state". The Constitution is the core and the foundation of the socialist legal system with Chinese characteristics. Chinese constitutions, from the 1954 Constitution to the 1982 Constitution, have all provided for the guiding ideology, the basic tasks, the political, economic and social systems, the state and government systems, the relationship between the central and local governments, and the citizen's rights and obligations, thereby fully affirmed the various achievements of socialist revolution and construction in China. From 1988 to 2004, China has revised the Constitution four times to affirm the successful experiences and positive results of opening up and reform in each new period of time. The constitution has the highest legal effect and is the basic legal basis of legislation in China. The formation of the legal system in China has confirmed and safeguarded the successful experiences and fruits of victory since the establishment of the PRC, especially since the reform and opening up in 1978, provided for the basic requirements of socialist modernization construction, recorded the main process of the common struggled carried out by Chinese people of all nationalities under the leadership of the CPC, and pointed out the objectives of struggle and basic tasks of the reform and opening up in China in the future. Especially, the formation on schedule of the socialist legal system with Chinese characteristics has embodied in the form of democratic legislation the will of the people, upheld the people's interest, thereby repeatedly reaffirmed and reinforced the legitimacy basis of the CPC's ruling power, effectively upheld the people' status as the masters of the country and safeguarded their human rights, and greatly promoted the construction of socialist material, political and spiritual civilizations.

3.2.3.2 The Formation of the Socialist Legal System with Chinese Characteristics Is a Major Result of the Legalization of the Basic Policies Adopted by the CPC Since the Reform and Opening up

Socialist laws in China are adopted by the people under the leadership of the CPC. They are not only the embodiment of the will of the people, but also the legalization of the Party's basic lines, principles and policies, and the legal manifestation of the unity of the propositions of the CPC and the will of Chinese people of all nationalities. In 1997, the CPC established "ruling the country by law" as the basic state policy and "construction of a socialist state under the rule of law" as the important objective of socialist modernization, and put forward the major task of formation of a socialist legal system with Chinese characteristics by the year 2010. In the legislative practice of the new era, the adoption of each amendment to the Chinese Constitution,[39]

---

[39]In practice, constitutional amendments are usually first proposed by the ruling CPC. For instance, after the Third Plenary Session of the Eleventh Central Committee, the CPC, while concentrating its efforts on the construction of the socialist legal system, has also been exploring the road of reforming the mode of exercise of the ruling power. At its Fourteenth National Congress, the CPC clearly stated that the objective of the economic reform in China is to establish the socialist market economic system. This was a major decision made by the CPC in the process of leading the Chinese

each five-year plan, and each important law...embodies the CPC's leadership over legislative work,[40] and the process of legalization through legislation of the Party's basic lines and policies and major decisions.

The Standing Committee of the NPC attaches high importance to the combination of legislation with economic and social development, to the integration of legislative decision-making with the major decision-making on the reform and opening up, and to the transformation through legislation into laws of the Party lines and policies. Since the reform and opening up in 1978, the NPC Standing Committee has, in light of the different situations in different periods of time, set various legislative tasks, such as "putting the emphasis of current economic legislation on the economic adjustment and institutional reform, so as to ensure the successful completion of the task of adjusting and reinforcing the results of economic reform"; "transforming into state laws through legal procedures the policies proved by practice to be correct and applicable for a long period of time, carefully studying various new situations and new problems emerged in the process of reform and opening up, and timely affirming in the form of law the successful experiences of reform and opening up"; "closely combining legislation with the actual needs of reform and development, confirming in the form of law those proved to be correct by practice, strengthening the results of reform and opening up, using the law to promote and safeguard the healthy advancement of reform, opening up and modernization construction";

---

people to carry out economic reform. To turn this decision into a guiding policy and principle to be implemented by state organs in their economic reform activities, the CPC Central Committee submitted a proposal on the revision of the Constitution to the Standing Committee of the Seventh NPC on February 14, 1993, so as to confirm by the Constitution the socialist market economic system. The Standing Committee of the Seventh NPC discussed the proposal and adopted a draft constitutional amendment at its thirtieth meeting and submitted the draft amendment to the first session of the Eighth NPC for deliberation. On March 29, 1993, the Eighth NPC approved the constitutional amendment at its first session, thereby enshrining the socialist market economic system in the Constitution. In September 1997, the CPC convened the Fifteenth Party Congress and adopted a political report, which put forward the basic state policy of constructing a socialist state under the rule of law. In order to turn the rule of law principle in this basic state strategy into a constant principle guiding the activities of state organs and on the basis of thorough investigation, research and solicitation of opinions, the CPC put forward the proposal on the amendment of the Constitution to the Standing Committee of the Ninth NPC on January 22, 1999. The Standing Committee of the Ninth NPC, after careful discussion, accepted this proposal at its seventh meeting and submitted the constitutional amendment to the Ninth NPC at its second session in accordance with the procedure of constitutional amendment. The deputies to the NPC, after careful deliberation, approved the constitutional amendment with an absolute majority vote, thereby establishing the principle of the rule of law in the Chinese Constitution. This shows that the CPC has taken a new step in ruling the country by law. See Hengshan (2003).

[40]The Decision of the Fourth Plenary Session of the Sixteenth CPC Central Committee pointed out that the CPC must adhere to the democratic, scientific, and lawful exercise of the ruling power. Exercising ruling power in accordance with law means that the Party must grasp the key link of institutional construction that is of fundamental, overall, stable and long-term importance, adhere to the strategies of ruling the country by law, leading the legislation, taking the lead in abiding by law, ensuring the enforcement of law, continuously promoting the standardization of economic, political, cultural, and social lives of the country and bringing them under the rule of law, and ensuring through laws and institutions the implementation of Party's lines principles and policies.

and "timely establishing in the form of law the successful experience gained in the reform, and revising provisions in current laws that are no longer compatible with the development of practice, so as to provide solid legal safeguard for the reform and development while at the same time leaving space for the deepening of the reform".

The formation of the socialist legal system with Chinese characteristics reflects the process of reform and socialist modernization construction and is the legal summarization of the basic experience of over 30 years of reform and opening up, the legal confirmation of the achievements of socialist modernization construction and of the basic lines, principles and policies adopted by the CPC in leading the Chinese people to carry out socialist construction and reform, and the legal generalization of the socialist road, theory and practice with Chinese characteristics. The formation of the legal system means that China's basic lines, principles and policies of reform and opening up are unchangeable, that China's choice of socialist road with its own characteristics is irreversible, that Chinese people's determination to strive for a relatively comfortable life and to pursue happiness is unshakable, and that the goal of the great rejuvenation of Chinese nation is bound to be realized.

3.2.3.3   The Formation of the Socialist Legal System with Chinese Characteristics Is an Important Indicator of the Comprehensive Advancement of the Rule of Law in China

A precondition of implementing socialist rule of law and the strategy of ruling the country by law is that there must be laws to go by. During the 30 years since the reform and opening up, strengthening the legislation has always been a priority in the construction of the rule of law in China and this phenomenon has been described by the legal scholars as "legislation-centered mode of construction of the rule of law". Under the guidance of Deng Xiaoping's thought on speeding up the legislative work, China has made remarkable achievement in legislation.

The period between 1978 and 1982 was a period of all-round restoration and development of legislation in China. During this period, the NPC and its Standing Committee, apart from comprehensively amending the Constitution in 1982, had also adopted and promulgated 22 currently effective laws (see Table 3.2).[41]

---

[41] According to the white paper China's Efforts and Achievements in Promoting the Rule of Law, promulgated by the Information Office of the State Council on February 29, 2008, by the time of the promulgation of the white paper, the NPC and its Standing Committee had adopted 229 current effective laws, among which, 23 had been adopted between 1978 and 1982 and the following six had been adopted before 1978: Organic Regulations of Urban Sub-district Offices (1954); Organic Regulations on Police Stations (1954); Resolution of the Standing Committee of the National People's Congress Approving the "Decision of the State Council on the Issue of Rehabilitation Through Labor" (1957); Resolution of the Standing Committee of the National People's Congress Approving the "Measures of the State Council on the Establishment of Schools with Donations of Overseas Chinese" (1957); Regulations of the People's Republic of China on Residence Registration (1958); and Regulations on Application for Use of the State-owned Wasteland and Barren Hills by Overseas Chinese (1955).

Table 3.2   Statistical analysis of the legislation by the NPC and Its Standing Committee during the Period between 1978 and 1982

	The Constitution and constitutional laws	Civil and commercial law	Administrative law	Economic law	Social law	Criminal law	Litigious and non-litigious procedure law
Number of laws adopted	7	3	6	2	2	1	1
Percentage of the total number of laws adopted in the same period (22)	31.82	13. 64	27.27	9.09	9.09	4.55	4.55
Percentage of the total in the same branch of law	17.95	9.38	7.59	3.70	11.76	100	14.29
Percentage of the total number of current effective laws (229)	3.06	1.31	2.62	0.87	0.87	0.44	0.44

The period between 1983 and 1992 was a period of legislation under the planned commodity economy. On the basis of the 1982 Constitution, the legislation in China had entered into a period of rapid development.

The legislative work had been carried out along two background threads: one was the reform of economic and political systems and the construction of democracy, the rule of law, and spiritual civilization; the other was the establishment of economic construction as the central task and the construction of an economic system that combines the planned economy with market regulation. During this period of time, the NPC and its Standing Committee, apart from revising the 1982 Constitution in 1988, had adopted and promulgated 70 current effective laws (see Table 3.3).

The period between 1993 and 2002 was a period of legislation against the background of the construction of socialist market economy. The main tasks in this period of time included strengthening the legislative work, establishing and improving the legal system of socialist market economy, especially speeding up the adoption and improvement of laws and regulations safeguarding the reform and opening up, strengthening macro economic management, and regulating micro economic activities. During this period of time, apart from revising the 1982 Constitution in 1993 and 1999, the NPC and its Standing Committee had adopted and promulgated 98 current effective laws (see Table 3.4).

The period from 2003 to now is a period of legislation against the background of comprehensively implementing the Scientific Outlook on Development. The guiding ideology and central task of the legislative work in China in this period has been embodying, safeguarding and implementing through legislation the requirements of the Scientific Outlook on Development. During this period, apart from the revision

Table 3.3 Statistical analysis of the legislation by the NPC and Its Standing Committee during the Period between 1983 and 1992

	The Constitution and constitutional laws	Civil and commercial law	Administrative law	Economic law	Social law	Criminal law	Litigious and non-litigious procedure law
Number of laws adopted	16	9	19	18	5	0	3
Percentage of the total number of laws adopted in the same period (70)	22.85	12.85	27.14	25.71	7.14		4.28
Percentage of the total in the same branch of law	41.02	28.12	24.05	33.33	29.41		42.85
Percentage of the total number of current effective laws (229)	6.98	3.93	8.29	7.86	2.18		1.31

Table 3.4 Statistical analysis of the legislation by the NPC and Its Standing Committee during the Period between 1993 and 2002

	The Constitution and constitutional laws	Civil and commercial law	Administrative law	Economic law	Social law	Criminal law	Litigious and non-litigious procedure law
Number of laws adopted	11	15	38	24	7	0	3
Percentage of the total number of laws adopted in the same period (98)	11.22	15.30	38.77	24.48	7.14		3.06
Percentage of the total in the same branch of law	28.20	46.87	48.10	44.44	41.17		42.85
Percentage of the total number of current effective laws (229)	4.80	6.55	16.59	10.48	3.05		1.31

Table 3.5 Statistical analysis of legislation by the NPC and Its Standing Committee during the Period between 2003 and 2008

	The Constitution and constitutional laws	Civil and commercial law	Administrative law	Economic law	Social law	Criminal law	Litigious and non-litigious procedure law
Number of laws adopted	3	5	12	9	3	0	0
Percentage of the total number of laws adopted in the same period (32)	9.37	15.62	37.50	28.12	9.37		
Percentage of the total in the same branch of law	7.69	5.62	15.18	16.66	17.64		
Percentage of the total number of current effective laws (229)	1.31	2.18	5.24	3.93	1.31		

of the 1982 Constitution in 2004, the NPC and its Standing Committee had adopted 32 current effective laws (see Tables 3.5 and 3.6).

After unremitting efforts made by China in the 60 years since the establishment of the PRC, especially in the 30 years since the reform and opening up, a socialist legal system with Chinese characteristics has finally taken form. The formation of this system is the full confirmation of the remarkable progresses made by the CPC in exercising the ruling power in accordance with law, by the legislative organs in democratic legislation, by administrative organs in the administration by law, by the judicial organs in the construction of a fair and just judicial system, and by all citizens in learning, abiding by and applying the law. It is the partial results of the efforts made by the whole nation from top to bottom in carrying forward the spirit of the rule of law, disseminating the culture of the rule of law, adhering to and implementing the basic strategy of ruling the country by law, and continuously improving the good platform provided by the socialist legal system with Chinese characteristics, and marks the new starting point of the comprehensive advancement of ruling the country by law and construction of a socialist state under the rule of law.

Table 3.6 Statistics on the legislation in China between March 2008 and September 2011

No.	Title	Time of issuance	Issuing authority	Adoption/revision
1	Law on the Protection of the Disabled	April 25, 2008	NPC Standing Committee	Revision
2	Circular Economy Promotion Law	September 2, 2008	NPC Standing Committee	Adoption
3	Law on the State-Owned Assets of Enterprises	January 20, 2009	NPC Standing Committee	Adoption
4	Fire Control Law	January 20, 2009	NPC Standing Committee	Revision
5	Patent Law	January 20, 2009	NPC Standing Committee	Revision
6	Food Safety Law	March 2, 2009	NPC Standing Committee	Revision
7	Amendment (VII) to the Criminal Law	March 2, 2009	NPC Standing Committee	Revision
8	Insurance Law	March 2, 2009	NPC Standing Committee	Revision
9	Postal Law	May 7, 2009	NPC Standing Committee	Revision
10	Rules of Procedure of the Standing Committee of the National People's Congress	May 7, 2009	NPC Standing Committee	Revision
11	Law on the People's Armed Police Force	September 4, 2009	NPC Standing Committee	Adoption
12	Law on the Mediation and Arbitration of Rural Land Contract Disputes	September 29, 2009	NPC Standing Committee	Adoption
13	Statistics Law	September 29, 2009	NPC Standing Committee	Revision
14	Law on Diplomatic Personnel Stationed Abroad	November 2, 2009	NPC Standing Committee	Adoption
15	Tort Law	December 30, 2009	NPC Standing Committee	Adoption
16	Island Protection Law	December 30, 2009	NPC Standing Committee	Adoption
17	Renewable Energy Law	December 30, 2009	NPC Standing Committee	Revision
18	Election Law	March 15, 2010	NPC Standing Committee	Revision

(continued)

Table 3.6 (continued)

No.	Title	Time of issuance	Issuing authority	Adoption/revision
19	National Defense Mobilization Law	March 18, 2010	NPC Standing Committee	Adoption
20	Copyright Law	March 18, 2010	NPC Standing Committee	Revision
21	Law on Guarding State Secrets	April 30, 2010	NPC Standing Committee	Revision
22	State Compensation Law	April 30, 2010	NPC Standing Committee	Revision
23	People's Mediation Law	April 30, 2010	NPC Standing Committee	Adoption
24	Reserve Officers Law	September 2, 2010	NPC Standing Committee	Revision
25	Administrative Supervision Law	October 18, 2010	NPC Standing Committee	Revision
26	Social Insurance Law	November 2, 2010	NPC Standing Committee	Adoption
27	Law on Choice of Law for Foreign-related Civil Relationships	November 2, 2010	NPC Standing Committee	Adoption
28	Organic Law of the Villagers Committees	November 2, 2010	NPC Standing Committee	Revision
29	Law on Deputies to the National People's Congress and Local People's Congresses at All Levels	November 2, 2010	NPC Standing Committee	Revision
30	Water and Soil Conservation Law	January 26, 2011	NPC Standing Committee	Revision
31	Amendment (VIII) to the Criminal Law	February 28, 2011	NPC Standing Committee	Revision
32	Intangible Cultural Heritage Law	February 28, 2011	NPC Standing Committee	Adoption
33	Vehicle and Vessel Tax Law	February 28, 2011	NPC Standing Committee	Revision
34	Coal Industry Law	April 25, 2011	NPC Standing Committee	Revision
35	Construction Law	April 25, 2011	NPC Standing Committee	Revision
36	Road Traffic Safety Law	April 25, 2011	NPC Standing Committee	Revision
37	Individual Income Tax Law	July 1, 2011	NPC Standing Committee	Revision
38	Administrative Compulsion Law	July 1, 2011	NPC Standing Committee	Adoption

3.2.3.4   The Formation of the Socialist Legal System with Chinese Characteristics Is Relative and Has Its Concrete Historical Position and Context

The socialist legal system with Chinese characteristics was formed at the primary stage of socialism. Compared with capitalist legal systems, it is characterized by the adherence to the state system of people's democratic dictatorship, the people's congress system, the socialist road, the socialist public ownership system and the system of distribution according to work, the construction of socialist spiritual civilization under the guidance of Marxist ideology, the leadership of CPC, and the system of multi-party cooperation under the leadership of the CPC. Therefore it is a legal system of socialist nature.

Compared with the rule of law (and the corresponding legal system) at the advanced stage of socialism envisaged by classic Marxist writers, it is the rule of law (and the corresponding legal system) at the primary stage of socialism, at which there are still some noticeable problems in the construction of democracy and the rule of law, the development of the rule of law is still not fully compatible with the requirements of the expansion of people's democracy and of social and economic development, and the reform of the political system still needs to be further deepened. This means that, after its formation, the socialist legal system with Chinese characteristics is still a legal system at the primary stage of development, with many imperfections and problems, and that the formation of a more perfect legal system will be a long and arduous process that requires continuous efforts.

Compared with the legal systems of the former socialist countries of the Soviet Union and Eastern Europe and those of other still existing socialist countries, such as Vietnam, North Korea and Cuba, it is a legal system with Chinese characteristics, which takes the integration of the universal Marxist doctrine of state and law with the Chinese practice of socialist modernization construction as the basic principle, the assimilation of the useful elements of the rule of law civilization around the world as an important approach, and the historical and cultural tradition and current national situation in China as the starting point.

The socialist legal system with Chinese characteristics was formed in the process of continuous reform and improvement of various economic, social and political systems in China. Since the law is the reflection of certain political, economic and social relations, legislation is the confirmation of the outcomes of political, economic and social reforms and changes.

As China continues to deepen economic reform, strengthen the construction of a harmonious society, and advance the reform of political system, the resulting adjustments and changes of economic, social and political relations will continuously set new standards and raise new demands on the review of existing laws, the adoption, revision and abolition of laws, and the improvement of the legal system, thereby enabling the legal system to be always in a relatively stable, yet constantly changing state. At this stage of social development, which takes all-round reform as its main characteristic, the formation of the legal system can only be a relative concept. What is absolutely necessary for China to do is to continuous improve the legal system, so as to satisfy the continuously changing needs of economic and social developments.

The socialist legal system with Chinese characteristics was formed in the process of constructing the socialist democratic political system and comprehensively advancing the rule of law. Currently the socialist democracy and socialist rule of law are still not perfect, and the basic strategy of ruling the country by law has not been fully implemented in China. This objective condition will inevitably affect the level of democratic and scientific legislation, the selection, function, content, technique and results of legislation, and ultimately the quality of the entire legal system. Therefore, measured by high standard and viewed from the perspectives of the form and content of legal system, the relationship between the part and the whole, and good law and good governance, the current socialist legal system with Chinese characteristics still has many defects and shortcomings and can only be said to have "taken initial or basic shape".

3.3 Main Legislative Experiences of the Formation of the Socialist Legal System with Chinese Characteristics

By reflection, the following six main legislative experiences can be summed up from the legislative practice in China since the founding of the PRC, especially since the reform and opening up:

3.3.1 Taking the Constitution as the Basis and the Overall Interest of the Country and the Basic Interest of the People as the Starting Point

The Chinese Constitution provides for the general principles on administering state affairs and ensuring social stability. It is the basic law of the country with supreme legal effect. All legislative activities must be carried out with the Constitution as the legal basis and may not contravene the spirit, the principles and the provisions of the Constitution. Adhering to legislation in accordance with Constitution is an inherent requirement of ruling the country by law, as well as an important precondition of ensuring the unity and authority of the rule of law. Only by taking the Constitution as the basis can we adopt laws that are compatible with the objective laws of social development and meet the needs of reform and construction in China.[42]

In the legislative process, legislative organs must strictly follow the principles and spirits of the Constitution, safeguard various rights of citizens, reasonably divide the competences of various state organs, regulate the behaviors of state organs and state personnel, and correctly handle the relationship between the lawful exercise of rights by the people and the lawful exercise of power by state organs. Legislation should

---

[42]See Tian (1996).

be aimed at the upholding the best interest of the greatest majority of the people; attention should be paid to preventing the inappropriate expansion of the powers and interests of state organs, and the infringement upon the lawful rights and interests of citizens; and efforts should be made to ensure that the laws adopted by legislative organs are compatible with the basic interest of the people of all nationalities and the overall interest of the state and conducive to the protection and promotion of the development of the productive forces.[43]

In order to adhere to the principle legislation in accordance with Constitution, it is necessary to correctly deal with the relations between the central interest and local interest, between the interest of parts and the interest of the whole, between long-term interest and immediate interest, between the interest of developed areas and that of the under-developed areas, and between the overall interest of the state and the basic interest of the people; make overall plans and take all factors into consideration, correctly understand different interest demands, properly handle the relationship between powers and rights, and protect the lawful rights and interests of citizens, legal persons and other organizations from infringement; give administrative organs necessary means to ensure the lawful and effective exercise of administrative power while at the same time regulate, restrict and supervise administrative power, so as to ensure that administrative organs exercise their power in a correct way and strike a balance between powers and rights; and correctly handle the relations between different powers, adhere to the unity of powers and responsibilities, embody the principle of close linkage between powers and responsibilities, and the total disconnection of power from interest; and appropriately handle the relations between different rights, make overall plans and take all interest demands into consideration, so as to promote social harmony and stability.

3.3.2 Taking Economic Construction as the Center of Economic Construction and Closely Combining Legislation with Major Decision-Making on Reform and Development

Taking economic construction as the center and adhering to the reform and opening up has been the theme of economic and social development in China since the reform and opening up. Another basic legislative experience in China is that legislation must meet the needs of economic and social development and reform and opening up.

Chinese legislators must clearly realize that legislation must be compatible with and create a good rule of law environment for reform, development and modernization. They should carefully summarize the basic experience of reform, opening up and modernization, affirm in the form of law these proved to be correct by practice, strengthen the positive results, so as to safeguard and promote sound and rapid eco-

---

[43] See Tian (1998).

nomic and social development. With respect to major reform decisions, they should adopt corresponding legal norms as soon as possible, so as to use legislation to guide, promote and safeguard the healthy development of reform, opening up and modernization;[44] adopt positive and cautious legislative polices, take legislation seriously, adopt laws only when conditions are ripe; refrain from adopting laws for which conditions are not yet ripe, so as to prevent premature laws from impeding the reform, avoid frequent revision of laws that have been adopted in a hasty way, and ensure the stability and authority of laws.

Different issues encountered in the legislation should be dealt with differently in light of actual conditions: with regard to those for which China has already accumulated comparatively mature experiences in the practice of reform and opening up, specific legal provisions should be adopted to deepen the experiences; with regard to those for which China has not gained mature experiences in the practice of reform and opening up, but there is an urgent need for legal regulation, provisions on general principles can be adopted, so as to leave rooms for further reform and development; and with regard to those on which no practical experience has been gained and no consensus reached, no legal provisions should be adopted until conditions are ripe.

In 1986, the State Council pointed out in the Report on the Seventh Five-Year Plan that: "With the deepening of economic reform, and the development of national economy, there is an increasing need to establish in the form of law more economic relations and norms of economic activities and to turn the law into an important means of regulating economic relations and economic activities."

In 1992, the CPC pointed out that: "An urgent task in the construction of socialist market economic system is to strengthening the legislative work, especially the adoption and improvement of laws and administrative regulations aimed at safeguarding the reform and opening up, strengthening macro-economic management, and regulating micro-economic activities."

In 1994, the CPC pointed out that: "reform decision-making should be closely combined with legislative decision-making. Legislation should embody the spirit of reform and laws should be used to guide, promote and safeguard the reform".

In 1995, the CPC stated that it would "adhere to the unity of reform and opening up and the construction of the legal system and closely combine reform decision-making with legislative decision-making".

In 1997 and 2002, the CPC further stated that it would "combine major decision-making on reform and development with legislation" and "strengthen the legislative work and improve the quality of legislation, so as to adapt to the new situation of the development of socialist market economy, the comprehensive progress of society and China's accession to the WTO, and form a socialist legal system with Chinese characteristics by the year 2010".

We can get a glimpse of the close combination of legislation with the reform and development from the work reports of the NPC Standing Committee (see Table 3.7).

---

[44]See Tian (1996).

Table 3.7 The combination of legislation with reform and development as demonstrated by the work reports of the NPC Standing Committee

Year	Main content in the reports relating to the combination of legislation with reform and development
1981	China is a large country with many ethnic groups and imbalanced political, economic, and cultural development in different areas. The legislators should take into consideration the concrete situation in different areas, which may differ in thousands of ways, and avoid rigid uniformity. Currently the economic legislation should be carried out around economic adjustment and institutional reform, so as to ensure the smooth realization of adjustment and strengthen the achievements of economic reform
1986	To meet the need of economic reform and socialist modernization, we must actively and responsibly speed up economic legislation in accordance with the order of priority and in light of concrete conditions. Currently, since comprehensive reforms of the economic, educational, scientific and technological systems are still in progress in China and some major reforms are still at the stage of accumulation of experience, laws in these fields should be adopted in a step-by-step way in light of actual conditions and on the basis of summarization of experience
1990	We should transform into state law through legal procedures policies proved in practice to be correct and having long-term applicability, carefully study various new situations and new problems emerged in the process of reform and opening up, and affirm in a timely way and in the form of law the successful experience of reform and opening up
1995	We will continue to speed up economic legislation, take an important step in the formation of a framework of legal system of socialist market economy and, in accordance with the requirement of closely combining legislative decision-making with reform decision-making, put the focus of legislation on the adoption of laws aimed at safeguarding and promoting reform and opening up and speeding up the establishment of socialist market economic system
1996	We should closely combine legislation with the practice of reform and development, affirm in the form law experiences that have been proved by practice to be correct, strengthen the results of reform and opening up, and use law to guide, promote and safeguard reform and development
1998	We will quicken the pace of legislation and speed up the adoption of laws on the socialist market economy, always pay attention to the combination of legislation with major decision-making on reform and development in the legislative work, carefully summarize the experience of reform, opening up and modernization, affirm in the form of law experiences proved to be correct by practice, strengthen the result of reform and opening up, and promote and safeguard the healthy development of reform, opening up, and modernization
2000	We will closely combine legislative work with the state's major decision-making on reform, development and stability and safeguard and promote the development of various undertakings through the establishment and improvement of the relevant legal systems

(continued)

Table 3.7 (continued)

Year	Main content in the reports relating to the combination of legislation with reform and development
2001	We will continue to take the main tasks of the state as the center and combine legislation with major decision-making on reform, development and stability, transform through legislation the Party's views into the will of the state and enable the legislative work to better serve the work of the state
2002	We will adopt and revise relevant laws in due time in light of the actual need of reform, opening up and construction of socialist market economic system, upgrade into law the successful practice and experiences of implementation of local regulations in various areas
2003	We will continuously strengthen and improve legislative work, more closely combine legislation with major state decision-making on reform, development and stability, carry out legislative work closely around the central task of the state, concentrate efforts on the adoption and revision of laws urgently needed in the country and laws indispensible to the formation of a legal system, and ensure that legislative work is subordinate to and serve the state work, and attach importance to both affirming the achievements of reform and leaving sufficient space for the deepening of the reform
2004	The basic thinking of legislative work is to carry out the work around the primary tasks of the Party and the state and serve the reform and opening up, pay attention to timely affirming in the form of law the successful experiences gained in the reform, revise provisions in current laws that are no longer compatible with the development of practice, and provide solid legal safeguard to reform and development while at the same time leaving sufficient space for continuous deepening of the reform, and to base the legislative work on national conditions in China and always take the great practice of reform, opening up and modernization as the basis of legislation
2007	We should accurately grasp the objective laws of reform, opening up and modernization, take into consideration the basic interests of the broadest masses of people, the common interest of the people and special interests of different groups at the current stage, and give full play to the regulating, guiding and safeguarding role of the law in the construction of a harmonious society
2008	In accordance with strategic arrangement and major decisions of the state and in light of the objective requirements of economic and social development, we will take the great practice of reform, opening up and modernization as the basis of legislation, focus on the adoption of laws that play an important role in the legal system with Chinese characteristics, are urgent needed in the social life, and for which relatively mature legislative conditions have been created, so as to solidify in the form of law the successful experiences of reform, opening up, and modernization. We will make comprehensive arrangements on legislative work by focusing on the objective of constructing a moderately well-off society in all respects, on major issues of reform, development and stability, and on hot and difficult problems that have caused great concern among the general public

China will adhere to the compatibility of legislation with reform, development and modernization, affirm by law the experiences proved by practice to be correct, strengthen the positive achievements of reform, development and modernization, safeguard and promote social and economic development, and create a good rule of law environment for reform, development and modernization.[45]

3.3.3 Adhering to the Chinese National Conditions and Characteristics and Drawing on Foreign Legislative Experiences

In legislative work, China must base itself on basic national conditions, have a deep understanding and correctly gasp of the characteristics of development in China at different stages, take economic construction as the center, adhere to reform and opening up, and carry out legislative work by focusing on the construction of a moderately well-off society in all respects and on the coordinated economic, political, cultural, and social development, so as to promote the smooth development of various undertakings in the country.

China is current at the primary stage of socialism and it will remain at this stage for a long period of time before it can realize industrialization and modernization. Although we have already made huge progresses in various fields since the reform and opening up, because of the huge population, weak economic foundation, and imbalance in development between urban and rural areas and between different regions, the situation of underdevelopment of the productive forces has not been fundamentally changed, the market economic system, the democratic system and the legal system are still not complete, problems of social injustice and corruption still exist, and the socialist system is still not mature. Although "through the unremitting efforts made since the founding of the People's Republic in 1949, particularly since the introduction of the reform and opening up policy, China has scored achievements in development that have captured world attention, and experienced far-reaching changes in the productive forces and the relations of production, as well as in the economic base and the superstructure, the basic reality that China is still in the primary stage of socialism and will remain so for a long time to come has not changed, nor has Chinese society's principal contradiction—the one between the ever-growing material and cultural needs of the people and the low level of social production."[46] Today, China is still a developing country. We must always keep this basic national condition in mind and take it as the basic starting point of the legislative work and unswervingly adhere to the legislation with Chinese characteristics.

China should base itself on its national conditions while at the same time carefully study and draw on the beneficial legislative experiences of foreign countries, but not blindly copy the legislative system of other countries. When adopting various laws,

---

[45]Li (1991, pp. 328–331).
[46]See Jintao (2007).

we should collect and sort out the relevant legal provisions in other countries, study and compare them and learn useful things from them. We should boldly assimilate and draw on those that reflect the universal laws of market economy, and the international norms and customs formed in international intercourse; those that are compatible with actual conditions in China can be directed transplanted and gradually improved in practice.[47] For example, in the field of civil and commercial laws, the General Principles of Civil Law, the Property Law, and the Contract in China have drawn on many basic systems from both common law countries and continental law countries, as well as many internationally accepted private law spirits and legislative principles. In the fields of administrative law, China has assimilated such general principles of modern administrative law as proportionality and trust protection. In the field of criminal law, the Chinese Criminal Law and Criminal Procedure Law have adopted such modern criminal law principles and spirits as legally prescribed punishment for a specified crime and open trial. In light of the new crime situation in the country, China has provided for many new crimes in the Criminal Law, such as funding terrorist activities, money laundering, insider trading, manipulating the dealing price of negotiable securities and futures, and impeding the management of credit cards. In the field of protection of intellectual property and the environment, China has also drawn on many foreign legislative experiences.[48]

On March 10, 2011, Mr. Wu Bangguo, the Chairman of the Standing Committee of the National People's Congress, announced that the construction of a legal system with Chinese characteristics has completed on schedule and pointed out that China will also attach importance to drawing on useful legislative experiences of foreign countries, but should never blindly copy them. Different countries have different legal systems; we should not construction the socialist legal system with Chinese characteristics by copying the laws of other countries because some foreign laws are not compatible with the national conditions in China while some other laws that are needed in the social life in China do not exist in foreign legal systems. One of the basic legislative experiences we have gained since the reform and opening up is to boldly learn from and draw on the positive results of the development of human rule of law civilization, including the two main western legal systems, while basing ourselves on the national conditions of China.

In the legislative practice of China, examples of drawing on the legislative experiences of foreign countries and those of Hong Kong, Macao and Taiwan are abundant[49]:

Example 1: In the deliberation on the draft amendment to the 1979 Law on Chinese-Foreign Equity Joint Ventures at the Third Session of the Fifth NPC in 1990, there were different opinions on whether the contract period of joint ventures may be decided differently according to their particular lines of business and circumstances. To study the issue of the contract period of Chinese-foreign joint ventures, the Research Department of the Legislative Affairs Commission of NPC Standing

---

[47] See Tian (1998).
[48] Information Office of the State Council (2008).
[49] Gu (2008).

Committee had consulted the laws on foreign invested enterprises in 18 foreign countries and in Taiwan. Among them, eight developed countries, namely the U.S., Japan, France, Germany, the Netherlands, Italy, Belgium and Luxembourg, had no special law on foreign investment. In these countries, foreign invested enterprises were regulated by the relevant provisions of the company law or civil law. The Soviet Union, Romania, Poland, Egypt, Chile, Indonesia, Thailand, and Singapore as well as Taiwan Province had adopted special law on foreign investment. The company laws and civil laws or foreign investment laws in the above two types of countries and regions had different provisions on the contract period of joint ventures. This information was used in the revision of Article 12 of the Law on Chinese-Foreign Equity Joint Ventures.

Example 2: The scope and period of protection by the Patent Law. China began to draft the Patent Law in 1979 and the draft was repeatedly revised in the following five years. In the deliberation on the draft law, there had been different opinions on the scope of protection of the Patent Law, namely whether it should cover utility models and designs in addition to inventions. Those opposed to the protection of utility models and designs argued that China still lacked the experience in patent protection and it was inappropriate for the Law to cover all three types of patents from the very beginning, whereas the proponents of the protection of utility models and designs held that all state parties to the Paris Convention should protect designs. To solve this problem, the Legislative Affairs Commission of NPC Standing Committee and the Patent Office consulted many foreign materials. They had learnt that, among the 158 countries that had implemented patent protection system, 38 provided for the protection of only inventions, 13 provided for the protection of inventions, utility models and designs, and 97 provided for the protection of inventions and designs—but most of them had included utility models in the category of inventions. As a result, the Patent Law adopted in 1988 provides for the protection of all three types of patents.

Example 3: The scope of regulation of the labor law. In July 1994, the Labor Law was adopted by the NPC Standing Committee. In the deliberation on the draft law, there had been many controversies, one of them being the scope of regulation of the labor law. Some people believed that the scope of regulation of the labor law should cover all workers. Although the relationship between state organs and their staff members is a special labor relationship, it is still a labor relationship. Others maintained that the relationship between enterprises and their employees is different in nature from the relationship between state organs and their staff members and, therefore, many of the provisions in the draft labor law do not apply to civil servants (for instance, civil servants are permanent employees of state organs and do not sign labor contract with the latter). In most countries of the world, such as the US, UK, Canada and Japan, the labor law does not apply to civil servants. As for public institutions and mass organizations, their relationships with their staff members are complicated. Whether the labor law should be applied to such relationships depends on whether such institutions or organizations have signed labor contracts with their staff members. The relationships between teachers, doctors, researchers and other professionals with their employers have their special characteristics and should be ` provided for by special laws.

Example 4: The Second Draft of the Tort Law had embodied the legislative guideline of "taking the relevant laws of the continental law system as the main body and those of the common law system as the application", successfully drawn on the legislative experiences and appropriately integrated the legislative advantages of the tort laws of both legal systems, thereby developing a set of relatively reasonable rules of tort law in China.

Table 3.8 shows the practice of the NPC and its Standing Committee of learning from and drawing on overseas legislative experiences in their legislation work.

In its legislative work, China has drawn on the beneficial legislative experiences of all countries in the world, including western countries. it has drawn on not only a large amount of western legislative experiences in the fields of economic, civil, commercial, environmental, energy, and social laws, but also some western experience in the fields democratic politics and administrative law; not only the experiences of the continent law system, but also those of the common law system and other legal systems; and not only foreign legislative experiences, but also those of Hong Kong, Macao and Taiwan. If it can be said that there is a Chinese legislative experience, this experience is the product of combination of Chinese national conditions and the legislative experiences of countries all around the world. It is an experience of China as well as an experience of the world.

3.3.4   Adhering to Democratic, Scientific and High-Quality Legislation

Democratic legislation is the inherent requirement of the principle of people being the master of the country, an important channel of fully expressing and effectively collecting the interests, the will and the propositions of the people and upgrading them through legislative procedure into the will of the state under the framework of democratic politics. Although the idea of democratization of legislation has been embodied to some extent in the legislative work in China since the reform and opening up in 1978, the term "democratic legislation" had not been formally used until the beginning of the 21st century. The work report of the NPC Standing Committee to the Fourth Session of the Ninth NPC stated that it would "strive to make the legislative decision-making more democratic and scientific". The Standing Committee of the Tenth NPC put forward the ideas of "adhering to the principle of legislation for the people" at its second session, the requirement of "making a new progress in the democratization of legislation" at its fourth session, and the task of "continuously advancing scientific and democratic legislation" at its fifth session. In 2007, the CPC further put forward of the principle of "adhering to scientific and democratic legislation" at its Seventeenth National Congress. From the above we can see that democratic legislation has gradually become a basic requirement of the legislative work and important legislative experience that should be adhered to for a long period of time in China.

Table 3.8 The practice of the NPC and Its Standing Committee of drawing on overseas legislative experiences in the drafting of 22 Laws

No.	Chinese Law	Time of adoption	Countries and regions whose legislative experiences China has drawn on	Main content of the law involved
1	Food Hygiene Law	Nov. 1982	Japan, US, Germany, Romania	Scope of application of the law; supervision over food hygiene; foods prohibited from selling; hygiene requirements on places and facilities of business; administrative punishments; criminal punishments
2	Water Pollution Prevention and Control Law	May 1984	US, Japan, Soviet Union, and Romania	Competent authority; adoption of various standards on water quality and pollutant discharge; the power to order an enterprise or facility that has discharged pollutants in excess of standard or caused a water pollution hazard to rectify within a certain period; or to stop operation or production; and legal responsibilities
3	Pharmaceutical Administration Law	June 1984	Soviet Union, Japan, US, UK, and Singapore	Competent authorities in charge of drug administration; permits or licenses for pharmaceutical production and sale and their term of validity; administration of imported drugs; and illegal drugs
4	General Principles of Civil Law	April 1986	US, UK, Germany, France, and Japan	Nature and roles of main laws regulating commodity economy: civil law; commercial law; economic law; labor law and social law

(continued)

Table 3.8 (continued)

No.	Chinese Law	Time of adoption	Countries and regions whose legislative experiences China has drawn on	Main content of the law involved
5	Enterprise Bankruptcy Law (for Trial Implementation)	Dec. 1986	UK, France, Italy, the Netherlands, Belgium, Germany, and Ireland	Conditions of bankruptcy; the initiation of the procedure of bankruptcy; classification of procedures of bankruptcy; jurisdiction over cases of bankruptcy
6	Standardization Law	Dec. 1988	Poland, Hungary, Czechoslovakia, Japan, France, Yugoslavia	Adoption of standard system and standards; implementation of standards; authentication of product quality; supervision over the implementation of standards; legal responsibilities
7	Environmental Protection Law	Dec. 1989	US, Japan, Soviet Union, Romania, South Korea, and Germany	Mode of legislation on environmental protection; definition of "environment"; pollutant discharge permit system; pollutant discharge fees; and time limitation for instituting an environmental action for damages
8	Law on Chinese-Foreign Equity Joint Ventures (Amendment)	April 1990	US, Japan, Germany, the Netherlands, Luxembourg, France, Italy, Poland, Egypt, Chile, Indonesia, South Korea, Thailand, Singapore, and Malaysia	Provisions on time limits of companies in the company law or civil law; and provisions on the contract period of joint ventures in foreign investment law
9	Copyright Law	Sept. 1990	US, France, Germany, Japan, Soviet Union, Italy, UK, Brazil, Romania, Yugoslavia, Continent Law System, and Common Law System	Works and authors protected by the copyright law; content of copyright; ownership of copyright; neighboring rights; restriction on copyright; copyright contract; tort; copyright of works created in the course of employment; etc.

(continued)

Table 3.8 (continued)

No.	Chinese Law	Time of adoption	Countries and regions whose legislative experiences China has drawn on	Main content of the law involved
10	Water and Soil Conservation Law	June 1991	US, India, Japan, Soviet Union, Australia, and New Zealand	Situation of water and soil loss; experience in water and soil conservation; measures for the control of water and soil loss; etc.
11	Law on the Administration of Tax Collection	Sept. 1992	US, UK, France, India, the Netherlands, Canada, Japan and Germany	Inquiring about the bank accounts of tax payers; control of the departure of taxpayers from the country; enforcement against the properties and bank deposits of defaulting taxpayers; coercive measures against suspected tax evaders; coercive measures of tax collection; constitutive elements of the crime of tax evasion; etc.
12	Maritime Law	Nov. 1992	International maritime organizations and British legal experts	International marine freight forwarding contract; the time of establishment of B/L transportation contract; application of laws on international marine freight forwarding and coastal transport; effect of registration of ownership and mortgage of ship; basic obligations of the carrier in B/L transportation; liability for damage in sea towage; maritime lien; special compensation for the rescue of oil tankers
13	Mine Safety Law	Nov. 1992	US, Japan, India and Taiwan Province	Mine safety law enforcement organs and their functions and powers; guarantees for safety in mine construction; report and disposition of accidents at mines; legal responsibilities

(continued)

Table 3.8 (continued)

No.	Chinese Law	Time of adoption	Countries and regions whose legislative experiences China has drawn on	Main content of the law involved
14	Trademark Law (Amendment)	Feb. 1993	US, France, Germany, Japan, Italy, and Thailand	Punishment of the acts of falsely using or counterfeiting the registered trademark of another person and selling goods bearing the registered trademark of others; the punishment of a legal person who counterfeits the registered trademark of another person; and the disposition of goods bearing counterfeited registered trademark
15	Anti-Unfair Competition Law	Sept. 1993	US, Germany, Japan, South Korea, and Hungary	Legislative style: separate legislation, unified legislation, and decentralized legislation; competent authorities and the functions and powers; acts of unfair competition; civil, administrative, and criminal responsibilities; etc.
16	Company Law	Dec. 1993	Germany, Japan, South Korea, France, UK, Norway, Sweden, Italy, Switzerland, Austria, US, Belgium, the Netherlands, and Denmark	Main differences between a joint stock limited company, a limited liability company, and a unlimited liability company; establishment of a company; shares, stocks; the transfer of the creditor's rights and stock rights of a company: organization of a company, board of directors, the board of supervisors and accountant of a company; annual accounting report of a company and its auditing; common reserve; dividend, holding companies and participating companies; transformation, merger, dissolution and liquidation of a company; foreign companies; and legal provisions on the punishment of companies
17	Budget Law	March 1994	Soviet Union, Romania, Spain, Japan, Germany, Thailand, UK, and South Korea	Balance of budget and deficit; examination, approval and adjustment of budget; supervision over the implementation of budget and final accounts; etc.

(continued)

Table 3.8 (continued)

No.	Chinese Law	Time of adoption	Countries and regions whose legislative experiences China has drawn on	Main content of the law involved
18	Labor Law	July 1994	US, Canada, UK, France, Japan, Romania, Russia, Bulgaria, Poland, Hungary, Mongolia, Iraq, etc.	The content, term, form, change, and termination of labor contracts; compensation for the termination of labor contracts; etc.
19	Arbitration Law	Aug. 1994	The Netherlands, Switzerland, Sweden, Japan, Model Law on International Commercial Arbitration	Setting aside of arbitration award; non-execution of arbitration award; etc.
20	Auditing Law	Aug. 1994	US, Austria, Spain, Canada, Turkey, Germany, France, Singapore, Japan, India, Sweden, Jordan, Saudi Arabia, etc.	The setup of auditing organs; the scope of auditing supervision; the competence of carrying out audit investigation; etc.
21	Contract Law	March 1999	US, Canada, Australia, Germany, UK, Italy, Spain, Japan, France, South Korea, etc.	Development of contract law: the principle of freedom of contract; effect of contract; business agent; change of circumstance; public interest donation; gift contract; loan contract; contract for work; freight transport contract; tourist contract; warranty against defects of goods; collect credit contract; franchise contract; entrustment contract; etc.
22	Legislation Law	March 2000	US, Germany, UK, France, Japan, Italy, Russia, and Belarus	Legislative competence; local legislation; legislative procedure; constitutional provisions on the legislative system; the legislative system; guiding ideology on legislation; basic principles of legislation; delegated legislation; legislative techniques; etc.

Main sources Gu (2009), Law Press China (2006), Law Press China (2002), and Zhang (2000); etc.

Adhering to scientific legislation is the basic requirement of legislation in China. Mao Zedong once said that "Formulating the constitution is like carrying out scientific research". To realize scientific legislation, we must adhere to the spirit of scientific legislation, adopt scientific method of legislation, abide by the rules of scientific legislation, follow the procedure of scientific legislation and improve the techniques of scientific legislation. Adhering to scientific legislation means to respect the rules of legislative work, to base the legislative work on the realistic feasibility of laws while at the same time paying attention to the proactive nature of laws, to affirm the achievement of reform through legislation while at the same time leaving space for deepening the reform, to quicken the pace of state legislation while at the same time giving full play to the initiatives of local peoples congresses in adopting local regulations, and to proceed from the national conditions in China while at the same time drawing on the foreign experiences in legislation, so as to ensure that the content of various laws are scientific, standardized and coordinated.[50] The legislative practice since the reform and opening up has shown that only democratic legislation can ensure the organic unity of the will of the people, the will of the Party and the will of the state; only scientific legislation can ensure that the legislation meets the scientific requirements of the law of nature, the law of development of Chinese society and the law of legislation itself; and only democratic and scientific legislation can ensure the fundamental improvement of the quality of legislation.

Although democratic legislation has been a fundamental principle always adhered to by China, due to various objective factors, it was only since the middle and late 1990s that Chinese legislative organs have gradually implemented the system of "open door legislation".

In March 2008, the Eleventh NPC stressed at its first session that, in legislative work, "We must adhere to the principle that all state powers belong to the people, improve the democratic system, enrich the forms of democracy, expand channels of democracy, promote the orderly participation in political affairs by citizens at various levels and in various fields, and ensure the exercise in accordance with law by the people of their rights of democracy election, democratic decision-making, democratic management, and democratic supervision". In April 2008, the Chairmen's Council of the NPC Standing Committee adopted a decision according to which all draft laws deliberated by the NPC Standing Committee should, as a rule, be published to extensively solicit opinions from the general public.

Between 1954 and 2008, the NPC and its Standing Committee had published the drafts of 20 laws (including the Constitution) to solicit opinions from the public. Among them, ten or 50% of the total were published between 2000 and December 2008, averaging 1.11 per year; four or 20% of the total were published between 1990 and December 1999, averaging 0.40 per year; five or 25% of the total were published between 1978 and December 1989, averaging 0.41 per year; and one (the Draft Constitution) or 5% of the total was published in 1954 (see Table 3.9).

On April 25, 2011, the Draft Amendment to the Individual Income Tax Law of the PRC was published on the website of the NPC to solicit opinions from the general

---

[50]Li (2003).

Table 3.9 The twenty draft laws published by the NPC and Its Standing Committee to solicit public opinions

Title	Date of publication	Time period of solicitation of public opinions	Results of solicitation of public opinions	Date of adoption
1954 Constitution	June 15, 1954	Over 2 months	Revisions had been made to the original draft	Sept. 20, 1954, (First Session of the First NPC)
The 1982 Constitution	Apr. 26, 1982	Apr. 26–end of Aug., 1982	Near 100 supplementary revisions had been made on the basis of the opinions received	Dec. 4, 1982 Fifth Session of Fifth NPC
Law on Industrial Enterprises Owned by the Whole People	Jan. 12, 1988	Jan. 12–Feb. 25, 1988	Many opinions and suggestions had been adopted	Apr. 13, 1988 (First Session of the Seventh NPC)
Administrative Procedure Law	Nov. 9, 1988	Nov. 9–end of Dec., 1988	Many revisions and supplementations had been made to the Draft Law on the basis of suggestions and opinions collected	Apr. 4, 1989 (Second Session of the Seventh NPC)
Law on Assemblies, Processions and Demonstrations	Jul. 6, 1989	Jul. 6, 1989–Aug. 10, 1989	The draft law was revised in light of the opinions collected	Oct. 31, 1989 (Tenth Meeting of the Standing Committee of the Seventh NPC)

(continued)

Table 3.9 (continued)

Title	Date of publication	Time period of solicitation of public opinions	Results of solicitation of public opinions	Date of adoption
Basic Law of Hong Kong SAR	Apr. 1988–Feb. 1989	Consultation Paper: five months; Draft Law: eight months	Over 100 revisions had been made to the Consultation Paper alone	Apr. 4, 1990 (Third Session of Seventh NPC)
Basic Law of Macao SAR	July 9, 1991–March 16, 1992	Consultation Paper: four months; Draft Law: four months	Over 100 revisions and supplements had been made to the Consultation Paper alone	March 31, 1993 (First Session of the Eighth NPC)
Land Administration Law	Apr. 29, 1998	Apr. 29–June 1, 1998	Many changes had been made to the draft law	Aug. 29, 1998 (the revised law adopted at the Fourth Meeting of the Standing Committee of the Ninth NPC)
Organic Law of Villagers' Committee	June 26, 1998	June 26–Aug. 1, 1998	draft law had been revised on the basis of the opinions received	Nov. 4, 1998 (Fifth Meeting of the Standing Committee of the Ninth NPC)
Contract Law	Sept. 4, 1998	Sept. 4–Oct. 15, 1998	The draft law had been revised in on the basis of the opinions received	March 15, 1999 (Second Session of the Ninth NPC)
Marriage Law	Jan. 11, 2001	Jan. 11–Feb. 28, 2001	Many revisions had been made to the draft law on the basis of opinions received	The revised law was adopted on Apr. 28, 2001 (21st Meeting of the Standing Committee of the Ninth NPC)

(continued)

Table 3.9 (continued)

Title	Date of publication	Time period of solicitation of public opinions	Results of solicitation of public opinions	Date of adoption
Property Law	July 10, 2005	July 10–Aug. 20, 2005	A total of 11,543 pieces of opinions and suggestions had been received, most of them accepted by the NPC	March 16, 2007 (Fifth Session of the Tenth NPC)
Labor Contract Law	March 20, 2006	Mar. 20–Apr. 20, 2006	A total of 191,849 pieces of opinions and suggestions received—a historical record in the legislative history of the NPC	June 29, 2007 (28th Meeting of the Standing Committee of the Tenth NPC)
Employment Promotion Law	Mar. 25, 2007	Mar. 25–Apr. 25, 2007	11,020 pieces of opinions and suggestions received, about 70% of them came from people at the grassroots level	Aug. 30, 2007 (the 29th Meeting of the Standing Committee of the Tenth NPC)
Water Pollution Prevention and Control Law	Sept. 5, 2007	Sept. 5–Oct. 10, 2007	Over 2400 pieces of opinions and suggestions and 67 letters had been received	Feb. 28, 2008 (32nd Meeting of the Standing Committee of the Tenth NPC)
Food Safety Law	Apr. 20, 2008	Apr. 20–May 20, 2008	A total of 11,327 pieces of opinions or suggestions received, including 9556 pieces submitted through the official website of the NPC, 37 articles published in newspapers and magazines; and 164 letters	Feb. 28, 2009 (Seventh Meeting of the Standing Committee of the Eleventh NPC)

(continued)

Table 3.9 (continued)

Title	Date of publication	Time period of solicitation of public opinions	Results of solicitation of public opinions	Date of adoption
Amendment (VII) to the Criminal Law	Aug. 29, 2008	Aug. 29–Oct. 10, 2008		Feb. 28, 2009 (Seventh Meeting of the Standing Committee of the Eleventh NPC)
Law on Protecting Against and Mitigating Earthquake Disasters	Oct. 29, 2008	Oct. 29–Nov. 30, 2008	A total of 7300 pieces of opinions and suggestions had been received	Dec. 27, 2008 (Sixth Meeting of the Standing Committee of the Eleventh NPC)
Insurance Law	Dec. 28, 2008	Dec. 28, 2008–Jan. 12, 2009		Feb. 28, 2009 (Seventh Meeting of the Standing Committee of the Eleventh NPC)
Social Insurance Law (Draft)	Dec. 28, 2008	Dec. 28, 2008–Feb. 15, 2009	A total of 70,501 pieces of opinions or suggestions received, including 68,208 pieces submitted through the official website of the NPC, 49 articles published in newspapers and magazines; and 2244 letters	

public. The Draft Amendment raised the tax exemption threshold from 2000 yuan to 3000 yuan and reduced the number of grade in the "scheme of progressive tax rates on amounts in excess of specified amounts" from nine to seven. By May 31, 2011, the number of opinions received from the general public had exceeded 230,000, which was a highest record of the number of opinions received on a single draft law in the history of the NPC.[51] On June 30, 2011, the Decision of the Standing Committee of the National People's Congress on Amending the Individual Income Tax Law of the People's Republic of China was adopted at the 21st meeting of the Standing Committee of the Eleventh NPC by a vote of 134 to 6, with 11 abstentions.

Legislative hearing is another important form of open door legislation. In 2005, before the initial deliberation by NPC Standing Committee on the 1500 yuan exemption threshold of individual income tax for wages and salaries, the NPC Law Committee, the NPC Financial and Economic Affairs Committee and the Legislative Affairs Commission of the NPC Standing Committee had held hearings in Beijing to extensively solicit public opinions on the appropriateness of this standard from people from all walks of life, including the broad masses of wage earners. This was the first legislative hearing held by state legislative organs in China.

At the level of local legislative organs, the practice, exploration and institutional building with respect to legislative hearing began much earlier.[52] In September 1999,

---

[51] As Mr. Ye Qing, a deputy to the NPC recalled: "The debate on the individual income tax law in the Great Hall of People was an unforgettable experience for me. It is a good example of the reform of individual income tax driven by public opinion." He wrote in his micro-blog that: "it was remarkable that the tax exemption threshold was raised by 500 yuan as a result of 230,000 pieces of opinions on the Draft Amendment. The debate on Monday lasted for about three hours. There were three different opinions among the deputies as to what to do with the draft amendment: some were in favor of adopting the amendment with the 3000 yuan threshold unchanged; some suggested that the vote on the draft amendment should be delayed until the next session of the NPC; and some others insisted that the tax exemption threshold in the amendment should be raised. I was of the opinion that, in light of the living cost, the opinions of netizens and the affordability by state finance in China, the threshold should be raised to 4000 yuan. Some deputies from developed areas proposed that the threshold be raised to 5000 yuan. Most deputies indicated that they would vote against the draft amendment if the 3000 yuan threshold were not raised. It was under this pressure that the threshold was finally set at 3500 yuan. The vote took place on Thursday. It took only 20 min for the revised amendment to be passed, with an overwhelming majority of the deputies voted in favor of it: only 10% of the deputies voted against it or abstained. This outcome should be mainly attributed to the appeal by netizens and the 83% dissenting votes against the original draft at the early stage of solicitation of public opinions." Mr. Ye said that this adjustment of individual income tax had to a large extent taken into consideration the public opinion: "The original 3000 yuan individual income tax exemption threshold basically reflected the opinions of government organs. The NPC needed to strike a balance of interest between government organs and the general public." At the next stage of adjustment, individual income tax should be changed from a classified tax collected on a monthly basis and with individual as the paying unit into a consolidated tax collected on an annual basis and with family as the paying unit. He admitted that: "the 230,000 pieces of opinions received during the revision of the Income Tax Law had played an important role in raising the threshold by 500 yuan. I hope this will become a model of hearing at people's congresses at various levels. The Internet has become an important channel by which ordinary citizens participate in public affairs. Public opinions can promote tax reform. In the future, we will also promote the openness and democratic management of public finance." See Yangzi River Daily (2011).

[52] See Wang (2003).

the Standing Committee of the People's Congress of Guangdong Province held a hearing on the (Draft) Regulations of Guangdong Province on the Administration of Invitation and Submission of Tenders of Building Projects, which was the first local legislative hearing in the country. According to incomplete statistics, by January 2006, a total of 45 legislative hearings had been held by the standing committees of the people's congresses of 31 provinces, municipalities directly under the Central Government, and autonomous regions on 45 pieces of draft local regulations that were closely related to the interests of the people.

Although legislative hearing plays an important role in soliciting public opinions on legislation and improving the quality of legislation, it still has many problems, such as lack of representativeness of the participants of hearings, the unreasonableness of hearing procedures, the nominal nature of the hearing, and the lack of importance attached to the result of the hearing. Moreover, legislative hearing has been held for less than 1% of the all the local legislations adopted. The above problems have affected to varying extents the democratic quality of open door legislation.

3.3.5 Attaching Equal Importance to the Adoption and Revision of Laws and Continuously Improving the Legal System

Since the reform and opening up, with the continuous evolution of economic and social relations, transformation of legal ideas and improvement of legislative techniques, China has been faced with increasingly heavier task of revision of laws. Attaching equal importance to the adoption and revision of law has become a main practice and basic experience of legislation in China. Among the 229 currently effective laws adopted by the NPC and its Standing Committee, 71 or 31% of the total have been revised. Statistics show that: of the one law in the criminal law branch, one or 100% has been revised; of the 32 laws in the civil and commercial law branch, 15 or 46.8% have been revised; of the 54 laws in the economic law branch, 21 or 28.8% have been revised; of the seven laws in the litigious and non-litigious procedure law branch, two or 28.5% have been revised; of the 79 laws in the administrative law branch, 22 or 27.8% have been revised; of the 39 laws in the constitution and other constitutional law branch, seven or 17.9% have been revised; and of the 17 laws in the social law branch, three or 17.6% have been revised.

As far as the year of revision is concerned, the rate of revision of the currently effective laws was zero between 1978 and 1982, with 22 laws adopted and none revised; 1.42% between 1983 and 1992, with 70 laws adopted and one revised; 33.67% between 1993 and 2002, with 98 laws adopted, 33 laws revised; and 115.62% between 2003 and 2008, with 32 laws adopted and 37 revised (see Table 3.10).

We can see from Table 3.10 that since 1979, more and more laws have been revised in China. After entering the 21st century, the number of revised laws has markedly

Table 3.10 Ranking of branches of law according to the number of revisions (71 revisions in total)

Ranking	Branch of law	1978–1982	1983–1992	1993–2002	2003–2008
1	Criminal law: one law adopted; one law revised: rate of revision: 100%			The Criminal Law (1997); NPC Standing Committee's Decision Concerning Punishment of Criminal Offenses Involving Fraudulent Purchase, Evasion And Illegal Trading of Foreign Exchange (1998); Amendment to the Criminal Law (1999); Amendment (II) to the Criminal Law (2001); Amendment (III) to the Criminal Law (2001); Amendment (IV) to the Criminal Law (2002); Amendment (V) to the Criminal Law (2005); Amendment (VI) to the Criminal Law (2006) (one law in total)	
2	Civil and commercial law: 32 laws adopted; 15 laws revised; rate of revision: 46.8%			Law on Chinese-Foreign Equity Joint Ventures (1990 and 2001); Marriage Law (2001); Trademark Law (1993 and 2001); Patent Law (1992 and 2000); Law on Wholly Foreign-Owned Enterprises; (2000); Law on Chinese-Foreign Contractual Joint Ventures (2000); Copyright Law(2001); Adoption Law(1998; Insurance Law (2002), (nine laws in total)	Company Law (1999, 2004 and 2005); Law on Commercial Banks (2003); Negotiable Instruments Law (1995 and 2004); Auction Law (2004); Partnership Enterprise Law (2006); Securities Law (2004 and 2005) (six laws in total)

(continued)

Table 3.10 (continued)

Ranking	Branch of law	1978–1982	1983–1992	1993–2002	2003–2008
3	Economic Law: 54 laws adopted; 21 revised; rate of revision: 28.8%			Statistics Law (1996); Forest Law (1998); Accounting Law (1993 and 1999); Grassland Law (2002); Water Law (2002); Law on Import and Export Commodity Inspection (2002); Law on the Administration of Tax Collection (1995 and 2001); Product Quality Law (2000); Agriculture Law (2002) (9 laws in total)	Foreign Trade Law (2004); Audit Law (2006); Law on the People's Bank of China (2003); Highway Law (1999 and 2004); Animal Epidemic Prevention Law (2007); Energy Conservation Law (2007); Seed Law (2004); Banking Supervision Law (2006); Fisheries Law (2000 and 2004); Mineral Resources Law (1996); Land Administration Law (1988, 1998 and 2004); Individual Income Tax Law (1993, 1999, 2005 and 2007) (12 laws in total)
4	Litigation and non-litigation procedure law: Seven laws adopted; two laws revised; rate of revision: 28.5%			Criminal Procedure Law (1996) (one law in total)	Civil Procedure Law (2007) (one law in total)
5	Administrative Law: 79 laws adopted; 22 laws revised; rate of revision: 27.8%			Military Serve Law (1998); Pharmaceutical Administration Law (2001); Customs Law (2000); Law on the Prevention and Control of Atmospheric Pollution (1995 and 2000); Archive Law (1996); Regulations on the Military Ranks of Officers of the Chinese People's Liberation Army (1994); Law on the Protection of the Rights and Interests of Returned Overseas Chinese and the Family Members of Overseas Chinese (2000); Surveying and Mapping Law (2002); Law on Officers in Active Service (1994 and 2000) (nine laws in total)	Compulsory Education Law (2006); Frontier Health and Quarantine Law (2007); Regulations on Academic Degrees (2004); Marine Environment Protection Law (1999); Cultural Relics Protection Law (1991, 2002 and 2007); Water Pollution Prevention and Control Law (1996 and 2008); Law on the Protection of Wildlife (2004); Lawyer's Law (2001 and 2007); Road Traffic Safety Law (2007) (13 laws in total)

(continued)

Table 3.10 (continued)

Ranking	Branch of law	1978–1982	1983–1992	1993–2002	2003–2008
6	Social Law: 17 laws adopted; three laws revised; rate of revision: 17.6%			Trade Union Law (2001) (one law in total)	Law on the Protection of Minors (2006) and Law on the Protection of Rights and Interests of Women (2005) (two laws in total)
7	The Constitution and other constitutional laws: 39 laws adopted; seven laws revised; rate of revision: 17.9%		Organic Law of People's Procuratorates (1983 and 1986) (one law in total)	Law on Regional National Autonomy (2001); Judge's Law (2001); and Public Procurators Law (2001) (three laws in total)	Organic Law of Local People's Congresses and Local People's Governments (1982, 1986, 1995 and 2004); Election Law for the National People's Congress and Local People's Congresses at All Levels (1982, 1986, 1995 and 2004); Organic Law of People's Courts (1983, 1986, and 2006) (three laws in total)

exceeded the number of newly adopted laws, indicating that Chinese legislation has entered into a period of major adjustment.

With respect to the number of revisions of the currently effective laws, by February 2008, two laws, or 2.8% of the total, had been revised five times or more; two, or 2.8% of the total, had been revised four times; four or 5.6% of the total had been revised three times; 14 or 19.7% of the total had been revised twice; and 49 or 69% of the total had been revised once.

The following statistics show the content, time and frequency of revision of laws in the seven main branches of law: (1) in the branch of the Constitution and other constitutional laws: seven laws had been revised. Among them, none had been revised five time or more; two or 28.57% revised four times; one or 14.28% revised three times; one or 14.28% revised twice; and three or 42.80% revised once; (2) in the branch of civil and commercial, a total of 15 laws had been revised. Among them, none had been revised four or more times; one or 6.66% revised three times; five or 33.33% revised twice; and nine or 60% revised once; (3) in the branch of administrative law, a total of 22 laws had been revised. Among them, none had been revised four or more times; one or 4.54% revised three times; four or 18.18% revised twice; and 17 or 77.27% revised once; (4) in the branch of economic law, a total of 21 laws had been revised. Among them, one or 4.76% had been revised five or more times; none had been revised four times; one or 4.76% revised three times; four or 19.04% revised twice; and 15 or 71.42% revised once; (5) three laws in the branch of social law and two in the branch of litigious and non-litigious procedure law had been revised, each for once; (6) the criminal law had been revised more than five times.

From the above statistics we can see that the majority of the laws in China had been revised once. This shows that legislative organs in China had taken a relatively cautious attitude towards the revision of laws.

3.3.6 Adhering to the Organic Unity of the CPC's Leadership, People's Democracy and Ruling the Country by Law

Adhering to the "organic unity of the three principles" is the most important and fundamental principle of developing socialist democratic politics with Chinese characteristics as well as the most important and fundament experience of legislative work in China. The CPC's leadership is the basic guarantee of people's status as the masters of the country, as well as of democratic, scientific, and high-quality legislation; people's status as the masters of the country is the essential requirement of socialist democratic politics as well as democratic, scientific, and high-quality legislation; ruling the country by law is the basic strategy adopted by the CPC for leading the people in administering state affairs; and having laws to go by is the precondition of ruling the country by law.

In China, laws are the concretization, standardization and legalization of the strategies and polices of the CPC that have been proved by practice to be correct, mature, and need to be implemented for a long period of time. The fundamental policies and the legislative proposals put forward by the CPC need to be transformed through legal procedures of the NPC into the will of the state and codes of conduct to be complied with by all members of society. In the legislative work, China must adhere to the correct political orientation, organically unify upholding the leadership of the CPC, the people being masters of the country and ruling the country by law, and guarantee through laws and institutions the implementation of the CPC's lines, strategies and polices. Only by adhering to the organic unity of the above three principles can we ensure the correct direction of the legislative work and realize the legislation by the people and for the people in the process of advancing the legislative work and improving the socialist legal system.

3.4 Continuously Improving the Socialist Legal System with Chinese Characteristics

The formation on schedule of the socialist legal system with Chinese characteristics indicates that the construction of the rule of law in China has entered into a new stage of having laws to go by. It has become an important milestone in the construction of socialist democracy and rule of law in China, and is of profound realistic and historical significance to strengthening and improving the legislative work at a new starting point, effectively safeguarding the implementation of the Constitution and laws, promoting the rule of law, and speeding up the construction of a socialist state under the rule of law.

Meanwhile, it should be noted that the socialist legal system with Chinese characteristics was formed in the process of strengthening socialist democratic political system and comprehensively promoting the rule of law and that a sound socialist legal system with Chinese characteristics should have at least the following characteristics: first, having laws to go by in every aspects of economic, political, cultural and social lives; second, the unity of and coordination between various kinds of laws in spirit, principle and concrete content and the minimization of contradictions and conflicts between different laws; third, the appropriateness in form and in content of each law, whether a code or separate law; and fourth, the timely discovery, revision, and supplementation of outdated, backward, and conflicting laws and realization of the synchronization of the change of laws with the development of situation. Therefore, measured by high standard, the formation of the socialist legal system with Chinese characteristics has only basically solved problem of "having no law to go by". The system "itself is not perfect" and still has some defects and shortcomings. Judging by the strategic objectives of building China into a moderately well-off society in all respects by the year 2020 and a socialist state under the rule of law by the year

2050, the formation of a more democratic and scientific socialist legal system with Chinese characteristics will be a prolonged and arduous task.

3.4.1 The Construction of the Rule of Law and the Realization of the "Five Transitions" of the Legislative Work

Firstly, after the solution of the problem of "having no law to go by", a basic task of China in the process of comprehensively promoting the rule of law should be to ensure the observance of law. The key to the construction of the rule of law is the transition from the legal system that takes the legislation as the center to the one that takes the down-to-earth implementation of the Constitution and laws as its center. The CPC and the government should attach more importance to and strengthen the implementation of the Constitution and laws, and realize the comprehensive and coordinated development of the implementation of the Constitution and laws and the construction of the legal system. On the one hand, China has made rapid progress in legislation and adopted a large number of laws, and now can proudly proclaim to the world that the construction of a socialist legal system with Chinese characteristics has already been completed in China. But on the other hand, many laws exist only in name or on paper in some places, fields and circumstances. Some government officials have never taken the law seriously and regard it as the tool for constraining others and "ruling the country by law" as a means of "ruling the people by law". Neither do some ordinary citizens take the law seriously. They believe in power, connection and petitions rather than law (that their problems cannot be solved unless they start a disturbance; their problems can only be partially solved if they start a small disturbance; and their problems can be completely solved if they start a big disturbance). At the current stage, the problem of "there being no law to go by" has already been basically solved and the main problem in the construction of the rule of law is the poor implementation of laws, which is manifested in such phenomena as non-compliance with law, slack enforcement of law, failure to bring lawbreakers to justice, violation of law by law enforcement officials, by those who are familiar with the law and by leading cadres. As a result, many laws and administrative regulations exist in name only. An especially prominent problem is the so-called "selective law enforcement", namely laws and administrative regulations that provide for certain obligations for citizens or prohibit citizens from engaging in certain activities, such as the Tax Law, the Criminal Law, the Traffic Regulations and the Regulations on Security Check, are implemented in a speedy, timely and strict way, whereas the laws and administrative regulations that regulate the behavior of government officials or require the state and the government to provide certain services or resources to citizens, such as the Law on Compulsory Education, the Labor Law, the Employment Promotion Law, the Environment Protection Law, and the Law on Food Hygiene, are generally not implemented in a timely and comprehensive way. The existence of such phenomena and problems has seriously undermined the effect of the implementation of and damaged the authority of the Constitution and laws. It is for this reason that an expert said during a session of the NPC and CPPCC that non-compliance with laws is even worse than having no law to go by. After the formation on schedule of the socialist legal system with Chinese characteristics, China should take the effective implementation of the Constitution and laws as the emphasis of the construction of the rule of law, realize its transition from the one centered on legislation to the one centered on the effective implementation of the Constitution and laws, promote the scientific development of the legal system with comprehensive coordination between the implementation of the Constitution and laws and the construction of the legal system. The statistics in Table 3.11 shows that more and more people have agreed that China should promote the construction of the rule of law by emphasizing the implementation of the Constitution and laws.

Secondly, after the basic realization of the rule of law objective of having laws to go by, China needs to advance in width and depth the implementation of the strategy of ruling the country by law and constructing the rule of law by taking legislation as the center, strengthening the construction of legal institutions and norms, cultivating the spirit, the idea and the consciousness of the rule of law, striving to turn the rule of law into people's value belief and mode of life, and realizing the comprehensive and coordinated development of the rule of law culture and the legal system. Law is an indispensable code of conduct in civilized society and the purpose of legislation and creation of legal norms is to give full play to the social functions of the law. If it can be said that practice is the criterion for testing truth, then the effect of the implementation of law is an important criterion for judging the soundness of the legal system. Therefore, we should carry out in-depth research on how to "adopt,

Table 3.11 On-line vote on the question "what should be the emphasis of the construction of the rule of law at the current stage?"

No.	Items	%	Votes
1	Advancing the strategy of ruling the country by law in a comprehensive way	10	1208
2	Establishing the idea of socialist rule of law	6	665
3	Enhancing the CPC's capacity for exercising the ruling power by law	9	1031
4	Advancing democratic legislation	5	598
5	Constructing a law-based government	10	1133
6	Deepening the judicial reform	11	1281
7	Strengthening the implementation of the Constitution and laws	28	3124
8	Deepening the publicity of and education on the legal system	2	222
9	Realizing the coordinated development of the rule of law	22	2587
	Total votes	100	11,849

Source www.iolaw.org.cn. Last visited on February 17, 2015

revise and abolish" laws from the point of view of comprehensively advancing the rule of law and constructing a socialist state under the rule of law and in light of the inherent requirements of the coordinated development of various links of the rule of law, including law enforcement, administration of justice, observance of law and legal supervision. The formation of the legal system means the basic solution of the long-existing problem of having no law to go by that has impeded the operation of the rule of law in China. After that, China should attach more importance to the linkage and coordination between legislation, administration of justice, observance of law and legal supervision while at the same time continue to pay attention to and strengthen legislative work. Attach more importance to giving full play to the role of the Constitution and laws in the political, economic and social lives, examine, assess and demand for the improvement and development of the legal system, so that it becomes the legal norms that not only exist on the paper, but also are improved and implemented in real life and believed in and complied with by all citizens.

Thirdly, after the formation of the socialist legal system with Chinese characteristics, China should transform its legislative work from one that attaches importance to the quantity of legislation to one that attaches importance to the quality of legislation by taking into consideration of not only the GDP of the quantity of legislation, but also the quality and actual effect of legislation, and not only of countless legal norms on the paper, but also the rule of law functions that can truly play their role in reality. In the past legislative work in China, there have been many abnormal phenomena that are more or less related to the practice of one-sidedly pursuing the quantity of legislation while ignoring the quality of legislation, such as "expanding powers and shirking responsibilities through legislation", "departmental protectionism and local protectionism" in legislation, repetitive legislation, overstepping one's legislative competence, "departmentalization of state legislation", "interest-driven departmental legislation", and "legalization of departmental interests". After the formation of the socialist legal system with Chinese characteristics, China should improve the quality of legislation in the following macro-dimensions: (1) Truly adhering to the principle of democratic and scientific legislation. Legislation is the embodiment of the people's will and the pursuit of democracy is the value orientation of modern legislation. Therefore, whether legislation can fully safeguard the people's right of participation and right to express their opinions, and whether it can truly embody the overall will of the broadest masses of people have become the criterion for judging the quality of legislation. In other words, this characteristic is in fact the manifestation and the embodiment in legislation of the principles of "the people being the masters of the country" and "exercising the ruling power for the people" as well as an important basis of the reasonableness and legitimacy of legislation in contemporary China. The mission of legislation in socialist China is to collect and express public opinions, enable the people to make decisions in accordance with legislative procedure and by legislative method, and then ensure the realization of the people's will through the enforcement and application of law. Whether a law has expressed the will of the people should be judged or determined not entirely by the legislators themselves, but mainly by the people and such judgment is expressed through such attitudes as welcome, acceptance, recognition, opposition, rejection, or resistance after the law is adopted. Any law that has been opposed, rejected, or resisted by the people, no matter how eloquent its language, how skilled its technique, how strict its logic, and how high-sounding its publicity, cannot be considered a piece of quality legislation, but should be regarded as a legislation of "negative value" or "negative quality". (2) Further improving the legislative procedure. The interest-balancing function and the democratic value of legislation are safeguarded and realized through legislative procedures. The relationship between legislative procedure and substantive values reflects the relationship between procedural justice and substantive justice and embodies the regulation and guidance of legislative value objectives by the legislative procedure. The systems of adoption, revision and abolition of laws, the systems of introduction of, and deliberation and voting on legislative proposals, the system of recordation and review of legislation, and the legislative interpretation system are all important parts of the legislative procedure. These procedural systems should be not only complete, but also able to meet the requirements of scientific and democratic legislation and compatible with national conditions in China. China should ensure, through the design of legislative procedures and the related institutional arrangements, that legislative procedures are scientific and conducive to the expression and collection of public opinions and that the principles of scientific legislation and democratic legislation are integrated and unified and implemented in every link of the legislative procedure and every concrete institution. In this respect, China has many successful experiences to be summed up and many practices to be review and improved. For example, legislative hearing is a system designed to solicit the opinions of all stakeholders on the legislative bill, so as to adjust relevant interest relations. However, in some localities, legislative hearing has often become a mere formality of legislative democracy because of such problems as asymmetry of legislative information, imbalance of legislative resources, and insufficiency of democratic participation. For another example, the legislative voting system in China has provided for no compulsory requirement on article-by-article or paragraph-by-paragraph vote on a bill of law, but only the vote on the entire bill. As a result, voters who are opposed to only one or a few provisions in a bill are faced with a dilemma: they have to either reject or accept the bill as a whole. Either choice may be against their legislative will. (3) Further strengthening the enforceability and operability of legislation. Law-making is a process of collection and expression of people's will whereas the implementation of law is the enforcement and realization of the people's will and the key to transforming the law from that written on the paper to that operating in real life. Practice is the only criterion for testing truth as well as a fundamental criterion for testing the quality of legislation. Under the precondition of good law and good governance, if a law cannot be effective implemented after it is adopted and, as result, becomes a mere scrap of paper and exists only in name, then it has no quality to talk about. After the formation of the legal system, the main problems to be solved by China in the construction of the rule of law are non-compliance with the law, unfairness in the enforcement of the law and failure to bring lawbreakers to justice. If we trace the root causes of poor or ineffective implementation of some laws in China, we will find out that many of them lie in the legislation itself: the defects, loopholes, gaps, and conflicts in legislation and the poor quality of legislation have led to non-enforcement or arbitrary enforcement of law. For example, local legislations prohibiting the setting-off of fireworks and firecrackers and restricting dog-raising in some areas have met with difficulties in enforcement, even resistance, by the people. This is to a large extent a result of the lack of public support for the legislation, rather than the ineffective law enforcement by administrative organs or the miscarriage of justice by judicial organs. (4) Further improving the overall coordination of legislation. The overall coordination of legislation mainly emphasizes the coordinated development of the legal system and the system of the rule of law. Such coordinated development includes: firstly, the internal coordination within each law, between laws at the same level, between laws and administrative regulations at different levels, and within the whole legal system; secondly, the coordinated development of legislation, mainly referring to the adoption, revision, supplementation, interpretation, compilation, and abolition of laws by legislative organs in appropriate time and, through these activities, the maintenance of the dynamic and coordinated development of the legal system. The so-called "appropriate time" could refer to the maturity of opportunity and conditions of legislation or the change of situation that necessitate the adoption, revision, supplementation, interpretation, compilation, and abolition of laws, including the adoption, revision or abolition of an upper-level law. Thirdly, the coordination between legislation and administrative law enforcement, administration of justice, legal supervision, and publicity of and education on the rule of law, namely the integrated construction and coordinated development of the entire system of the rule of law. In the sense of political science, the legislative process is a process of political decision-making and the result of legislation is the result of political decision-making. The quality of such decision-making affects the overall design and construction of the system of the rule of law and determines the direction, the path, the speed and the quality of the development this system. Therefore, while enthusiastically engaging in the research on and planning of the reform of various systems relating to the rule of law, such as the reform of the system of a law-based government, the judicial system, and the legal supervision system, we must have the macro thinking and consciousness of the rule of law, pay more attention to making unified planning and arrangement of the overall reform and coordinated development of the system of rule of law by improving the quality of legislation, so as to avoid the situation in which the more thorough and successful local reforms, the further away from the overall objective of unified and coordinated development of the rule of law. In our daily life, we can often see such slogans as "In a task so important for generations to come, we must use every means to ensure good quality in the work" or "quality is life", which reflect people's aspiration and demand for high-quality daily products. Similarly, in the political life and the field of construction of the rule of law, legislation is a kind of special political and rule of law product. The quality of legislation is the key to people's democracy and rule of law and directly determines the quality of the political life of the people as masters of the country and the fate of the construction of the rule of law and socialist political civilization in China.

Fourthly, after the formation of the legal system in China, the emphasis of the legislative work in China should be shifted from the making of laws to the coordinated development of the making, compilation, interpretation, revision, supplementation, and abolition of laws, so as to make the legal system more scientific, stable, and authoritative and give it more vitality.

Fifthly, after the formation on schedule of the legal system, the mode of legislative work in China has been transformed from that of "wading the river by groping for stones" and "formulating a law or a provision in a law whenever conditions are ripe" to that of scientific planning, unified arrangement, and coordinated development and from one that evades the crucial point and chooses the easier task in the selection of legislative projects, to one that "picks hard nuts to crack" and "tackles difficult problems head on", so that legislation can truly become an art of distribution of social interests, adjustment of social relations, and resolution of social conflicts.

After the formation of the socialist legal system with Chinese characteristics, the emphasis of the legislative work in China is on the further improvement of this system in accordance with the Scientific Outlook on Development and the requirement of comprehensively advancing the rule of law at a new historical starting point, which is an even more difficult and arduous task.

3.4.2 Establishing a Stricter and More Scientific Standard on the Socialist Legal System with Chinese Characteristics

To further improve the socialist legal system with Chinese characteristics, it is necessary to find overall solutions to legislative problems, establish higher legislative standards, and raise the legislative quality to a new level.

3.4.2.1 Improving the Socialist Legal System with Chinese Characteristics Means to Bring Various Basic Social Relations Under the Scope of Regulation by Law

Law is the regulator of social relations and distributor of social interests. In the improvement of the legal system, China should bring every aspects of the economic, political, cultural, social and international relations of the state into the scope of regulation by law, so as to ensure that there are laws to go by in the main aspects of the political, economic, social and cultural lives of the country. Currently, there are still some legislative gaps, and, as a result, many social relations have not yet been brought under the scope of legal regulation in China. We can catch a glimpse of these legislative gaps from the following list of laws that, according to some scholars and experts, should be adopted by China in recent years: the press law, the law on association, the law on community self-governance, law on the declaration of assets by public officials, law on organizational establishment, law on household registration, law on emergence response, law on the correction of illegal acts, law on administrative procedures, law on administrative compulsion, law on macroeconomic regulation, general principles of commercial law, law on the registration of real estate, e-commerce law, food law, energy law, social insurance law, law on basic medical security, mental health law, law on the safeguarding of farmers' rights and interests, law on housing security, law on legal aid, law on social assistance, law on financial regulation, charity law, law on volunteer service, social credit law, individual information protection law, island protection law, law on natural preservation zones, land frontier law, assess evaluation law, etc.

Of course, while stressing and attaching importance to legislation, we must also be aware of the inherent limitation of legislation and prevent excessive legislation. In adjusting social relations, legislation should be like a good fishnet: although it has sparse meshes, but no fish escapes from it. There should be an appropriate and balanced proportion between civil, criminal, administrative, economic and social legislations. Just as famous British legal historian Sir Henry Maine said, we can tell the level of civilization of country from the proportion between its civil law and criminal law. In general, the proportion of criminal law is larger than that of the civil law in a semi-civilized country, and the opposite is true in a civilized country.[53] China should change as soon as possible the current situation of social legislation lagging behind economic legislation, legislation on human rights legislation lagging behind administrative legislation, and civil legislation lagging behind criminal legislation.

3.4.2.2   Improving the Socialist Legal System with Chinese Characteristics Means to Link up Various Parts of the System to Form an Organic Whole, and Ensure that There Is No Legislative Gaps, Ornamental Legislation, Outdated Legislation, or Other Major Legislative Defects in the System

From the perspective of the requirements of scientific legislation and legislative techniques, China, in improving the socialist legal system with Chinese characteristics, should realize harmonious relations between different kinds of laws, such as those between codes and separate laws, between revised laws and original laws, between interpretative laws and original laws, between lower-level laws and upper-level laws, between new laws and old laws, between special laws and general laws, between procedure laws and substantive laws, between local laws and central laws, and between international laws and domestic laws, so that all these laws constitute an organic and unified whole. In 2010, Professor Liang Huixing put forward the proposal to revise the Succession Law, which was adopted 25 years earlier, so as to expand the scope of inheritance, improve the system of forfeiture of the succession right, revise the scope and sequence of statutory successors, provide for the equal effect of various kinds of will, supplement the succession system and the will execution system, further improve the systems of partitioning of heritage, succession by subrogation, and legitim. Besides, many other laws, such as the Civil Procedure Law, the Criminal Procedure Law, the Administrative Procedure Law, the Forestry Law, the Organic Law of the Urban Residents Committee, the Organic Law of the National People's

---

[53] See Li (1959).

Congress, the Advertisement Law, the Budget Law, and the Postal Law, need to be revised. With the advancement of economic reform and social transition to a new starting point, a large number of laws adopted at the early stage of reform and opening up have reached the end of their life cycle. With the comprehensive implementation of the basic strategy of ruling the country by law and the enhancement of legislative ability, China has now entered into a period of attaching equal importance to the adoption and revision of laws. The task of improving existing laws is as arduous as that of adopting new laws. It should take such legislative measures as legislative review and the revision, interpretation, supplementation, and abolition of laws to minimize the gaps, contradictions, conflicts, loopholes, repetitions, backwardness and other defects in the legal system.[54]

3.4.2.3 Improving the Socialist Legal System with Chinese Characteristics Means to Realize the Rule of Good Law and Good Governance

In China, legislation itself is the collection and expression of people's will and the key to distributive justice. If the legislation itself is unfair and there are such phenomena of legislative corruption as departmental protectionism, then the better the implementation of the law, the further away we are from the value objective of ruling the country by law. Under the condition of ruling the country by law, stress must be laid not only on having laws to go by and abiding by the law, but more importantly, also on advocating and realizing good law and good governance. "Only by embodying the law of nature and the aspirations of the people and conforming to the tide of historical development can the laws be truly believed in and consciously abided by, and become fundamental, comprehensive, stable and long-term social instruments."[55] The legal system in China is both the legalization of socialist value principles and the systematization of basic social code of conduct.

After over 30 years of unremitting efforts, the construction of the legal system in China will be completed soon and the problem of having no law to go by in the construction of the rule of law has been basically solved. But how is the current situation of implementation of law in China? I am afraid to say that the situation of the compliance with, implementation and application of various laws in the legal system is not optimistic. After the formation on schedule of the legal system and with the continuous increase of the number of laws, the implementation of law is lagged behind the development of legislation, and the more laws adopted, the less effective the implementation of the laws. Therefore, the most important criterion for judging the soundness of a legal system is not the number of laws adopted, or the GDP of legislation, but the actual effect of the laws after their adoption. In a sound legal system, laws of various branches, at levels, and in various forms should all play

---

[54]http://www.legaldaily.com.cn/index_article/content/2010-03/11/content_2080384htm?node= 5955.
[55]Zhu (2010).

their due role in social life. Legislators should avoid the situation in which the laws they adopted exist only in name or on paper and perform practically no function. The socialist legal system with Chinese characteristics should be respected, abided by and implemented and become the guidance of people's behaviors and the laws in real life. The legislative purposes can be truly realized only if the state and the legislators ensure through good laws and good governance the compliance with laws and the protection of human rights.

3.4.3 Strengthening the Research on the Legislative Theory of the Socialist Legal System with Chinese Characteristics

In China, legislation is the embodiment of the unity of the propositions of the Party, the will of the people and the will of the state, the reflection and recordation of the achievements of social and economic development and institutional reforms, and the standardization and legalization of various important guidelines and policies adopted by China since the reform and opening up. Meanwhile, the formation of the legal system marked the new developments of and raised new demands for the further improvement of the legislative theory in China.

Legislative practice is the motive force directly propelling the continuous enrichment and development of legislative theory whereas legislative theory is the guidance that ensures the continuous progress of legislative practice. The level and quality of legislation and the soundness of the legal system are closely related to the conditions of the culture, concept, and theory of legislation.

As far as historical origin is concerned, the construction of the rule of law, including the legislative theory and practice in China, is apparently influenced by the socialist legal system in the Soviet Union. During the early years of the People's Republic, China had carried out a wholesale transplantation of the legal system from the Soviet Union. Since the reform and opening up, China has made major adjustments to its thinking of legislative work. On the one hand, China has speeded up the legislative process by proceeding from the national conditions and practice, focusing on the central tasks of economic construction and social development, and adopting such methods as "crossing a river by feeling the way over the stones", "revising and supplementing laws whenever conditions permit" and "extensive rather than intensive legislation". This process is similar to process of the reform and opening up and the exploration of the road of socialism with Chinese characteristics and this legislative mode has enabled China to complete the construction of the legal system with Chinese characteristics in only 30 years. In the legislative practice of reform and opening up, China has gradually accumulated precious legislative experiences and put forward many important legislative theories and ideas, thereby providing the theoretical support to the formation of the socialist legal system with Chinese characteristics in China.

On the other hand, in the process of borrowing the socialist legislative theory from the Soviet Union, China has discarded many of its outdated elements and, by combining it with the beneficial elements of western legislative practice, has gradually formed a socialist legislative theory with Chinese characteristics. With respect to its origin, the theory of construction and method of division of the legal system in China were borrowed from the Soviet Union. Its theoretical characteristic of the economy under the ownership by the whole people and its political ideology of class struggle had to a certain extent affected, even impeded the self-improvement and comprehensive development of the legal system on the basis of construction of socialist market economy and harmonious society.

With respect to the theory on the construction of the legal system, China has not adopted the theory of division of the legal system by public law, private, economic law and social law, which is commonly used in western countries, but basically adopted the socialist theory on the legal system from the Soviet Union.

Needless to say, because of the weak basis of legislation and the lack of sufficient legislative theoretical research and practice, the current legal system in China is still imperfect, and far from meeting the requirements of socialist modernization, the people's strong demand for legislation, the basic requirement of having laws to go by in the process of ruling the country by law and constructing a socialist state under the rule of law, and the standards of democratic, scientific and high-quality legislation.

In improving the socialist legal system at the new historical starting point, China should further strengthen the research on the theory of construction and the method of division of legal system, and promote the innovative development of the legal system. The following examples show that many important questions still urgently need to be studied and answered in the theory of construction socialist legal system with Chinese characteristics. We should take the essence of traditional Chinese legal culture and the beneficial experience of world legal culture as the cultural basis for improving the current legal system, the one country (the PRC), two systems (socialist and capitalist systems), three legal systems (socialist legal system in mainland, the common law system in Hong Kong SAR and continental law system in Macao SAR and Taiwan) and four jurisdictions (the Mainland, Hong Kong, Macao, and Taiwan) as the whole object in the study and construction of Chinese legal system, the innovative, open, scientific and inclusive thinking as the method and principle of improving the current legal system, and the public law, private law, social law, comprehensive law and international law as the basic categories for the division of the legal system, so as to realize the comprehensive and sustainable development of socialist legal system both in theory and in methodology, both form and content, and both in borrowing from and in transcending foreign experiences.

We should further strengthen the research on basic theory of legislation in China by focusing on theories of legislative philosophy, legislative politics, legislative sociology, legislative economics, legislative values, legislative powers, legislative subjects, legislative relations, legislative systems, legislative procedures, legislative techniques, legislative behaviors, legislative interpretation, and comparative legislation, and, through systematic and in-depth research on basic legislative theory, gradually construct a theoretical system of socialist legislation with Chinese characteristics, thereby providing more scientific and rational ideological guidance and theoretical support for the continuous improvement and further development of the legal system in China.

3.4.4 Adopting and Implementing Scientific Legislative Development Strategies and Legislative Plans

If it can be said that China basically adopted the legislative method of "crossing the river by feeling way over the stones" in the early years of reform and opening up and began to attach importance to legislative planning and scientific legislation in the mid period of reform and opening up, then in the future, China should attach more importance to proactive and scientific legislation, carefully study and adopt national legislative development strategy, more conscientiously adhere to scientific, democratic and high-quality legislation, and scientifically formulate and earnestly implement legislative plans, so as to further improve the socialist legal system with Chinese characteristics.

Firstly, China should continue to implement Deng Xiaoping's strategic conception and the "three-step" strategic arrangement, and strive to raise China's level of average per capita GNP to that of moderately developed countries, basically realize modernization, and build itself into a prosperous, democratic, civilized and harmonious socialist state by 2050. It should, in light of the general trend of development of world situation and in accordance with the strategic objective of completing the construction of political, economic, social, cultural and ecological civilizations, especially the strategic objective of building China into a socialist state under the rule of law by the year 2050, carefully study and design the national legislative development strategy in the next 40 years, adopt and continuously improve the "timetable" and "road map" for improving the socialist legal system with Chinese characteristics, and enable the Chinese legal system to realize the development objective of making itself more democratic and effective, so as to better guide, serve, regulate and safeguard the smooth realization of the objective of socialist modernization.

Secondly, China should comprehensively implement the Scientific Outlook on Development and, in accordance with the objective of building China into a moderately well-off society in all respects by 2020—by then China will basically realize industrialization, markedly enhance comprehensive national strength, and lead the world in the overall size of domestic market; comprehensively increase the level of people's wealth, markedly improve people's quality of life and ecological environment, enable the people to fully enjoy democratic rights and have higher cultural quality and spiritual pursuit, and becomes a more stable and united country with better institutions and more vitality, and a country more open to the outside world, having more affinity and able to make greater contribution to the human civilization—and in light of the tasks of comprehensively promoting the rule of law in each period of time, carry out research on and adopt national legislative plan for the period of 2010–2020 and measures for its annual implementation, strive to transform into laws the lines, principles and policies on the construction of a moderately well-off society in all respects, and provide legal safeguard for the realization of national strategic objectives by 2020; it should concretize each year's legislative tasks, including the adoption, revision, and abolition of laws, attach importance to not only the adoption of new laws, but also the cleanup and the codification, revision, supplementation, interpretation and abolition of existing laws, and institutionalize and normalize the work of adoption, revisions and abolitions of laws; and strive to eliminate the defects of departmental legislation by improving the relevant institutions and procedures, stabilize the number of legislation, enhance the quality of legislation, improve legislative procedures and techniques, optimize legislative structure, coordinate the relationship between legislation and economic and social development, institutional reform, the construction of ecological civilization and the promotion of people's welfare.

Thirdly, we should attach high importance to the democratic, scientific, authoritative and solemn nature of legislative plans and give them the necessary legal effect, so as to ensure the completion of various kinds of legislative work with high quality. In 1991, the Standing Committee of the Seventh NPC adopted the first official legislative plan—the Legislation Plan of the Standing Committee of the National People's Congress (October 1991–March 1993). The Standing Committee of the Eighth NPC also attached great importance to the planning of legislative work by adopting a five-year legislative plan and annual legislative plans. The Standing Committee of the Ninth NPC further pointed out that "annual plans, five-year plans, and long-term programs" should be adopted for the legislative work. Legislative planning is an important precondition of the guidance and arrangement of the legislative work and an important safeguard for the improvement of the socialist legal system with Chinese characteristics. "Planned legislation is able to highlight the priorities of the legislative work and adapt it to the needs of reform, opening up, and modernization drive, increase initiatives and prevent repetition, dispersion and omission in the legislative work, avoid unnecessary legislative activities, help the relevant government departments to participate in legislative activities in a coordinated and prepared way, thereby improving the quality of legislation."[56] Careful implementation of legislative plan is crucial to improving the quality and efficiency of legislation. In the process of further improving legislative planning, China should try to strengthen the mechanisms for the full and democratic participation by public and social interest groups in the formulation and adoption of legislative plans and prevent legislative plans from being controlled by the will of some individual leaders or a few interest groups; ensure that the development of legislative planning complies with the laws of scientific development and legislation, prevent subjective and arbitrary adoption of legislative program; enhance the authority of state legislative organs in the formulation of legislative plans, prevent the power to adopt legislative plan from falling into the hands of other organs or individuals, and minimize "departmental legislative planning"; strengthen the role of the state in the implementation of legislative plans,

---

[56]Wang and Liu (2008).

and prevent the tendency of "taking up the minor issue to evade the major one" or "picking easy jobs and shirking hard ones" in the implementation of legislative tasks. When a change of situation makes it necessary to change or adjust legislative plan, such change or adjustment, whether the addition, reduction, postponement or merger of legislative projects, must undergo strict demonstration, review and approval procedures.

Fourthly, China should carefully implement the legislative plans of the NPC Standing Committee. In October 2008, the Standing Committee of the Eleventh NPC adopted a five-year legislative plan, according to which China will adopt or revise 64 laws in the next five-year period. Among them, 49 are listed as Category I legislative projects, namely draft laws to be submitted to the NPC for deliberation during its term of office; fifteen are listed as Category II legislative projects, namely draft laws that need to be prepared and submitted to the NPC for deliberation when conditions are mature. This five-year legislative plan has the following characteristics: First, the realizing the compatibility between legislative plans and economic and social development, being people-oriented, promoting scientific and harmonious development, adhering to unified planning and rational arrangement, and embodying and implementing the Scientific Outlook on Development in the adoption of laws aimed at strengthening legislation in the social field, improving socialist market economic system, advancing the construction of democratic political system, and building a resources-conserving and environment friendly society. Second, continuing to strengthen social legislation. The plan includes a total of six pieces of social legislation: Social Insurance Law, Law on Basic Health Care; Mental Health Law, Social Assistance Law, Charity Law, and Law on Safeguarding the Rights and Interests of the Elderly (revision). After the promulgation of these laws, the legislation in the social field, especially legislation relating to the safeguarding of people's livelihood, will become more complete and people's social rights will be better protected. Third, attaching equal importance to the adoption and the revision of laws. In this legislative plan, the number of projects on the adoption of new laws has decreased to 64 while the number of legislative projects on the revision of laws has increase to 28.

The NPC Standing Committee attaches high importance to the implementation of legislative plans, strives to improve the quality of legislation, and to implement legislative projects with respect to "task, time, organization and responsibility", so as to provide important safeguard to the formation on schedule and the further improvement of the socialist legal system with Chinese Characteristics.

3.4.5   Quickening the Pace of Codification

Codification, also called compilation of codes of law, is a legislative activity whereby the state adopts systematic legal norms to adjust a particular type of social relations through the promulgation of a unified, logically complete and internally consistent code of law. The so-called a code of law refers to a comparatively systematic legislative document resulting from the codification of the legal norms in a certain branch of law. In China, the earliest comparatively systematic code of law was the Book of Law (Fajing) compiled by Li Kui, the Prime Minister of the State of Wei in the Warring States Period in the Fifth Century BC. The Code of Hammurabi of Ancient Babylon in the 18th Century BC, and Codex Justinianus compiled under the order of the Byzantine emperor Justinian in the Sixth Century BC were famous western law codes in ancient times. The term "codification" was invented, or at least introduced into Britain, by the British political jurist Jeremy Bentham, who believed that codes of law should be complete and comprehensive, and may not be supplemented or revised unless through legislative procedure. Bentham had advocated codification of law and called for legislative reform, but received no response. As a result, Britain had made no progress in the codification of law during Bentham's lifetime. It was only after Bentham's death in the late 19th Century that some parts of traditional common law were codify, namely turned into statutory laws, for example, the Bills of Exchange Act (1882) and Sale of Goods Act (1893). During the same period, Justice Westbury tried to compile the Collection of Laws of Great Britain and appointed a Royal Committee in 1866 to examine the role of compilations of laws. However, the report submitted by the Committee in 1867 led to the abortion of the compilation plan. Later, Sir James F. Stephen draft the Code of Evidence, but the draft code was shelved after only the first reading in the Parliament. In 1879 he also drafted the Criminal Code and Criminal Procedure Code, the latter was submitted to the Parliament, but also met with the fate of being shelved. In 1965, the Law Committee was appointed with the task of codification of laws but had achieved no substantive progress. The French comparative jurist Rene David pointed out in his book English Law and French Law: A Comparison in Substance that there are many compilations of laws and decrees in UK that cover a whole branch of law. At the first look, their structure is not different from that of codes. However, "the English statutory law consists of countless individual laws, decrees and regulations adopted by the Parliament in the past 500 years that are contradictory to each other."[57] Meanwhile, the case law developed by courts had already become a deep-rooted tradition in UK. This historical background, interwoven with other conditions, had determined that the codification of law in UK was a very difficult one.

In France and other continental European countries and in the US, codification of law had gained popularity. In the end of the 17th and in the 18th centuries, France had adopted a series of ordinances, each of them the codification of a branch of law. They included the 1667 Ordinance on the Reform of Civil Procedure, which was in essence a civil procedure code, the 1670 Ordinance on Criminal Procedure, the 1673 Commercial Ordinance, and the 1681 Maritime Ordinance. After the breakout of the French Revolution, there had been a widespread demand for eliminating the phenomenon of disorder and unsystematic local customs and laws, and for promoting national unity through the establishment of a national legal system. In 1800, Napoleon appointed a committee consisting of four jurists to be responsible for the drafting of the Civil Code, which was promulgated in 1804. Later, the committee had also

---

[57]Marx and Engels (1956, p. 702).

compiled the Civil Procedure Code, the Commercial Code, the Criminal Code and Criminal Procedure Code.

In Germany, Anton Friedrich Justus Thibaut published an essay entitled On the Necessity of a National Code for Germany in 1814, advocating the adoption of a code covering the civil law, the criminal law and the procedural law and applicable in all parts of Germany. However, Friedrich Carl von Savigny was strongly opposed to the codification of laws in Germany, maintaining that the development of law should take the inherent strength of national spirit as its basis. Finally, the German Empire adopted the Civil Code in 1896 and the Code came into force on January 1, 1900. Apart from Germany, other continental European countries had also followed the example of France in adopting the civil code. They included: Austria (1810), the Netherlands (1818), Italy (1865), Portugal (1867), Spain (1889), Switzerland (1898/1907) and Greece (1940). Non-European countries that had adopted civil code included: Turkey (1869/1876), Egypt (1875/1881), Iran (1927/1935) and Japan (1898).

Codification is an important indicator of the level of the rule of law civilization, especially legislative civilization, in statutory law countries. It is also an inevitable requirement of democratic, scientific and high-quality legislation and the improvement of socialist legal system with Chinese characteristics. Currently, the level of codification of law in China is still very low, many basic codes, such as civil code, commercial code, administrative code, administrative procedure code, social code, economic code, intellectual property code, human rights code, and military code, have not yet been adopted. Without doubt, the large-scale review and cleanup of laws at the previous stage has created a good condition for the codification of law. However, review and cleanup of law itself does not necessarily lead to the codification of law, but is only a basic, initial preparatory work for the codification.

In the codification of basic laws, China should attach importance to the following conditions or factors:

Firstly, whether the economic and social relations to be adjusted by the codes have already been stabilized. If the large-scale reform of economic, social and cultural institutions in China has not yet been completed and economic and social relations are in a condition of constant change, the stability and authority of codification cannot be guaranteed. Therefore, the relative stability of objects of adjustment is a precondition of codification.

Secondly, the legislation in the field to be adjusted by a code should be basically complete. This is the basis as well as the precondition of codification of laws. A major gap or insufficiency in the relevant legislation will bring great difficulties to the codification of law.

Thirdly, the legal theories, legislative ideas, and legislative techniques needed for the codification must be basically mature and in place so as to provide scientific and mature theoretical support to codification.

Fourthly, in order to carry out codification, China must have corresponding accumulation of legislative techniques and experiences. The cleanup of laws plays an important role as the basis and precondition of codification, but it does not necessarily lead to codification of law, which has higher demand and is more difficult than the cleanup of laws.

3.4.6 Promoting the Institutionalization and Normalization of Cleanup of Laws

The so-called cleanup of law means the systematic review by competent authorities of current laws to determine which are still applicable, which need to be supplemented or revised, and which need to be abolished. Cleanup of laws is an important means by which the state coordinates and harmonizes various parts of the legal system. Because cleanup of law is of the nature of legislation, only organs that have the power to adopt laws and administrative regulations or the organs authorized by these organs have the competence to cleanup current laws and administrative regulations.

Since the founding of the New China, the Chinese government has attached importance to the work of cleanup of laws. As early as in January 1955, Zhou Enlai pointed out at an executive meeting of the State Council that: "It is an important work to carry out a timely cleanup of the various laws and regulations promulgated by the former Government Administration Council and various organs under it and to establish a procedure for the regular complication of laws and regulations on the basis of cleanup of current laws and regulations."[58] In 1956, in accordance with the decision of the meeting and Zhou Enlai's instruction, the former Legislative Affairs Bureau of the State Council, with the support of various departments under it, carried out an initial cleanup of the 250 pieces of laws and regulations promulgated or approved by the former Government Administration Council. The results of this cleanup can be divided into the following five categories: (1) 42 pieces of laws and regulations that were still applicable, including those that were still applicable but a few of their provisions needed to be revised in the future; (2) 64 pieces of laws and regulations that were still applicable be must be revised; (3) 55 pieces of laws and regulations that needed to be reformulated or merged. Most of these laws and regulations had basic principles that were no longer compatible with current conditions and policies and therefore needed to be replaced with new ones. In some cases, different laws and regulations had conflicting provisions on the same issue and they needed to be replaced by a unified law or regulations. (4) 42 outdated laws and regulations; and (5) 47 laws and regulations that had already been specifically abolished or naturally lost their validated as a result of the abolition or change of a certain institutions or organizations. In 1980, Mr. Peng Zhen, the Vice Chairman of the NPC Standing Committee, discussed the cleanup of the 1500 pieces of laws, decrees and relevant provisions promulgated by the New China before 1980 at the fifteenth meeting of the Standing Committee of the Fifth NPC.[59] Although he did not use the term "cleanup", but the term "review", but the effect was the same. At the meeting, Mr. Peng said that the laws and degrees adopted since the establishment of the People's Republic of China, with the exception of those that are contradictory to the Constitution, laws, or decrees adopted by the Fifth NPC and its Standing Committee, continue to be valid. During the 17 years after the establishment of the People's Republic, China

---

[58]The Bulletin of the State Council of the People's Republic of China, No. 5.
[59]Peng (1980).

has adopted over 1500 laws, decrees and administrative regulations, many of them are still applicable or basically applicable today. Under the condition of heavy legislative task and lack of resources, reaffirming the validity of the existing laws and regulations enables us to concentrate our efforts on the adoption of laws and regulations that are urgently needed, especially economic laws and regulations. This was an important measure for improving the socialist legal system. The laws, decrees and administrative regulations adopted in the past can be divided into three categories: First, those that have already completed its historical mission and naturally lost their validity as a result of historical development, such as the Land Reform Law and the Interim Regulations on Private Enterprises. Some of those laws have already been replaced by new laws. For example, the 1953 Election Law and the 1954 Organic Law of People's Courts and Organic Law of People's Procuratorates have already been replaced by the corresponding laws adopted at the Second Session of the Fifth NPC. Second, those which are still applicable or basically applicable but need minor revisions or supplementations. There are many examples of such laws and regulations, such as the Regulations on Administrative Penalties for Public Security, Decision of the State Council on Issues concerning Reeducation through Labor, the Interim Provisions of the State Council on Awarding and Punishment of Personnel in State Administrative Organs, and Organic Regulations of Urban Residents' Committees. Third, those which need to be fundamentally revised or abolished. The number of such laws and regulations are small. The questions of which laws and regulations are still applicable and which need to be revised or supplemented should be decided on the basis of extensive investigation and research and in light of the actual situation in the country. Currently the NPC, the State Council and various organs under them are reviewing and cleaning up laws and regulations in accordance with this spirit. Carrying out the necessary cleanup of existing laws and regulations to determine which of them are still applicable and which need to be revised or abolished is of great significance as it lays the foundation for the work of large-scale legislation.

At the end of 1987, the Legislative Affairs Commission of the NPC Standing Committee carried out a review and cleanup of the laws (including decisions concerning legal issues) adopted by the NPC and its Standing Committee before the end of 1978. Among the 134 laws reviewed, 111 had already become invalid and 23 were still effective or still effective but under revision. Besides, by the end of 1978, the NPC Standing Committee had approved 48 organic regulations of people's congresses and people's committees of national autonomous areas. After the adoption of the 1982 Constitution, the Organic Law of People's Congress and People's Governments at Various Levels, and the Law on Regional National Autonomy, various regional national areas had adopted or were in the process of formulating regulations on the exercise of autonomy and the above-mentioned organic regulations had lost their effect as a result of the change of situation.

Moreover, between 1984 and the beginning of 1987, the former Legislative Affairs Bureau of the General Office of the State Council and the Legislative Affairs Bureau of the State Council, in accordance with the unified arrangement of the State Council, organized the various departments under the State Council to carry out a complete and systematic cleanup of the 3298 pieces of administrative regulations promulgated or approved by the State Council (or the former Government Administrative Council) between October 1949 and the end of 1984. Among the 3298 administrative regulations, 442 were found not to meet the criteria of administrative regulations and therefore treated no longer as administrative regulations, but as ordinary documents. The remaining 2856 pieces of administrative regulations were divided into the following four categories: (1) Those that have been specifically abolished or declared invalid by the State Council. There were a total of 1604 pieces of administrative regulations in this category, including 446 that had been replaced by new regulations or were contradictory to the current administrative policies or law and 1158 that had lost legal effect as a result of expiration of their time periods of application or the disappearance of the objects regulated by them. (2) Those that needed major revision. There were a total of 279 pieces of regulation in this category. They had been gradually listed into the legislative plans of the relevant departments under the State Council for revision or redrafting. (3) Those that continued to be valid. There were 661 pieces of regulations in this category. They included those all the provisions of which were still applicable and those the basic principles and most provisions of which were still applicable, but only a few individual provisions of which were problematic and needed interpretation before they could be applicable again. These regulations, together with the 96 effective administrative regulations promulgated by the State Council in 1985, were later classified by type and compiled into different volumes of the Compilation of the Current Administrative Regulations of the People's Republic of China, which was and published both in China and abroad. (4) Currently effective internally implemented or secretly issued regulations. There were 312 pieces of regulations in this category. Because these regulations had confidential content in the fields of military affairs, foreign trade and foreign affairs, they were compiled into internal documents and applied only by the relevant personnel. Meanwhile, the various departments under the State Council and the people's governments of various provinces, autonomous regions and municipalities under the Central Government had also carried out cleanup of tens of thousands of departmental and local rules and regulations.

Cleanup of laws is an important technical means of improving the legal system in China. On March 10, 2011, Mr. Wu Bangguo, Chairman of NPC Standing Committee, stated in a work report of the Committee that the problems of maladjustment, incongruity and incompatibility also existed in currently effective laws and regulations in China. For this reason, the relevant legislative organs in China, on the basis of the cleanup work in 2009, carried out a cleanup of current laws and regulations under the supervision and guidance of the NPC Standing Committee in 2010. The State Council and local people's congresses attached high importance to the cleanup of laws and regulations and carried out cleanup within their respective scope of competence. By the end of 2010, they had revised a total of 107 administrative regulations and 1417 local regulations, and abolished seven administrative regulations and 455 local regulations, thereby completing the cleanup of administrative regulations and ensuring the formation on schedule of the socialist legal system with Chinese characteristics by 2010.

The comprehensive cleanup of the current system of law organized by the NPC Standing Committee is a very important measure for improving the legal system and advancing the rule of law in China. Every cleanup of laws and improvement of the legal system is carried out for the purpose of adapting the laws and the legal system to the economic and social conditions at a certain stage of development. It is a legislative measure for enabling the legal system to better adapt itself to economic and social development.

In June 2009, the Chairman of the NPC Standing Committee put forward a bill on the cleanup of laws, proposing the abolition of eight laws and the revision of 141 provisions in 59 laws: "This cleanup is focused on the legal provisions adopted in the early years of the New China and during the early period of reform and opening up, which are apparently no longer compatible with economic and social development, and on the prominent problem of obvious inconsistency and incongruity between different laws. It is mainly aimed at solving the inherent problems in laws." As far as technique is concerned, this cleanup mainly adopted the method of "packaging" in dealing with laws that needed revision, namely "solving the problem of the revision of 59 laws with the adoption of one law". Of course, this was not the largest scale cleanup of laws since the establishment of the New China. Nevertheless it was the largest one since the beginning of the new century.

The purpose of cleanup of laws is to provide technical and institutional safeguards for the construction and improvement of the socialist legal system with Chinese characteristics. Whenever economic, political and cultural development enters into a new stage or reaches a turning point, it will raise new demands on the improvement of the existing legal system. On the other hand, a cleanup also needs to be carried out if it is found out that certain laws and administrative regulations at certain stage of implementation are no longer compatible with actual situation or economic and social development. In the legislative process, legislators limited by their foresight and technical means, are unable to foresee various problems, especially some new situations and problems that would emerge in the process of social development and as a result of the tension between limited legislative foresight and ever-changing situation of economic and social development, a cleanup of law is needed from time to time to adapt the legal system to economic and social development.

The key to the cleanup of laws is the cleanup of higher-level laws, which have widespread impact and high legal effect. Therefore, the improvement of lower-level laws should be driven by the revision of high-level laws. From perspectives of the content and branches of law, highlight should be given to the following three key aspects: first, laws and legal norms relating to state institutions and the operation of public powers; second, institutions, procedures and legal norms relating to respecting and safeguarding human rights; and third, legal norms relating to coordinated economic and social development.

In the process of cleanup of laws, it is necessary to establish relevant standards, procedures and competences. After the cleanup, the Legislative Affairs Commission of NPC Standing Committee or the NPC Law Committee should study the opinions of all sides on the cleanup and form a document on the results of the cleanup. Further study still needs to be carried out as to whether the results of the cleanup should be submitted to the NPC Standing Committee or the NPC itself for decision, or send to the organs that have adopted the laws or regulations for review and confirmation, or whether the NPC Standing Committee should be authorized to carry out review of all the results and adopt a bill on the cleanup.

In particular, the cleanup of laws should be institutionalized and normalized. Since China has not yet established a comprehensive constitutional review mechanism, it is very difficult to timely discover and effectively rectify contradictions, conflicts, inconsistency and defects in the legal system through daily law enforcement and judicial activities. As a result, carrying out "campaign-style" or "package" cleanup of laws from time to time is of great importance to the improvement of the legal system. However, because the concentrated cleanup of the legal system is often faced with such problems as tight schedule, heavy task and difficulties in finding out the problems, there will often be "fish escaping from the net" in the cleanup. For example, the Procurator General of the Supreme People's Procuratorate pointed at a NPC Session in 2011 that "Even today, the Organic Law of People's Procuratorates still contains provisions on cracking down on counterrevolutionaries, which are apparently incompatible with the current situation of economic and social development, reform and opening up, as well as with the current legal requirements. Because as early as in the revision of the Criminal Law in 1997, the crime of counterrevolution was changed into the crime of endangering national security; and the 1999 Amendment to the Constitution also changed the term 'counterrevolution' to 'endangering national security'". There are many other such examples. Under the current system, an effective way of preventing and resolving such problems is to institutionalize and normalize the cleanup of laws. More specifically, the following approaches can be considered: firstly, every bill on the adoption of a new law or revision of an existing law should attach a detailed list of all the other laws and regulations that will be affected by the adoption or revision of the law and, as a result, also need to be revised or adjusted. The list shall be taken as reference for legislators in the deliberation of or vote on the bill; secondly, legislative organs should include a report on the cleanup of laws and regulations in the previous year in their annual work reports to people's congresses; thirdly, the Supreme People's Court and the Supreme People's Procuratorate should include a report on the cleanup of the legal system in their annual work reports to the NPC; and fourthly, China should implement the system of "open door cleanup of laws", and encourage citizens, the mass media and people from all walks of life to report to legislative organs the laws and regulations that need cleanup and put forward suggestions on cleanup.

References

A deputy to the NPC talks about his personal experience in the debate on the reform of the individual income tax, saying it was remarkable that the tax exemption threshold was raised by 500 yuan in three days. Yangzi River Daily, 11 July 2011

Biwu D (1985) On the question of new democratic political power (speech given at the seminar on people's political power on October 10, 1948). In Biwu D (ed) Selected works of Dong Biwu. People's Publishing House, Beijing

Biwu D (ed) (2001) Editorial Group for Collected legal works of Dong Biwu. Law Press China, Beijing

Bonfante P (1992) A textbook on Roman Law. Chinese edition (trans: Huang F). China University of Political Science and Law Press, Beijing

Coicoud J-C (2002) "Preface", Légitimité et Politique. Chinese edition (trans: Tong X and Wang Y). Central Compilation and Translation Press, Beijing

Deng X (1975–1982) Neither democracy nor the legal system should be weakened. In: Selected works of Deng Xiaoping, vol II. People's Publishing House, Beijing, pp 146–147

Editorial Department for Law Teaching Materials (1982) Basic theory of legal science. Law Press China, Beijing

Encyclopedia of China Publishing House (1984) Encyclopedia of China: law science. Encyclopedia of China Publishing House, Beijing

Gu A (2006) Legislative note. A review of the process of the making of some laws in China (1982–2004). Law Press China, Beijing

Gu A (2008) A witness to the thirty-years' legislation in China since the reform and opening up. Law Press China, Beijing

Gu A (2009) A retrospect of my experience of carrying out legislative work. Law Press China, Beijing

Han Y, Zhaoru C (eds) (1981) Selected legal documents adopted in revolutionary areas during the period of new democratic revolution in China, vol 1–2. China Social Sciences Publishing House, Beijing

Hengshan STZ (2003) On the exercise of the ruling power by the Communist Party of China in accordance with Law. Soc Sci China 1

Information Office of the State Council (2008) China's Efforts and achievements in promoting the rule of law, February 28

Jintao H (2007) Hold high the great banner of socialism with Chinese characteristics and strive for new victories in building a moderately prosperous society in all respects, report to the Seventeenth National Congress of the Communist Party of China on October 15

Law Press China (2002) Construction of democracy and the legal system in the People's Republic of China. Law Press China, Beijing

Lazarev BB (1999) General theory of law and state. Chinese edition (trans: Wang Z et al). Law Press China, Beijing

Lenin VI (1959) Complete works of Lenin, vol 36. Chinese edition. People's Publishing House, Beijing

Li P (ed) (1991) Theory and practice of socialist legislation in China. China Legal System Publishing House, Beijing

Li B (ed) (2000) Jurisprudence. Economic Science Press, Beijing

Li P (2003) Work report of the NPC Standing Committee Given at the First Session of the Tenth NPC

Maine H (1959) Ancient law. Chinese edition (trans: Shen J). The Commercial Press, Beijing

Mao Z (1964) New-Democratic Constitutional Government. In: Selected works of Mao Zedong. People's Publishing House, Beijing

Mao Z (1977) Selected works of Mao Zedong, vol 5. People's Publishing House, Beijing

Marx C, Engels F (1956) Complete works of Marx and Engels, vol. 1. Chinese edition. People's Publishing House, Beijing, p 702

Marx C, Engels F (1958) Complete works of Marx and Engels, vol 4. Chinese edition. People's Publishing House, Beijing

Peng Z (1980) Work report of the standing committee of the Fifth National People's Congress People's Republic of China

Peng C (1993) Work report of the Standing Committee of the Eighth National People's Congress of the People's Republic of China

Raz J (2003) The concept of a legal system. Chinese edition (trans: Wu Y). China Legal System Publishing House, Beijing

Secretariat of the Second Session of the First National People's Congress of the People's Republic of China (ed) (1955) The proceedings of the second session of the First National People's Congress of the People's Republic of China. People's Publishing House, Mao

The Code Napoleon (The French Civil Code) (1979) Chinese edition (trans: Li Haopei et al). The Commercial Press, Beijing

Tian J (1996) Work report of the NPC Standing Committee to the Fourth Session of the Eighth National People's Congress

Tian J (1998) Work Report of the NPC Standing Committee to the First Session of the of the Ninth National People's Congress

von Hayek FA (2000) Law, legislation and liberty, vol 1. Chinese edition (trans. Zhenglai D et al). China Encyclopedia Publishing House, Beijing

Wang Q (2003) Studies on legislative hearing. Peking University Press, Beijing

Wang L, Liu B (2008) An authoritative interpretation of the Fifth Legislative Plan of the Standing Committee of the Eleventh National People's Congress. The Procuratorate Daily

Wu D, Ren Y (1984) A brief introduction to Debates over the system of law in the Soviet Jurisprudential Circle. In Zhang Y et al (eds) A collection of theses on jurisprudence. Mass Publishing House, Beijing, p 287

Wu D, Zongling S (eds) (1987) Basic theory of socialist law. Law Press China, Beijing

Wu D et al (1984) Issues relating to socialist legislation in China. Masses Publishing House, Beijing

Yang J (2003) The legislative system, legal system and legislative principles in China, a lecture given to the Standing Committee of the Tenth NPC on April 25

Zane JM (2002) The story of law. Chinese edition (trans: Sun Y). China Braille Publishing House, Beijing

Zhang C (2000) An introduction to the legislation law of the People's Republic of China. Law Press China, Beijing

Zhang Y et al (1984) Collected theses on jurisprudence. Masses Publishing House, Beijing

Zhu W (2010) The quality of legislation determines the quality of the rule of law. People's Daily

Zweigert K (1992) Introduction to comparative law. Chinese edition (trans: Pan H et al). Guizhou People's Publishing House, Guiyang

Chapter 4
Contemporary Chinese Model of the Rule of Law from the Perspective of Comparative Law

One of the important reasons for the significant development of the rule of law and the legal research in China since the reform and opening up in 1978 is the rapid popularization and extensive application of comparative law. The application of such methods of comparative law as "seeking commonness among differences" and "seeking differences among commonness", whether in the fields of legislation, law enforcement, administrative of justice or legal supervision, has provided China with broader vision, deeper understanding, more choices and more effective reference in the construction of the rule of law and legal research, and given it wings for the take-off of the modernization of the legal system in China. During the 20 years of reform and opening up, China has emphasized the research on, study of, and borrowing from the common law system and the continental law system in the construction of the rule of law and legal research. In the 21st Century, with the continuous deepening of the reform and expansion of the opening up, legal research in China needs to have more globalized and diversified vision and perspective, break away from the set pattern of the mainstream legal culture and rule of law mode of the common law system and continental law system, extensively learn from other more globalized and diversified rule of law models, civilizations and experiences, so as to advance in a comprehensive way the development of the rule of law civilization in China.

4.1 A Discussion on the "China Model" and "China Model of Rule of Law"

4.1.1 Different Opinions on the "China Model"

From the perspective foreign academic circles, the "China Model" is relative to European-American Model, the Soviet Model, and the Latin American Model, and usually used as a summarization of the Chinese experience of development. Some

© China Social Sciences Press and Springer Nature Singapore Pte Ltd. 2018
L. Li, *The Chinese Road of the Rule of Law*, China Insights,
https://doi.org/10.1007/978-981-10-8965-7_4

Chinese scholars hold that the "China Model" was first put forward by Mr. Joshua Cooper Ramo, a senior editor of the Time magazine in his article The Beijing Consensus: The "China Model", published in May 2004. Actually, Deng Xiaoping had repeated mentioned the China Model as early as in the 1980s. For example, Deng pointed out in May 1980 that "The Chinese revolution was carried out not by adopting the model of the Russian October Revolution but by proceeding from the realities in China, by using the rural areas to encircle the cities and seizing power with armed force. Since the Chinese revolution succeeded by integrating the universal principles of Marxism with the concrete practice of China, we should not demand that other developing countries, let alone the developed capitalist countries, adopt our model in making revolution."[1] In May 1988, Deng Xiaoping further pointed out that: "It is impossible to solve all the problems in the world with only one model. Just as China has its own model, Mozambique must also find its own model."[2]

What is the "China Model"? In the eyes of some foreign scholars, the China Model has the following characteristics: first, originality. It is independently created by China on the basis of his own national conditions and it is a "practical model" for solving the economic problems in China. Second, progressive or incremental reform. "It adopts a step-by-step, explorative, and accumulative method to carry out reform in a progressive way that proceeds from the easy to the difficult and assimilates all the excellent thoughts and experiences in the process". Third, affinity to the people. It is aimed at realizing the interests of the greatest majority of people. And fourth, stability. It means strong government dominance and political stability.

In the opinion of some Chinese scholars, the "Chinese model" is different from either the Soviet model or the social development model of western developed countries, but has its own prominent institutional characteristics: China implements not a system of full privatization, but a system of mixed ownership, which is dominated by the economy of public ownership and allows diverse forms of ownership to develop side by side; although China has introduced the market economic system, the extent of adjustment and intervention by the government is must large than that in the western countries; with respect to the political party system, China does not implement the two-party or multiparty system, but adheres to the system of one-Party leadership by the CPC. Nevertheless, it is not a "one-party political system", but a political system of "single party leadership and multi party co-operation"; China implements the people's congress system and the system of democratic centralism, rather than the system of parliamentary politics, the system of separation of three powers, or the bicameral system; it implements the socialist system in the Mainland, but allows Hong Kong, Macao and Taiwan to implement the capitalist system; although China allow the existence of different schools of thought, it always adheres to the dominant position of Marxism in the ideological field, thereby leading to the situation of coexistence of the monism of political ideology and pluralism of social ideological trend.

---

[1]Deng (1994, p. 318).
[2]Deng (1993, p. 261).

Although the concept of the "China model" is recognized and used by many foreign scholars, it is denied by some others. For example, Professor Thomas Heberer, Director of Political Institute/Institute of East Asian Studies of University of Duisburg-Essen in Germany, pointed out that, since "China is in a period of transitional from planned economy to market economy, I do not believe that there exists a so-called China model. This transitional period will be accompanied by drastic social transformation and political reform and this process is gradual and incremental. Under such a condition, it is still too early to talk about Chinese Model". Meanwhile, he also admitted that "China's development process has its distinctive, even unique, characteristics."[3] Professor Arif Dirlik, a China expert at University of Oregon, held that "the China Model is only an idea, rather than a concept or thought, because it does not have much close relationship with the latter. The simple accumulation of mutual or common understandings does not necessarily constitute a consensus."

Many other foreign scholars are also opposed to the so-called "China Model" because, in their opinion, the reason for China's success is exactly the absence of any "model". The concept of "China Model" masks the most important reason of China's economic success, namely the seizure of opportunities. The method of reform is perhaps more interesting than actual policies in China. If there is really an experience, it is the correct attitude towards reform and opening up, namely seeking truth from fact.

Some Chinese scholars are also opposed to the concept of the "China Model", arguing that the term "model" has the meaning of setting an example for others, which China has no intention of doing.[4] They explain that: "The relevant systems in China have not been finalized and are still under exploration. Talking about the "China Model" under this circumstance has the effect of finalizing the existing systems, which is both incompatible with the fact and dangerous."[5] They prefer to replace the "China Model" with "the China Case" or "Chinese characteristics". The reasons for the skepticism or negation of the concept of "China Model" are very complicated. They mainly include the followings: firstly, China has suffered greatly from "models" in the past. After the establishment of the People's Republic, China had blindly copied the "Stalin Model" from the Soviet Union. As a result, it has met with difficulties and made mistakes in the construction of the country. The reform carried out after 1978 was mainly aimed at remedying the defects in the Soviet socialist model. Secondly, the concept of "China Model" was first put forward by foreign scholars, whose interpretations of the model are affected by their motivations (for example, using this concept to advocate the "Theory of China Threat"). This, combined with the differences in cultural background, has inevitably led to biased explanations by foreign scholars of the "China Model", which are not accepted by Chinese scholars. Thirdly, there has been a worry among Chinese scholars that too much publicity of the "China Model" will offend other countries, affect China's foreign relations, and

---

[3] Heberer (2005).
[4] Zhao (2009).
[5] Li (2009).

damage its international image. And fourthly, some people believe that the "China Model" is still in the process of formation and development and faced with many challenges. Therefore, it is still too early to talk about the "China Model".

4.1.2 The "China Model of the Rule of Law"

Since the establishment of the People's Republic, especially since the implementation of the policy of reform and opening up in 1978, China has made huge achievements in the construction of the rule of law and ruling the country by law. It is an undisputed fact that the rule of law has played an important role in guiding, regulating and safeguarding the reform of the economic, social, political, cultural, health and educational systems in China. With the disputed "formation" of the "China Model", the issue of the "China Model of the Rule of Law" has also gradually emerged. Influenced by different opinions on the "China Model" in the theoretical circle, Chinese scholars has not been able to carry out extensive and in-depth discussion or publish much research results on the "China Model of the Rule of Law". In the discussions that have already been carried out, the following three opinions have been put forward:

According to the first opinion, China has found out through exploration a road to the development of the rule of law compatible with its own national conditions, accumulated positive and negative experiences, put forward and implemented the basic state policy of ruling the country by law, and realized the intended objectives of construction of the rule of law at the current stage. Therefore, the "China Model of the Rule of Law" has already taken form.

According to the second opinion, although China has made huge achievements in constructing the rule of law and ruling the country by law and accumulated the experiences of and created a road to the development of a system of the rule of law compatible with national conditions, it is still too early to judge whether these experiences and this road constitute the "China Model of the Rule of Law". More cautious observations need to be made before such a conclusion can be made.

According to the third opinion, China has implemented the state policy of ruling the country by law for only ten years and the constructed the rule of law for only 30 years. Many basic problems (such as those relating to judicial independence, equality before the law, presumption of innocence, and the standardization and predictability of law) still have not yet solved, and the system of the rule of law in China is still in the process of development and evolution and, therefore, far from being finalized. Under this circumstance, the formation of the "China Model of the Rule of Law" is out of the question.

From the above we can see that today it is still too early to declare the formation of the "China Model" or the "China Model of the Rule of Law". However, from the perspectives of the actual functions of the rule of law and the achievement made by China in the implementation of the state policy of ruling the country by law, it seems that the concept or the term of "China Model of the Rule of Law" can be used to describe the phenomenon of the construction and development of the rule of law in China or the understanding of the current situation of ruling the country by law in China in the communication and exchange between China and foreign scholars.

4.2   Historical Origins of the Contemporary "China Model of the Rule of Law"

China is an ancient country with a 5000-year-old civilized history and a long-standing and well-established legal system. The customary law of slavery system emerged in China as early as in the 21st century BC. The first statutory law was adopted and a systematic code of law emerged in China during the Spring and Autumn Period (770–221 BC). In the Tang Dynasty (618–907 AD), China had developed a relatively complete feudal law code, which had been inherited and developed by succeeding feudal dynasties. The Chinese legal system had become a distinctive legal system in the world and ancient China had made important contribution to world legal civilization. After the Opium War in 1840, China had gradually been reduced to a semi-colony and semi-feudal society. To Change the miserable fate of the state and the nation, some people with lofty ideals tried to transplant the rule of law model of modern western countries into China. However, their efforts ultimately failed because of various historical reasons.

The establishment of the PRC in 1949 opened a new era in the construction of the rule of law in China. In the beginning of reform and opening up in 1978, China had established the principle of "developing socialist democracy and perfecting socialist legal system" and adopted the sixteen-character guideline for the construction of the legal system, namely: "There must be laws to go by, the laws must be observed and strictly enforced, and lawbreakers must be prosecuted." In the first 30 years of reform and opening up, the emphasis and priority of the construction of the rule of law was to adopt a large amount of laws and regulations and establish a socialist legal system with Chinese characteristics, so as to solve the problem of "having no law to go by". In 1997, China established "ruling the country by law" as a basic strategy of state governance and "construction of a socialist state under the rule of law" as one of the important objectives of socialist modernization. In 1999, China enshrined the objective of "ruling the country by law and constructing a state under the rule of law" into the Constitution, thereby opening a new chapter in the construction of the rule of law in China. After entering into the 21st Century, China has continued to advance with and made remarkable achievements in the construction of the rule of law. Especially after the Eighteenth CPC Congress in 2012, China has put forward a series of new objectives of and new demands on the construction of a law-based country, including comprehensively advancing the rule of law, speeding up the construction of a socialist state under the rule of law, adhering to the principles of scientific legislation, strict law enforcement, impartial administration of justice, observing the law by all citizens, adhering to the integrated construction of a law-based state, a law-based government and a law-based society, simultaneously promoting governance by law, exercise of the ruling power by law, and administration by law, respecting and safeguarding human rights, upholding the authority of the Constitution and laws, deepening in a comprehensive way the reform of administrative law enforcement system and the judicial system, and constructing a country under the rule of law… The above ideas, demands and reform measures have summarized the basic Chinese experience of construction of the rule of law, laid out the road map of the future development of the rule of law in China, and contributed to the gradual formation of a Chinese model of construction of the rule of law.

The contemporary "China model of rule of law" is not a groundless conjecture or a castle in the air, but has gradually formed and developed on the basis of inheriting and drawing on the achievements of the development of the rule of law civilization, both ancient and modern, Chinese and foreign. Before 1958, China had mainly borrowed from and transplanted the relevant contents of the socialist model of legal system from the Soviet Union. Since the reform and opening up in 1978, especially since the 1990s, China has mainly drawn on the rule of law models and legal systems of US, UK, Germany, France, Japan and other western countries. Generally speaking, the contemporary "China model of the rule of law" originated from the following four historical sources:

First, the influence of the Soviet model of socialist legal system. Mao Zedong said that: "The Russian October Revolution helped progressive intellectuals in China, as throughout the world, to adopt the proletarian world outlook as the instrument for studying a nation's destiny and considering anew their own problems. Follow the path of the Russians—that was their conclusion."[6] The adoption of the Soviet ideology and state system means the wholesale acceptance of the Soviet models, including the Soviet model of legal system.

In 1931 the CPC established the political and legal systems of Chinese Soviet Republic, which were mainly copied from the Soviet Union. A series of laws and regulations promulgated by the Chinese Soviet Republic, including the Outline of Constitution, the Regulations on Marriage, the Organic Law of the Government, the Organic Law of the Central Government, the Organic of Local Governments, the Election Law, the Interim Organic Regulations of Military Tribunals, the Interim Procedures for Dealing with Cases of Counterrevolution and the Establishment of Judicial Organs, and Interim Organic Regulations of Department of Adjudication, had laid the legal foundation for the establishment of the Chinese Soviet political power and the formation of its legal system. The content of many of these laws and regulations were introduced from the Soviet Union by Liang Botai[7] and others.

---

[6]Mao (1991, p. 1472).

[7]Liang Botai (1899–1935) joined the China Socialist Youth League in 1920, began his study at the Communist University of the Toilers of the East in Moscow in 1922 and became a member of the CPC in the same year. He went to work in Vladivostok in 1924, becoming a judge in the Court of Khabarovsk and devoting himself to legal research and judicial work. After coming back to China from the Soviet Union in 1931, he worked in the Soviet Government of Western Fujian Province as the director of Political Security Bureau and elected a member of Central Executive Committee of the first and second "National Soviet Congress". He was appointed Vice Chairman of People's Judicial Committee in April 1933, Vice Chairman of the People's Committee on Internal Affairs

Since the establishing of the PRC, China had adopted the polices of "inviting in", "going out" and "leaning on one side" to comprehensively transplant the Soviet model of legal system. For example, the 1954 Constitution was basically drafted with the 1936 Soviet Constitution as the blue print. In a report on the Draft of the 1954 Constitution, Liu Shaoqi pointed out that, in the drafting of the Constitution, China has drawn on different versions of the Soviet Constitution and the constitutions of different people's democratic countries. Apparently, the experiences of the Soviet Union and other advanced socialist countries were of great help to China. The Draft Chinese Constitution integrated the Chinese and international experiences. A comparison between the 1954 Constitution and the 1936 Constitution of the Soviet Union shows that the two constitutions were very similar in terms of constitutional system, constitutional provisions, and the system of political power.

In the field of legislation, China had introduced a large number of legal institutions from the Soviet Union, attached importance to the making of land law, marriage law, and criminal law, and accepted the concept of economic law. For example, unlike most other countries in the world, which divide the legal system into public law, private law and social law, China, influenced by the Soviet Union, refused to take the public or private nature of laws as the criterion for the division of the legal system, but accepted the Soviet model and adjusted it in light of its own national conditions. Currently, the socialist legal system with Chinese characteristics is divided into seven branches of law: the Constitution and other constitutional laws, civil and commercial law, administrative law, economic law, social law, criminal law, and litigious and non-litigious procedure law.

In the judicial field, the judicial systems in China, such as those relating to the setup of courts, relationship between higher and lower courts, people's assessors, the organization of trial, principles of criminal trial, and trial procedure, had all been transplanted from the Soviet Union. The system of independent procuratorial organs with the functions and powers of legal supervision was completely copied from the Soviet Union. The socialist legal theory, the model of legal system, and the system of law of the Soviet Union became very important sources of the legal system in the New China.[8] In the early years of the People's Republic, China had basically taken the road of "wholesale Sovietization" and the Soviet model of legal system became the most important historical source of the Chinese legal system.

Second, the experience of construction of the legal system gained by the CPC in the process of leading the Chinese people to establish the people's political power. The experiences continuously accumulated by the CPC in the process of constructing the people's democratic political power and the legal system by proceeding from the national conditions, the Chinese practice and the central tasks of the state and by drawing on the Soviet model of legal system were the main historical source and

---

in July 1933, and Vice Chairman of the Central People's Judicial Committee and a chief justice of the Supreme Court in February 1934. He had tried a series of important criminal cases during the period of the Soviet Areas, thereby contributing to the construction of the legal system in Soviet areas. In March 1935, he was arrested and executed by the Kuomintang Government in March 1935 after being wounded while leading his army to get through the enemy line.

[8] See He (2002).

practical basis of the Chinese legal system, where many principles, institutions and practices of the contemporary "China model of the rule of law" have originated. Many of the unique institutional designs and judicial principles in the current legal system in China, such as the public trial system, the circuit court system, the principle of attaching importance to evidence and procedure, and the mediation system, have all originated from the legal system of the Chinese Soviet Republic. The "Ma Xiwu Trial Mode" and the practice and principle of supplementing trial with mediation during the War of Resistance against Japanese Aggression had exerted important influence on the construction of the legal system in New China and become an important source of the "rule of law model" of contemporary China.

The "Ma Xiwu Trial Mode" is a trial mode named after the President of the Higher Court of Shaanxi-Gansu-Ningxia Border Region during the period of War of Resistance against Japanese Aggression. Its main content includes simplification of litigation procedure, implementation of the system of circuit trial and on-the-spot trial of cases. This trial mode has the following characteristics: first, going down to the grassroots units to carry out investigation and find out the facts of the case, never listening only to or readily believing in one party to a case or handling a case in a hasty way; second, trying cases on the spot, not following any set form of trial, handling cases with the participation of the masses of people and for the convenience of the people, and trying cases in public; third, streamlining trial procedures for the convenience of the people; fourth, adhering to the relevant principles and combining the spirit of law with people's demands. This trial mode was popularized within the jurisdiction of the government of the Border Region, but later had abandoned for a long period of time. Since the implementation of judicial reform in the beginning of the 21st century, China has again vigorously advocated and implemented the Ma Xiwu Trial Mode.

Third, the influence of traditional Chinese legal culture and system. China is an ancient country with a more than 5000 years long history of civilization and a long-standing and well established legal system. Judicial activities backed by state power and mainly aimed at the resolution of social disputes emerged as early as in the Xia Dynasty (cir. 21–16 BC), and after several thousand years of development, evolved into a complete Chinese legal system and an oriental judicial cultural tradition with the Confucian Doctrine of the Mean as its core. The legal system in ancient China had the following characteristics: introducing Confucianism into laws and combing Confucianism with law; the law being considered to originate from the monarch, be subordinate to power, and family-oriented, and must embody ethics; unity of heaven and man and integration of human feeling, reason and law; combining criminal law and civil law in a single code and attaching great importance to criminal law but looking down upon civil law; no separation of judicial function from administrative function and subordination of judicial function to administrative function; extorting a confession by torture and basing conviction on confession; trying cases in accordance with law and by analogy; pursuing the elimination of lawsuits and settling disputes through mediation (elimination of lawsuits was the highest value objective of ancient judicial system and a symbol of peace, prosperity and simple and honest folkway); and managing government officials according to law and clearly defining their competences and accountability. In the development of "China model of rule of law", China must abolish several-thousand-year-old feudal autocratic system and feudal culture while at the same time absorbing the cultural nutrients from the long-standing and well established Chinese legal system, so as to make the past serve the present and bring forth the new through the old. For example, in line with the criminal law tradition of "controlling government officials with heavy criminal punishments" of ancient China, Article 238 of the current Chinese Criminal Law contains the following provision on the crime of unlawful detention: "Where an employee of a state organ abuses his authority to commit any of the three aforementioned crimes, he is to receive a heavier punishment in accordance with the stipulations stated in the three preceding paragraphs." In ancient China, there had been a legal tradition and system of "resolving disputes through mediation", so as to realize the ideal social condition in which "there is no lawsuit". In real life, however, it is very difficult to avoid various disputes and conflicts. In order to narrow the gap between ideal and reality and realize social harmony and stability, the ruling class in ancient China had explored the ways and methods of "elimination of lawsuit" and established legal mechanisms for "resolving disputes through mediation". The mediation in contemporary China includes people's mediation, administrative mediation, mediation by the court, and arbitral mediation.[9] In August 2010, the NPC Standing Committee adopted the People's Mediation Law, thereby turning this "Flower of the Orient" into an institution, a law, and a will of the state. In the past, people did not have a deep understanding or attach sufficient importance to the traditional Chinese legal culture and legal system, which had been denounced and negated, rather than accepted and carried on. As a result, their influence on contemporary "China model of the rule of law" has been very limited.

Fourth, the influence of western legal culture and rule of law model. In the reform carried out by the Qing Dynasty in 1900 and during the rule of the Kuomintang Regime after 1911, China mainly tried to borrow, through Japan, from the legal systems of western continental law countries. But this effort had never truly been successful. The CPC, in the construction of people's legal system—from the creation of the legal system in the revolutionary basis in 1931 to the establishment of a national

---

[9]The mediation in contemporary China refers to the mediation established by people's political power. It is a system consists of four parts: (1) People's mediation. Also called non-government mediation, it is the mediation of disputes among the people by a people's mediation committee. It is a kind of mediation outside judicial proceedings. (2) Court mediation. It is the mediation by a people's court in a case of civil or economic dispute or a minor criminal case accepted by the court. It belongs to the category of mediation within judicial proceedings. For marital cases, mediation within judicial proceedings is a compulsory procedure. For other civil cases, mediation is not compulsory, but optional. A mediation decision made by a people court has the same effect as a judgment. (3) Administrative mediation. It can be further divided into two categories: first, mediation of ordinary disputes among the people by a grassroots people's government, namely by the people's government of a township or a town. It is a kind of mediation outside judicial proceedings. Second, mediation of certain civil, economic, or labor disputes by a state administrative organ in accordance with legal provisions. It is also a kind of mediation outside judicial proceedings. (4) Arbitral mediation. It is the mediation by an arbitral body in a case accepted by it. If the mediation fails, the arbitral body will make an arbitral decision. It is also a kind of mediation outside judicial proceedings.

people's legal system in the early years of the People's Republic—had mainly learned from the experience of the Soviet Union. In the late 1950s, the Chinese-Soviet relationship deteriorated and, because of complicated historical reasons and conditions, China gradually embarked on a road of ignoring the legal system and practicing the rule of man. After the reform and opening up in 1978, especially after the collapse of the Soviet Union and the drastic changes in Eastern Europe, China began to pay more attention to drawing on and borrowing from the useful experiences of western developed countries in the process of strengthening the construction of socialist rule of law, implementing the basic strategy of ruling the country by law, developing the legal system, and deepening the judicial reform. For example, many laws made by China in the field of civil and commercial law, such as the General Principles of Civil Law, the Property Law, and the Contract Law, have adopted the basic systems of common law and continental law countries, embodied internationally accepted spirits and legislative principles of private law, recognized the principles of freedom of contract, autonomy of will, and equality of subjects, and safeguarded public property and the lawful private property of citizens; in the field of administrative law, China has accepted many universally recognized principles of modern administrative law, such as the principle of proportionality and the principle of trust protection; and in the criminal law field, the Chinese criminal law and criminal procedure law have embodied many basic principles and spirits of modern criminal law, such as legally prescribed punishment for a specified crime and open trial. Faced with new crime situations, China has, by drawing on the foreign experiences of criminal legislation, provided for many new crimes in the Criminal Law, including financing terrorist activities, money laundering, insider trading, manipulating the dealing price of negotiable securities and futures, and impairing the management of credit cards; in the field of protection of intellectual property and environmental protection, China has also drawn on many foreign legislative experiences.

After the reform and opening up, China has basically abandoned the practice of learning from the Soviet model of legal system, and has been increasingly drawing on, borrowing from, even transplanting the rule of law model and experiences of the US, the UK, Germany, France, Japan and other western developed countries. On the other hand, it has not made sufficient effort in proceeding from national conditions and adhering to the Chinese legal culture and tradition. In fact, modern western legal cultural or system is a double-edged sword to the construction of the rule of law in China: on the one hand, absorbing and borrowing from the achievements of legal civilization of all mankind, including western legal civilization, is conducive to speeding up the construction of the rule of law and the legal system and to advancing the judicial reform in China; but on the other hand, blindly copying western rule of law model and legislative experience without proceeding from the actual situation in China would affect, even impede the construction of the rule of law and the judicial reform in China.

4.3 Main Characteristics of the Contemporary "China Model of the Rule of Law"

The contemporary China model of the rule of law refers to the model of socialist rule of law or the road of the development of the socialist rule of law with Chinese characteristics. In analyzing the main characteristics of the contemporary "China model of the rule of law", four important reference systems with respect to political philosophy and political system must be taken as the preconditions of comparative analysis.

Firstly, the "China model of the rule of law" is the rule of law model of the people's democratic republic, rather than that of feudal Chinese empire, or western constitutional monarchy. The "China model of the rule of law" adheres to the people's status as the masters of the country and implements the system of the people's republic. It not only rejects feudal autocracy or feudal monarchy, but also strives to eliminate the pernicious influence of feudalism and "the rule of man" in the fields of ideology, culture, politics, law, institutions, behavior, attitude and style of work.

Secondly, it is a socialist, rather than capitalist, rule of law model. Therefore, the "China model of the rule of law" not only adheres to the "Four Cardinal Principles", namely the principles of adhering to the CPC's leadership, the people's democratic dictatorship, the socialist road, and Marxism, especially the CPC's leadership and the socialist road, but also resolutely opposes the road of wholesale westernization and mechanical imitation of the western model of the rule of law.

Thirdly, the "China model of the rule of law" is a rule of law model at the primary stage of socialism, rather than the rule of law model at the advanced stage of socialism. Currently, the "China model of rule of law" is still incomplete, underdeveloped, and immature. It still has many problems and defects, such as non-compliance with law, slack law enforcement, impunity for law-breakers, perversion of justice for a bribe, dereliction of duty, and abuse of power. Long-term and continuous efforts still need to be made to oppose the rule of man, improve the legal system, reform the judicial system, cultivate the culture of the rule of law, and establish the authority of law. Especially, some non-socialist social phenomena and economic factors should be allowed to exist in China under certain circumstances.

Fourth, the "China model of rule of law" is a socialist model of rule of law with Chinese characteristics, rather than the socialist model of the rule of law of the Soviet Union or Eastern European countries. Therefore, it must proceed from the actual national conditions in China, embody the essence of traditional Chinese legal culture, and draw on the achievements of the development of the rule of law civilization around the world, but never blindly copy the rule of law model of western countries.

To sum up, the "China model of the rule of law" has the following main characteristics.

4.3.1   Taking Economic and Social Construction as the Center and Strengthening the Construction of the Rule of Law

Taking economic construction as the center and adhering to reform and opening up is the theme of economic and social development in China. One of the basic characteristics of the "China model of the rule of law" is that the legislation and the rule of law must adapt to and serve the needs of economic and social development and the reform and opening up. In the 30 years of reform and opening up, the work in the fields of legislation, administrative law enforcement, administration of justice, legal supervision, legal service, legal education and legal research have all been basically carried out around the center of economic construction, reform and opening up. After 2002, China has attached more importance to social harmony and gradually shifted the center of the construction of the rule of law from economic construction to better and quicker economic and social development.

Taking economic construction as the center has been the guiding principle of the reform and opening up since 1978, as well the central task of the construction of the rule of law and legislation. For example, the NPC pointed out in 1980 that China must concentrate its efforts on adopting laws and regulations, especially those in the economic field, that were still lacking and urgently needed. In order to meet the need of the construction of the "four-modernizations", China must strengthen the work of economic legislation. In 1985, the NPC Standing Committee pointed out when summing up its legislative work that, in the previous five years, it had strengthened economic legislation, and drafted the Law on Chinese-Foreign Contractual Joint Ventures, the Law on Wholly Foreign-owned Enterprises, the Customs Law, the Maritime Law, the Company Law, the Law on Mineral Resources, the Labor Law, the Land Law, and many other important laws. Because the institutional reform was still at the stage of exploration, experimentation, and accumulation of experiences, some laws might take longer to formulate. In a big country like China, there is a serious problem of imbalance between different areas in political, economic, and cultural developments. Therefore, laws can only solve the most basic problems. They should not be made too specific or detailed. Otherwise, it would be very difficult to apply them in the whole country. Local governments of different areas should report to the NPC Standing Committee the legal problems encountered and the laws need to be adopted in the process of opening up to the outside world and reforming the urban economic system, so that the Committee can speed up the economic legislative work in a planned way, in order of priority and in light of concrete conditions.

In 1986, the State Council pointed out in the Report on the Seventh Five-Year Plan that: "With the deepening of economic reform and further development of the national economy, there has been increasing demand for finalizing, in the form of law, more economic relations and codes of economic activities, so as to turn the law into an important means of adjusting economic relations and regulating economic activities." In 1987, the report of the Thirteenth Party Congress clearly pointed out that China must attach equal importance to economic construction and the construction of the legal system. The construction of the legal system must run through the whole process of the reform…In the construction of the legal system, we must ensure that the economic construction and the reform are carried out in an orderly way, and strengthen the achievements of reform through adoption of laws or creation of institutions. In 1992, the report of the Fourteenth Party Congress demanded that China: "must strengthen the legislative work, especially speed up the adoption and improvement of laws and regulations that safeguard the reform and opening up, strengthen macro-economic regulation, and standardize micro-economic activities—which are urgently demanded by the construction of a socialist economic system." In 1994, the CPC demanded that: "Reform decision-making must be closely combined with legislative decision-making. Legislation must embody the spirit of reform and laws must be able to guide, promote and safeguard the reform." In 1995, the CPC further demanded that: "China must adhere to the unity of reform, opening up and the construction of the legal system and closely combine decision-making on reform and development with legislative decision-making."

In 1997 and 2002, the CPC again demanded that: "China must combine major decision-making on reform and development with legislation", "adapt to the new situations of the development of socialist market economy, comprehensive social progress, and the accession to the WTO, strengthen the legislative work, improve the quality of legislation, and realize the formation of the socialist legal system with Chinese characteristics by the year 2010." The close combination of legislation with reform and development is embodied in the work report of the NPC Standing Committee. One of the basic characteristics of the "China model of rule of law" is adhering to the compatibility between legislation, reform, development, and modernization, confirming through the adoption of law the experiences proved to be correct by practice, strengthening the positive results of reform, opening up and modernization construction, safeguarding and promoting sound and rapid economic and social development, and creating a good rule of law environment for reform, development and modernization construction."

In the more than 30 years of reform and opening up, the rate of economic growth and the rate of the growth of national income in China have far exceeded the world averages and today China has become the second largest economy in the world. The achievements made by China in the reduction of poverty population in the past 30 years have far exceeded those made by India and Vietnam. Statistics of the World Bank show that the percentage of the poor in Chinese population had decreased drastically from 65% in 1981 to 18% in 2001, which was very rare in the world. China established four special economic zones in 1980, accepted market economy in 1992, joined the WTO in 2001, and successfully dealt with the international financial crisis in 2008. It is the most successful developing country in the transition to the market economy and in the process of economic globalization. In the process of rapid economic growth, the China model of rule of law has gradually taken form and played an indispensable guiding, regulating and safeguarding role.

4.3.2 Proceeding from the National Conditions in China and Drawing on All Beneficial Results of the Development of the Rule of Law Civilization in the World

Since the modern times, the construction of the rule of law in China had mainly relied on the transplantation of law. After the reform and opening up in 1978, large-scale borrowing from and transplantation of western legal systems have remained to be one of the main measures under the "China model of rule of law". However, a major task faced by China in the construction of the rule of law is to create a legal system and develop a rule of law model with Chinese characteristics on the basis of its own national conditions. In this respect, China adheres to the following basic principle: proceeding from its national conditions and draw on (transplant) all beneficial results of the development of rule of law civilization of mankind.

In the process of developing the "China model of rule of law", China has drawn on and transplanted a large amount of legal concepts and systems from western countries, the Soviet Union and Eastern European countries. For example, many legal concepts and principles currently used in China, such as legislation, administration, administration of justice, democracy, the rule of law, human rights, constitutionalism, company, judge, time limitation, rights, obligations, legal relation, legal responsibility, legal act, emergency, legally prescribed punishment for a specified crime, presumption of innocence, equality before the law, and safeguarding human rights, even the concept of law school and concepts of classification of disciplines, such as constitutional law, administrative law, civil law, criminal law and procedure law, have all come from western legal culture. The people's procuratorial system in China was mainly copied from the Soviet Union whereas the unified professional qualification examination for judges, procurators, lawyers, and notaries public are the result of drawing on the practice of the common law system.

On the other hand, China must always base itself on its own national conditions and refrain from blindly copying western rule of law experience and model in the construction of the rule of law. It must adhere to its own characteristics and proceed from its own actual needs. For example, China must implement the people's congress system, rather than the system of separation of three powers, and the system of regional national autonomy, rather than the federal or confederation system, adopt the policy of "One Country, Two Systems" to solve the problems of Hong Kong, Macao and Taiwan, and implement the people's mediation system, the system of complaint by letters and visits, the Ma Xiwu Trial Method and other dispute resolution systems with Chinese characteristics.

Currently, the China model of development of the rule of law is undergoing an important transition from an imitative model that emphasizes the borrowing from western legal system to an autonomous model that aims at solving practical problems in China by proceeding from the concrete national condition and establishing itself through self-development and independent innovation.

4.3.3 The Development of the Rule of Law Characterized by Government Dominance, Combination of Higher Levels with Lower Levels, and Steady Advancement

China has its own unique national conditions and the China model of rule of law must also have its own characteristics. Different from the rule of law model of any other country, it is a rule of law model characterized by "government dominance, combination of higher levels with lower levels, participation by all parties, and steady advancement". In most cases, each advancement made by China in the development of the rule of law, whether the advocacy of the development of democracy and the improvement of the legal system during the early years of reform and opening up or the establishment of the basic state policy of ruling the country by law in mid and late 1990s, whether the nationwide campaign on the popularization of law or the construction of cities under the rule of law, and whether the advancement of administration by law or the reform of the judicial system, has been initiated, dominated, and supported by the government, and the result of combined efforts made by the central and local governments, the government and enterprises, the government and citizens, and leaders and followers. The most prominent Chinese characteristic of this model is that: calls are made by the Central Government and responded by local governments; plans are adopted and orders issued by the government and implemented or followed by citizens, enterprises and society; and instructions are given by leaders and executed, abided by or implemented by followers.

Generally speaking, the construction of the rule of law in China is dominated by the government: it has been implemented from top to bottom by organizational and educational means after the highest decision-makers at the central level decided to implement the policy of ruling the country by law and constructing a socialist state under the rule of law. It was initiated by the Central Government and mainly implemented at the local, grassroots and industry levels. The construction of the rule of law was promoted by the government, not spontaneously demanded by the people. Therefore, its prospect is determined to a large extent by the government's strategic design and the steps of its implementation, as well as the determination of and the planning by the state, especially state leaders.

This government-dominated mode of promoting the rule of law has the advantage of being easy to initiate: under the unified order by the Central Government, local governments at all levels and people of all walks of life can be quickly mobilized to devote themselves to the cause of ruling the country by law. The government can make use of the authority and human, material and financial resources of the state, and mobilize and organize the whole society to participate in the work of ruling the country by law, and is able to see the results and produce sensational effect in a short period of time.

However, this mode of promoting the strategy of ruling the country by law has many defects, the biggest one being that ruling the country by law is considered an act of the government implemented by way of a campaign or movement, in which non-governmental forces are not truly mobilize and the government often puts itself above the rule of law and treats society and the people as the objects of governance. If this act of the government is not understood and accepted by the people, it is not sustainable and cannot be institutionalized and legalized. This, combined with such factors as improper methods of organization and leadership, ineffective publicity and education, lagging institutional reform, and weak practical operation, can lead to the abortion of the rule of law.

In China, the construction of the rule of law and ruling the country by law are actually regarded as an important content of political development and an important aspect of political reform. In China, it is very difficult to separate politics from law both in ideology and in fact, and politics is always put before and considered superior to law (the rule of law), as demonstrated by the widespread use of such concepts as "university of politics and law", "political and legal affairs committee" and "political and legal work". Therefore, all the guiding ideology, principle requirements and operational steps applicable to political reform are also applicable to the construction of the rule of law and ruling the country by law. For example, the basic principle to be adhered to in the political reform in China is to carry out the reform under the leadership of the CPC, in an orderly, organized, active yet prudent, and step-by-step way. The same principle also applies to the construction of the rule of law in China, which must be carried out in a step-by-step manner by adhering to and strengthening the CPC's leadership and coordinating with economic, social and cultural development. For another example, the political reform must meet the requirements set by Deng Xiaoping, namely being conducive to invigorating the CPC and the country, to mobilizing the enthusiasm, the initiatives and the creativity of the masses of people, to upholding the national unity and social stability, and to promoting economic development and social harmony and progress. The same is also true for ruling the country by law, which means that the people, under the leadership of the Party, and in accordance with provisions of the law, manage the affairs of the sate through various channels and in various forms, manage economic and cultural undertakings and social affairs, ensure that various kinds of work are carried out in accordance with law, gradually realize the institutionalization, standardization, and routinization of socialist democracy, so that this system and law will not change with the change of state leaders or the change of view or focus of attention of state leaders. Ruling the country by law is an objective requirement of the development of socialist market economy, an important symbol of the progress of civilization, and an important safeguard for long-term stability of the country.

4.3.4 Combining the Rule of Law with the Rule of Virtue, with the Rule of Law Playing the Leading Role

In Chinese history, the rule of law and the rule of virtue have always been two basic means of state governance, just like the two wheels of a cart or the two wings of a bird—each of them plays an important role in maintaining social order. The rule of virtue in traditional Chinese society mainly refers to a mode of state governance. It has two basic meanings: firstly, it refers to the state governance mode that attaches importance to the educational role of ethics and realizes social and state governance through the educational and regulating role of ethics. Confucius once said that: "If the people be led by laws, and uniformity sought to be given them by punishments, they will try to avoid the punishment, but have no sense of shame. If they be led by virtue, and uniformity sought to be given them by the rules of propriety, they will have the sense of shame, and moreover will become good."[10] Secondly, it refers to a state governance mode that attaches importance to the moral examples set by the rulers and realizes state and social governance through such moral examples. "The rule of virtue, as an important content of the Confucian political and ethic thoughts, had a very clear position in ancient China: ethics is superior to law and the rule of virtue superior to the rule of law, namely "virtue dominates and law supplements".

In the construction of the rule of law in contemporary China, the rule of law and the rule of virtue have always been closely integrated, but the emphasis of the integration is different in different periods of time. In the beginning of the 21st century, Chinese leaders put forward the idea of "combing the rule of law with the rule of virtue". However, this idea was questioned by the law circle. As far as general principle is concerned, the Chinese jurisprudential circle is not opposed to the combination of law with ethics and the rule of law with the rule of virtue and holds that, from the perspective of the maintenance of social stability, law and ethics are of equal importance and they are connected to and supplementary to each other. Ethical norms and legal norms should be integrated and jointly play their role. Good moral quality enables the people to conscientiously support the good and oppose the evil, and is conducive to the cultivation of a good social climate of pursuing nobleness and encouraging advancement, thereby ensuring the healthy development of the socialist market economy and the improvement of the overall quality of the Chinese nation. However, China, as a country with several thousand years old feudal tradition of the rule of man, lacks the tradition of democracy, the rule of law and the historical basis of the rule of law. Since China established the basic strategy of ruling the country by law in 1997, the importance and necessity of ruling the country by law began to be understood and accepted by the people. Under this circumstance, emphasizing the combination of the rule of law with the rule of virtue will greatly weaken the people's respect for and understanding of and the implementation of the basic strategy of ruling the country by law, even lead to the restoration of the rule of man under the camouflage of ruling the country by virtue. The actual situation in China is that: the rule of law, as the minimum standard of human behavior, has far from been observed or realized; the number of violations of law and crimes is increasing with each passing day; social conflicts and disputes are piling up one after another; the legal order is frequently challenged, and the authority of the rule of law is weak. Under this circumstance, in which the rule of law is still unable to play its role, stressing the role of ethics and highlighting the idea of ruling the country by virtue deviates from the reality of in China and is unable to solve any practical problem

---

[10]The Analects: Weizheng.

in the country. Therefore, the Chinese legal scholars should adopt the following attitude towards the relationship between the rule of law and the rule of virtue: on the one hand, they should recognize that there is a close and mutually supplementary relationship between the two and that the rule of law does not negate the importance of ethics and stress that ethics is the indispensable ideological condition and cultural basis of the rule of law; on the other hand, they should also recognize that at the current stage China must adhere to the basic strategy of ruling the country by law and to the dominant position of the rule of law and oppose any attempt to replace or weaken the rule of law with the rule of virtue.

4.3.5 Adhering to the Unity of the Rule of Law and the Unity of Diversity

China is a unitary state and the unity of the rule of law is one of the basic principles enshrined in the Chinese Constitution. Under the principle of unify of the rule of law, local governments must obey the central government, local legislation may not contradict the central legislation, lower-level laws may not contravene upper-level laws, both courts and procuratorates operate under a unified judicial system and apply unified standard on the application of law, unified principle on the interpretation of laws, and unified legal procedures for the implementation of laws. The withdrawal of the power to review death sentences by the Supreme People's Court from provincial higher people's courts further unified and standardized the conditions of and criteria on the application of the death penalty, thereby putting the death penalty under strict control. The implementation of the case guidance system by the Supreme People's Court has reduced the arbitrariness of trial. Under the precondition of the unity of the rule of law, the rule of law in China allows a certain degree of diversity, so as to adapt to such national situations as a vast territory, diversity of ethnic culture, and uneven economic and social developments.

Firstly, with respect to the state system, China implements the "One Country, Two Systems" policy, namely to implement the socialist system in the Mainland, but the capitalist system in Hong Kong, Macao and Taiwan. More specifically, China implements the socialist mode of legal system in the Mainland (according to the standards on the division of legal systems in the world described by the French comparative jurist Rene David in his book Main Legal Systems in Contemporary World and by the German comparative jurist Konrad Zweigert in his book An Introduction to Comparative Law), common law mode of legal system in Hong Kong Special Administrative Region, and the continental law mode of legal system in Macao Special Administrative Region and in Taiwan Province.

Secondly, with respect to the legislative system, China implements a unified pluralistic legislative system, namely under the unified national legislative system, there is a division of legislative functions and powers between the central and local legislative organs: some legislative matters can only be dealt with by central legislative organs. The people's congresses of provinces, provincial capitals and larger cities and their standing committees have the local legislative power; those of Hainan Province and the cities of Shenzhen, Zhuhai, Xiamen and Shantou have the special legislative power of special economic zone; and the people's congresses of ethnic autonomous areas have the power to adopt regulations on the exercise of autonomy and separate regulations, which can contain certain adaptations to the laws and regulations adopted by the central legislative organs and upper-level laws. According to Article 75 of the Legislation Law of the PRC, regulations on the exercise of autonomy and separate regulations can contain adaptations to laws and administrative regulations under the following two circumstances: First, adaptation is specifically authorized by a state law. By the year 2012, over ten current laws and three current administrative regulations, including the Marriage Law, the Inheritance Law, and the General Principles of Civil Law, have authorized ethnic autonomous areas to make adaptive or supplementary provisions under the precondition of not violating the basic principles of the law. Second, the regulations on the exercise of autonomy and separate regulations of an autonomous area can contain adaptations to the provisions of a law which is not entirely compatible with the actual conditions of the area, even if there is no specific authorization by the law. By the end of 2010, a total of 139 pieces of effective regulations on the exercise of autonomy and 777 pieces of effective separate regulations had been adopted by 155 ethnic autonomous areas. Among them, 75 had made adaptations to the relevant provisions of laws and administrative regulations in light of local conditions. These adaptations mainly involve such matters as marriage, inheritance, development of resources, family planning, protection of minors, public security, environmental protection, and land, forest and grassland administration.

Thirdly, with respect to the national judicial examination system, in recent years, the Ministry of Justice has been continuously taking new measures for reforming and improving the system in light of the new developments of situation. These measures include: first, striving to solve the problem of shortage of legal professionals in central and western regions and at grassroots level by implementing special policies in these regions and ethnic minority areas, and appropriately lowering the application requirements and the passing score for candidates from these areas or those at the grassroots level. For example, the passing score in the national judicial examination in 2013 was 360 in most parts of the country, but only 280 in Tibetan Autonomous Region. Separate passing scores were set for candidates of ethnic minorities taking the examination using examination papers in ethnic minority languages. Second, expanding the scope of candidates. Beginning from 2004, permanent residents of Hong Kong and Macao special administrative regions who hold Chinese citizenship have been allowed to take part in the examination; beginning from 2008, senior students of regular institutions of higher learning in the Mainland and residents of Taiwan have also been allowed to take part in the examination. In 2013, a total of 436,000 persons took part in the examination, 32,000 more than the previous year. Moreover, in the field of dispute resolution, there are a large number of (unwritten) local laws in many areas in China in contrast to the (written) state laws made by the central and local governments. These "local laws" sometimes conflict with provisions of state laws, but they are effective and low-cost and play an import role in the resolution of many conflicts and disputes in remote, backward rural and ethnic minority areas.

4.3.6 Adhering to the Organic Unity of the CPC's Leadership, the People's Democracy and Ruling the Country by Law

In 2002, the Report of the Sixteenth Party Congress established the development of socialist democracy and the construction of socialist political civilization as important objectives of the strategy of building a moderately prosperous society in all respects and pointed out that: "The key to developing socialist democracy is to organically combine the Party's leadership, the status of people as the masters of the country, and ruling the country by law". In 2005, the White Paper on Political Democracy in China clearly pointed out that: "In building political democracy, China will abide by the following principles: upholding the unity of the leadership of the CPC, the people being the masters of the country and ruling the country by law. This is the most important and fundamental principle for developing socialist political democracy in China." The 2008 white paper China's Efforts and Achievements in Promoting the Rule of Law, in summarizing China's experience in the construction of the rule of law, once again stressed that: "Chinese people have realized that the following principles must be observed in the process of carrying out the fundamental policy of governing the country by law: adhering to the leadership of the CPC, the people as the masters of the country and ruling the country by law, ensuring that the CPC always plays the role as the core of leadership in directing the overall situation and coordinating the efforts of all quarters in legal construction, upholding the people's position as masters of the country according to prescriptions of the Constitution and the law, and making sure that all work is carried on according to law." "The organic unity of the three" has undoubtedly become the most fundamental and most important characteristic of the democratic political system and the rule of law model in China.

The CPC's leadership is the basic guarantee of people's status as the maters of the country and the implementation of the strategy of ruling the country by law. Deng Xiaoping once said that: "China must be led by the CPC and the socialist modernization construction in China must be carried out under the leadership of the CPC. This is an unshakable principle. Once this principle is abandoned, China will disintegrate and slip into chaos and it would be impossible to realize the modernization." People being the masters of the country is the basic requirement of socialist democratic politics and ruling the country by law is the basic strategy by which the ruling party leads the Chinese people to govern the country. The "organic unity of the three" represents a major adjustment of the direction of the political reform in China, namely from one that takes the "separation of the Party from the government" as the objective, to one that takes the "organic unity of the three" as the objective and characteristic, and provides guidance for dealing with the relationship between ruling the country by law and the leadership of the CPC. For example, some people asked: if both ruling the country by law and adhering to the CPC's leadership are to be emphasized, which one of them has the superiority, the Party's leadership or the Constitution and laws? This is a question about how to appropriately deal with the relationship between the two. Under the principle of "the organic unity of the three", the Party's leadership over the state and society is mainly realized by such means as adopting fundamental policies, putting forward legislative proposals, taking the lead in observing the law, ensuring the implementation of law, and recommending important cadres. The principle emphasizes ensuring the socialist orientation of the construction of democracy and the rule of law through the Party's leadership, ensuring the Party's progressiveness and the justness of the rule of law in China through the development of people's democracy, and ensuring the Party's leadership and the people's position as the masters of the country through the implementation of the rule of law.

4.4   A Comparative Study on the Level of Development of the Rule of Law in China

The construction of the rule of law can be assessed in two dimensions: vertical and horizontal. In the vertical dimension, compared with 10, 30 and 60 years ago, China has made world-famous achievements whether in the theory of socialist rule of law or in the practice of socialist democratic rule of law, whether in the construction of socialist legal system with Chinese characteristics or in the building of a system of socialist rule of law with Chinese characteristics, whether in legislation, law enforcement and administration of justice, or in learning the law, applying the law and observing the law, whether in legal system and procedures or in the spirit and mechanism of the rule of law, and whether in leading cadres' capacity for acting according to law, or the citizens' consciousness of law and the rule of law. In the horizontal dimension, huge achievements have been made by China in the construction of the rule of law in the past 60 years and, in many aspects, the rule of law in China today is not inferior to the rule of law in western developed countries.

The following international, Hong Kong and mainland indices of the rule of law conditions (level) can be used as reference systems in the assessment of the current level of the rule of law in China.

4.4.1   The Rule of Law Index of the World Justice Project

The World Justice Project was initiated by American Bar Association in association with United Nations Lawyer's Association, Pan-America Lawyers' Association, and Pan-Pacific Bar Association at the World Justice Forum held in Vienna, Austria on July 3–5, 2008. The Forum was attended by 500–700 prominent leaders and experts from all parts of the world and aimed at articulating the concept of the rule of law and developing a standard for evaluating the situation of the rule of law in different countries. The purpose of the "rule of law index" is to form a unified global standard to be used to assess the extent to which a given country adheres to the rule of law.

The World Justice Project puts forward the following four "fundamental principles" for the assessment of the rule of law: first, everyone, including the government and its officials and agents, are accountable under the law; second, the rule of law is a system based on fairly adopted, publicized, widely understood, and stable laws; third, the process by which the rule of law is enforced is fair and enables everyone to have access to justice; and fourth, there is a contingent of competent, independent, and ethical attorneys or representatives and judges with all the necessary knowledge.

On the basis of these principles, the World Justice Project's rule of law index contains fourteen main indicators, which can be divided into three parts: the first one emphasis constitutionalization and institutionalization of the rule of law, so as to ensure that the ruling power is constrained; the second part concerns legislation, including parliamentary legislation and administrative legislation; and the third part concerns the enforcement of law, including the enforcement and administration of laws and regulations.

The WJP rule of law index stresses that the assessment of the situation of the rule of law in a country should be based not only on the provisions of laws, but also on the actual situation of enforcement of laws; the process of the adoption of law must be open, so as to draw on the wisdom of the masses, and to pass information to ordinary citizens through the mass media and other independent channels; laws must protect fundamental human rights, including civil and political rights, economic, social and cultural rights; laws must be clear, coherent, easily understood, and have foreseeability; the fairness and impartiality of the rule of law depends on the support by independent and responsible lawyers and judges.

4.4.2 World Bank Rule of Law Assessment Standard

The World Bank holds that the essence of the rule of law lies in the extent to which people trust and observe the law of the country, the degree of fairness and foreseeability of law, and the ways in which property rights are safeguarded. Therefore, the main indicators in the assessment the situation of the rule of law should include crime rate, judicial efficiency, the foreseeability of law, and implementation of contracts. The rule of law index is an important content of the annual "global index of government regulation" published by the World Bank.

4.4.3 Hong Kong Rule of Law Index

Hong Kong is the first city in China to use index to assess its own condition of the rule of law. The Hong Kong Rule of Law Index contains seven elements of the rule of law and their components, which are considered to be the minimum standards and requirements of the rule of law (see Table 4.1).

Table 4.1 Hong Kong rule of law index

Classified rule of law indices	No.	First-level conditions of the rule of law	Second-level conditions of the rule of law
	1	The current laws meet the basic requirements of a sound law	General requirements on laws: openness; stability; definiteness; non-retroactivity; no demanding for impossible act; compatibility with general social values
	2	The government acts by the law	
	3	There exist rules and procedures for preventing the arbitrary exercise of power by the government	
	4	Equality of everyone before the law	
	5	Fairness of law enforcement	Compatibility between government's behavior and published laws; judicial independence
	6	Universal judicial fairness	Fair court trial; independence of judges; procedures for bringing lawsuits against the decisions and administrative acts of the government
	7	Procedural justice	The principle of presumption of innocence, the principle of natural justice; rules of evidence; fair trial

The assessment of the rule of law index in Hong Kong is mainly carried out through the grading by elites, supplemented by public opinion poll.

4.4.4 Rule of Law Assessment Systems of Shanghai, Beijing, Nanjing and Yuhang District of Hangzhou City

Shanghai Rule of Law Index System consists of ten components: judicial indices, law enforcement indices, publicity of law indices, legal supervision indices, public security indices, social participation indices, legal resource indices, legal service indices, basic indices, and other indices.

Beijing Rule of Law Environment Assessment Index System is a hierarchical structure consists of indices in the following four aspects: legislation, law enforcement and administration of justice, material input safeguards, and protection of citizens' rights.

Nanjing Rule of Law Assessment Standard consists of the following assessment systems: the sincerity and good faith assessment standard system, with government good faith indices, enterprise good faith indices, intermediary organization good faith indices and individual good faith indices as the concrete standards; the security assessment standard system with urban political stability, economic security, the safety and peacefulness of people's life, and the safety of urban ecology as the concrete indicators; and the assessment standard system with the levels of legalization of urban political, economic, cultural and social lives as the concrete indicators.

The rule of law assessment system of Yuhang District, Hangzhou City, Zhejiang Province consists of the following standards: exercise of the ruling power by Party committees, administration by law, judicial fairness, protection of rights in accordance with law, a standardized and orderly market, a sound supervisory system, a sound democratic political system, the improvement of quality of the whole people, and social stability and harmony.

4.4.5 Principles on the Comparison (Assessment) of the Level of Development of the Rule of Law

The comparison of the development of the rule of law between China and foreign countries can be carried out at the following three levels.

First, the political guiding ideology of the construction of the rule of law. Compared with the rule of law in western countries, the rule of law being constructed in China is of the socialist nature. There are essential differences between the two. Compared with the rule of law in other socialist countries, the rule of law in China is a socialist rule of law with Chinese characteristics, which must be based on the national conditions of China and proceed from the reality of the primary stage of socialist in China. In carrying out qualitative comparison at this level, we must pay special attention to the class nature, political nature and socialist characteristics of the rule of law. China should never practice western capitalist rule of law.

Second, historical and cultural conditions of the construction of the rule of law. Different historical and cultural conditions have influenced and determined the establishment of different legal systems, such as the continental law system, the common law system, the Scandinavian law system, the Chinese law system, and the Islamic law system. The legal system in China belongs to the family of socialist legal system but with obvious characteristics of the continental law system. In assessing the rule of law condition in a country, we must take into full consideration the historical and cultural traditions and the social, political and cultural realities of the country. In carrying out comparison at this level, we should advocate "seeking commonness among differences and finding differences between similarities", and never improperly belittle ourselves or become self-conceited.

Third, the principles, institutions and procedures of construction of the rule of law. At the level of the form of realization of the rule of law and the operation and techniques of the rule of law, there are some concepts, values, principles, norms and procedures that are common to the rules of law in different countries all around the world. At this level, the rules of law in countries of different ideologies, different cultural traditions and different social systems have relatively high comparability and referentiability. It is at this level that the development of the rule of law can be assessed by taking western rule of law as the reference system. However, assessment made at this level must be combined with the assessment at the above-mentioned two levels in order to come to a comprehensive conclusion.

In making the comparison and assessment, we must make it clear that the rule of law in China must be a democratic socialist rule of law with Chinese characteristics, rather than a western rule of law under bourgeois dictatorship; we must adhere to the people's congress system, and never practice western system of "separation of three powers" or bicameralism; we must adhere to the system of multi-party cooperation and political consultation under the leadership of the CPC, and never practice western two-party or multi-party system. In a word, we must adhere to the organic unity of the principles of the CPC's leadership, the people being masters of the country and ruling the country by law. In the followings I will conduct a preliminary comparison of the form of realization of the rule of law between China, Russia, Japan, France, Germany, and US in the following six dimensions: the road of development, legislation, administrative law enforcement, administration of justice and observance of law (see Tables 4.2, 4.3, 4.4 and 4.5).

Through the comparison with some western countries, we can come to the following preliminary conclusion: China has caught up with western countries in the legislation on the rule of law, but it is still lagged far behind the western countries in law enforcement, administration of justice, legal supervision, observance of law and the consciousness of rule of law.

Table 4.2 Development of the rule of law: a comparison between China and Russia

No.	Matters to be compared	China	Russia
1	Cultural background of the rule of law	China has a long feudal tradition, and no tradition of democracy and the rule of law in history; after the establishment of the People's Republic, China has adhered to the Marxist political and legal outlook, and constructed a socialist legal system by learning from the Soviet Union. Since the reform and opening up, China has adhered to the strategy of constructing a state under socialist rule of law with Chinese characteristics by proceeding from national conditions and drawing on the achievements of political civilization of all mankind, including western rule of law civilization	Russia has a long tradition of feudal serfdom; after the October Revolution, Russia adhered to Marxist Leninist ideology of state and law and established the first socialist system of the rule of law in the world; after the dissolution of the Soviet Union, Russia has completely accepted the western ideology of the rule of law and legal system. After coming into power, Putin has made some adjustments to the policy of wholesale acceptance of western institutions in the economic field, but few adjustments have been made in the field of the rule of law
2	Standard of construction of the rule of law	Chinese-style Marxist and socialist ideology of the rule of law; socialist road of democratic politics with Chinese characteristics and "the organic unity of three"; main principles: popular sovereignty, safeguarding of human rights, unified authority of the rule of law, exercising the ruling power by law, democratic legislation, administration by law, judicial fairness, conscientious observance of law, and supervision over and restraint of power	Wholesale acceptance of western standards: general election, multi-party system, separation of three powers, and freedom of the press

(continued)

Table 4.2 (continued)

No.	Matters to be compared	China	Russia
3	Legislation	The NPC has the power to adopted and revised basic laws; the NPC Standing Committee has the power to adopt and revise ordinary laws; the State Council has the power to adopt administrative regulations; people's congresses at the provincial level and their standing committees have the power to adopt local regulations; people's congresses of larger cities and their standing committees also have the power to adopt local regulations; people's congresses of special economic zones and their standing committees can adopt regulations of special economic zones in accordance with special authorization; people's congresses of national regional autonomous areas have the power to adopt regulations on the exercise of autonomy and separation regulations, which may contain adaptations to certain provisions of laws and administrative regulations; the ministries and commissions under the State Council have the power to adopt ministerial rules; and local people's governments with legislative power can adopt local rules	The legislation system of the Russian Federation consists of the followings: the Constitution of Russian Federation; federal constitutional laws; articles of confederation; federal laws; codes of law; normative documents issued by the President of Russia; normative documents issued by Federation Council and State Duma, Federal Government, various ministries, national commissions and other competent departments of the Russian Federation; authorization agreements between the federation and federal subjects; international treaties and inter-governmental agreements concluded by the federal government. The Federal Constitution and federal laws have the highest legal effect in the Federation, and play the role of ensuring the unity of the federal legal system. Federal laws can be further divided into the constitutions and laws of republics; constitutions and laws of krais, states and federal cities; and constitutions and laws of autonomous okrugs and oblasts

(continued)

Table 4.2 (continued)

No.	Matters to be compared	China	Russia
4	Administrative law enforcement	The transition of guiding ideology of administrative law enforcement from that of control-oriented government to that of service-oriented government and from governance by administrative means to governance by rule of law means; the adoption of the Program for Comprehensively Promoting Administration by Law, which has administrative binding force, and the emphasis on administration by law and construction of service-oriented and law-based government; strengthening and improving administrative legislation; improving administrative justice mechanism; safeguarding the lawful exercise of administrative power; and supervising the exercise and preventing the abuse of administrative power	(1) the transition of the guiding ideology of administrative law enforcement from that of "administration law" in the Soviet era to that of "power control—balance law" in the era of Russian Federation; (2) the content of administrative law: state administration; local autonomy; subjects of administrative law; state affairs; administrative illegality; administrative punishment; administrative coercion; administrative litigation; administrative procedure; administrative review; and administrative justice; (3) bases of administrative law enforcement: Law on the Filing of Charges against Acts and Decisions Infringing upon Citizens' Rights and Freedoms; Civil Procedure Law of Russian Federation; and Arbitral Procedure Law of Russian Federation; (4) litigation organs: some administrative cases are tried by ordinary courts, and some are tried by arbitration courts

(continued)

Table 4.2 (continued)

No.	Matters to be compared	China	Russia
5	Administration of justice	Under the unitary political system, the rule of law and the judicial system in the whole country are unified. The court system consists of the Supreme Court, higher courts, intermediate courts, and grassroots courts. China implements a trial system whereby the second instance is final In the ten-year judicial reform, China has achieved some successes in the reform of judicial concepts, institutions, procedures, systems, and mechanisms, but also met with many new problems and challenges How to deepen judicial reform, improve the justiciability and effectiveness of the Constitution and laws, and build fair, efficient and authoritative judicial organs in the process of deepening the political reform and implementing the basic strategy of ruling the country by law has become a major question to be carefully studied and answered at the next stage of judicial construction and reform	The federal judicial system consists of the federal courts and courts of constituent entities of the Russian Federation. The federal courts system consists of three parts: the Constitutional Court of Russian Federation, ordinary courts, and arbitration courts Judicial reform: (1) reform of trial principles: the principle of simultaneous use of different trial systems (the jury system, the system of trial by judges and people's assessors, the system of sole-judge trial, and system of trial by collegial panel); the principle of jury plus court trial; the principle of protection of the rights of the defendant; and the principle that court proceedings must be conducted and judicial documents must be issued in Russian language; (2) reform of the system of execution of judgments: establishment of the judicial police system and the compulsory execution system; (3) reform of the system of status of judges: judges enjoy independent organizational, legal, financial, social material guarantees and guarantee of continuing education; reform of the system of supervision over judges: the establishment of Judge's Council and the Highest Appraisal Committee for Judges. The Russian President has the power to appoint judges, but does not have the power to dismiss judges. Only the Appraisal Committee for Judges has the power to remove judges. Every year, about 50 judges are discharged from their posts by the Committee According to the Law on the Constitutional Court of the Russian Federation and the Law on the Judicial System of the Russian Federation, the Constitutional Court is the judicial organ responsible for constitutional supervision and the interpretation of the constitution. Its functions and powers include the power to try constitutional cases (cases relating to the constitutionality of legal documents, disputes over functions and powers, the constitutionality of the application of law in concrete cases, and the impeachment of the Russian President), the power to interpret the Constitution, the power to put forward legislative bills, etc.

(continued)

Table 4.2 (continued)

No.	Matters to be compared	China	Russia
6	Observance of law	Although the situation of observance of law in China is still not satisfactory, generally speaking China is in the process of gradually solving the existing problems and the situation is taking a turn for the better. With the comprehensive implementation of the basic strategy of ruling the country by law and the deepening of judicial reform and publicity and education on the rule of law, the situation of observance and implementation of law will become even better	The judiciary is corrupt and inefficient; the law enforcement environment, the implementation of law, and the situation of public security are poor; human rights are not safeguarded; citizens have lost their subject consciousness and are suffering from belief crisis; pan-liberalism and anarchism are on the rise; nationalism, terrorism, splitism, and racial conflicts are seriously impeding the development of the rule of law in Russia; citizens have weak legal consciousness. Especially the young people have lost their faith; legal nihilism has become prevalent; the rate of alcoholism, violence and crime are continuously rising and the situation is aggravated by the unscrupulous mass media which are filled with violence and pornography and seriously affecting the physical and mental health of the youth in Russia
Comparison of similarities	(1)	In the past, both countries belong to the family of socialist legal system. The legal theories and legal systems of the two countries have many similar contents	
	(2)	The construction of the rule of law in both countries has been influenced by the rule of man	
	(3)	Both countries combine western ideas of the rule of law idea with their national conditions in the development of the rule of law	
Comparison of differences	(1)	Adhering to, developing and innovating socialist legal theory	Abandonment of socialist legal system and whole-sale westernization
	(2)	developing socialist democratic rule of law with Chinese characteristics	Constructing the rule of law in accordance with western standards
	(3)	Combining western experience and national conditions in the construction of the rule of law	Whole-sale westernization in the development of the rule of law
	(4)	Implementing state-control model of the rule of law	Implementing the social-control model of the rule of law
Overall assessment		Generally speaking, the development of the rule of law in China and that in Russia each has its own merits. However, the public security condition under the Chinese rule of law and the trend of development of the rule of law in China are apparently better than in Russia	

Table 4.3 Development of the rule of law: a comparison between China and Japan

No.	Matters to be compared	China	Japan
1	Cultural background	The traditional Confucian culture values obligations over rights, the state (collective) over the individual, the rule of man over the rule of law, and mediation over litigation	Before Meiji Reform, Japan had a cultural tradition very similar to that in China. After the Reform, it has been learning more and more from the West, while at the same time preserving many aspects of its own political cultural tradition, such as Tennoism and the emphasis on the mediation as a means of dispute resolution
2	Road of development of the rule of law	In the late Qing Dynasty legal form, China began the large-scale learning from western countries, especially from Germany and Japan; in the early years of construction of the legal system led by the CPC, China mainly learned from the legal system of the Soviet Union; after the reform and opening up, China has obviously increased the learning from the western rule of law	Japan began large-scale transplantation and acceptance of western rule of law culture and systems after the Meiji Reform. Before World War II, Japan had been influenced by French, British and especially German laws. Many legal institutions and legal thoughts in Japan came directly from Germany. After World War II, US law has had important influence on Japan and many Japanese systems have been reformed according to the US model. After many years development, Japan has become a modern country under the rule of law with a legal system that has the characteristics of both the continental law system and the common law system
3	Legislation	Chinese legislative system is based on the people's congress system; emphasis has been laid on the learning from the legislative experiences of Japan, Germany, US, UK and other western countries	Under the precondition of separation of three powers, Japan has mainly learned from German and US legislative systems. It implements a bicameral legislative system and has strengthened administrative legislation and local autonomous legislative power. In doing so, it attaches importance to proceeding from its own national conditions and preventing mechanical imitation of foreign systems

(continued)

Table 4.3 (continued)

No.	Matters to be compared	China	Japan
4	Administrative law enforcement	China lacks a set of clear and stable legal norms and administrative establishment; the enforcement of administrative law and the supervision over administrative power need to be strengthened	Japan has adopted strict provisions on administrative organizations to ensure the effectiveness of administrative law enforcement and attaches importance to the application of the formal and informal procedures of administrative licensing, administrative punishment, and administrative coercion, the openness of the operation of administrative power and the supervision over the activities of administrative organs
5	Administration of justice	China adheres to the nature and characteristics of socialist judicial system with Chinese characteristics and reforms the judicial system by drawing on western experiences; the review of constitutionality and legality is carried out by legislative organs	Japan learns from modern western judicial systems, emphasizes judicial independence, implements a unified judicial examination system; carries out judicial reform and practices American-style constitutional review system
6	Observance of law	Generally Chinese people do not take rules very seriously, but their consciousness of observance of law has been gradually enhanced; they value mediation over litigation and resolve their disputes by resorting first to feelings, then to reason, and finally to law	The Japanese people attach importance to rules and esprit de corps, have a strong consciousness of observance of law, and stress and advocate harmony among the people and mediation as a means of dispute resolution. A large number of disputes have been resolved through mediation
7	Basic conclusions	China should give priority to learning from the Japanese experience over the experiences of other western countries in the modernization of the system of the rule of law, proceed from its own national conditions and the socialist nature of the country, and give full play to the advantages and characteristics of traditional Chinese culture	

Table 4.4 Development of the rule of law: a comparison between China and France and Germany

No.	Matters to be compared	China	France	Germany
1	Cultural background	The legal thoughts and systems in France and Germany have had an important influence on the development of the rule of law in China As far as its nature is concerned, the rule of law in China belongs to the family of socialist legal system. But as far as its legal form is concerned, it basically belongs to the family of continental law system. The development of the rule of law in China has been heavily influenced by such French political and legal thinkers as Montesquieu, Rousseau and Duguit and by such documents as the Civil War in France, Declaration of the Rights of Man and of the Citizen and the French Civil Code. Duguit visited China in the 1930s to help the Nationalist Government draft its constitution. German thinkers such as Marx, Hegel and Kant, German jurists such as Savigny and Jhering, and important German legal documents such as the German Civil Code and Weimar Constitution have all had an important influence on the development of the rule of law in China In late Qing Dynasty, Mr. Shen Jiaben, the minister in charge of the revision of the Qing Code, personally visited various European countries to investigate the history and current situation of capitalist rule of law and introduce western laws into China. Under his sponsorship, over 33 laws and legal works from Russia, France, Germany, Holland, Italy, Japan, Belgium, Switzerland and Finland had been translated into Chinese	France is one of the places of origin of the continental law system. Many important codes, institutions and principles of modern law, such as the first civil code, criminal code, commercial code, criminal procedure code and civil procedure code in modern history, the institutions of bankruptcy, company, notary public, trademark, civil agency, litigation preservation and the principles of equality before the law, separation of three powers, non-retroactivity of law, free evaluation of the evidence by judges, and justifiable defense, all originated in France	Germany is a typical continental law country. In accordance with the Roman Law tradition, its legal system consists of public law and private law. Private law takes party autonomy as its basis and the regulation of the relationship and resolution of conflicts of interest between private persons as its fundamental tasks. Public law takes the state as its basis and the establishment of the basis and the limitation of the state power as its main task. Public law disputes are under the jurisdiction of constitutional court and administrative courts whereas private law (civil and commercial law) disputes are under the jurisdiction of common courts
2	Road of development of rule of law			

(continued)

Table 4.4 (continued)

No.	Matters to be compared	China	France	Germany
3	Legislation		Legislation takes the forms of laws, emergency regulations, regulations, and departmental rules. The National Assembly adopts an average of 100 laws each year—half of them are related to international treaties; the other half of them are domestic laws. Normally, a law is supported by about ten pieces of detailed rules on its implementation. Each year, the government adopts about 500 pieces of detailed rules on the implementation of laws. The Constitutional Committee is responsible for the review of constitutionality of laws	Germany has developed a legal system consisting of various branches of law, including constitutional law, criminal law, criminal procedure law, civil law, commercial law, civil procedure law and administrative law. Normally each branch of law takes a code as its basis and core and numerous separate laws as supplements. The German Party Law, as the earliest party legislation in the world, is aimed at restraining and regulating the behavior of political parties
4	Administrative law enforcement		Administrative courts have history of over 200 years in France and play an important role in preventing the abuse of political power and protecting the lawful rights and interests of citizens; case law has an important position in administrative law; the principle of the rule of administrative law is the core principle of the French administrative law; France has achieved marked results in the supervision over administrative law enforcement	After the World War II, Germany entered into a period of "administration of social rule of law state", in which the state has extensive social administrative functions. Main developments in contemporary administrative law enforcement in Germany include: attaching importance to administrative efficiency and service-oriented administration; strengthening administrative legislation; continuously developing economic administration law; reforming administrative organization, expanding the social and economic functions of the government and its functional departments; strengthening government intervention in social economy; reforming administrative means; improving the efficiency and transparency of administrative activities; reforming the civil servant law; and strengthening the judicial remedy system

(continued)

Table 4.4 (continued)

No.	Matters to be compared	China	France	Germany
5	Administration of justice		France has established two court systems: administrative court system and common court system (judicial court system), which are independent from and operate parallel to each other. In 2001, the judicial court system dealt with a total of 9,936,950 criminal cases and 2,297,462 civil and commercial cases; the administrative court system accepted a total of 151,371 cases and concluded 146,181 cases. In November 2005, there were a total of 7402 judges in France. Among them, 5584 or 77.77% were trial judges, 1818 or 32% were prosecutors; in 2005, a total of 44,054 lawyers were registered a various lawyers' societies in France. Among them, 21,473 or near half were in the Paris Ile-de-France Region	German courts adhere to the principle of judicial independence. Judicial power is exercised by independent courts. Judges are appointed for life and obey only the law in the trial of cases. Ordinary courts are divided into four levels: primary courts; district courts, state courts, and federal courts; judicial power can be divided into five different types—criminal, civil, administrative, fiscal and social—which are exercised by five different courts. There are four levels of ordinary courts: local courts, regional courts, state courts and the Federal Court of Justice; three levels of administrative courts: lower, higher and federal; two levels of fiscal courts: state fiscal courts and the Federal Fiscal Court; three levels of labor courts: lower labor courts, state labor courts and the Federal Labor Court; and three levels of welfare courts: lower welfare courts, state welfare courts and the Federal Welfare Court. And there is a Federal Constitutional Court, which supervises over the observance of the Basic Law and decides on the disputes between the Federation and a state and between various organs of the Federal Government
6	Observance of law		The total population in France was 61 million in January 2006. In 2006, the total number of criminal cases occurred in Metropolitan France was 3,725,588 and the crime rate was 61.03‰. Among these criminal cases, 55.83% were cases of theft, 8.97% were cases of fraud and economic or financial crimes, 10.08% were cases of infringement on personal rights, and 25.12% were other cases of crimes, including drug-related crimes. Among those prosecuted for a criminal offense, 84.92% were male, 15.08% were female, 81.67% were adults, 18.33% were minors, 79.27% were French nationals, and 20.73% were foreigners	German people have a relatively high consciousness of the rule of law and good habit of observance of law. This consciousness and habit are inseparable from the school education in Germany. The education law of each state contains provisions on training students to abide by the law and observe public morality. German schools teach students about their obligations as citizens and moral standards, and cultivate their sense of responsibilities as citizens. Family education has a profound influence on the formation of outlook on life and morality

(continued)

Table 4.4 (continued)

No.	Matters to be compared	China	France	Germany
7	Overall assessment		Constitutional Council—the system of constitutional review; effective supervision over public power; legislative innovation: the recognition by the criminal law of crimes committed by legal persons embodies certain utilitarian tendency; France attaches importance to drawing on some systems in the common law system and socialist legal system, such as the plea bargain system in common law countries and the mediation system in China	The gap between China and Germany in legislation in the field of rule of law is also gradually narrowing. However, many problems still exist in the construction of rule of law in China, such as low quality of legislation, ineffective law enforcement, unfair administration of justice, and low consciousness of the rule of law among the general public. Compared with Germany, which has an effective law enforcement system and strong public consciousness of rule of law, China still has a long way to go

Table 4.5 Development of the rule of law: a comparison between China and the US

No.	Matters to be compared	China	US
1	Cultural background	In the construction of the rule of law, China mainly draws on the experience of western continental law countries on the basis of preserving traditional legal culture and mainly draws on the Soviet experience of socialist rule of law on the basis of adhering to the socialist system	common law system; British common law tradition; the national condition and actual needs after the establishment of the United States; the rule of law ideals of Montesquieu and others; and the efforts made by founding fathers of the United States
2	The road of development of the rule of law	The people's congress system; the system of multi-party cooperation and political consultations under the leadership of the CPC; people's democracy; adherence to the guiding role played by Marxism with Chinese characteristics in the construction of the rule of law and in legal research, to the "organic unity of three" and to the principle of the gradual advancement of democracy, human rights and the rule of law	The implementation of the system of separation of three powers; the two-party system; the presidential system; and the general election system; individual freedom and utilitarianism running through the rule of law and legal research; the gradual and step-by-step realization of rights and development of the rule of law
3	Legislation	the legislative system under the system of people's congress system; the strengthening of administrative legislation; the increasing supplementary role played by judicial interpretation in legislation; and the exercise of the power of constitutional review by the NPC	legislation dominated by the Congress; the strengthening of administrative legislation; the obvious role played by judges in law-making; constitutional review playing an important role in coordinating the relations between various laws
4	Administrative law enforcement	China is in the process of advancing administration by law and construction of a law-based government, but the realization of these goals takes a long time. Violation of law in the process of law enforcement occurs occasionally	The President has a strong power; law enforcement organs attach importance to administration by law; despite strict supervision over administrative power, violation of law by police officers and other law enforcement officials is still a prominent problem

(continued)

Table 4.5 (continued)

No.	Matters to be compared	China	US
5	Administration of justice	China adheres to the nature and characteristics of socialist administration of justice with Chinese characteristics and pursues fair, efficient and authoritative administration of justice; courts have no power of constitutional review; judicial interpretation is playing too big a role while lawyers not play a big enough role in the administration of justice	Separation of federal judicial power from state judicial power; judicial independence (the independence of judges); judges-made law; the exercise of judicial review by courts; lawyers playing a relatively big role in administration of justice
6	Observance of law	China has no tradition of democracy and the rule of law in history and the people generally lack respect for rules, but their consciousness of observance of law has been gradually enhanced; they value mediation over litigation and resolve their disputes by resorting first to feelings, then to reason and finally to law	The US has a solid cultural basis of the rule of law; citizens, enterprises and mass organizations all have a strong consciousness of the rule of law and solve their disputes by resorting first to law, then to reason, and finally to feelings. However, the crime rate is still high and public security situation is worrying in the US
7	Overall assessment	China has made remarkable achievements in the construction of the rule of law. However, it is obviously lagged behind the US in the regulation of administrative power, judicial independence, the construction of the lawyer's profession, and legal research and education. An American professor pointed out that the levels of technique and procedure of the rule of law and the degree of realization of the rule of law in China today are roughly the same as those of the US in the first half of the 20th Century	After 200 years of development since its establishment, the United States has already established relatively a mature legal structure, legal system and legal profession; citizens have a strong consciousness of law and the development of rule of law in the US has reached a high level

References

Deng X (1993) Selected works of Deng Xiaoping, vol 3. People's Publishing House, Beijing

Deng X (1994) Selected works of Deng Xiaoping, vol 2. People's Publishing House, Beijing

He Q (2002) Reflections on the transplantation of the soviet judicial system by the New China. Peking Univ Law J 3

Heberer T (2005) Research on some issues relating to the China Model, vol 5, Contemporary World and Socialism

Li J (2009) Scholars should be cautious in using the term 'China Model', in *Study Times*, 7 Dec 2009

Mao Z (1991) Selected works of Mao Zedong, vol 4. People's Publishing House, Beijing

Zhao Q (2009) China has no intention of exporting any "Model", in *Study Times*, 7 Dec 2009

Chapter 5
Realizing Fairness and Justice Through the Rule of Law

5.1 What Is Fairness and Justice in the Legal Sense

Fairness and justice is a core value of socialism as well as the soul of the rule of law in China. Fairness is the lifeline of the rule of law. In order to advance in an all-round way ruling the country by law, we must adhere to the principles of relying on the people, benefiting the people, protecting the people, taking the safeguarding of people's basic rights and interests as the starting point and ultimate goal, ensuring that people enjoy extensive rights and freedoms and assume corresponding responsibilities, upholding social fairness and justice and promoting common prosperity in the process of construction of the rule of law. Judicial fairness plays an important guiding role in the realization of social justice whereas miscarriage of justice has a fatal destructive effect on social justice. Therefore, it is necessary to improve judicial administration system and the mechanism for the operation of judicial power, regulate judicial behavior, strengthen the supervision over judicial activities, and strive to let people to feel fairness and justice in every judicial case tried. In comprehensively advancing ruling the country by law, China must take the promotion of fairness, justice and the welfare of the people as the starting point and ultimate goal. So, what is fairness and justice in the legal sense?

Fairness and justice is one of the eternal questions of value philosophy as well as one of the most controversial questions in human social life. Since time immemorial, almost all questions relating to value judgment in the people's ideological understanding, the interests and rights pursued by the people, and the determination of merits and demerits in the people's social activities have all been closely related to fairness and justice. The concept of fairness and justice has been given many different, even opposite, definitions and interpretations by people of different historical times, social groups, fields of specialization, schools of thought, and social classes, and from different interest positions and point of views. Just as the famous Austrian jurist Hans Kelsen pointed out: "What is justice is a question that has existed since time immemorial. To answer this question, countless people have shed their precious

© China Social Sciences Press and Springer Nature Singapore Pte Ltd. 2018
L. Li, *The Chinese Road of the Rule of Law*, China Insights,
https://doi.org/10.1007/978-981-10-8965-7_5

blood and bitter tears and countless distinguished thinkers, from Plato to Kant, have racked their brains. However, the question remains unanswered today, just as in the past."[1] American jurist Edgar Bodenheimer also said that: "Justice has a Protean face, capable of change, readily assuming different shapes, highly variable features. When we look deeply into its face, trying to find out secrets hidden behind its outward appearance, bewilderment befalls us."[2]

In the Chinese context, the question of justice involves three key words: fairness, impartiality and justice.

The so-called fairness is a term of reciprocity that normally applies to people with equal status. It refers to fairness of opportunity, process and result of citizens' participation in economic, political and social affairs.

Impartiality normally refers to the stand and attitude that should be adopted by social authorities and individuals in handling social affairs. "Take the legal relationship between the judge (arbitrator) and the parties in a case as an example. The concept of fairness emphasizes the enjoyment and upholding of the rights of the parties, whereas impartiality emphasizes the equal-handedness and selflessness of the intermediary; the core of fairness is equality, namely similar cases should be treated similarly, whereas impartiality takes selflessness and neutrality as its core. It means that, in deciding a case, the intermediary should be influenced neither by his own emotion, nor by any outside pressure or the status or background of any party to the case."[3]

The so-called justice mainly refers to the affirmative judgment on questions of right and wrong and good and evil in the political, legal and moral fields. Justice is the philosophical connotation of fairness. It includes social justice, political justice, and legal justice. As a moral category, justice has the same meaning as "fairness", mainly referring to behaviors that comply with certain social moral standard. As a legal category, justice is sometimes also expressed as "fairness and justice". It includes formal and substantive legal justice, mainly referring to activities that comply with norms on legal procedure and substantive legal provisions, especially judicial trial activities.

Related to the concept are the concepts of social justice and social fairness. The former means "giving everyone what he or she deserves" whereas the latter means to treat all persons and matters equally without discrimination. Here, social justice has an obvious "moral value orientation", emphasizes the "basic value orientation" of society, and stresses the legitimacy of such value orientation, whereas social fairness has obvious instrumentality. It emphasizes the "same criterion" for judging all persons and matters, or giving equal treatment without discrimination and preventing the application of different standards to different persons or matters. As for the reasonableness or legitimacy of the criterion, it is outside the scope of consideration of fairness. Therefore, all things that are just must also be fair, but not necessarily all

---

[1] Quoted in Zhang (1996, p. 575).
[2] Bodenheimer (1999, p. 252).
[3] Ma (2012, p. 5).

things that are fair are also just. This, in the opinions of some scholars, is the most important distinction between social fairness and social justice.

In fact, in the opinions of some western scholars, "'fairness' should be used to explain 'justice', but the word closest in meaning to 'justice' in ordinary sense is 'desert'. If one person gives another person his desert, then what the former has done to the latter is just."[4] The understanding of justice is often embodied in moral assessment of what things "should" or "ought" to be, which come from the moral system formed in the cultural tradition of a society. Plato held that justice is "good", "this concept of good controls every person and influences his soul, even though he has made some mistakes. If so, every act done is consistent with such good, and every part of human nature is controlled by good, then we have to call it justice. This is the best part of human life."[5] The Institutes of Justinian states at its every beginning: "Justice is the set and constant purpose which gives to every man his due."

The famous British jurist Friedrich Hayek used a large space of his book Law, Legislation and Liberty to discuss the issue of justice. In his opinion: "To speak of justice always implies that some person or persons ought, or ought not, to have performed some action; and this 'ought' in turn presupposes the recognition of rules which define a set of circumstances wherein a certain kind of conduct is prohibited or required."[6] In other words: "It is universally considered just that each person should obtain that (whether good or evil) which he deserves; and unjust that he should obtain a good, or be made to undergo an evil, which he does not deserve."[7] However, Hayek tended to have a negative attitude towards the concept of social justice. He said that John Stuart Mill regarded "social justice and distributive justice as synonyms." "Society should treat all equally well who have deserved equally well of it, that is, who have deserved equally well absolutely. This is the highest abstract standard of social and distributive justice; towards which all institutions, and the efforts of all virtuous citizens should be made in the utmost degree to converge."[8] He pointed out that: "Not only 'social justice' but also 'social democracy', 'social market economy' or the 'social state of law' (or rule of law-in German sozialer Rechtsstaat) are expressions which, though justice, democracy, the market economy or the Rechtsstaat have by themselves perfectly good meanings, the addition of the adjective 'social' makes them capable of meaning almost anything one likes. The word has indeed become one of the chief sources of confusion of political discourse."[9] "The most common attempts to give meaning to the concept of 'social justice' resort to egalitarian considerations".[10] "Though we have no positive criteria of justice, we do have negative criteria which show us what is unjust."[11] He further explained that:

---

[4]Beauchamp (1990, pp. 327–328).

[5]Plato (2001, p. 295).

[6]von Hayek (2000b, p. 52).

[7]See John Stuart Mill, *Utilitarianism*, Chap. V.

[8]von Hayek (2000b, p. 118).

[9]Ibid., p. 140.

[10]Ibid., p. 142.

[11]Ibid., p. 65.

"If it is not the intended or foreseen result of somebody's action that A should have much and B little, this cannot be called just or unjust… We shall see that what is called 'social' or 'distributive' justice is indeed meaningless within a spontaneous order and has meaning only within an organization,"[12] because "Justice is thus emphatically not a balancing of particular interests at stake in a concrete case, or even of the interests of determinable classes of persons"[13] In his opinion, "Justice is an attribute of human conduct…strictly speaking, only human conduct can be called just or unjust. If we apply the terms to a state of affairs, they have meaning only in so far as we hold someone responsible for bringing it about or allowing it to come about. A bare fact, or a state of affairs which nobody can change, may be good or bad, but not just or unjust. To apply the term 'just' to circumstances other than human actions or the rules governing them is a category mistake."[14]

Famous American political thinker John Rawls proposes in his book *A Theory of Justice* that all basic social values—the basis of freedom, opportunity, income, wealth and self-respect—should be distributed equally, unless the unequal distribution of one or all the values is in the interest of every individual of society. From this idea of justice, he derived two principles of justice: the first one is the principle of equality; the second one is the difference principle and fair equality of opportunity. The first principle is not difficult to understand. The difference principle means that the distributed justice should be "to the greatest benefit of the least advantaged members of society". Justice is realized through the reasonable distribution of various institutions, including the legislation. The value orientation of distribution is the realization of justice, whereas the external form of justice is equal interests—various tangible or intangible interests. Apparently Rawls tried to understand formal justice as correspondent of substantive justice: formal justice means "similar cases are treated similarly, the relevant similarities and differences being those identified by the existing norms. The correct rule as defined by institutions is regularly adhered to and properly interpreted by the authorities. This impartial and consistent administration of laws and institutions, whatever their substantive principles."[15] As far as its content is concerned, formal justice include such natural justice precepts as "ought implies can", "similar cases are treated similarly", "*nullum crimen sine lege*", and upholding the integrity of judicial process. In this sense, formal justice is also the rule of law.

Chinese legal scholar Professor Zhuo Zeyuan points out that impartiality can be understood as the synonym of fairness or the synonym of justice, or as general term for both fairness and justice. In Chinese language, there is a big difference between fairness and justice. The former seems to emphasize more the reasonableness and impartiality of adjudicative subjects or rules of adjudication whereas justice seems to emphasize more the ultimate reasonableness and compliance with moral principles…in the relevant dictionaries, fairness and justice are often placed side by

---

[12]Ibid., p. 53.

[13]Ibid., p. 60.

[14]Ibid., p. 50.

[15]Rawls (1988, p. 58).

side to each other.[16] In view of the usage of Chinese language and for the convenience of writing, I will not make distinctions between the different Chinese words for "justice" in this chapter, unless there is a special need to do so.

Since "we do not have any conclusive knowledge about what is justice and what is injustice"[17] and "since no one can determine what is just, someone must decide what is legal",[18] then we must let the law to determine the concrete content of justice, the mode of behavior, and the criteria of rights and obligations, and realize fairness and justice through legal method and legal procedure.

Compared with the justice in the moral sense, justice in the legal sense has the following characteristics: First, explicitness. Justice in the legal sense is explicit about its subjects, objects, and content and has explicit legal bases for the determination of such questions as who enjoy rights, who bear responsibilities, how to perform duties and carry out actions, and how legal relations are formed and changed. Second, normativity. Justice in the legal sense is abstractly summarized, concretely expressed and clearly provided for by the constitution, laws, administrative regulations and local regulations. It is usually manifested in such relationships as rights and obligations, powers and responsibilities, and interests and actions. Legal provisions and legal basis are the basic criteria of justice as well as the basic standards for distinguishing justice from injustice. Third, unity. The justice in the legal sense adheres to the principle of the unity of the rule of law and the principle of equality of everyone before the law. All subjects within the sovereign power of a state and the areas covered by law are treated equally. Judicial organs treat similar matters in a similar way; and no privilege or special interest is allowed outside the law. Fourth, justiciability. Justice in the legal sense is clear, concrete and foreseeable. A subject of legal relationship who believes that he himself has been treated unequally or unfairness or that his rights has been infringed upon can and ought to seek remedy through judicial procedure. The court is the last line of defense for the justice in the legal sense.

5.2 Why Should Justice Be Realized Through the Rule of Law?

In western culture, law is a science of justice and injustice. Justice is the highest value pursued by law. In western languages, "jus" is a polysemous word that has the meanings of justice, fairness, uprightness, law and rights. It refers to views, behaviors, activities, thoughts and institutions that are just and reasonable. The minimum requirement of justice is that the distribution of social interests and undertaking of social obligations are not arbitrary, but must following certain norms, procedures and standards. The universality of justice requires the equal distribution of social interests and obligations in accordance with certain standards (equality in terms of

---

[16]Zhuo (2013, p. 161).

[17]MacCormick et al. (1994, p. 266).

[18]von Hayek (2000b, pp. 71–72).

quantity, contribution or status). Distributors of social interests and obligations must keep certain degree of neutrality. Justice can also be used to express the good individual and social ethical conditions, such as security, order, harmony, tolerance, respect, and happiness. In this sense, the pursuit and the safeguarding of the value objective of justice is one of the important reasons human society need law and the rule of law civilization.

In the West, the words "law" in English, "ius" and "lex" in Latin, "droit" and "loi" in French, and "recht" and "gestz" in German can all be used to express the concept of law, whereas the words "ius", "droit", "recht" also have the connotations of rights, fairness, and justice. It can be said that in the western context, there is an inherent connection between law and justice. It is even believed that the law is a tool for realizing justice. Aristotle said that: "it is evident that in seeking for justice men seek for the mean or neutral, for the law is the mean."[19] And ancient Roman jurist Celsus said that: "Law is the art of the good and the equitable (*Ius est ars boni et aequi*)".

In China, the word "law" also has the meaning of justice. According to the book Shuowen Jiezi (Analytical Dictionary of Chinese Characters), the ancient form of the Chinese character "law" is "灋", which means criminal punishment. It consists of three parts: "氵", which literally means water, suggesting the law is as even as the surface of water, namely it treats everyone with equality; "廌" refers to a mythical cattle-like beast with one horn that settled disputes by ramming the party at fault"; and "去", which means to drive away those who are unjust."[20] This means that the word "law" has the meaning of "passing fair judgment on what is right and what is wrong" and has the authority of "trial by god". So what is law? Ancient Chinese politician Guanzi said that: "The law is a standard, just like a carpenter's line marker, gauge, or scale"[21]; that "The so-called laws are the rules used to regulate various social behaviors, distinguish right from wrong, and safeguard people's life and property"; and that "Laws and decrees are the code of conduct for both the people and public officials"[22]; and that: "law is like a parent to the people."[23] Mozi said that: "The artisans make square objects according to the square, circular objects according to the compasses; they draw straight lines with the carpenter's line…Thus all artisans follow the standards in their work."[24] Mencius said that: "Without the compass and square, one could not make squares and circles." And Shang Yang said that "Law is the standard for the determination of right and wrong in a country".[25]

From the above we can see that, in both Chinese and western legal cultures, laws are the fundamental basis for the judgment and determination of right and wrong,

---

[19] Aristotle (1981, p. 169).

[20] Quoted in Qichao (1999, p. 1258).

[21] See Guanzi: Qifa.

[22] See Guanzi: Qizhuqichen.

[23] See Guanzi: Fafa.

[24] See Mozi: On the Necessity of Standards.

[25] See Shang Jun Shu: Cultivation of the Right Standard.

violations of law and crimes, rights and obligations, and liabilities and punishments, as well as the rules and criteria on the resolution of disputes. Law has not only such behavioral characteristics as normativity, definitiveness, and operability, but also value characteristics related to justice, rationality, and freedom. It is an important institutional arrangement that concretizes, normalizes, unifies and standardizes morally indeterminate justice and fairness. In contemporary Chinese society, we can often see the following phenomena: in cities, when some peccant buildings are demolished by administrative law enforcement organs in accordance with law, the owners of such buildings would often put up such signs as "seeking justice" and "upholding human rights" to resist the administrative law enforcement action and demand compensation and restoration of the buildings"; in the countryside, the secretary of a village Party committee who had been removed from his office and expelled from the Party in the 1950s or 1960s for using public funds on gambling is today demanding not only political rehabilitation, but also compensation for the "economic losses" he has suffered in the past fifty years, including the "economic losses" he has suffered as a result of loss of opportunity to hold a higher position; in universities, those who have not been conferred senior academic titles complain that they have been treated unfairly by the leaders of the university or the evaluation committee of professional titles; those who have been conferred senior professional titles also have complaints because they believe that they should have been conferred the professional titles a long time ago; in government organs, those who get promoted to a higher position complain that their colleagues who have less qualifications have been promoted to the same position many years ago; those who have not got promoted complain even more because they believe they deserve the titles by virtue of their hard work, even if they have made no contribution in their fields of specialization; in the business circle, those who have made big money complain that they have been working too hard without a strong backing or patron in the government and that their money are hard-earned; those who have not earned big money have even more complaints, blaming the government and everybody else for their poverty and being full of hatred towards government officials, the rich people and society as a whole; in the courtroom, those who have won the case complain about the strict judge, the black-hearted lawyers, the high litigation fees and the tedious proceedings, whereas those who have lost the case complain about miscarriage of justice, judicial corruption, and judges who pervert justice for a bribe; some people curse the government and society while enjoying the achievements of reform and opening up; some others curse when the real estate price rises and create a disturbance when the real estate price falls… It seems that, in front of the interest cake of social justice, less and less people are satisfied or content with what they have and more are dissatisfied, complaining, cursing and creating disturbances. The causes behind these chaotic phenomena are numerous and complicated, but most of them are related to the misjudgment and incorrect understanding of the value of social justice. Friedrich Hayek had noticed the social limitation of the concept of "social justice" a long time ago: "When we ask what ought to be the relative remunerations of a nurse or a butcher, or a coal miner and a judge at a high court, of the deep sea diver and the cleaner of sewers, of the organiser of a new industry and a jockey, of the inspector of taxes and the inventor of a life-saving drug, of the jet-pilot or the professor of mathematics, the appeal to 'social justice' does not give us the slightest help in answering this question."[26]

Today, many individuals, even groups, in China take "social justice" as their moral banner and justification to make all kinds of demands on society, which is represented by the government. For example, those who have been laid off often demand for a job, salary, subsidies, welfare, compensation, etc.; those who have lost a lawsuit often demand for justice, human rights, the rule of law, the punishment of a certain judge, the change or abrogation of a judgment, etc.; those who are dissatisfied with the compensation for housing demolition and resettlement often demand for the cancellation of housing demolition and resettlement, substantial increase in compensation, arrangement for relocation and employment, or punishment of corrupt officials, etc.; those who believe that they are treated unfairly in employment, salary, welfare, medical service and pension often raise economic demands directly relating to employment, salary, welfare, medical service and pension. If these demands are not met, they might upgrade their demands from economic ones to political ones, such as the opposition to "corrupt officials", the government, the system or certain policies or laws. All these demands raised under the banner of "social justice" involve a core question: what is "social justice"? The state and society have provided no uniform moral standard, let along an objective and generally accepted standard, that can be used to answer this question. As a result, every individual or group can raise demands on the government or society on ground of "social justice", regardless of whether these demands are reasonable or whether they are supported by laws and policies. Especially under the influence of such negative ideas as "the law cannot be enforced when everyone is an offender", when more and more people join a demand for social justice, it seems the justifiability, reasonableness and legitimacy of a demand are strengthened with the increase of the number of people making the demand. This logic of "the more people making a demand, the more reasonable the demand is" has been used repeatedly and even popularized in many large-scale mass disturbances, and become a kind of negative "social consensus".

With the deepening of the nationwide legal education work, the rise of the rights protection "movement", and the rapid spread of the behavior pattern of "seeking justification and gains by creating a disturbance", social justice, as a lofty value concept, while continuously enhancing the morality and moral cognition of the general public, has often been misunderstood or abused and become the "excuse" or "basis" for various acts of challenging political authorities and disrupting legal order, and used a shield, even a moral weapon, by those who commit all kinds of injustice.

Looking from another angle, even in situations where individual interests are actually harmed as a result of the defects in the exercise of public powers, such as improper method of law enforcement, insufficient compensation for housing demolition and resettlement, lack of transparency in judicial proceedings, inappropriately light or heavy sentencing, error or delay in the implementation of policies and laws, or as a result of adjustments of interests in the process of social transition, such as adjustment of policies, revision of laws, change of standards, restructuring of enter-

---

[26]von Hayek (2000b, p. 135).

prises, dissolution of institutions, and sudden change of situation in the market, the demands raised by individuals whose interests are actually affected should still be compatible with the spirit of the rule of law and the principle of balance of interests. Even if their demands are supported by law, such demands must be proportionate to the harms to their rights and interests. They should never raise unreasonable demands. The situation in which those who create a big disturbance get a big compensation, those who create a small disturbance get a small compensation, and those who create no disturbance get no compensation must be changed.

In view of the facts that justice in the sense of value philosophy, being mainly a moral judgment and pursuit, has great subjectivity, randomness, and uncertainty, that people's understandings of and demands for social justice in today's pluralistic Chinese society are diversified, complex and variable, that the market economy in China encourages people to pursue the maximization of economic and other interests in a lawful way, thus inevitably leading to pluralism of value and conflicts of interests, that the deepening of the reform and social transition will inevitably lead to frequent occurrence of various social conflicts, in which all parties try to occupy moral high ground and justify their own acts by holding high the banner of "justice", that the understandings of social justice by the government, society and individual citizens may be very different from, even opposite to, each other as a result of their different roles and perspectives, and that contemporary Chinese society lacks basic consensus and criteria for the determination of "justice", it is even more necessary to attach importance to the realization of justice through the rule of law.

It should be recognized that justice in a society under the rule of law is relative in value attribute because, firstly, people's understanding of justice is relative. What is believed to be just by the majority of people, in one society, or during one period of time may not be considered so by the minority of people, in another society, or during another period of time; secondly, as a result of conflicting interest relations, legislators, in the application of the principle of justice, generally can only realize the formal (procedural) justice, but cannot ensure the complete *de facto* justice. Procedural justice is usually pre-established. In a democratic society under the rule of law, procedures must be discussed by the public and agreed upon by the majority of the people and rules on the distribution of interests must be established. Then the concrete distribution of interests should be carried out through the application of procedures in accordance with the principle of equality of everyone before the rules (laws). Before the formation of rules (procedures), the main characteristics of justices procedural justice mainly refers to the democratic nature of discussion, the possibility of bargaining, and the diversity of the expression of interests; after the formation of rules (procedures), procedural justice mainly refers to the openness, universality, definitiveness and abstract nature of rules and equality and consistency of their application; thirdly, just premises do not necessarily lead to just results whereas unjust results are often caused by unjust or just premises. What the legislation is able to do is neither to completely eliminate the gap between the premises and the results, nor directly unify just premises of legislation and just results of application of law. Such value objectives can only exist in ideal conditions, but cannot be achieved by any legislation. What legislation is able do is to narrow the gap between the two through preventive and remedial measures. For example, the state law that guarantees the lawfulness and inviolability of private property is unfair to those who have no or little private property because it provides a possibility or a strong possibility of protection, but actual excludes those who have no private property from its scope of application. This legal guarantee also has little meaning to people with little private property. Under this circumstance, what legislators can do is to ensure through such mechanisms as taxation, social welfare and redistribution that the state, while safeguarding private properties, also strives to realize justice in result, namely the relative sharing of social wealth. Fourthly, people with different personalities and needs have different, even opposite, understandings of the same results. Therefore, the justice that is manifested in the form of fairness can only get increasingly closer to, but could never reach, absolute justice. What the legislators can pursue is only a relative justice. Apparently, what is understood by legislators to be justice is not necessarily considered to be justice, or even can be considered to be injustice, by the majority of the people. Therefore, what a society under the rule of law should pursue is relative justice, procedural justice or justice of rules. A society under the rule of law advocates de facto justice and justice of result, but cannot ensure the realization of such justice. A society under the rule of law pursues justice in the form of rights, opportunity, process, and procedure. China will be able to achieve this justice as long as it is able to comprehensively advance ruling the country by law and truly realize scientific legislation, strict law enforcement, impartial administration of justice, observance of law by the whole people, good law and good governance, and safeguarding of human rights.

The justice pursued by a society under the rule of law is concrete, relative, based on law, and can be safeguarded and remedied through legal procedures. In a society under the rule of law, nobody should advocate justice in an abstract way, pursue justice outside legal rules, or even seek the realization of justice in a way that undermines legal order or violates the rights of others.

"In the face of human imperfection, we articulate the rule of law partly in terms of procedures designed not to secure that absolute justice will be done, but to be a safeguard against the worst sort of injustice. Injustice rather than justice 'wears the trousers' in political philosophy, because, being fallible, we cannot say in advance what the just decision will always be, and, living among selfish men, we cannot always secure that it will be carried out, so for the sake of definitiveness, we adopt a negative approach, and lay down procedures to avoid certain likely forms of injustice, rather than aspires to all forms of justice."[27]

To realization justice through the rule of law, it is necessary to meet four requirements: firstly, to give full play to the functions of the rule of law and reconstruct the basic system of assessment of social justice. The law is a general code of conduct that embodies the will of the state and a distributor of social interests and social resources. More importance should be attached to giving full play to the basic role of the rule of law as the guidance in the judgment of social values and the standard of social behavior, so as to bring the public interest demands for justice under the

---

[27] von Hayek (2000b, p. 101).

rule of law. It is necessary to transform through scientific legislation abstract reasonable demands for justice into concrete and clear legal rights and interests, and safeguard through strict law enforcement and impartial administration of justice the lawful rights and interests of the people. The public should uphold and realize by legal means the justice manifested in the form of their legal rights and interests. The legislature should, on the basis of giving full play to democracy and fully understanding various interest demands of the public, sum up and make a list of "rights ought to be", so as to systematize and clarify public interest demands for justice. Then, in light of state and social resources and in order of priorities, gradually transform through democratic legislative procedures the "rights ought to be" in the list into legal rights and bring the public interest demands on justice into the orbit of rights and the rule of law. Secondly, to reasonably provide for the rights and obligations of citizens, rationally distribute various resources and interests, and scientifically allocate various powers and responsibilities through fair and justice substantive laws, so as to realize substantive distributive justice. Thirdly, to adopt through democratic, scientific and effective procedural law the procedural rules that fully reflect public opinions and are accepted by the majority of people, realize through procedural law the allocation of resources, balance of interests, resolution of contradictions, alleviation of conflicts, and achievement of the procedural justice. And fourthly, to resolve various disputes and conflicts of interest through various legal procedures and mechanisms, including judicial procedures, so as to realize both substantive justice and procedural justice, or at least judicial procedural justice, under the rule of law.

5.3   Transforming Moral Demands for Justice into Law Through Democratic and Scientific Legislation

Law is an important tool of state governance and good law is the precondition of good governance. In the construction of a socialist system of the rule of law with Chinese characteristics, China must adhere to the principle of adopting legislation in advance, giving full play to the guiding and promotional role of legislation, and taking the improvement of the quality of legislation as the key. It must ensure that legislation is people-oriented and for the people and implements the socialist core values, so that every piece of legislation is compatible with the spirit of the Constitution, reflect the people's will, and be supported by the people. It must also ensure that the principles of justice, fairness, and openness run through the whole process of legislation, improve the legislative mechanism, attach equal importance to the making, revision, abolition, and interpretation of laws, and enhance the timeliness, systematicness, pertinence, and effectiveness of laws and administrative regulations. Legislation is the collection and expression of the people's will. Its main function is to reasonably distribute social interests and adjust social interest relations. Through democratic methods and legal procedures, it reasonably allocates social resources, assigns rights and obligations, arranges such substantive interests as powers and responsibilities, establishes the relevant procedures, adopts codes of conduct, delimits the boundaries of behaviors, and defines behavioral patterns, so as to realize the objectives of distributive justice. Aristotle believed that the process of legislation is the distribution of justice. Hayek stressed that: "The criteria of justice should be determined through legislation."[28] Because "people believe that all that can be decided by legislative decision must be a question of justice, and that it is the will of the legislature which determines what is just."[29]

In order to realize distributive justice in legislation, a modern society needs to give full play to people's democracy, allow various interest groups to participate in legislation and fully and effectively express their interest demands and opinions while at the same time listen to the interest demands of others, enable various social forces and social interests to fully participate in game-playing, make compromise to each other, reach consensus and embody such consensus in the law. "Fairness in real and genuine sense is the spirit and soul of all laws. Positive law is explained by it and rational law derives from it… The principle of fairness under statutory law means treating similar cases similarly and the principle of fairness above statutory law means to make fair judgment in accordance with human reason and emotion."[30]

Although western scholars who advocate taking justice as the inherent value of legislation, such as Aristotle and Rawls, give different interpretations to "justice", they all recognize the existence of a value criterion that can be taken as the basis of legislation and that the legislation is just a process of legalization of justice. Some western scholars who adhere to the natural law theory take reason, fairness and equality as the inherent value of law and maintain that legislation is only the concrete activity that follows and embodies these value principles. Applying the values that belong to the category of moral philosophy to legislation and evaluation of laws is the main characteristic of the theory of legislative value because the recognition or denial of value of behavior and the value orientation of social relations in the legislative process all embody the people's demand for social morals and value orientation. Utilitarianism, which takes interest as the inherent value of legislation, essentially takes interest as a core standard of value to raise demand and pass judgment on legislative activities, and takes the confirmation of "the best interest of the greatest majority of people" as the value orientation of legislation. Many value conflicts in western society, such as those between the safeguarding of human rights and restriction of freedom for the achievement of certain objectives, between women's right to abortion and the fetus' right to life, between wiretapping for the purpose of protecting public security and the freedom of communication, between the right to carry a gun and the safeguarding of the right to life, between the right to privacy and public security, between the freedom of speech and prohibition of libel, and between the patient's demand for euthanasia and the doctor's moral and legal obligation of healing the wounded and rescuing the dying, have all been unfolded around the core value of justice. It can be said that the most important function of the law as a

---

[28] von Hayek (2000b, p. 135).

[29] Ibid., pp. 49–50.

[30] Kim (1989, p. 79).

regulator of social relations is to resolve various value conflicts through legislation, thereby realizing the justice in the legal sense.

The Marxists holds that the law is the embodiment of certain economic relations, and "economic relations in each society are first of all manifested as interest."[31] "Both political and civil law-makings are but the manifestations and recordings of demands of economic relations."[32] In a certain sense, economic relations can be boiled down to interest relations, which obviously affect, restrict or drive the judgment and choice of value in legislation. They are the incentives that motivate legislators to make laws and the value objectives that guide legislators to carry out legislative activities. In order to strike a balance among various interests in legislation, it is necessary to introduce a higher standard, namely the value standard of justice, and use it to distribute various interests and ensure that the distribution can be basically accepted by various parties. If attention is paid only to the interest value of legislation, the legislation might slip into the mires of utilitarianism, resulting in intolerable inclination of its interest value, excessive partiality to private properties and a polarized society in which "the poor get poorer and the rich get richer". The phenomenon of unfair distribution of social wealth and the polarization of the society also exist in China. Analyzed from the point of view of legislative value, the interest-inclination policy of "letting some people get rich first", although stresses getting rich through labor and in accordance with law, has nevertheless led to the following question: who "let" some people to get rich first, the government or the market? A further question is: what rules are followed by the government, or what mechanisms are used by the market, in "letting" some people get rich first? Different rules or mechanisms can lead to very different results. If the government is partial, for example, practices departmental or regional protectionism, or negligent—"doing a bad thing out of good intention"–in legislation, or if the legislation is manipulated by some interest groups to become "inclined" to themselves, then such legislation will probably lead to corruption, bureaucracy, or "abuse of legislation for personal gains" in the process of "letting some people get rich first". Under many circumstances, the polarization between the rich and the poor in society is caused by unfair legislations, institutions and policies. Therefore, the principle of getting rich in accordance with law does not necessarily ensure the fairness of distribution of interests. Only legislations that meet the value requirements of justice can ensure the appropriate distribution of the interest value of legislation, and the reasonableness and the genuine legitimacy of the policy of "getting rich through labor and in accordance with law". Democratic legislation is a process of interest game-playing and bargaining, in which "people can go to legislative organs to frankly discuss interests".[33] Even if the interests are definitively distributed by the market, such distribution still needs to be regulated by fair legislation. Although the market itself has the function of distributing interests according to the law of value, it is inherently motivated by the maximization of interests, even "seeks nothing but interest". The market only provides the driving force and certain basis of calculation

---

[31] Marx and Engels (1995, p. 209).
[32] Marx and Engels (1958, pp. 121–122).
[33] Lawrence (1994, p. 265).

in the distribution of interests, but cannot ensure that the process and the result of distribution of interest are generally accepted by society as just. Only by enabling people to first reach a consensus through such social consultation mechanisms as full expression of will, bargaining, and mutual compromise, then transforming the consensus into norms and laws, and finally carrying out market distribution of interest in accordance with such legal rules and established procedures, will it be possible to achieve the justice in the market distribution of interest that can be recognized by social evaluation.

Legislation is the precondition of construction of the rule of law and realization of good law and good governance, the embodiment of the unity and transformation into state will of the Party's propositions and the people's will, as well as a process of providing legal basis for the realization of social justice through legislative justice in China. The formation on schedule of the legal system has provided solid legal basis for the construction of the rule of law and good precondition for comprehensively advancing strict enforcement of law, fair administration of justice, and observance of law by the whole people in China. However, because of many problems in the legislation in China, some laws are unusable, inoperable, difficult to implement, apply, or comply, or even exist only in name after their adoption. These problems include: first, emphasizing the quantity, the efficiency, and the form of legislation while ignoring the quality, the democratic nature and the actual effect of legislation, even treating legislation as a vanity project, making laws and regulations without considering whether they can be effective implemented. Second, the phenomena of domination of legislation by administrative organs, manipulation of legislation by special interest groups, and infiltration into legislation by big foreign corporations and consortiums, which have to a certain extent affected the fairness, authority and credibility of legislation. The problems of "departmentalization of administrative power, profitization of departmental power, and legalization of departmental interest" still exist, and some legislations bearing the obvious impress of departmental interest or special interest have legalized abnormal interest structure or power relations. Third, the degree of diversity, effectiveness, and normalization of the institutions, mechanisms, and procedures designed to enable citizens and stakeholders to participate in legislation still falls short of the requirements of democratic legislation. Citizens and social organizations often become "disadvantaged groups" in the legislative process. As a result, some legislations are unable to fully reflect and embody popular will. Fourth, because of such phenomena as "negative legislation", "passive legislation", "legislation that blurs the line between right and wrong and avoids the important and dwells on the trivial" and the fact that legislative organs are afraid, unable, and unwilling to use legislation to solve difficult problems, some laws have "congenital" defects that impede the strict enforcement of law, fair administration of justice and observance of law by the whole people. Fifth, as a result of the unsatisfactory operation of the mechanisms for reporting legislation to competent authorities for the record, for decision and for review and the unsound legislative supervision mechanism, legislative conflicts still exist, which have a negative impact on the application of laws and the authority of legislation. Sixth, the recent changes in the quality, ability, behavioral mode, interest demand, and political ethics of deputies to people's congresses have resulted in complicated situations of local legislation in which the principle of legislation for the people and embodying the unity of the Party's propositions and the people's will is not strictly followed, thus leading to "legislative corruption".

In order to realize justice through democratic and scientific legislation, it is necessary to change the idea and the mode of legislation. In legislation, attention should be paid to fully representing people's will, embodying people's interest, reflecting people conditions, resolving social problems and distributing social wealth in a fair way, and preventing departmental and local protectionisms, the legalization of abnormal interest structure and power relations, and the corruption of legislative power, so as to uphold people's interests at the source of institutions and norms. The legislative idea should be changed from one that takes economic construction as the center to one that emphasizes the comprehensive and coordinated economic, political, social and cultural development, from one that one-sidedly pursues the quantity of legislation while ignoring the quality and the actual effect of legislation to one that gives priority to the quality and actual effect of legislation, and from one that over-emphasizes the adoption of new laws to one that attaches equal importance to the adoption, revision, supplementation, interpretation, cleaning up, abolition, codification and translation of laws. Attention should also be paid to giving full play to the auxiliary role of interpretation of the Constitutional and laws in promoting the implementation of the Constitution and laws.

Meanwhile, efforts should be made to promote democratic legislation, expand the channel for different interest groups to publicize their opinions and express their interests, enable the public to fully express their legislative will and interest demands, so as to realize justice through legislative game playing. China should establish and further improve the mechanism for more extensive solicitation of public opinions on draft laws. In principle, all legislative affairs that involve public interest should be made public and mechanisms should be established for the explanation of and feedback on the situation of adoption of public opinions on legislative affairs. Legislative hearing system should be further improved. Legislative hearing should be held on draft legislations that have major impact on public interest, so as to ensure that all stakeholders are able to fully participate in the legislation and effectively carry out legislative game playing, and that the public is able to fully express their legislative demands. China should establish a system whereby lawyers and legal experts provide professional consultation and legal aid on the participation in legislative hearing to the stakeholders of draft legislations; promote legislative openness, establish systems whereby representatives of the public can audit the meetings of the standing committees of people's congresses and special committees in which drafts of laws, administrative regulations and local regulations are deliberated. At such meetings, representatives of the public should have the right to speak, so as to guarantee the right of the public to know and to supervise the legislation.

Legislation deals with various conflicts of interest in accordance with the principle of justice. It distributes interest not for the sake of interest, but for the sake of justice and it takes justice as the criterion to distribute interest and evaluate the distribution of interest. Therefore, legislators must take into consideration the value requirements of justice when they design and deliberate on the inclination or balance of different interests. Just as Paul A. Freund said: "The criteria applied by judges in adjudication are consistency, equality, and foreseeability, whereas the criteria applied by legislators in law-making are equitable sharing, social utilitarianism, and equal distribution."[34] In any case, legislation is a process in which the legislators coordinate interests, balance relations, mediate contradictions and reduce conflicts, and in which different values stand out and compromise with each other. Except under extreme circumstances, legislators who act arbitrarily are bound to fail.

In achieving justice through democratic and scientific legislation, importance must be attached to the following principles: (1) The principle of freedom. Legislation is a process of concentrated expression of the will of the people. The interests to be distributed by legislators concern the whole or part of the people. Legislators must listen carefully to opinions and suggestions of the people, respect their choice of the way in which their interests are distributed, and safeguard the full and free expression of their will. (2) The principle of giving consideration to different interests. In situations where different interests conflict with each other, legislators must give consideration to all stakeholders in the distribution of interests. Although there is an order of priority among different interests, proper consideration should be given to all interests. (3) The principle of fairness. Legislators should treat all parties fairly in the choice of the value of legislation and uphold both the formal justice and the justice of result. (4) The principle of necessary differences. In the distribution of interests, legislators can apply the principle of differential treatment if there are sufficient and necessary reasons to do so. For example, they can restrict some freedoms of citizens for the purpose of protecting national security. However, while safeguarding the best interest of the largest majority of people in the legislation, appropriate remedies should be given to the minority whose interest is harmed by the legislation. Of course, the concrete application of these principles is difficult and further analysis needs to be carried out on these principles through the choice of the value of specific interests in order to enable them to have practical significance. For example, how should legislators make a fair value choice between individual interest and state interest, which are in a relationship of mutual contradiction and mutual dependence? On the whole, the individual-oriented or state-oriented outlook on value is the basic premise of the implementation of the value. If this premise is considered to be absolute and irreconcilable, then the value choice between individual interest and state interest is probably redundant. But the problem is: whichever party the legislators give priority to in the distribution of interest, the interest of the other party should never be ignored. Individual or state interests are not abstract. Individual interest can be divided into personality interest and material interest, whereas state interest can be divided into sovereign interest and economic interest (all these interests can be further divided and quantified). It seems that the distinction between individual and state interests enables us to make the following qualitative comparison and choice: under the state-oriented system, the state's sovereign interest overrides the individual's personality interest and the state's economic interest overrides the individual's material and personality interest. However, no such generalized formula can be followed in the quantitative

---

[34] von Hayek (2000a, p. 197).

comparison and choice. If the state's economic interest and individual's material interest are placed in the civil law relations, it is even more necessary to make the value choice in legislation in accordance with the principles of equality and free will.

5.4 Realizing Justice Through Implementation of Law

The life and authority of law lie in the implementation of law. After the formation of the socialist legal system with Chinese characteristics in 2011, the emphasis of the construction of the rule of law in China has shifted from making the law to upholding the authority of Constitution and laws and comprehensive and effective implementation of law has become the central task of China in ruling the country by law. Implementation of law refers to the activities of realizing the requirements of legal norms in social life through such ways and means as the enforcement, application, observation, and utilization of laws. It is an important link in ruling the country by law and constructing the rule of law in China, the concrete manifestation of the realization of the purposes and objectives of justice. The key to implementation of law is to realize justice through strict enforcement of law, fair administration of justice and conscientious observance of law.

5.4.1 Realizing Justice Through Strict Enforcement of Law

If it can be said that the main function of legislative organs is to express the will of the people, then the main function of administrative organs is to execute the will of the state (which of course embodies the will of the people and the will of the ruling party).[35] In China, 70% of civil servants who "live off government money" work in administrative organs; 80% of all the laws in China are implemented by administrative organs and their staff. Therefore, the key to ruling the country by law and realizing the will of the people and the ruling intentions of the ruling party is strict enforcement of law and administration by law. According to modern political theory, in a conflict between the state and the individual or between the government and the citizen, the citizen, as an individual, is always in a disadvantaged position and the powerful administrative power can easily infringe upon the rights of the citizen. The most effective way of realizing people's supervision over the government is to require the government to exercise administrative power in accordance with the law, which embodies the will of the people, so as to bring both the abstract and concrete administrative acts of the government on the track of institutions and laws. Administration by law stressed by the strategy of ruling the country by law usually contains the following requirements: "(1) the role of administrative power may not contradict the law; (2) administrative organs may not impose obligations on the

---

[35]Goodnow (1987, p. 9).

people or restrict the people's rights without legal basis; (3) administrative organs may not exempt anyone from his legal obligations or grant him any right without legal basis; (4) in cases where the law allows administrative organs to make discretional decisions, such decisions may not exceed the scope prescribed by law."[36] In cases where the unlawful or inappropriate act of an administrative organ harms the lawful rights and interests of a citizen, a legal person, or other organization, the latter has the right to apply for administrative reconsideration or bring the matter directly to a people's court, so as to rectify the unlawful or inappropriate administrative act and seek administrative compensation for the damages caused by such act through administrative reconsideration or litigation procedures. Only in this way can we be able to effectively regulate administrative power and administrative acts and truly ensure the realization of justice.

According to the modern rule of law thinking, the most important, basic and effective way of upholding and realizing justice is to ensure that administrative organs and civil servants act in strict accordance with law, conscientiously implement administration by law, and strive to construct a government under the rule of law. All the following acts of administrative organs and civil servants run counter to justice: duplicate law enforcement, multi-level law enforcement, non-enforcement of law, arbitrary law enforce, entrapment law enforcement, uncivilized law enforcement, restrictive law enforcement, selective law enforcement, campaign-style law enforcement, weak law enforcement, and tardy law enforcement; disobeying orders and defying prohibitions, administrative omission, dereliction of duty, unlawful administration, knowingly violation of the law, rent-seeking, taking bribes and bending the law and, and acting as protective umbrella for "dark and evil forces"; and the enforcement of the law by some administrative organs in such a rude and brutal way in land expropriation and housing demolition that intensifies social conflicts, even leads to mass disturbances and extreme and vicious incidents.

Some people hold that those who exercise judicial power should pursue justice whereas those who exercise administrative power should pursue efficiency, rather than justice. This view is incorrect. Firstly, any public power must adhere to the principle of justice, which is not only a basic requirement of popular sovereignty and the democratic state, but also a basic requirement of citizen's interests and basic human rights; secondly, although the core value pursued by legislative power is democracy, that pursued by administrative power is efficiency and that pursued by judicial power is justice, justice is also indispensible to legislative and administrative powers, only its position in the order of priority of different state powers is not the same, which does not mean that it is not important; finally, administrative power is a kind of "active power" that can easily and frequently infringe upon the rights and interests of citizens and society, as well as an aggressive power that can easily leads to conflicts between public powers and private and social rights. Only by taking the principle of justice as the standard and requirement can we be able to put administrative power into the cage of laws and institutions. In a certain sense, the abuse of administrative power or administrative omission can easily cause serious

---

[36]Han et al. (1993, p. 32).

harm to fairness and justice. Therefore, it is more important for the administrative power to adhere to and uphold fairness and justice.

5.4.2   Realizing Justice Through Judicial Fairness

Party Secretary General Xi Jinping pointed out that administration of justice is the last line of defense for social justice. He said that I have once quoted the British Philosopher Francis Bacon by saying that: "One foul sentence does more hurt than many foul examples. For these do but corrupt the stream; the other corrupts the fountain." There is a profound reason in this saying. If administration of justice, as the last line of dense, has lost public trust, then social justice will be under universal skepticism, and social harmony and stability will be hard to safeguard. Therefore, justice is the lifeline of the rule of law; judicial fairness plays an important leading role in upholding social justice and miscarriage of justice has a fatal destructive effect on social justice. The value of justice originally belongs to the category of ethics, but has become the principle of judicial activity and the criterion for the assessment of administration of justice after it was introduced into the judicial field. Courts in western countries boast about their judicial fairness by taking sword and scale as their symbols, with the former symbolizing the authority of state power and the latter symbolizing impartiality, fairness and justice. Under the socialist system in China, judicial fairness is an essential requirement made by socialist society on administration of justice. Judicial organs must take facts as the basis and law as the criterion, handle cases in strict accordance with law, punish crimes and safeguard the lawful rights of citizens. "A value or fact conflict must be resolved by some third party... A judge decides cases on a clear-cut, all-or-nothing basis; one side wins, the other loses... The third party, then must appeal to facts, norms, or standards. To bind the two parties, he must appear independent, impartial—and strong."[37] Administration of justice is a kind of remedy for the realization of justice, the last line of defense for justice. Any social conflict or dispute that cannot be resolved by other ways and means should be able to be resolved in a fair way through the judicial channel. In the field of law, people's social interests often manifest in various rights. People need judicial remedy when their rights are infringed upon. The essence and ultimate objective of administration of justice is the realization of justice. In contrast to the distributive justice pursued by legislation and justice of realization pursued by law enforcement, the justice pursued by the administration of justice is a corrective justice. That is to say, when people's rights and interests are subjected to unlawful infringement and all other remedies have failed, there should be judicial remedies to stop the infringement, rectify the wrongs, restore the rights, and bring everything back on the track of the rule of law. Using the rule of law thinking to pursue justice means to resolve conflicts by making full use of the judicial system and judicial procedures, rather than by making trouble and creating a disturbance. "...to bring a

---

[37]Lawrence (1994, pp. 264–265).

lawsuit, a party must convert his interests into demands and phrase the demands in terms of claim of right or disputes of fact... Many claims before a court are merely claims of interest, transformed on paper into claims of right."[38] "It is necessary to distinguish between two kinds of demand: interests and claims of rights. Two people have a conflict of interest when they both want the same valuable object: two men in love with one woman; two politicians running for a single office; two cities vying for a convention. Conflicts of interest arise out of scarcity. In the examples given, both parties have a legitimate claim...In a lawsuit, two parties each claim title to a single tract of land. Each party will insist in the pleadings that his claim is right and the other party's wrong, that the opponent misconceives the rules. The argument will be couched in terms of rights, not interests—facts, norms, and 'law'".[39] There are consequences for distinguishing between rights demands and interest conflicts. "Parties can easily compromise conflicts of interest, less so conflicts of values or fact. In a sense, a contract is the resolution of a conflict of interest. One man wants to buy a horse for a low price; the other wants to sell but very high. The two sides bargain, and agree when they feel they have gotten all they could. Usually, neither one is 'morally involved'. Courts of law do not resolve conflicts of interest. A party would have to convert his claim into a conflict of value or fact before he could go to law."[40]

Judicial fairness is the last line of defense for legal justice. It means that infringed rights must be protected and remedied and violations of law and crimes must be punished. Law has the function of settling disputes and judicial trial has function of making neutral, passive and final decisions on disputes. American jurist Martin P. Golding holds that formal justice is procedural justice, especially litigious justice, whereas substantive justice is the justice of distribution of legal rights and obligations. The standards of litigious justice include: (1) neutrality, including: "a person who has personal interest in a case should not be a judge in that case", "the resolution to a dispute should not contain the personal interest of the person who solves the dispute"; and "the person who resolves a dispute may not have prejudice for or against a party to the dispute"; (2) "persuasive disputes", including "giving equal attention to both parties to the dispute", "paying attention to the arguments and evidence of both parties to the dispute", "the person who resolve the dispute should hear the opinions of one party in the presence of the other party", and "all parties to a dispute should have fair opportunity to respond to the arguments raised and evidence produced by the other party"; (3) "solution", including "the conditions of the solution of the dispute must be based on rational deduction" and "reasoning should touch upon the arguments raised and evidences produced by the parties".[41] In deepening judicial reform, China should guide the public to bring their demand for justice into judicial procedure; courts should deal with each case that has entered into judicial proceedings in an open and fair way in accordance law, try to resolve each dispute through fair

---

[38] Ibid., p. 265.

[39] Ibid., pp. 263–264.

[40] Ibid., p. 246.

[41] Golding (1987, pp. 240–241).

administration of justice, and enable the public to feel the fairness and justice in each judicial case. However, the question of whether the public can truly feel justice in each case should be answered through concrete analysis. "Principles that are exactly opposite to each other have often been regarded as justice at the same time by people in different social strata, by people belonging to different groups that are far away from each other in relationship or in distance, or even by two persons who are very close in relation to each other. Two opposing parties in a lawsuit usually both firmly believe in the justifiability of their own causes of action because they are resorting to different kinds of justice…among these different and conflicting ideas of justice, there is always only one that can triumph over all the others."[42] "What people demand the court to do is not to implement justice, but to provide certain protection against major injustice".[43]

In the process of realizing justice through judicial fairness, efforts should be focused on the solution of the following two kinds of problems: first, the influence on and interference in the handling of judicial cases from various external factors, such as power, connection, money, and favor, which take such forms as the review and approval of the trial of cases by a local Party committee, deciding judicial cases by a Party committee or by the political and legal affairs commission under a Party committee, instruction by Party and government leaders on the handling of case by the court, intervention by a local people's congress in individual judicial cases, intercession by relatives and friends, etc. Second, problems resulting from the defects in the internal systems and mechanisms of judicial organs, including the abuse of such judicial powers as the powers of investigation, arrest, interrogation, prosecution, adjudication, execution, and legal supervision. They take such forms as extorting a confession by torture, presumption of guilt, unjust verdict, abuse of discretional power, accepting bribes from both the plaintiff and the defendant, bending the law for personal gain, backlog of court cases, difficulties in the execution of judgments, judicial arbitrariness, miscarriage of justice and judicial corruption. Special efforts should be made to solve the institutional problems that lead to judicial tyranny and miscarriage of justice.

Administration of justice is the last and strongest remedy for social stability and justice. As far as administrative power is concerned, "an independent judicial power is able to handle all the problems resulting from the implementation of the rule of law by government organs".[44] In a country under the rule of law, judicial fairness is a basic indicator for judging whether the political system in the country is democratic and civilized. If the administration of justice is not fair, then this country is not a state or society under the rule of law. The realization of judicial fairness mainly depends on the independent exercise of the adjudicative and procuratorial powers by judicial organs free from interference by any administrative organ, social organization or individual. We must "resolutely implement the following principles in the whole country: once a law is put into force, it must be observed and strictly enforced and

---

[42] Ehrlich (2009, p. 260).

[43] von Hayek (2000b, p. 101).

[44] Wheeler (1983, p. 50).

violators must be brought to justice; everyone is equal before the law; whoever
violates the law must be investigated by public security organs and dealt with by
judicial organs in accordance with law; and no one is allowed to interfere in the
implementation of law."[45]

5.4.3 Realizing Justice Through Conscientious Observance of Law

Aristotle said that: "We must remember that good laws, if they are not obeyed, do
not constitute good government. Hence there are two parts of good government; one
is the actual obedience of citizens to the laws, the other part is the goodness of the
laws which they obey."[46] Only when every citizen acts in accordance with laws and
conscientiously abides by laws, can laws truly be implemented and justice truly be
realized.

Why should citizens abide by law? Plato held that obeying the law is an obligation
and duty of every citizen, because "The city-state gives every citizen an equal part
of interest in the forms of life, provisions, education, or due rights. When a citizen
has passed the test for citizenship and has observed the affairs of the city and the
Laws, if this does not satisfy him he is free to take his belongings and go wherever
he wants. He can go to a colony or settle in another city-state. Those who choose
to stay have actually entered into a contract with laws, expressing their willingness
to obey the laws of the city-state. Those who disobey the laws are guilty of a triple
sin: disobedience to their parents, disobedience to their benefactors who have raised
them, and breach of contract."[47] The obligation to abide by the law is based on the
social contract of a civil society. It is the basic legal obligation a citizen, as a member
of society, must fulfill in order to enjoy justice and the main way of realizing justice
in the legal sense. "A practically unlimited number of illustrations might be given,
drawn from either the earlier or the later Middle Ages, of this conviction that the law
belongs to the people whom it governs and is evidenced by their observance of it or,
in case of doubt, by the statement of some body properly constituted to determine
what the law is."[48]

In China, people are the subjects of the state, society and the strategy of ruling
the country by law. The Constitution and laws are the concentrated embodiments of
the will of the people and the institutional expressions of people's interest demands.
Therefore, to abide by the Constitution and laws is to respect the will and uphold the
interest of the people. Conscientious observance of law by all citizens can be truly
realized only under the socialist system. However, at the primary stage of socialism,
it will take a long period of time and arduous efforts to turn this ideal condition of

---

[45] Xiaoping (1994, p. 254).

[46] Aristotle (1981, p. 199).

[47] Plato (1983, p. 109).

[48] Sabine (1986, p. 249).

implementation of law from a theory into a reality, and make the obedience to the law a conscientious choice, rather than a forced behavior, of every citizen. There are mainly four different conditions of observance of law by citizens in China: first, the conscientious observance of law, which reflects citizens' belief in the rule of law, their pursuit of the value and the spirit of law, their firm conviction in justice, and their high-degree consciousness and rational approval of observance of law. It is the highest-level condition of universal observance of law, but is also the most difficult one to achieve. Second, the condition of unwilling to violate the law, which embodies citizens' respect for law, their belief in the authority of the judicial power, their reverence for state public power, and their voluntariness and high-degree approval of observance of law. Third, the condition of unable to violate the law, which reflects citizens' trust in the legal system, their acknowledgment of judicial fairness, and their belief in legal responsibilities and legal consequences. Legal control of one's own behavior is a perceptual approval of observance of law. Fourth, the condition of being afraid to violate the law, which reflects citizens' fear of the rule of law and of the compulsory punishment by law. It is the minimum requirement of the observance of law, the passive acceptance of law by citizens, a primary condition as well as a relatively common mentality of observance of law.

To realize justice, we should concentrate our efforts on changing the ideas, habits and institutions of disorderly observance of law. All organizations and individual must act within the scope of the Constitution and laws. In other words, all organizations and individuals must abide by law. Observance of law is realized when every social organization or individual conscientiously abide by law and carry out activities in accordance with law. Its concrete manifestation is that state organs, enterprises, public institutions and individual citizens conscientiously act within the scope of Constitution and laws.

A just person is a person who obeys the law. With respect to the observance of law, every citizen must start with himself, with small things around him, and with his own concrete behavior and habits, refrain from doing anything that are prohibited by law, treat positively the things that are advocated by law, and do things that are protected by law in accordance with law. "Liberty is a right of doing whatever the laws permit, and if a citizen could do what they forbid he would be no longer possessed of liberty, because all his fellow-citizens would have the same power."[49] Every citizen must develop a law-abiding consciousness and the habit of trusting in the law, abiding by the law, and cherishing the law, strive to become a qualified citizen in a society under the rule of law, implement the obligation of abiding by the law in his daily life, and gradually form a stable and effective culture of observance of law. China should "strive to create a good rule of law environment in which people act in accordance with law, apply the law to solve their problems, and resolve their conflicts and promote various kinds of work on the track of the rule of law", "strengthen the implementation of the Constitution and law, uphold the unity, dignity and authority of socialist legal system, and create a rule of law environment in which people are

---

[49]Montesquieu (1961, p. 154).

unwilling, unable and afraid to violate the law."[50] We should resolutely change the situation of "low cost of violation of law and high cost of abiding by the law", let violators of law pay a higher price for the violations that for the observance of law, so as to create a rule of law environment in which people are unwilling, unable and afraid to violate the law.

References

Aristotle (1981) Politics. Chinese Edition (trans: Wu S). The Commercial Press, Beijing

Beauchamp TL (1990) Philosophical ethics: an introduction to moral philosophy. Chinese edition (trans: Lei K et. al.). China Social Sciences Press, Beijing

Bodenheimer E (1999) Jurisprudence: the philosophy and method of the law. Chinese edition (trans: Deng Z). China University of Political Science and Law Press, Beijing

Ehrlich E (2009) Fundamental principles of sociology of law, Chinese edition (trans: Shu G). Encyclopedia of China Publishing House, Beijing

Golding MP (1987) Philosophy of law. Chinese edition (trans: Qi H). SDX Joint Publishing Co., Beijing

Goodnow FJ (1987) Politics and administration. Chinese edition (trans: Wang Y). Huaxia Publishing House, Beijing

Han L et al (1993) On administration by law. Social Sciences Academic Press, Beijing

Kim H (1989) Fundamental legal concepts of china and the west: a comparative study, chinese edition (trans: Chen G, Wei X, Li C). Liaoning People's Publishing House, Shenyang

Lawrence M (1994) Friedman, legal system. Chinese edition (trans: Li Q, Lin X). China University of Political Science and Law Press, Beijing

Ma B (2012) Social justice and governance: between ideal and reality. Social Sciences Academic Press, Beijing

MacCormick N, Weinberger O, Detmold MJ (1994) An institutional theory of law: new approaches to legal positivism. Chinese edition (trans: Zhou Y). China University of Political Science and Law, Beijing

Marx C, Engels F (1958) Complete works of Marx and Engels, Chinese edition, vol 4. People's Publishing House, Beijing

Marx C, Engels F (1995) Complete works of Marx and Engels, Chinese edition, vol 2. People's Publishing House, Beijing

Montesquieu (1961) The spirit of laws, vol 1. Chinese edition (trans: Zhang Y). The Commercial Press, Beijing

Plato (1983) Euthyphro/Apology/Crito. Chinese edition (trans: Yan Q). Commercial Press, Beijing

Plato (2001) Law. Chinese edition (trans: Zhang Z, He Q). Fudan University Press, Shanghai

Qichao L (1999) Complete works of Liang Qichao. Beijing Publishing House, Beijing

Rawls J (1988) A theory of justice. Chinese edition (trans: Huaihong H et al). China Social Sciences Press, Beijing

Sabine GH (1986) A history of political theory, vol 1. Chinese edition (trans: Sheng K et. al.). Commercial Press, Beijing

von Hayek F (2000a) Law, legislation and liberty, vol 1. Chinese edition (trans: Deng Z et al). China Encyclopedia Publishing House, Beijing

von Hayek F (2000b) Law, legislation and liberty, vol 2–3. Chinese edition (trans: Deng Z et al). China Encyclopedia Publishing House, Beijing

Wheeler H (1983) Constitutionalism. In Greenstein FI, Polsby NW (eds) Governmental institutions and procedures. Chinese edition. Youth Cultural Enterprise Co. Ltd., Taipei

---

[50]Xi (2012, p. 12).

Xi J (2012) Speech given at the conference of representatives of all circles in Beijing in commemoration of the thirtieth anniversary of the implementation of the current constitution. People's Publishing House, Beijing

Xiaoping D (1994) Selected works of Deng Xiaoping, vol 1. People's Publishing House, Beijing

Zhang W (1996) Studies on trends of western philosophy of law in the 20th century. Law Press China, Beijing

Zhuo Z (2013) Justice as rule-of-law value in a harmonious society. In: Li L et al (eds) The rule of law basis of the construction of a harmonious society. Social Sciences Academic Press, Beijing

Chapter 6
Ruling the Country by Law and Promoting the Modernization of State Governance

Since the Decision on Several Major Issues Concerning Comprehensively Deepening the Reform (hereinafter referred to as the Decision), adopted at the Third Plenary Session of the Eighteenth CPC Central Committee, puts forward for the first time in history the reform objective of "promoting the modernization of the state governance system and capacity", "state governance" and "the modernization of state governance", as two important concepts of political science, have quickly become "hot words" that have attracted much attention from the Chinese academic circle and led to heated discussions in which all kinds of opinions have been put forward. Actually state governance is an "old concept". Otherwise, there is no need to 'modernize" it. It is more a proposition of legal science than a concept of political science. Otherwise, it would be difficult to explain how state and society had been run in the thousands of years before the emergence of the concept of "state governance". In other words, we can ask the following question: had there been any form of social management (including rule, control, administration or regulation) or social order in the thousands of years before the appearance of the concept of "state governance"? The answer is of course yes. Then, what is the relationship between state governance and ruling the country by law (the rule of law)? Two further questions are: what are the position and the role of ruling the country by law (the rule of law) in the new context of "promoting the modernization of the state governance system and capacity"? And how should we advance ruling the country by law and speed up the construction of the rule of law in China in light of the requirement of modernization of state governance?

6.1 The Relationship Between Ruling the Country by Law and Promoting the Modernization of State Governance

The Decision states that "The overall goal of comprehensively deepening the reform is to improve and develop socialism with Chinese characteristics, and to promote the modernization of the state governance system and capacity." Ruling the country

© China Social Sciences Press and Springer Nature Singapore Pte Ltd. 2018   221
L. Li, *The Chinese Road of the Rule of Law*, China Insights,
https://doi.org/10.1007/978-981-10-8965-7_6

by law is a basic principle enshrined in the Chinese Constitution and a basic strategy by which the CPC leads the people in administering state affairs. Ruling the country by law and state governance interact with each other and complement each other, reaching the same goal by different means. Against the background of comprehensively implementing the strategy of ruling the country law and constructing a socialist system of rule of law with Chinese characteristics and in the historical process of transforming China from a country with a big system of law to a country with a sound system of the rule of law, high importance should be attached and full play should be given to the role played by the strategy of ruling the country by law in the modernization of state governance.

6.1.1 The Meanings of Ruling the Country by Law and State Governance

How should a state be governed? This is not a new or small question, but an old and major question that has existed ever since the emergence of the state, a fundament question to be answered by Marxist state theory,[1] and a core issue to be dealt with by both political science and law science. According to Marxist state theory, the question of state and state governance should be analyzed and answered from the perspectives of state system, polity, political model, and basic strategy. From the perspective of state system, class analysis of the nature of the state should be carried out to determine whether it is a rule of the majority over the minority or the opposite—which is the primary question of state governance. From the perspective of polity, the state governance must answer the question of whether a state adopts the system of republic or constitutional monarchy, the federation system or the unitary system, the head of state responsibility system or the cabinet responsibility system, or the people's congress system, namely the question concerning the form of the organization of political power. From the perspective of political model, state governance must answer the question of what political model a state should adopt: director election, multi-party system, separation of three powers, the bicameral system, the combination of direct and indirect elections, the combination of one-party leadership and multi-party cooperation, the combination of intra-party democracy of the ruling party and people's democracy, democratic centralism, or other political models?

---

[1] Marxists hold that "The state is nothing but a machine used by one class to oppress the other class and, in this respect, there is no difference between a democratic republic and a monarchy." (Marx and Engels 2009, p. 111); "The state is the product and manifestation of the irreconcilability of class contradiction") (Lenin 2012, p. 114); therefore, "the special organ that systematically uses violence and coercion to force the people to submit themselves to violence…is called the state" (Lenin 2009, p. 285); "political rule anywhere is based on the performance of certain social functions and it can continue to exist only when it performs such social functions" (Marx and Engels 2012, pp. 559–560) "The state is a structure separated from society and made of people who are specialized, almost specialized, or mainly specialized in administration. People are divided into two groups: the administrators and the administrated." (Lenin 2009, p. 288).

From the perspective of basic strategy, state governance must answer the question of what path dependence and ruling strategy a state should adopt: dictatorship, the rule of man, autocracy, democracy, the rule of law, republic, or other strategies?

The CPC has, in the great practice of leading the Chinese people in wining the victories of revolution, construction and reform, on the basis of the founding of the People's Republic of China and implementation of socialist system, and in the form of the state constitution, laws and the Party constitution, established the people's democratic dictatorship led by the working class and based on the alliance of workers and peasants as the state system of the PRC, the people's congress system as the polity of the PRC, the leadership of the CPC, the democratic centralism, the people's congress system, the system of regional national autonomy, the system of multi-party cooperation and consultation, and the system of democratic self-government at the grassroots level as the main content of the political model of the republic, ruling the country by law as the basic strategy of state governance, and the rule of law as the basic mode of state governance,[2] and continuously developed socialist democratic politics with Chinese characteristics and promoted ruling the country by law and the modernization of state governance.

In the general sense, ruling the country by law means to adhere to and implement the rule of law, restrict power by law, administer state affairs in accordance with law, and oppose the rule of man and autocracy.[3]

---

[2] At the First Plenary Session of the Chinese People's Political Consultative Conference on February 15, 1978, Mr. Liang Shuming pointed out that: "It is a good thing that now we are again able to discuss the Constitution and take part in the adoption of the Constitution…My personal experience is that the Constitution has often been a mere scrap of paper and state governance has mainly relied on the rule of man, rather than the rule of law, in China. In the 30 years since the founding of the PRC, although we have adopted our own Constitution, but the Constitution has not been regarded as the highest authority in the country, nor has it been universally observed. This conclusion is based on the actual situations of several main historical periods in the past 30 years…But now I want to point out that the time for the rule of man has already gone. Today we no longer have great leaders like Mao Zedong, who had high prestige among the people, and such a leader will not emerge any time soon. Therefore even if someone wants to practice the rule of man, it would be difficult for him to do so. Moreover, after many years of practice, especially after the ten-year lesson of "Cultural Revolution", which had been paid in blood, the Chinese people have had a personal experience of the harms of the rule of man and their desire and demand for the rule of law have become increasingly strong. Therefore, it is very necessary and important that we discuss the Constitution today. We must treat this issue with utmost care and seriousness. China is now in a gradual transition from the rule of man to the rule of law. Today is a turning point. From now on, we must gradually rely on the authority of the Constitution and laws in ruling the country. Ruling the country by law has become a historical trend that nobody can stop." Wang (2004, pp. 297–298).

[3] At a seminar on the theory of the rule of law, organized by the Law Institute of Chinese Academy of Social Sciences in April 1996, the majority of the participants agreed that: "Ruling the country by law, namely the rule of law, means to run a country in accordance with the will of the people and with laws that reflect the objective law of social development and that the political, economic, and social activities of the state and citizens' activities in all areas must all be carried out in accordance with law, and not subject to the interference, impediment and sabotage by any individual. Its basic requirements are: legislative organs exercise legislative power in accordance with law; government organs exercise administrative power in accordance with law; judicial organs exercise judicial power

State governance"[4] refers to the institutional arrangement and process whereby the people, as masters of the country, take control the political power, exercise the state power, and administer state affairs through the NPC and local people's congresses at various levels, whereby all state organs, the armed forces, all political parties and public organizations and all enterprises and institutions, under the leadership of the ruling party, jointly participate in the political, economic and social lives of the state, jointly administer state and social affairs, manage economic and cultural undertakings, jointly promote the comprehensive political, economic, social, cultural and ecological development in accordance with the Constitution, laws, and other norms, institutions and procedures, and whereby the ruling party adheres to the principle of exercising the ruling power in accordance with the Constitution and laws, commands the whole situation and coordinates various efforts, support state organs to perform their functions independently and in accordance with law, leads and supports various social subjects to implement systematic governance, law-based governance, comprehensive governance and governance at the sources of problems.

6.1.2 The Relationship Between Ruling the Country by Law and State Governance

What is the relationship between ruling the country by law and state governance?[5] We hold that ruling the country by law is mainly a concept of law science whereas state

---

in accordance with law; citizens' rights and interests are truly protected by law; and the power of state organs are strictly controlled by law." Li (2005, p. 462).

[4]Currently no consensus has been reached in Chinese theoretical circle on the definition of the concept of "state governance". Different people have different understandings of and give different definitions to this concept. An article published in the journal Seeking Truth holds that: "State governance means that the Party leads the people to administer state affairs and manage economic, cultural and social undertakings through various channels and in various ways in accordance with the law." See Qiu (2014). Professor Wang Puqu of Peking University holds that: "'State governance' is actually the system and process whereby the CPC represents and leads the people to take control of political power and exercise the ruling power. It means the administration of state and social affairs by the CPC in a scientific, lawful and effective way under the precondition of adhering to, strengthening, and improving the basic political and economic systems and the framework under which the CPC runs the country by commanding the whole situation and coordinating various efforts." See Puqu (2014). This author holds that, in the Chinese discourse system, the description and definition of the concept of "state governance" should be closely centered around the "organic unity of the three principles", which is not only the essential characteristic of socialist democratic politics with Chinese characteristics, but also the key to understanding the concept of "state governance".

[5]An examination of the history of human civilization shows that law, legal system, rule of law, ruling the country by law or ruling the country in accordance with law have been the main and effective way of state and social governance, establishment of order, and adjustment of social relations ever since the emergence of state in human history. Most of the modern developed countries in contemporary time are countries under the rule of law, whereas "state governance", which emerged in mid and late 20th Century, is only an idea and method that overlaps with the concept of a state under the rule of law. It is a supplement, improvement and innovative development, but not a replacement, of the rule of law or ruling the country by law. Today, most countries of the world generally do

governance is mainly a concept of political science, science of public administration and sociology. Although the two belong to different discourse systems and have slight differences in connotation and extension, they have the same essence and objective and similar subjects and objects and ways and methods, and they reach the same goal of good law and good governance by different means.

More specifically, ruling the country by law and state governance have the following commonalities:

First, they both adhere to the system of socialism with Chinese characteristics, to the leadership of the CPC, to the exercise of the ruling power in accordance with the Constitution and laws, and to their own advancement and implementation by the sovereign state within the framework state constitution.

Second, they both adhere to the principle of popular sovereignty and the principle that people being the masters of the country and the subjects of ruling the country by law and state governance, rather than the objects of governance, control and rule.

Third, they both stress the importance, stability and authority of state governance system, demand the development of a complete, sound, mature and modernized institutional system of state governance, which mainly includes a legal system that embodies the will of the state and takes the constitution as the core.

Fourth, they both take the political rule of people's democratic dictatorship as their premise, involve such governance modes as "heteronomy", "autonomy", and "jointnomy", and comprehensively use "rule", "administration" and "regulation" as indispensable ways and means of state governance. Understood from the point of view of classification of law, "rule" is mainly used in the fields of public law relations, such constitutional law and criminal law, "administration" is mainly used in the fields of public law relations, such administrative law and economic law, as well as in fields of public-private law relations; and "governance" is mainly used in the fields of social law and private law relations.[6] The three of them co-exist in the legal system or legal relations in a state, and are all important ways of regulating social relations and administering state affairs.

Fifth, their targets (objects) of "administration" and "regulation" are more or less the same and they both involve such fields and aspects as politics, economy,

---

not emphasize the idea and the system of "state governance", but by adhering to the rule of law or ruling the country by law, have achieved the expected objectives of state governance. In China, state governance and ruling the country by law are in essence largely identical but with minor differences, and they reach the same goal by different means.

[6]In the 1995 Report entitled *Our Global Neighborhood*, the Commission on Global Governance gives the following definition to "governance": Governance is the sum of the many ways individuals and institutions, public and private, manage their common affairs. It is a continuing process through which conflicting or diverse interests may be accommodated and co-operative action may be taken. It includes formal institutions and regimes empowered to enforce compliance, as well as informal arrangements that people and institutions either have agreed to or perceive to be in their interest. It has the following four characteristics: it is neither a whole set of rules, nor a kind of activity, but a process: the basis of governance is not control, but coordination; governance involves both public and private sectors; governance is not a formal institution, but a continuous interaction. Therefore, the term "governance" mainly stresses a kind of social law and private law relationship. It cannot express or reflect all connotations of state rule, administration and regulation.

culture, society and ecology, internal affairs, national defense and foreign relations, reform, development and stability, running of the Party, the state and the armed forces, adjustment of social relations, regulation of social behaviors, allocation of social resources, coordination of social interests, resolution of social conflicts, safeguarding of private rights and restriction of public powers.

Sixth, the direct objectives pursued by both of them require the realization of good law and good governance and stress that there should not only be sound and complete laws and legal systems of state governance, but also the full and effective implementation of such laws and legal systems in real life.

Seventh, both aim at developing people's democracy, invigorating society, establishing good social order, promoting justice, realizing the Chinese dream of national prosperity, people's happiness, and rejuvenation of the Chinese nation, and building China into a democratic, prosperous, powerful and civilized modern socialist country.

The differences between ruling the country by law and state governance are the followings: First, state governance stresses the differences between "governance" and "administration" in terms of subjects, source of power, operation, and scope, and holds that the development from "administration" to "governance" is an ideological leap forward and practical innovation.[7] Second, state governance not only adheres to the rule of law as the basic way and ruling the country by law as the basic strategy of governing the country, but also attaches importance to the role of such means as politics, the rule of virtue, norms of self-government, contract and discipline. Third, state governance adheres to jointnomy, namely the equal participation in governance by various social subjects, as the main form of governance, and emphasizes the equality, free will, commonality and participation of the subjects of governance, whereas ruling the country by law adheres to systematic and comprehensive governance, adopts not only methods of heteronomy (such as public security law enforcement, industrial and commercial law enforcement and health law enforcement) and autonomy (such as grassroots and community self-government), but also such methods of jointnomy as participation by everyone and joint administration by relevant government functional departments. Finally, the scope of state governance covers not only areas directly regulated or adjusted by state law and the rule of law, but also some matters within political parties, social organizations, armed forces, enterprises, public institutions and society that are not covered by law and the rule of law.

Despite the above differences, ruling the country by law and state governance have more in common than in difference. When understanding the relationship between the two, we should, first of all, see them not as the opposites to or replacements of each other, but as two things that supplement each other and reach the same goal by different means; secondly, we should not separate the two from each other. We should neither one-sidedly stress the position and role of ruling the country by law, nor overemphasize the value and function of state governance. The two are in a relationship of interconnection and interaction; thirdly, we should not give one-sided interpretations

---

[7] See Keping (2014), He (2014), and Li (2014).

to the three concepts of "governance", "administration", and "rule". They are not in a relationship of contradiction, mutual exclusion or successive replacement, but in a relationship of coexistence, mutual influence and interaction.[8] However, there are different orders of priority in the use of these three concepts during different periods of time, under different conditions, in different contexts, or from different disciplinary perspectives.

6.1.3 The Key to the Modernization of State Governance Is Bringing It Under the Rule of Law

State governance has at least two aspects: the system of state governance and the capacity for state governance.[9]

State governance system refers to the system of institutions of state administration under the leadership of the CPC, including various institutional mechanisms and arrangements of laws and regulations in the fields economy, politics, culture, society, ecological civilization and Party building, which constitute a whole set of closely linked and coordinated state systems. The formation of a complete, scientific, standardized and effective state institutional system is one of the important objectives of the modernization of the state governance system. State governance capacity is the capacity for utilizing state institutions to administer affairs in various aspects of society, such as reform, development and stability, internal affairs, foreign relations and national defense, and running of the Party, the state and the armed forces.[10] Party Secretary General Xi Jinping points out that state governance system and state governance capacity are the concentrated embodiments of the institutions and institutional implementation capacity. The two are complementary to each other and state governance is impossible without any of them.

---

[8] In fact the Chinese Constitution uses the word "administer" (or manage) in more than 20 different places—for example Article 2 of the Constitution provides that "The people administer state affairs and manage economic, cultural and social affairs through various channels and in various ways in accordance with the law"—but never uses the word "governance". Among the 240 currently effective laws in China, over a dozen have the word "administration" in their titles, for examples, Public Security Administration Punishments Law, Law on the Administration of Exit and Entry of Citizens, and Law on the Administration of Entry and Exit of Foreigners, but none of them contains the word "governance" in its title.

[9] Some scholars hold that the concept of state governance should also include such content as the idea, process, and effect of state governance.

[10] See Yao (2014).

Modernization of state governance[11] means to democratize, scientize and informatize governance system and capacity and, most importantly, to bring them under the rule of law.[12]

On the one hand, we must try to bring the state governance system under the rule of law. Dong Biwu once said that: "Just as its name implies, the system of state laws and institutions is a legal system".[13] In a country under the rule of law, most institutions and mechanisms in the state governance system have already been incorporated into the system of state law and manifest themselves as legal norms and legal systems. Therefore, developing and improving the system of state law and constructing a complete and scientific legal system are effective ways of promoting the legalization, standardization and finalization of state governance system and the formation of a complete, scientific, standardized and effective state institutional system. On the other hand, it is necessary to bring the state governance capacity under the rule of law. In a country under the rule of law, state governance capacity mainly refers to the capacity for administration or governance in accordance with law, including the capacity for utilizing the legal system to administer state and social affairs and manage economic and cultural undertakings in accordance with the Constitution and laws, the capacity for scientific legislation, strict enforcement of law, and fair administration of justice, and the capacity for applying the rule of law thinking and method to deepen the reform, promote development, resolve conflicts and uphold stability. As American Jurist Lon Fuller pointed out: "Law is the purposive enterprise of subjecting human conduct to the governance of rules."[14] The ultimate goal of bringing state governance capacity under the rule of law is to strengthen the power (right) capacity and capacity for act, the capability for enforcing and abiding by the Constitution and laws, and the capacity for operation and implementation of the state institutional system. China should attach high importance and give full play to the important role of the basic strategy of ruling the country by law in state governance. Ruling the

---

[11] Mr. Shi Zhihong, Vice Chairman of the Committee for Social and Legal Affairs of Chinese People's Political Consultative Conference, calls "the modernization of state governance system and state governance ability" "the fifth modernization". He believes that the modernization of state governance system relies on sound institutions, superior state governance capacity and a contingent of high quality cadres. In this sense, the modernization of state governance system and state governance capacity can be considered the "fifth modernization", in addition to the "four modernizations" (modernization of agriculture, industry, national defense and science and technology) put forward by the CPC. This means that the governance system and capacity of the Party and state in China are developing towards the goals of keeping pace with the times, following the objective law of development, and displaying great creativity (Shi 2013).

[12] See Qiu (2014). Another scholar holds that "The rule of law is a criterion for evaluating the maturity of an institution as well as a basic way of promoting the finalization of a institution…without a reliable rule of law safeguard, an institution would lack authority and executive capacity, the modernization of state government system would be out of the question, and state governance ability would be like flower's reflection in the mirror or moon's shadow on the water." (Zhang 2014). Hu Jianmiao holds that: "Modernizing state governance means making it more democratic, scientific and civilized and, most importantly, bringing it under the rule of law." (Hu 2014).

[13] Biwu (1979, p. 153).

[14] Fuller (1969, p. 106).

country by law is not only the main content of the modernization of state governance, but also an important way and a basic method of advancing modernization of state governance that plays the role of leading, regulating, promoting and safeguarding the modernization.

6.2 Promoting the Modernization of State Governance by Giving Full Play to the Important Role of the Rule of Law

In applying the rule of law thinking and method to promote the modernization of state governance under the new situation of comprehensively advancing the strategy of ruling the country by law and constructing a socialist system of the rule of law with Chinese characteristics, more attention should be paid to giving full play to the role of the strategy of ruling the country by law (rule of law), implementing the strategic arrangement of comprehensively deepening the reform and the overall requirement of the "five-in-one construction", realizing the general reform objectives of improving and developing the system of socialism with Chinese characteristics, and adhering to the organic unity of the Party's leadership, the people being masters of the country and ruling the country by law.

6.2.1 Promote the Modernization of State Governance by Giving Full Play to the Functions of the Constitution as the General Rules on Administering State Affairs and Ensuring National Security

The constitution is an important indicator of the level of civilization and the progress of a country. It is the fundamental law of a country and the general rules on administering state affairs and ensuring national security. It is a law that has the highest legal status, authority and effect and is of fundamental, global, stable and long-term nature.[15] The most basic way of advancing the modernization of state governance, shaping a systematic, scientific, standardized and effective state governance system, and achieving the maturity and finalization of various institutions of state governance is to uphold the authority and ensure the implementation of the Constitution, and give full play to its role as the general rules on administering state affairs and ensuring national security.

The Chinese Constitution establishes in the form of basic state law the road, the theoretical system and institutional system of socialism with Chinese characteristics, provides for the fundamental system and task of the state, the core leadership and

---

[15]Xi (2013).

guiding ideology of the state, the basic systems of the state and the relevant principles and institutions, such as the system of Patriotic United Front, the basic strategy of ruling the country by law, the principle of democratic centralism, and the principle of respecting and safeguarding human rights. We must adhere to, thoroughly implement and continuously develop these institutions and principles. Adhering to and implementing these constitutional institutions and principles and the principle of ruling the country and exercising the ruling power in accordance with the Constitution is conducive to promoting the standardization and finalization of state governance system at the level of top-level design and strategic arrangements in accordance with the requirement of the Constitution and to enhancing the authority and effectiveness of state governance capacity. For example, the Preamble of current Chinese Constitution requires the "steady improvement of various socialist institutions", which is an overall constitutional requirement on the reform and improvement of the state governance system, as well as a fundamental constitutional basis of the modernization of state governance system.

The key to the modernization of state governance system is the modernization of the people. In a socialist country, the people are the masters of the state and state governance is the people's own undertaking. The modernization of state governance in the sense of people's democracy can be realized only by mobilizing the people, relying on the people, and organizing the people to administer state and social affairs. The Constitution is the general rules on and general basis of state governance. Comprehensively implementing the Constitution, extensively mobilizing and organizing the people to exercise the state power through people's congresses at various levels, to administer state affairs and manage economic, cultural and social affairs through various channels and in various ways in accordance with the law, and to govern, build, share and develop together, and ensuring that the people are the masters of the state, society and their own destiny are conducive to mobilizing the people's enthusiasm and initiatives and to giving full play to their role as subjects of state governance and the rule of law.

The progress of civilization[16] is both an important objective of national development and an important indicator of the modernization of state governance. In order to promote the modernization of state governance, it is necessary to strengthen the construction of material civilization, reinforce the economic foundation of socialism, promote the development of productive forces, strengthen the construction of political civilization (especially institutional civilization), improve the superstructure of socialism, uphold the lawfulness and legitimacy of state political power,

---

[16] According to a study by Chinese scholars, the word "civilization" first appeared in modern British history. In the beginning of the 18th Century, after Scotland was united with England, the civil law of Scotland was integrated into the common law of England, and word "civilization" was created to refer to law or trial. The 1755 Dictionary of the English Language defined civilization as "an expert of civil law or a professor of Roman law." In the second half of the 18th Century, enlightenment thinkers used the world "civilization" as the opposite of "barbarism" to denounce the rule of darkness in the Middle Ages. Therefore, the progress and development of law, private law and judicial trial has become the most important indicator of the development of human civilization. Today, the civilization of rule of law is indispensable in the evaluation of modernization of state governance.

strengthen the construction of spiritual civilization, carry forward socialist core values, and promote the prosperity and development of advanced culture. The Chinese Constitution clearly provides that the state promotes the coordinated development of socialist material, political and spiritual civilizations, and contains special provisions on basic social, economic, political, and cultural systems, ideology, morality, and citizens' rights and obligations. Only by truly respecting and effective implementing the Constitution, will China be able to actively promote the progress of civilization and the modernization of state governance.

6.2.2 Guiding the Modernization of State Governance by Giving Full Play to the Value Judgment Function of the Rule of Law

The law of a modern state is not only a system of code of conduct, but also a system of value judgment, as well as the institutionalized embodiment of mainstream values of society. By promoting through the rule of law such basic values as freedom, equality, fairness, justice and human rights, the state carries forward the spirit of the rule of law, disseminates the idea of the rule of law, and leads social progress. "The rule of law means not merely the establishment of a set of institutional systems, or the adoption of a constitution and a set of laws. The most important component of the rule of law is perhaps the spirit of the rule of law embodied in the culture of a country."[17] The Chinese Constitution provides that China must adhere to the leadership of the CPC, the socialist system, the state guiding ideology and the polity of people's democratic dictatorship. The socialist theory of the rule of law stresses that China must adhere to the organic unity of the three principles, proceed from national conditions, draw on all the beneficial results of development of political and rule of law civilizations of mankind, gradually realize the modernization of industry, agriculture, national defense, science and technology and state governance, but never blindly copy the democratic political model and the rule of law model of western capitalist countries. These affirmative and prohibitive provisions in the Constitution have determined the nature and pointed out the correct direction and path of development of state governance in China.

The rule of law advocates such basic values as democracy, freedom, fairness, justice, equality, good faith, human rights, dignity, order, security, happiness, and peace, adheres to such basic principles as popular sovereignty, the supremacy of the constitution and laws, safeguarding human rights, restricting power, exercising the ruling power by law, administration by law, judicial fairness, and universal observance of law, and follows such basic objective rules as universality, definitiveness, standardization, unity, stability, predictability, and justiciability.[18] In a report entitled

---

[17]Gibson and Gouws (1998, pp. 38–39).

[18]"Justiciability" in the sense of the rule of law has two aspects: from the citizen's point of view, it means that a citizen whose legally prescribed rights are infringed upon should be able to file a

Our Global Neighborhood, the Commission on Global Governance, an international organization known for its advocacy and promotion of global governance, calls for "a common commitment to core values that all humanity could uphold: respect for life, liberty, justice and equity, mutual respect, caring, and integrity", so as to improve the quality of global governance.[19] Apparently, the core values advocated by global governance are consistent with the basic values pursued by the rule of law. However, global governance and state governance have a marked difference: the former pursues its value ideals mainly through such moral advocacy methods as appeals, publicity and public opinions whereas the latter mainly realize its value objectives by relying on the force of the rule of law. Therefore, by advancing the modernization of state governance in accordance with the basic values, principles and objective laws of the rule of law and through the application of methods of the rule of law, we will be able to ensure the consistency between the value choice of state governance with that of the rule of law, and promote the integration of the modernization of state governance and the rule of law, thereby realizing the good governance of the state and society.

6.2.3 Promoting the Modernization of State Governance by Giving Full Play to the Regulating Functions of the Rule of Law

Law is an important tool of state governance and a code of conduct for adjusting social relations. Marx said that "Law is not a means for suppressing freedom, just as the law of gravitation not a means for stopping movement... on the contrary, laws are affirmative, definitive, and universal norms...law codes are people's bibles of freedom."[20] Normativity is the basic characteristic of the rule of law. Through such norms as permissive norms, authorizing norms, and prohibitive norms, it tells subjects of legal relations what they should not do, what they should do, and how should they do them, so as to achieve the objectives of adjusting social relations, regulating social behaviors, and maintaining social order.

In the process of safeguarding and promoting the modernization of state governance, the normative function of the rule of law can play its role in the following ways: firstly, to ensure through the implementation of procedures and institutions of constitutionality and legality that the construction of the institutional system of state

---

lawsuit at the court to seek protection and remedy of his rights in accordance with law; from the court's point of view, it means that the court may accept a case and make corresponding judgment in accordance with specific provisions of law. Currently, among the more than 240 effective laws in China, only about 40 can be taken as the basis of adjudication by the court and be cited in a judgment. Another interpretation of "justiciability" is that a subject of legal relationship who believes himself subjected to unfair treatment and his rights infringed upon can and should seek remedy through legal proceedings in accordance with law and that the court should be the last resort for achieving fairness and justice in the legal sense.

[19]Quoted in Keping (2014, p. 32).

[20]Marx (1995, p. 176).

governance and the enhancement of state governance capacity are carried out in the framework of the Constitution and on the track of the rule of law, so as to prevent behaviors and phenomena of violation of the Constitution and laws. For example, the Constitution, the Legislation Law, the Law on Regional National Autonomy, the Trade Union Law, the Organic Law of Villagers' Committees, and the Law on Industrial Enterprises Owned by the Whole People all clearly provide for the leadership position and the leading role of the CPC.[21] The ruling party should, in accordance with the above laws, improve the institutional system relating to the exercise of ruling power and promote the modernization of the system of exercising ruling power. Secondly, to confirm and finalize the institutional elements and institutional innovations of state governance in the form of substantive and procedural law norms on rights and obligations, powers and duties, behavioral models and consequences, so as to making them more rigorous in logic, more scientific in content, more complete in form, and more coordinated in system. Thirdly, to promote the full implementation of the Constitution and other legal norms in various forms and through channels, such as strict law enforcement, fair administration of justice, universal observance of law, acting in accordance with law, governance by law and comprehensive treatment, so as to continuously enhance the authority and enforceability of the institutional system of state governance. For example, the task of "dealing with cases of complaint by letters and visits that involve law or lawsuit by bringing them under the rule of law and establishing the system of termination in accordance with law of cases of complaint by letters and visits that involve law or lawsuit", put forward by the CPC at the Third Plenary Session of the Eighteenth CPC Central Committee, embodies the thinking of applying the rule of law method to deal with cases of complaint by letters and visits that involve law or lawsuit. Fourthly, to give full play to the deviation-rectification mechanism of the rule of law to enable competent state organs to respond to and deal with the deviation of some innovations on state governance system from the correct path, the conflicts between different state governance mechanisms, and obstacles encountered in the implementation of the institutional system of state governance, so as to ensure the more orderly and smooth advancement of the modernization of state governance.

---

[21] For examples, the Legislation Law provides in Article 3 that: "Legislation shall be conducted under the fundamental principles laid down in the Constitution…and in adherence to the…leadership of the Communist Party of China"; the Organic Law of Villagers' Committees provides in Article 4 that: "The grassroots organizations of the Communist Party of China in the countryside shall work in accordance with the Constitution of the Communist Party of China, play its role as the leading core, guide and support villagers' committees in their exercise of functions and powers, and, under the Constitution and the law, provide support and safeguard to villagers in their self-government activities and in their direct exercise of democratic rights"; and the Law on Industrial Enterprises Owned by the Whole People provides in Article 8 that "Grassroots organizations of the Chinese Communist Party in an enterprises shall guarantee and supervise the implementation of the guiding principles and policies of the Party and the state in the enterprise."

6.2.4 Promoting the Modernization of State Governance by Giving Full Play to the Coercive Function of the Rule of Law

The most important difference between law and other social norms is that law is manifested as the will of the state and its implementation is guaranteed by the coercive force of the state. The will of the state and the coercive force are the two important characteristics of law. In China, law is the norm of social behavior that embodies the unification of the ideology of the Party and the will of the people, and is transformed into the will of the state through the legislative procedure. The implementation, application and operation of law take the coercive force of such state organs as police, courts, prisons, even armies, as their ultimate guarantee. Therefore, subjects of legal relations who fail to fulfill their legal obligations or perform their legal duties or violate the relevant provisions of law can be sanctioned, punished or coerced by law enforcement or judicial organs in the name of the state.[22]

Promoting the modernization of state governance by giving full play to the coercive function of the rule of law means that, on the one hand, bringing the establishment, reform and abolition of the relevant institutions in the state governance system on the track of the rule of law and relying on the coercive force of the rule of law to safeguard and advance the creation and innovation of state governance system, for examples, establishing the National Security Council and the Intellectual Property Court, carrying out ministerial-level reform and deepening the reform of the administrative law enforcement system, abolishing outdated institutions and mechanisms that impede economic and social development, such the "sheltering for investigation" system and the "rehabilitation through labor" system, and reducing the number of items of administrative approve and the number of crimes punishable by death in the Criminal Law; on the other hand, comprehensively advancing strict enforcement of law and fair administration of justice, relying on coercive law enforcement and judicial institutions and mechanisms to guarantee the effective implementation of the state governance system and to enhance the enforceability of the legal system of state governance, for examples, severely and speedily cracking down on the crime of terrorism in accordance with law, implementing the criminal policy of tempering justice with mercy, investigating the criminal responsibilities of Party members and leading cadres who violate state laws; etc.

Of course, the intervention by the rule of law in the field of state governance should be carried out in accordance with the following principles: firstly, "the public powers

---

[22]In an article entitled "State Governance and Basic State Capacities", Professor Wang Shaoguang puts "coercive capacity" at the top of the list of eight basic capacities of state governance. He writes that: "Coercion does not sound very nice, but the biggest difference between the state and other human organizations is that the former can lawfully monopolize violence and use coercive force. Externally, such coercive force must be able to defend the country against foreign threat, thus requiring the state to establish and maintain a regular army; internally, this coercive force must be able to maintain peace and stability, thus requiring the state to establish a contingent of well-trained, well-funded, highly disciplined and uniformly dressed professional police." See Wang (2014).

are prohibited to do anything that is not authorized by law whereas the private persons are free to do anything that is not prohibited by law"; secondly, legal norms should be distinguished from ethics, discipline, internal regulations, rules on self-governance, and other social norms; thirdly, the coercive function of a state under the rule of law should be distinguished from the restraining force of other social norms. The coercive function of the rule of law, which represents the will of the state, can only operate within the scope of law and in accordance with law. We should not substitute it for functions of ethics, discipline and other social norms, let alone forcibly turn all other social norms into laws and the will of the state.

6.2.5   Promoting the Modernization of State Governance by Giving Full Play to the Function of Democratic and Scientific Legislation

Aristotle held that the essence of legislation is distributive justice, which is realized through the establishment of rights, obligations, powers and responsibilities, adjustment of social relations, allocation of social resources, distribution of social interests and regulation of social behaviors. According to modern theory of democracy, the basic function of legislation is to express the will of the people, the basic function of administration is to execute the will of the people, and the basic function of the administration of justice is to judge the will of the people. The above three functions are combined in the framework of constitution and jointly realize the effective governance of the state and society.

Just as Wang Anshi, a politician in ancient China, said: "Implementation of good laws in a country brings peace and stability to the country and implementation of good laws in the world brings peace and stability to the whole world".[23] In China, legislation is the embodiment of the ideology of the Party and the will of the people, the concretization and legalization of the Party's lines, principles and policies and the institutionalization, normalization and legalization of political, social and economic reforms and developments. It is a process in which the Party leads the Chinese people to distribute justice through legislative procedures, in which the people express their will and interest demands as the masters of the country, and in which rules are laid down for the people of the whole country and basis are established for state governance. It is an engine that powers the creation of institutional norms for state activities, and the main way of constructing the state legal system and modernizing the state governance system. Therefore, comprehensively advancing democratic and scientific legislation and giving full play to the guiding and promotional role of legislation is a process in which state legislative organs create, elaborate, improve and develop the state governance system through the application of legislative thinking, method, procedures and techniques.

---

[23] See *Collected Works of Wang Wengong*: the Chapter on the Duke of Zhou.

Under the new situation of the formation of the legal system and comprehensive deepening of reform in China, the manifestations of the role played by legislation in guiding and promoting state governance are the followings: first, innovation on ideas. More importance should be attached to applying the rule of law thinking and method to bring state governance system and capacity into the framework of the Constitution and onto the track of the rule of law. The innovation on state governance system should not contravene the Constitution and laws. The revision of relevant laws should be carried out before the reform, so as to ensure that major reforms are carried out in accordance with law. Activities of state governance should not violate the Constitution and laws, but should be carried out in strict accordance with laws and regulations. Second, more importance should be paid to combining major decisions on the reform and innovation of state governance system with legislative decisions, so as to transform through legislation the reform decisions into the will and the institutions of the state and ensure the legitimacy and institutionalization of reform decision-making. Third, more importance should be attached to timely creating new laws and institutions, revising or abolishing outdated laws and regulations through comprehensive application of various legislative methods, such as adoption, revision, abolition and interpretation of laws, in light of the inherent demands of the modernization of state governance system, so as to continuously enhance the normativity, systematicness, pertinence and effectiveness of the institutional system of state governance. Fourth, more importance should be attached to the supervision over the implementation of the Constitution and supervision over legislation, so as to discover and rectify in a timely way "reform decisions" and "institutional innovations" that contravene the Constitution or laws and provide powerful rule of law guarantee for the improvement of the institutional system of state governance.

6.2.6 Promoting the Modernization of State Governance by Ensuring the Exercise of the Ruling Power by the CPC in Accordance with the Constitution and Laws

The modernization of state governance is an arduous and complicated systems engineering project that can succeed only by adhering to the exercise of ruling power by the CPC in accordance with the Constitution and laws. Firstly, the CPC should firmly establish the idea and strengthen the consciousness of the ruling party, organically unify the principles of adhering to the Party's leadership, the people being the masters of the country and ruling the country by law, enhance its ability to govern the country by applying the rule of law thinking and the method, and raise the level of exercise of ruling power in accordance with the Constitution and laws, so as to continuously promote the institutionalization and legalization of state governance by linking Party regulations with state systems and combining Party policies with state laws. Secondly, the CPC should give full play to its role as the leading core to command the whole situation and coordinate the efforts of all quarters, adhere to the basic strategy of ruling the country in according with law and the basic method of exercising the ruling power in accordance with law, be good at ensuring that Party policies fully reflect and embody the people's will by giving full play to democracy, transforming through legal procedures Party's policies and ideologies into the will of the state, enabling candidates recommended by Party organizations to be elected leaders of organs of state power, realizing the Party's leadership over the state and society through organs of state power, and supporting organs of state power, administrative organs, adjudicative organs and procuratorial organs to exercise their functions and powers independently and in coordination with each other, so as to better uphold the authority of the ruling party and the state political power, the authority of the constitution of the ruling party and the state constitution and state laws, and the authority of the Party's leadership and the rule of law, fully embody the Chinese characteristics and institutional advantages of the modernization of state governance, and continuously enhance the authority and the enforceability of the state governance system. Thirdly, the CPC leads the Chinese people to adopt and implement the Constitution and laws. It should act within the scope of the Constitution and laws, take the lead in abiding by laws, and be honest in performing its official duties, so as to lead the whole society to continuously enhance their consciousness of rules, procedures and responsibilities, strengthen their awareness of the state, institutions and the rule of law, and develop a good behavioral habit of acting in accordance with law, dealing with their problems and resolving their disputes by relying on laws, thereby creating a good environment of the rule of law. Finally, in the long practice of revolution, construction and reform, the CPC has accumulated rich experiences in political, organizational and ideological leadership, explored the way of scientific, democratic and law-based exercise of ruling power, and developed the basic strategy of ruling the country by law. By adhering to the theory, the path and the institutional self-confidence of socialism with Chinese characteristics and the principles of exercising the ruling power in accordance with the Constitution and laws and enhancing its capacity for leading the legislation, ensuring the enforcement of law, upholding administration of justice, and taking the lead in abiding by the law, the CPC will be able to apply the rule of law thinking to lead the theoretical innovation on the modernization of state governance and rely on the rule of law method to promote the institutional and practical innovation on the modernization of state governance.

As Party Secretary General Xi Jinping pointed out: "In a modern society, people cannot do without law. But law is not omnipotent."[24] We should give full play to the role of the rule of law in guiding and promoting the modernization of state governance, but should not go against the objective law and the thinking of the rule of law, exaggerate the role played by the rule of law, or be stuck in the ideological rut of "omnipotence of the rule of law".[25]

---

[24]See the Speech Given by Party Secretary General Xi Jinping at the Second Collective Study Session of the Politburo of the Eighteenth CPC Central Committee.

[25]In adjusting social relations through legislation, we should ensure that "Justice is slow but sure" and that proportions of civil law, the criminal law, administrative law, economic law and social law in the legal system are balanced and appropriate. Just as famous British jurist Maine said: the level

6.3   Comprehensively Implementing the Strategy of Ruling the Country by Law and Speeding up the Construction of Rule of Law in China in Accordance with the General Reform Objective of Modernization of State Governance

The CPC pointed out at the Third Plenary Session of its 18th Central Committee that it would speed up the institutionalization, standardization and proceduralization of socialist democratic politics, build a socialist state under the rule of law, develop the people's democracy with wider, more adequate and sound participation, and shape a set of institutions and systems that are structurally complete, scientifically standardized and operationally effective, make institutions in all areas more mature and complete, comprehensively implement the strategy of ruling the country by law, and speed up the construction of rule of law in China, so as to achieve the objectives of full implementation of the basic strategy of ruling the country by law, the basic completion of the construction of a government under the rule of law, the continuous enhancement of judicial credibility, the effective respect for and safeguarding human rights, and bringing various aspects of the work of the state under the rule of law by 2020, the year in which China becomes a moderately prosperous society in all respects.

These are the general demands on the modernization of state governance, as well as the general objectives of the strategy of ruling the country by law in an all-round way and speeding up the construction of the rule of law in China. China should make an overall planning for ruling the country by law and state governance, strive to achieve the general objective of building China into a country under the rule of law in the process of modernizing state governance and realizing the modernization of state governance in the process of implementing in an all-round way the strategy of ruling the country by law and constructing China into a country under the rule of law.

6.3.1   Strengthening the Authority of the Rule of Law and of Good Law and Good Governance and Bringing State Governance Under the Rule of Law

The authority of the rule of law means that the operation of laws and the legal system is in a dominant and supreme position in the whole social adjustment mechanism and social norm system and that all subjects of public power must act within the scope of the constitution and laws and no one should have any privilege above the

---

of civilization of a country can be judged by the proportion between its civil and criminal laws in this country: a semi-civilized country has less civil law but more criminal whereas a civilized country has more civil law but less criminal law.

constitution and laws. The famous American thinker Thomas Paine wrote in his book Common Sense that: "…as in absolute governments the King is law, so in free countries the law ought to be King".[26] The supremacy of the constitution and laws is the concentrated manifestation of the authority of modern rule of law. The CPC pointed out at its Eighteenth National Congress that: "We should give greater scope to the important role the rule of law plays in the country's governance and in social management, uphold the unity, sanctity and authority of the country's legal system." The Chinese Constitution and laws are the embodiment of the unity of the Party's ideology and the will of the people and, as such, has the supreme position and authority in the country. Therefore, upholding the authority of the Constitution and laws and strengthening the authority of the rule of law is the concentrated manifestation of upholding and strengthening the authority of the people, the ruling party and the state and an inevitable requirement of the general objective of bringing state governance under the rule of law.

The rule of law is the key to state governance and bringing state governance under the rule of law is the core of the modernization of state governance. Bringing state governance under the rule of law means to take the Constitution and laws as the highest authority and main basis in state governance and public administration and ensure their effective implementation in the political, economic and social lives of the country. It contains requirements in many different aspects. However, understood from the perspective of the combination of state governance system and state governance capacity, its essence is good governance by good law. Expressed in the language of modern political science, "good law" refers to a whole set of mature and complete institutions and systems, mainly the legal system, that are structurally complete, scientifically standardized and operationally effective. "Good governance" refers to the capacity for and the process and results of applying state laws and institutions in state governance and management of various affairs of society. In order to bring state governance under the rule of law, it is necessary to strengthen good law and good governance.

Good law is the precondition and basis of good governance. If a country wants good governance, it must first have good laws. Just as Party Secretary General Xi Jinping once pointed out: "Not any law can be used to rule the country. Not any law can be used to rule the country well."[27] This means that the state and society must be governed by good laws that are structurally complete, scientifically standardized and operationally effective. It requires the state to establish a whole set of complete, scientific and effective institutions and systems, especially a legal system. The basic value of the rule of law advocated by the strategy of bringing state governance under the rule of law is an important criterion for judging whether a law is good or not, the value pursuit of the creation of a good legal system, and the ethical orientation of the realization of good law and good governance. A "good law" contains the following five aspects of requirements and criteria on legislation: first, legislation should have

---

[26]Paine (1981, pp. 35–36).

[27]See the Speech Given by Party Secretary General Xi Jinping at the Second Collective Study Session of the Politburo of the Eighteenth CPC Central Committee.

good and just value orientation and conform to such value criteria as justice, fairness, freedom, equality, democracy, human rights, order, and security; second, legislation should be the collection and expression of the will of the people. An important criterion for judging whether a law is "good" or "bad" is whether the people is able to participate and express their opinions in legislation and whether the legislation can embody the overall will of the people and uphold the fundamental interest of the people; third, the legislative procedure should be scientific and democratic, so as to ensure the creation of good law; fourth, legislation should be compatible with the actual situation of the development of economic and social relations. It should be targeted, enforceable and operable; fifth, legislation should be coordinated as a whole and internally unified and should not be self-contradictory.

Good governance is the effective implementation of good law and the ultimate objective of state governance. "Good governance" in the sense of political science contains ten elements: first, legitimacy; second, the rule of law; third, transparency; fourth, accountability, namely the administrators should be accountable for their own acts; fifth, responsiveness, namely public administrators and public administrative organs must give timely and responsible responses to citizens' demands; sixth, effectiveness; seventh, participation, namely extensive political and social participation by citizens; eighth, stability; ninth, integrity; and tenth, justice.[28]

"Good governance" in the sense of law science means to implement well-made constitution and laws, to ensure the effective execution and operation of various systems embodied in legal norms and the fair, reasonable and timely application of laws in state governance, and to realize the value pursuit of "good law" through the effective operation of the rule of law. Since the people are the masters of the country and subjects of society, good governance is first of all the majority rule of the people, rather than the authoritarian rule of the minority. Good governance is mainly the rule of institutions, rules and laws, rather than the rule of man.

In order to bring state governance under the rule of law through good law and good governance, it is necessary to carry forward the spirit of the rule of law, uphold the authority of the rule of law, strengthen the constitutionality and legality of state governance, adhere to scientific legislation, strict enforcement of law, fair administration of justice, universal observance of law, and equality of everyone before the law, and ensure that there is law to go by, the laws are observed and strictly enforced, and lawbreakers are prosecuted.

6.3.2 Strengthening the Construction of the People's Congress System and Promoting the Democratization of State Governance

The democratization of state governance means that "public administration and the relevant institutional arrangement must guarantee popular sovereignty or people

---

[28]See Keping (2014, pp. 59–60).

being masters of the country. All public policies must fundamentally embody the will of the people and the subject status of the people."[29] Professor Francis Fukuyama, a senior researcher at Stanford University and the author of the book The End of History and the Last Man, pointed out that: "Currently an orthodox opinion is that there is a relationship of mutual promotion between democracy and good governance."[30] Good governance is inseparable from democracy and extensive political and social participation by citizens and social organizations.

People's democracy is the life of socialism and the essential characteristic of ruling the country by law and the modernization of state governance. The people's congress system is a basic institutional platform whereby people exercise their democratic rights as masters of the country and administer state affairs and manage economic, cultural and social affairs. It is the fundamental institutional basis of the modernization of state governance and the basic institutional guarantee for the comprehensive advancement of ruling the country by law. Deng Xiaoping said that, without democracy, there will be no socialism or socialist modernization to talk about.[31] To realize the modernization of state governance, we must promote the democratization of state governance, unswervingly adhere to, strengthen, and improve the people's congress system.

In strengthening the construction of the people's congress system against the background of advancing the democratization of state governance, attention should be paid to the study and handling of the following issues: first, actively exploring ways of normalizing, institutionalizing and bringing under the rule of law the organic unity of the Party's leadership, people being masters of the country and ruling the country by law, namely organically unifying the three principles in the platform of the Constitution and the people's congress system, bringing them into the basic political system of state governance, and applying the Constitution and the people's congress system to ensure the smooth advancement of the modernization of state governance on the road of socialist democratic politics with Chinese characteristics; second, adhering to and upholding the people's status as masters of the country, comprehensively implementing the constitutional power, constitutional functions and constitutional status of the National People's Congress as the highest organ of state power, and strengthening and promoting the modernization of state governance system through the construction of basic political system; third, further strengthening and enhancing the power capacity (right capacity) and capacity for act of organs of state power and their deputies, including the legislative power, the power to decide on major matters, the power of appointment and removal of personnel, and the power of supervision, so as to ensure that people's congresses at various levels, their standing committees and their deputies have the necessary powers, capacities, and responsibilities to enable them to play their due roles in ruling the country by law and in state governance; fourth, striking a balance between democracy and efficiency in the construction of the people's congress system, giving equal consideration to the demands of demo-

---

[29] Yu (2013).

[30] Fukuyama (2013, p. 5).

[31] Deng (1994, p. 168).

cratic legislation and those of scientific legislation, and further improving the various systems of people's congresses, including the session system,[32] the system of convening of meetings, the meeting system, the system of openness, the voting system, the hearing system, the auditing system, the inquiry system, the investigation system, and the legislative assistance system, in light of the new demands of democratization of state governance.

6.3.3   Improving the Chinese Legal System and Providing Legal Support for the Formation of a Structurally Complete, Scientifically Standardized and Operationally Effective State System

The rule of law is an indicator of the progress of human civilization. Laws are the standardized, proceduralized and fixed carriers of state governance system. State institutions and systems in various aspects and at various levels are the main content of law. From the perspective of state governance, the completeness of the legal system reflects the ability of the ruling party to exercise the ruling power in accordance with law, as well as the leadership capacity, the cohesion capacity and governance capacity of the political power. The more developed the legislation in a country, the more complete, standardized and mature the state governance systems and institutions in that country. In China, the formation on schedule of the socialist legal system with Chinese characteristics is a sign that there are laws to go by in various aspects of economic, political, cultural, social and ecological construction of the country and that there are institutions to be used, laws to be applied, rules to be obeyed and procedures to be followed in all aspects of state governance, and that a state governance system with the Constitution as the core and the system of law as the basis has already formed, and that the state governance system is basically mature and complete.

Improving the socialist legal system with Chinese characteristics is an important task of legislation put forward by the CPC at its Eighteenth National Congress and the Third Plenary Session of its Eighteenth Central Committee as well as the inevitable requirement of the modernization of the state governance system. To improve the legal system against the background of advancing the modernization of state governance system, China must, on the basis and in the process of strengthening the construction of the people's congress system, adhere to scientific legislation, comprehensively promote democratic legislation, innovate legislative theory, update

---

[32]In legislative science, the session system is a system on the space of time between two sessions of a legislative organ and the time duration of each session. This system is usually provided for in the Constitution and relevant laws. The duration of the session of a legislative organ begins on the date the legislative organ is convened and ends on the date the session is closed. Currently the duration of the annual session of the NPC is too short (less than ten days), which is not conducive to the implementation of democratic legislation and to the performance of functions by the NPC.

legislative ideas, change legislative mode, adjust legislative mechanisms, perfect legislative procedures, improve legislative techniques, popularize legislative assessment, strengthen legislative supervision, continuously raise the quality and level of legislation, so as to provide powerful legislative guarantee and legal support for the formation of a structurally complete, scientifically standardized, operationally effective, mature, complete and modernized system of state institutions.

6.3.4 Strengthening the Implementation of the Constitution and Laws and Enhancing the State's Capacity for Governance by Law

The authority and the life of the constitution and laws lie in their implementation. Good implementation of the constitution and laws is a basic content and an important indicator of the modernization of state governance. The Chinese Constitution and laws contain provisions—some of them are very detailed—on the various requirements and various aspects of state governance and its modernization. Therefore, the good implementation of the Constitution and laws is in essence the effective operation and implementation of state governance system. The guarantee by the ruling party and the state of the enforceability of the Constitution and laws is in essence the comprehensive embodiment of the capacity for state governance. "The life of laws lies in its implementation. If laws are not implemented or not effectively implemented and, as a result, are not complied with and law-breakers are not brought to justice, then laws are of no use at all, no matter how many of them have been adopted." "If laws are not effectively implemented, they are just mere scraps of paper, no matter how many of them are made, and ruling the country by law is nothing but an empty talk." "Implementation is the life of institutions. Slack implementation of institutions will result in the broken window effect."[33] The key to modernizing state governance capacity is to enhance the capacity for ruling the country by the Constitution and laws, the capacity for governance by law, and the capacity for implementing the Constitution, laws and various institutions. More importance should attached to the implementation of the Constitution and laws, to transforming the laws on the paper into laws in real life, and to turning the institutions in legal provisions into activities in social life, and continuously improve the capacity for and the quality of governance by law through the application of the rule of law method and the implementation of law.

In order to enhance the capacity for governance by law, further develop the mechanisms and procedures for the supervision over the implementation of the Constitution and laws, and take the implementation of the Constitution to a new level, China should, apart from conscientiously implementing the reform arrangements made at the Third Plenary Session of the Eighteenth CPC Central Committee, consider the adoption of the following measures: further strengthening the CPC's leadership over

---

[33] Quoted in Zhang (2014).

and overall planning and coordination of the implementation of the Constitution and the legislative work; promoting the implementation of the Constitution through legislation; establishing mechanisms for the simultaneous promotion of interpretation of laws and interpretation of the Constitution; including a report on the situation of implementation of the Constitution in the annual work report of the NPC Standing Committee; improving the mechanisms for the review of the constitutionality and legality of laws and administrative regulations; establishing and improving the mechanisms for the review of the constitutionality and legality of intra-Party regulations and institutions; and strengthening the theoretical research on the revision of the constitution and the establishment of the Constitution Supervision Committee.

6.3.5 Implementing the Index System of Construction of the Rule of Law and Enhancing the Efficiency of State Governance by Law

Professor Francis Fukuyama points out in the article "What is Governance?" that governance is "the capacity of the government for adopting and implementing rules and providing services"[34] and governance or good governance needs to be measured (measurement of governance). He suggests that the quality of state governance should be measured from the perspectives of procedure, capacity, output and the autonomy of bureaucratic system. The Worldwide Governance Indicators of the World Bank, the Governance Indicators Project of the UNDP, and the World Justice Project initiated by American Bar Association and other lawyers' organizations all point out that state governance must be quantitatively measurable. Governance not quantitatively measured is not scientific governance, and the degree of quantitative governance determines the level of modernization of state governance.

The CPC pointed out at the Third Plenary Session of its Eighteenth Central Committee that, in order to build scientific index systems and assessment criteria on the construction of the rule of law, China should proceed from its own national conditions, design a set of index in accordance with requirements of the strategy of ruling the country by law and modernization of state governance, and apply it to carry out scientific and quantitative assessment of the results of the construction of the rule of law and modernization of state governance in the country. State governance can be divided into three basic component parts: state governance system, state governance capacity, and state governance cost. With respect the state governance system, concrete indices include the scientificity, standardization, effectiveness, maturity and completeness of constitutional norms, legal system, state institutions and relevant systems; with respect to the state governance capacity, concrete indices include the capacity of the ruling party for exercising the ruling power in accordance with law, the capacity of the people for being the masters of the country, the capacity of administrative organs for administration by law, the capacity of judicial organs for fair admin-

---

[34]Fukuyama (2013, p. 5).

istration of justice, and the capacity of subjects of public power for implementing the Constitution, laws and regulations, running the Party, the state and armed forces, administering internal, foreign and national defense affairs, carrying out reform, promoting development, and maintaining political and social stability. With respect to the cost of state governance, concrete indices include tax burden, consumption of resources, legislative cost, law enforcement cost, judicial cost, stability maintenance cost, risk cost, trial-and-error cost, operational cost, and anti-corruption cost. The adoption of a whole set of scientific and reasonable indices of the GDP of the rule of law[35] has made it possible to carry out actual measurement and concrete assessment of the quality of rule of law and modernization of state governance.

6.3.6 Promoting the Modernization of State Governance in the Process of Constructing China into a Country Under the Rule of Law

The construction of China into a country under the rule of law is a major practice and innovative development of the rule of law civilization in contemporary China, a new historical starting point in the process of carrying forward and rejuvenating the fine tradition of Chinese legal culture, an important part of the task of modernizing state governance and bringing it under the rule of law, and the comprehensive inheritance, strategic upgrading and major development of the basic policy of "there must be laws to go by, the laws must be observed and strictly enforced, and lawbreakers must be prosecuted" and the basic strategy of "ruling the country by law and constructing a socialist state under the rule of law".

In constructing China into a country under the rule of law, we must adhere to the combination of the universal principles of the rule of law civilization and the road of socialist democracy and rule of law with Chinese characteristics, to the organic unity of the Party's leadership, people being masters of the country and ruling the country by law, to the complementary relationship between ruling the country by law and modernization of state governance, to the comprehensive development of scientific legislation, strict enforcement of law, fair administration of justice, and universal observance of law, to the simultaneous advancement of ruling the country by law, exercising the ruling power by law and administration by law, and to the unified construction of a law-based state, a law-based government and a law-based

---

[35] In recent years, Professor Ma Huaide has been advocating the idea of "the rule of law GDP" in mass media, claiming that "the rule of law GDP" is more important than "economic GDP" and calling for the establishment of "the rule of law GDP" and using it to promote the rule of administrative law and to assess the performance of the government. Explorations on the quantitative assessment of indices of local rule of law have been carried out in some cities, including Shenzhen, Wuxi, Kunming, Chengdu and Yuhang District of Hangzhou City. The "Index System for the Assessment of Social Governance in China", presided over by Professor Yu Keping, and the "Awards for the Construction of Law-based Government in China", presided over by Professor Ying Songnian and Professor Ma Huaide, have both achieved positive results.

society, truly uphold the authority of the Constitution and laws, effectively regulate and restrain powers, fully respect and safeguard human rights, and realize social justice in accordance with law.

In constructing China into a country under the rule of law, we must actively yet prudently deepen the legal reform, make special efforts to solve the main problems in the construction of the rule of law, including wrongful legislation,[36] slack law enforcement, miscarriage of justice, disorderly observance of law, and weak rule of law, comprehensively implement the strategy of ruling the country by law, speed up the construction of a socialist state under the rule of law, so as to transform China from a country with a complete system of law into a country under the rule of law, basically complete the construction of China into a country under the rule of law by the year 2020, the year in which China becomes a moderately prosperous society in all respects, and fully complete the construction of China into a country the rule of law by the year 2049, the 100th anniversary of the founding of the People's Republic of China.

References

Biwu D (1979) On socialist democracy and legal system. People's Publishing House, Beijing

Deng X (1994) Selected works of Deng Xiaoping, vol 1. People's Publishing House, Beijing

Fukuyama F (2013) What is governance?. Chinese version (trans: Liu Y et al). In Yu K (ed) China governance review, vol 4. Central Compilation & Translation Press, Beijing

Fuller LL (1969) The morality of law (revised edition). Yale University Press

Gibson JL, Gouws A (1998) Support for the rule of law in the emerging South African democracy. Int Social Sci J (Chinese edition), 2

He Z (2014) Understanding state governance and its modernization. Marxism and Reality, 3

Hu J (2014) The key to the modernization of state governance is to bring it under the rule of law. Study Time, 14 July 2014

Keping Y (2014) On the modernization of state governance. Social Sciences Academic Press, Beijing

Lenin VI (2009) A special collection of Lenin's Works. Chinese edition. People's Publishing House, Beijing

Lenin VI (2012) Selected works of Lenin. Chinese edition, vol 3, People's Publishing House, Beijing

Li L (2005) Summary of the seminar on ruling the country by law and constructing a socialist state under the rule of law. In Li L (ed) Evolution of the rule of law and constitutionalism. China Social Science Press, Beijing

Li Z (2014) Modernization of governance: scientific connotation and standard setting. People's Tribune, 7

---

[36] Since this author is uncertain about the formulation of "legislative corruption", but has indeed witnessed such phenomena as "departmentalization of administrative power, profitization of departmental power, and legalization of departmental interest", legislations with obvious marks of departmental interest or the interest of special groups, and legalization of abnormal interest pattern or power relations in the legislative process, the term "wrongful legislation" is used here to describe the above phenomena. Moreover, any power not subjected to supervision will inevitably lead to corruption. Today, the phenomenon of corruption has emerged in all fields of public power, but the corruption in the field of legislative power has not yet been paid enough attention to in China.

Marx C (1995) Debates on freedom of the press and publication of the proceedings of the assembly of the estates. In: Complete works of Marx and Engels, vol 1. Chinese edition. People's Publishing House, Beijing, p 176

Marx C, Engels F (2009) Collected works of Marx and Engels. Chinese edition, vol 3. Beijing: People's Publishing House

Marx C, Engels F (2012) Selected works of Marx and Engels. Chinese edition, vol 3. People's Publishing House, Beijing

Paine T (1981) Selected works of Thomas Paine, Chinese edition (trans: Ma Q et al). The Commercial Press, Beijing

Puqu W (2014) A scientific understanding the meaning of "state governance". Guangming Daily, 18 June 2014

Qiu S (2014) The modernization of state governance: breaking away from the rule of man and marching towards the rule of law. Seeking Truth, 1

Shi Z (2013) Vice chairman of the committee for social and legal affairs of chinese people's political consultative conference, discusses 'the fifth modernization'. Beijing Daily, 9 Dec 2013

Wang D (2004) An Record of questions and answers with Liang Shuming. Hubei People's Publishing House, Wuhan

Wang S (2014) Sate governance and basic state capacities. J Huazhong Univ Sci Technol (Social Sciences Edition), 3

Xi J (2013) Speech given at the conference of representatives of all circles in Beijing in commemoration of the thirtieth anniversary of the promulgation and implementation of the current constitution. People's Publishing House, Beijing

Yao L (2014) New trends in the study of state governance ability. Study Time, 9 June 2014

Yu K (2013) Promoting the modernization of state governance system along the road of democracy and the rule of law. Newsxinhua, 1 Dec 2013. Available at: http://news.xinhuanet.com/politics/2013-12/01/c_125788564.htm, last visited 9 June 2017

Zhang X (2014) Promoting the modernization of state governance system and ability. Cass J Polit Sci, 2

Zhang W (2014) Major tasks of construction of the rule of law in China. Legal Daily, 11 June 2014

Chapter 7
Comprehensively Promoting Ruling the Country by Law and Striving to Build China into a Country Under the Rule of Law

The convening of the Eighteenth CPC Party Congress and the adoption of a series of major strategic arrangements at the third and the fourth plenary sessions of the Eighteenth CPC Central Committee have sounded the bugle call for the advancement of economic, political, social, cultural and ecological constructions in China, declared the beginning of a new historical period of development of the great cause of comprehensively ruling country by law and building a state under the rule of law, and indicated that the great practice of comprehensively deepening the reform, promoting development, building a moderately prosperous society in all respects, and realizing the great rejuvenation of the Chinese nation has entered into a new stage. At this new historical starting point, the Chinese people have reached the following consensus: ruling the country by law is the basic strategy by which the ruling party leads the Chinese people to carry out state and social governance; the rule of law is the basic method by which the ruling party governs the country; and the construction of the rule of law in China by the ruling party is an indispensable component of the great Chinese dream. In order to build China into a socialist state under the rule of law as soon as possible and realize the Chinese dream of rule of law, China must comprehensively deepen the legal reform, advance ruling the country by law in an all-round way, and adhere to the organic unity of the Party's leadership, the people being masters of the country and ruling the country by law, to the coordinated development of scientific legislation, strict enforcement of law, fair administration of justice, and observance of law by the whole people, to the simultaneous advancement of ruling the country by law, exercising the ruling power by law, and administration by law, to the integrative construction of a law-based state, a law-based government and a law-based society, and to giving fully play to the role played by the ruling Party in leading the legislation, ensuring the enforcement of law, supporting administration of justice, and taking the lead in abiding by the law.

7.1 The Great Strategic Significance of Comprehensively Advancing Ruling the Country by Law at the New Historical Starting Point

The Decision on Major Issues Pertaining to Comprehensively Advancing Ruling the Country by Law (hereinafter referred to as the Decision), adopted at the Fourth Plenary Session of the Eighteenth CPC Central Committee, has for the first time in Chinese history made an overall strategic arrangement in the form of the highest-level political document and highest-level decision of the ruling party, for further guiding and safeguarding the construction of socialism with Chinese characteristics, for advancing the modernization of the state governance system and capacity by comprehensive advancing ruling the country by law and speeding up the construction of the rule of law in China, and for actively and prudently deepening various institutional reforms on the track of the rule of law, thereby providing important institutional and legal safeguards for building China into a moderately well-off society in an all-round way and for realizing the Chinese dream of the great rejuvenating the Chinese nation. It is of great strategic and practical significance to strengthening the construction of the socialist system of rule of law with Chinese characteristics, comprehensively advancing ruling the country by law and speeding up the construction of a socialist state under the rule of law.

In October 2014, the CPC, as the ruling Party in China, held a special session of its Central Committee to study and discuss the construction of socialist rule of law with Chinese characteristics and political development in the country and made a special decision on major issues concerning the comprehensive advancement of ruling the country by law in China. This was an unprecedented event in the 160-year history of International Communist Movement, in the 90-year history of the CPC, in the 60-year history of the People's Republic of China and especially in the 30-year history of reform and opening up in China. The convening of the Fourth Plenary Session of the Eighteenth CPC Central Committee and adoption of the Decision shows that the CPC, as the biggest ruling party in the world, has lifted the implementation of the basic strategy of ruling the country by law and the basic method of the rule of law to the new historical height of governing the country by the ruling party and advancing the modernization of state governance. It shows that the new generation of central collective leadership in China led by Party Secretary General Xi Jinping is attaching more importance to giving full play to its leadership role in the construction of the rule of law, to using the rule of law thinking and the rule of law method to govern the country, to upholding the authority of the Constitution and laws and applying them in running the Party, the state and the armed forces, to bringing state governance under the rule of law, to constructing a law-based state, a law-based government, and a law-based society, and to leading the Chinese people in creating a new life of political openness, social harmony, and economic prosperity, that the construction of socialist rule of law with Chinese characteristics and ruling the country by law have been unprecedentedly combined with the practice of reform and opening up, with the economic, political, cultural, social and ecological construction, and with the strategic objectives of building Chinese into a moderately prosperous society in all respects and realizing the Chinese dream of great rejuvenation of the Chinese nation, that the CPC and the Chinese government have had a more profound understanding, a more scientific grasp, and more a positive control of the construction of socialist democracy and rule of law with Chinese characteristics and the political reform in China, that the construction of the rule of law has reached a new starting point and entered into a new stage of comprehensive advancement, systematic construction, breakthrough at key points, and deepening of the reform, and that the construction of socialist rule of law with Chinese characteristics is entering into the second spring of comprehensive and rapid development and systematic and coordinated advancement.

Comprehensive advancement of ruling the country by law is an important content of construction of a socialist modern state with Chinese characteristics. The Chinese Constitution provides that China will develop socialist democracy, improve the socialist legal system, modernize the country's industry, agriculture, national defense and science and technology step by step, and build itself into a socialist country that is prosperous, powerful, democratic and culturally advanced. Construction of a modernized socialist big power with Chinese characteristics is the objective of struggle of the Chinese dream of great rejuvenation of the Chinese nation, as well as an inherent objective of ruling the country by law and modernizing the state governance.

In the early days of reform and opening up, Chinese people, based on the scientific conclusion that "without democracy, there will be no socialism or socialist modernization to talk about", the bitter experience of "taking class struggle as the key link" and the Cultural Revolution,and the actual needs of bringing order out of chaos, and implementing reform, opening up and socialist modernization, decided that China must develop people's democracy, improve the legal system and bring democracy under the framework of the legal system. Today, based on the new realization that "without the rule of law, China will not be able to modernize state governance, build a moderately prosperous society in all respects, or realized the Chinese dream of great rejuvenation of the Chinese nation", the new understanding that the rule of law "is of great importance to the exercise of ruling power by the CPC, the rejuvenation of the Chinese nation, the happiness and welfare of the people, and the lasting political stability in the country", the new judgment that "the building of a moderately prosperous society in all respects has entered a decisive stage, that the reform has entered the deep-water zone where tough challenges must be met, that the current international situation is complex and volatile and that the Party is faced with unprecedentedly heavy tasks of carrying out reform, promoting development and maintaining stability, and unprecedented numbers of contradictions, risks and challenges", and the new thinking that the position and the role of ruling the country by law has become even more prominent in the overall work of the state and the Party, the Chinese people have realized that they must take the comprehensive advancement of ruling the country by law as the key to the implementation of the overall strategy of development of the state and the Party, unfold the work of carrying forward the spirit of the rule of law and cultivating the culture of the rule of law in the larger context of establishment of socialist core values, uphold the authority and guarantee the implementation of the Constitution and laws in the bigger framework of upholding the authority of state governance, strengthening the ruling basis of the Party, safeguarding people's fundamental rights and realizing social fairness and justice, and implement the basic requirements of constructing the system of rule of law and giving full play to the functions of the rule of law in the concrete practice of guiding the reform, promoting comprehensive development, building an orderly society, and guaranteeing lasting peace and stability.

Comprehensively advancing ruling the country by law is the basic guarantee of the development of the people's democracy under the new situation. Under the principle of popular sovereignty, the people are always the subjects of ruling the country by law, rather than the objects to be punished and controlled. Ruling the country by law should never be allowed to degenerate into "controlling the people by law". The essence of ruling the country by law is to realize people's democracy by fighting corruption, administering public officials by law and supervising and restraining public power. Therefore, the starting point and the ultimate goal of ruling the country by law must be developing the people's democracy, safeguarding the people's political status and sovereign rights as subjects of the state and society. The new demands posed by the development of people's democracy on ruling the country by law are manifested not merely in political democracy and political rights, such as right to vote and the right to stand for election, the right to administer public affairs, the right to know, the right of political participation, and the right of supervision, but more importantly also in social democracy and social rights, such as the right of self-governance, social security, medical service, pension, housing, employment, education, health, and public services, as well as in economic democracy and economic rights, such as participation in economic decision-making and management, the right to acquire property or shares of enterprises, the right to join trade unions, equality of men and women, equal pay for equal work, paid leave, adequate living standard, and production safety. The broad masses of people need not abstract, vague and remote democratic political rights and democratic political participation, but concrete, real, equal and fair democratic political rights by which they will be able to participate and be respected in the administration of public affairs. They do not need democratic political rights on the glass ceiling that are inaccessible to them, but concrete, tangible and practical rights and interests, such as personal and property rights, economic and social rights and the rights to safe environment, ecology and food.

Comprehensively advancing ruling the country by law is an important content and the main way of realizing the modernization of state governance. The relationship between ruling the country by law and state governance is that of interacting with each other, supplementing each other, and reaching the same goal by different means. Ruling the country by law is an important content as well as an important means of realization of the modernization of state governance. To modernize state governance means to democratize, scientize and informatize state governance system and capacity and, most importantly, to bring them under the rule of law. On the one hand, state governance system should be brought under the rule of law. Most institutions, systems and mechanisms of the state governance in a country under the rule of law have already been embodied in the state law system through legislative procedure and manifested as legal norms and legal systems. Therefore, developing and improving the state law system and constructing a complete and scientific system of legal institutions is in essence promoting the legalization, normalization, and finalization of state governance system and the formation of a structurally complete, scientifically standardized and operationally effective state institutional system. On the other hand, state governance capacity must also be brought under the rule of law. State governance capacity in a country under the rule of law mainly refers to the capacity for governance by law, including the capacity for relying on state legal system to administer state and social affairs and manage economic and cultural undertakings in accordance with the Constitution and laws, the capacity for ensuring scientific legislation, strict law enforcement, fair administration of justice and observance of law by the whole people, and the capacity for using the rule of law thinking and method to deepen the reform, promote development, resolve conflicts and uphold stability. Bringing state governance capacity under the rule of law ultimately means to enhance the power (rights) capacity and capacity for act in state governance, strengthen the enforceability and the observance of the Constitution and laws, and the operability and enforceability of state institutional system. High attention should be paid to giving full play to the role of the strategy of ruling the country by law and the rule of law method in promoting the modernization of state governance. Ruling the country by law in a comprehensive way is not only an important content of the modernization of state governance, but also an important way and a basic means of modernization of state governance that plays an important role of guiding, standardizing, promoting and safeguarding the modernization.

Comprehensively advancing ruling the country by law is an inherent requirement of deepening market economic reform. The market economy is in essence an economy under the rule of law because market subjects need to be confirmed by law, market behaviors need to be regulated by law, property rights need to be protected by law, market order needs to be upheld by law, the operation of the market needs to be macro-controlled by law, and market disputes needs to be adjudicated in accordance with law…. The objective law of historical development both in China and abroad shows that no country is able to realize the effective operation and sustainable development of the market economy under the condition of long period of absence of the rule of law. Market economy stresses the decisive role played by the market in the allocation of resources, namely the realization of effective and reasonable allocation of market resources through the division of labor in society, fair competition, and free equal-value exchange. Therefore, in order to give full play to the functions of the market, it is necessary to regulate government activities, put power into the cage of laws and institutions, prevent improper and excessive government interventions in economic activities, guarantee the autonomous and decentralized decision-making by market subjects, protect property rights and personal freedom, safeguard the equal status of market subjects, realize fair competition, implement the principle of good faith, reduce the cost of transaction, ensure strict enforcement of law, fair administration of justice, and effective resolution of disputes, and uphold market order. In order to enable the market to play a decisive role in the allocation of resources and further promote the economic development, it is necessary to comprehensively advance ruling the country by law, improve the system of the rule of law, create good rule of law environment, realize the equality of rights, equality of opportunities, equality of rules, and equality of everyone before the law, realize distributive justice in the initial link of allocation of resource through democratic and scientific legislation, as well as executive justice and corrective justice through strict law enforcement and fair administration of justice, and enable the administration of justice, as the "stabilizer" of society, to provide a mitigation mechanism in the market economic reform.

Comprehensive advancement of ruling the country by law is an inevitable requirement of the construction of rule of law in China. The construction of the rule of law in China is a process of pursuit by Chinese people of such values as freedom, equality, human rights, fairness, justice, security, order, dignity, and happiness, a process of establishing theoretical self-confidence, path self-confidence and institutional self-confidence, improving socialist system with Chinese characteristics, modernizing state governance, and bringing various aspects of the state work under the rule of law, and a process of administering state and social affairs, allocating resources, safeguarding human rights, taming powers, and realizing good law and good governance in accordance with the Constitution and laws. To comprehensively advance ruling the country by law, we must implement in a deep-going way the decisions of the third and fourth plenary sessions of the Eighteenth CPC Central Committee, adhere to the socialist system with Chinese characteristics, implement the theory of socialist rule of law with Chinese characteristics, strengthen the construction of the system of socialist rule of law with Chinese characteristics, develop a complete system of legal norms, a highly efficient rule of law implementation system, a strict rule of law supervision system, and a powerful rule of law safeguarding system, shape a complete intra-Party regulation system, adhere to the simultaneous advancement of ruling the country by law, exercising the ruling power by law, and administration by law and the integrated construction of a law-based state, a law-based government, and a law-based society, realize scientific legislation, strict enforcement of law, fair administration of justice, and observance of law by the whole people, and promote the modernization of state governance system and capacity. In comprehensively advancing ruling the country by law, China must continuously deepen the legal reform, strengthen the construction of the system of socialist rule of law with Chinese characteristics, advance ruling the country by Constitution, truly respect and uphold the authority of the Constitution; promote democratic and scientific legislation, continuously improve the system of law with Chinese characteristics, promote administration by law, and speed up the construction of a law-based government; promote judicial fairness, build an independent, impartial, efficient and authoritative judicial system; promote observance of law by the whole people and speed up the construction of a law-based society; run the armed forces in accordance with law and ensure the absolute leadership of the Party over the armed forces; advance the construction of local rule of law and strengthen the practical foundation of ruling the country by law; carry out international cooperation in the field of the rule of law and improve the new international order of rule of law; and, most importantly, comprehensively advance the exercise of ruling power by law and truly strengthen and improve the Party's leadership over and guarantee of the work of ruling the country by law.

Comprehensively advancing ruling country by law is the basic way of realizing justice. Justice is a common value pursuit of contemporary Chinese society. However, with respect to the question of what is justice, different people have different opinions, and there is no consensus on the "greatest common divisor" of justice. Against this social background, we should not advocate justice in an abstract way, but should express and realize operable justice through law and the rule of law: we should give full play to the indispensable and unique function of the rule of law, reconstruct the basic system of evaluation of social justice, and bring the interest demands for justice of social organizations and the broad masses of people under the rule of law; transform through scientific legislation their reasonable abstract demands for justice into concrete and specific legal rights or interests, and effective safeguard their lawful rights and interest through strict enforcement of law, fair administration of justice and administration by law; enable social organizations and the general public to uphold and realize fairness and justice that manifest as their legal rights and interests through the rule of law method and in accordance with law; reasonably provide for the rights and obligations of citizens, distribute various resources and interests, scientifically allocate various powers and responsibilities, and realize substantive distributive justice through the adoption of fair and just substantive laws; adopt through democratic and scientific procedural law procedural rules that fully reflect the will of the people and are accepted by the majority of people, so as to distribute resources, balance interests, reconcile contradictions, resolve conflicts, regulate behaviors, and realize procedural justice; and rely on various rule of law procedures and mechanisms, including judicial procedures, to resolve various conflicts of interest, and realize both substantive and procedural justice, or at least procedural justice, under the rule of law.

Comprehensive advancement of ruling the country by law is the fundamental solution to the problem of corruption and abuse of power. Corruption of power is the mortal enemy of socialist rule of law and the biggest obstacle to comprehensive advancement of ruling the country by law and construction of a socialist state under the rule of law. China should attach more importance to comprehensively advancing ruling the country by law, put power into the cage of laws and institutions, improve the mechanisms for controlling and supervising power, give full play to the role of the rule of law thinking and method in the fight against corruption and abuse of power, and put under control and solve the problem of corruption of power through the improvement of relevant institutions and mechanisms and through the construction of the rule of law. The phenomenon of corruption is infinite in variety and ever changing, but it root cause is the corruption of public power, because unrestrained power inevitably leads to corruption and absolute power leads to absolute corruption. Therefore, all countries under the rule of law must separate and control powers. The corruption of public power takes many forms and has many causes, but its ultimate form and root cause is power rent-seeking, namely the corruption by various holders and exercisers of public power—basically all of them are government officials and civil servants. Therefore, all countries under the rule of law must not only control public power in accordance with law, but also strictly control and administer government officials in accordance with law. In China, regulating public power and government officials in accordance with law is an inevitable requirement of comprehensively ruling the country by law, exercising the ruling power by law and administration by law, as well as an inevitable requirement of anti-corruption and power control under the rule of law thinking. The fight against corruption depends on the control of power, which in turn depends on the implementation of the rule of law.

7.2 Deepening Political Reform by Comprehensively Advancing Ruling the Country by Law

In adhering to the socialist road of political development with Chinese characteristics, China must actively and prudently deepen the political reform, comprehensively implement the strategy of ruling the country by law, and speed up the construction of a socialist state under the rule of law. The CPC stated at the Third Plenary Session of its Eighteenth Central Committee that it will deepen the political reform closely around the organic unity of the Party's leadership, the people being masters of the country and ruling the country by law. Political reform is a basic policy always adhered to by the CPC and the Chinese government since the Third Plenary Session of the Eleventh CPC Central Committee. It is the self-improvement of the socialist political system with Chinese characteristics as well as the sound development of the legal system in China.

7.2.1 The Essence of Comprehensive Advancement of Ruling the Country by Law Is the Reform of the Political System

Ruling the country by law is a basic strategy by which the Party leads the Chinese people to administer state affairs. From the perspective of developing democratic politics, ruling the country by law means that the people, as masters of the country, administer state and social affairs and manage economic and cultural undertakings in accordance with the Constitution and laws; from the perspective of strengthening and improving the Party's leadership and exercise of the ruling power, ruling the country by law means that the Party must act within the scope of the Constitution and laws, administer state affairs in accordance with the Constitution and laws and exercise the ruling power in accordance with the Constitution and law; from the perspective of the internal function and values of the rule of law, ruling the country by law means to regulate power and government officials in accordance with law, respect and safeguard human rights, and bring various kinds of the work of the state under the rule of law; and from the perspective of promoting the modernization of state governance system and capacity, ruling the country by law means to continuously improve the legal system and legal institutions, ensure their effective operation, and realize good law and good governance.

Comprehensive advancement of ruling the country by law can be achieved only through the coordination of political, economic, cultural and social resources, with the assistance of such means as education, administration, economy, ethics, discipline and custom. However, from the perspective of the institutional level of the state governance system, legal reform is political reform. In a certain sense, the essence of comprehensive advancement of ruling the country by law is the deepening of the reform and the self-improvement of the political system in China.

In the process of comprehensive advancement of ruling the country by law and construction of the rule of law, China must adhere to the organic unity of the Party's leadership, people being masters of the country and ruling the country by law, to the comprehensive strengthening of scientific legislation, strict law enforcement, fair administration of justice and observance of law by the whole people, to the simultaneous advancement of ruling the country by law, exercising the ruling power by law and administration by law, and to the integrated construction of a law-based state, a law-based government, and a law-based society. All the above requirements, when implemented in the modernization of state governance system, will inevitably lead to the reform of relevant political institutions and mechanisms. China must have clear understanding of and make sufficient preparation for these reforms.

Without any doubt, the institutional form of "the organic unity of the three" is the socialist democratic political system with Chinese characteristics, with the adherence to the CPC's leadership and exercise of the ruling power as its core and the people's congress system as its fundamental system. Various reform measures and designs and proposals relating to the implementation of the strategy of ruling the country by law will all inevitably touch upon, either directly or indirectly, the Party's leadership system, the people's congress system, and China's political system. The promotion of scientific legislation involves not only various institutional issues, such as how to improve the system, procedure, technique, quality and the actual effect of legislation and the legal system, but also such underlying institutional issues as how to further improve the quality of deputies to people's congresses, implement the constitutional power of people's congresses, strengthen the supervision by people's congresses, and development the democracy of people's congresses. Promoting strict enforcement of law involves not only the reform and improvement of the systems, mechanisms and method of administrative law enforcement and the strengthening of the regulation and control of the discretional power of administrative law enforcement, but also a series of underlying institutional issues, such as deepening the reform of administrative system, transformation of government functions, advancement of administration by law, and construction of a law-based government. Advancement of fair administration of justice inevitably demands the comprehensive deepening of judicial reform, even taking judicial reform as the breakthrough point of political reform. Advancing administration by law, implementing the principle that the CPC leads the legislation, ensures the enforcement of law at the institutional level, upholds administration of justice, and takes the lead in abiding by the law is in itself a comprehensive revolutionary transformation of the CPC from a revolutionary party to a ruling party, and a most profound political reform in which the CPC carries out revolution against itself.

Characterizing the comprehensive advancement of ruling the country by law as political reform means that China is actively adapting its political system to the needs of economic and social development and comprehensive deepening of the reform, and realizing self-improvement and optimized development of the political mechanism within the framework of the Constitution and on the track of the rule of law. It means that the CPC and the Chinese government, after more 60 years of exploration since the founding of the PRC, especially after over 30 years of practice since the reform and opening up, have finally found a reliable approach to carrying out political reform in an organized, active, steady and step-by-step way under the leadership of the CPC, which is the only way of continuous development and self-perfection of the socialist democratic political system with Chinese characteristics that is compatible with the national conditions in China.

Comprehensively implementing the strategy of ruling the country by law and applying the rule of law thinking and method to carry out political reform in an active and steady way is of great significance to China. Firstly, it formally puts on the agenda of the Party and the government various political reforms that have already been carried out in practice under the precondition of adhering to the Party's leadership and ensuring national unity and social stability, thereby creating a harmonious and orderly social environment and good atmosphere for the political reform; secondly, it brings the people's reasonable demands on institutional reform (especially the reform of the political system) into the scope of the rule of law through the adoption, revision, abolition, and interpretation of laws, and reaches broad consensuses through the application of legal reason, transforms these consensuses into laws through democratic legislative procedure, and expresses and solidify through the legal system the results of political reform and various other reforms, so as to avoid the necessity of radical reforms; thirdly, it continuously improves the socialist legal system with Chinese characteristics and the legal institutions, procedures and mechanisms in the fields of legislation, law enforcement, administration of justice, observance of law, and upholding of the authority of law, ensures the effective implementation of the Constitution and laws, upholds social fairness and justice, human rights and fundamental freedoms, thereby promoting the modernization of state governance system and bringing it under the rule of law and further adapting the political and legal superstructure to the needs of economic and social reform and development; and finally, it enables China to firmly grasp the power of discourse and the initiatives in the political reform, response to people's reasonable demands on political reform and development, rebuke the slanders and distortions of the democratic politics and the political reform in China by western hostile forces and hostile elements, confidently declare to the world that the reform in China is a comprehensive and in-depth reform that touches upon all aspects of social life—not just a reform of the economic, social and cultural systems, but also a reform of the political system that is centered closely around "the organic unity of the three" and takes ruling the country by law as its main path dependence.

Comprehensive advancement of ruling the country by law is in essence promotion of political reform. Therefore, China should not let down its guard, but should attach high importance to this issue, strengthen the leadership over the reform and prevent domestic and foreign hostile forces and elements from taking advantage of the legal reform, especially the judicial reform, to advocate and peddle western democratic values and judicial models, and infiltrate the legal reform in China. Meanwhile, China should also strengthen the positive guidance of the relevant theoretical researches and publicities by domestic academic circle and mass media, pay close attention to people's interest demands on the political reform, prevent certain people who have an ulterior motive from utilizing the political reform to instigate street politics, large-scale mass incidents and other activities against the rule of law.

7.2.2 Comprehensive Advancement of Ruling the Country by Law Is the Only Road to Deepening Political Reform in China

In a peaceful and rational society, political reforms, such as Li Kui's Reform, Wu Qi's Reform, Shang Yang's Reform, Wang Anshi's Reform and the One Hundred Day Reform in ancient and modern Chinese history, usually take the form of legal reform, namely all these reforms have tried to improve the political system through the change of the existing legal systems and institutions. These legal reforms, as the carriers of political reform, are neither violent revolution, nor change of regimes, but improvement, amelioration and restoration of the existing system, the reform and self-improvement carried out by the state legal and political systems at their own initiatives under the precondition of not changing the existing basis of political power and political rule. Revolution, on the other hand, is a profound qualitative change of social and political system, which uses "revolt", "uprising" and other extremely violent means to overthrow all the existing political power and realize the regime change.

Under the Chinese constitutional system, comprehensive advancement of ruling the country by law and speeding up of the construction of the rule of law in China is an important component and main path dependence of political reform, as well as the legal guarantee of the active and prudent deepening of political reform. Comprehensively advancing ruling the country by law, regulating power and government officials in accordance with law, fully guaranteeing people's democracy, and respecting and safeguarding human rights are the effective ways of actively and prudently carrying out orderly reform of the political system through the reform and improvement of the legal system. The constitution is the top-level design and the concentrated embodiment of the state political system. The good operation of the political system means carefully implementing the constitution, ruling the country and exercising the ruling power in accordance with the constitution, and upholding the authority of the constitution. To revise and interpret the constitution is to actively and prudently deepen the political reform at the level of fundamental legal norms of the state. Especially modern democratic politics is the rule of law politics regulated and safeguarded by laws and institutions under command of the constitution. Adhering to the institutionalization and legalization of democracy, advancing ruling the country by law, exercising the ruling power by law and administration by law, constructing a law-based country, a law-based government, and a law-based society, promoting the adoption, revision, abolition and interpretation of laws and the judicial reform, and strengthening the supervision over powers are in essence all measures of self-perfection and self-reform of the political system within the framework of the constitution.

During the 30 years of exploration and practice since the reform and opening up, the Chinese people have increasingly realized that the political reform must be carried out simultaneous with economic, social and cultural reforms, that the relationship between reform, development and stability must be dealt with in a proper way, and that the political reform must be actively and prudently deepened in light of the national conditions in China. It has been proved in practice that political reform involves great risks, but, without it, it would be difficult for other reforms to be deepened or successful. To carry out the political reform in an active, orderly and efficient way and prevent and control the possible risks of the reform, China must adhere to the fundamental principle of organic unity of the Party's leadership, people being masters of the country, and ruling the country by law, and the basic strategy of realizing the main objectives of the reform through comprehensive advancement of ruling the country by law and construction of the rule of law in China within the framework of the Constitution and on the track of the rule of law. Comprehensively advancing ruling the country by law and deepening political reform in the process of constructing the rule of law in China is the only way of strengthening the construction of democracy and the rule of law and realizing the self-perfection and deepening the reform of the political system under the new situation in China.

Firstly, comprehensive advancement of ruling the country by law is a major reform of the political system. Ruling the country by law means that the broad masses of people, under the leadership of the CPC, administer state and social affairs and manage economic and cultural undertakings in accordance with the Constitution and laws and bring various aspects of work of the state under the rule of law. The process of ruling the country by law is a process in which people exercise their democratic political rights as the masters of the country, in which the state political power is held and exercised in accordance with laws and regulations, and in which the state political system is constructed, operated and improved in accordance with law. Since 1978, the development of China from a country under the rule of man, to a country with a legal system, and ultimately to a country ruled by law is a process of major reform of the way in which the CPC leads the Chinese people in governing the state as well as a process of deep-level political reform in which the political system is made increasingly more democratic and scientific and gradually brought under the rule of law. Comprehensively advancing ruling the country by law and upholding the Party's leadership and the people's position as masters of the country through the rule of law thinking and method will ensure that the state machinery and the political system operate in an orderly and effective way and that the government functions by the mandate of the people, empathizes with the feelings of the people, and works for the well-being of the people.

Secondly, there will be no democratic politics without the rule of law. The rule of law is the institutionalization and legalization of democracy and the institutional safeguard of democratic politics. Today, a legal system has already taken form in China, providing legal basis for activities in all aspects of economic, political, social and cultural lives of the country, and marking the comprehensive establishment and continuous improvement of the socialist system with Chinese characteristics. The various political systems in China, including the system of the CPC's leadership, the system of people's democratic dictatorship, the people's congress system, the system of regional national autonomy, the system of grassroots democratic self-governance, the system of democratic election and democratic consultation, the state administrative system and the judicial system, are all provided for and guaranteed by the Constitution and laws and are established, operated and modified in accordance with law. Comprehensive advancement of ruling the country by law and continuous improvement of the systems of the constitution, laws and legal norms will speed up the process of standardizing the political system and bringing it under the rule of law, effectively put political powers and political activities under the scope of legal control and legal safeguard, realize the reform, improvement and development of various institutions, procedures and norms in the political framework and on the track of the rule of law, and deepen through the rule of law method the political reform in the practice of ruling the country by law.

Thirdly, advancing scientific legislation is in itself a "reform". Strengthening the legislative work, continuously improving the legal system and the rule of law basis on which the political system depends for its existence is in itself a reform that can propel the continuous development of political civilization in China at its source in order orderly way, promote the continuous standardization of political activities, and realize the continuous perfection of the political system. The amendment of the Constitution and the adoption, revision, abolition, and interpretation of laws will inevitably promote the establishment, improvement, change, or even cancellation of certain political institutions. For example, the adoption of the Administrative Litigation Law gave birth to the administrative litigation system whereby ordinary citizens can sue government organs; and the revision of the election law enabled rural residents to have equal rights with urban residents in the election, thereby improving the election system in China. Apparently, the adoption, revision, abolition, interpretation of laws in the process of ruling the country by law is a process of continuous self-improvement and self-development of the legal system, as well as a process of reform and improvement of various institutions, including the political institutions, in China.

7.2.3 Deepening Political Reform in the Process of Comprehensive Advancement of Ruling the Country by Law

Under the current national situation and political, social and cultural conditions in China, political reform is not a dreadful monster. The Chinese people, by relying on their political wisdom and rationality, are fully able to harness and control this kind of reform. Therefore, there is no need to turn pale at the mere mention of political reform. But on the other hand, political reform is not something that people can do arbitrarily as they please. The adherence to the socialist system with Chinese characteristics and ruling the country by the Constitution laws are the preconditions, boundaries, and guarantees of political reform in China. No one is allowed to incite trouble and create confusion by taking advantage of the political reform.

As far as the essence of political reform is concerned, deepening political reform through the comprehensive advancement of ruling the country by law means the readjustment and redistribution of a series of major interests under the framework of the Constitution by taking the rule of law as the guarantee and justice as the orientation. The law is a distributor of social interests. As far as various subjects of public power are concerned, carrying out political reform under the rule of law, breaking down the barriers that solidify interests means in essence the reduction of various private interests obtained through the abuse of public power and the increase of responsibilities and services; the reduction of arbitrariness and increase of supervision and restrictions; the reduction of the opportunities of corruption and the increase of honesty and self-discipline; and the reduction of dereliction of duty and slackness and increase of democracy and efficiency; as far as citizens, enterprises, ordinary social organizations and other subjects of private rights and social rights are concerned, political reform in essence will not harm their major interest, but will bring them more freedom, equality, democracy, the rule of law, fairness, justice, honesty, and efficiency. In China, the people are the masters of the state, the society and their own fate. Deepening the political reform in an orderly way by implementing the strategy of ruling the country by law is compatible with the basic and long-term interests of the people. In the political reform, they have nothing to lose but the oppression and exploitation by bureaucrats and the holders of privileges, and they have justice, fairness, democracy and the rule of law to win. Therefore, they are the supporters, participants and beneficiaries of political reform and the force that the political reform must rely on. Only a few people, government departments and local authorities with vested interests would fear, oppose or impede political reform. To carry out political reform in the process of ruling the country by law is to enable the power given by the people to serve the people, and enable the people to share the interests and benefits created by the people themselves.

As far as the content of political reform is concerned, deepening the political reform through the advancement of ruling the country by law requires the adjustment and change of a series of important political and social relations in state and social lives, including: the relations between political parties, the people and the state, which are mainly manifested in the relations between the Party's power, civil rights and political power; the relations between politics, democracy and the rule of law, mainly manifested in the organic unity of the three; the relations between the central and local governments, mainly manifested in the separation of powers and functions between the two; relations between the government, society and the individual, mainly manifested in the relations between administrative power, social rights and individual rights; the relation between the government and the market, mainly manifested in the relation between administrative power and the law of market economy; the relations between people's congresses, adjudicative organs and procuratorial organs, mainly manifested in the division of labor and cooperation between the government, the people's court and the people's procuratorate under the unified leadership of the legislative power; and the relations between administrative organs, adjudicative organs and procuratorial organs, mainly manifested in the division of labor, the cooperation and the check and balance between the three. The law is the adjustor of social relations. The political reform carried out in the process of advancement of ruling the country by law aims at further adjusting and improving political and social relations through the application the rule of law thinking and method, bringing a series of basic relations in the political system into the scope of adjustment, regulation and supervision by the Constitution and laws, promoting the deep-level reform and global optimization, and bringing the state governance system under the rule of law.

As far as the objects of the political reform are concerned, deepening the political reform through the comprehensive advancement of ruling the country by law never means to abandon the socialist direction and the socialist road, or change the fundamental political system or basic political institutions, or implement the western multi-party system or the system of separation of three powers, but to reform and improve political systems, procedures, methods and mechanisms that can no longer meet to the need of economic and social development and are no longer acceptable to the broad masses of people under the precondition of adhering to the socialist direction and road and on the basis of upholding the fundamental political systems and basic political institutions of the country. It means to apply the rule of law thinking and method to promote the reform, improvement and innovative development of such concrete political system and mechanisms as the Party and state leadership system, the legislative system, the administrative system, the judicial system, the election system, the intra-Party regulation system, the democratic administration system, the democratic supervision system, and the democratic participation system in accordance with the provisions and under the guidance of the Constitution and laws. The problems and defects in the above institutions and mechanisms are the main targets of the deepening of the political reform, as well as the key problems to be paid attention to and solved in the process of comprehensive advancement of ruling the country by law.

As far as the method of the political reform is concerned, deepening the political reform through the comprehensive advancement of ruling the country by law means not to carry out the lawless "big democracy" or the "Cultural Revolution" style deconstructive political movement of "destroying the old and establishing the new", or violent political revolution or political struggle, but to adhere to the constructivism in the sense of democracy and the rule of law, reform and improve the political system in a constructive, active and prudent way in the process of advancement of ruling the country by law; to carry out top-level design of political reform on the basis of fully developing democracy and through the rule of law thinking and method, to give full play to the innovative spirit of the broad masses of people in the exploration of the reform, to integrate the people's demands for political reform into the practice of comprehensive advancement of ruling the country by law, and unify people's different understandings of political reform in the overall arrangements for speeding up the construction of the rule of law in China, and to actively and prudently advance the reform of various political institutions through ruling the country by law and on the track of the rule of law.

7.3 The Strategic Reform Objectives of Comprehensive Advancing Ruling the Country by Law and Building China into a Country Under the Rule of Law

Comprehensively advancing ruling the country by law, striving to construct China into a country under the rule of law, and continuous deepening the legal reform in China are of great significance to the comprehensive deepening of reform at both the state and the social levels because the rule of law has the following two functions.

7.3.1 The Rule of Law Is an Important Content of Socialist Democratic Politics and the Advancement of Ruling the Country by Law Is an Important Means of Implementing Political Reform in China

Without socialist rule of law, there will be no socialist democratic politics to talk about. Therefore, comprehensively advancing ruling the country by law and continuously deepening the legal reform are not only an important content of the innovative development and the standardization, institutionalization and legalization of socialist democratic politics with Chinese characteristics, but also an important way of actively and prudently deepening political reform in a comprehensive way within the current constitutional framework and on the track of socialist rule of law. Under the Chinese political system and constitutional framework, the content, characteristics and functions of the rule of law have determined that the process of strengthening the construction of the rule of law, the process of advancing ruling the country by law, the process of deepening the legal reform, and all other processes of the rule of law (legal system) are not merely processes of improvement of laws and development of the rule of law. They involve not merely legal issues, but also issues of political development and the reform of the political system, which belong to the category of politics.

Since the reform and opening up, China has made unprecedented achievements in the construction of the rule of law and the CPC and the Chinese government have established the basic strategy of ruling the country by law; the capacity of the ruling party for exercising the ruling power in accordance with the Constitution and laws has been markedly enhanced; the construction of the socialist legal system with Chinese characteristics has been completed on schedule; human rights and democracy have been reliably safeguarded by the rule of law; the rule of law environment that promotes economic and social development has been continuously improved; the level of administration by law and judicial fairness have been continuously raised; the control of and the supervision over powers by the rule of law have been strengthen; marked processes have been made in the publicity of and education on laws and in the provision of legal services; innovative development has been continuously made in the advancement of local rule of law and administration of industries in accordance with law; the policy of "one country, two systems" and the basic laws of Hong Kong and Macao special administrative regions have been effectively implemented; the rule of law consciousness of the whole society has been generally enhanced, and there has been rapid developments in the fields of legal research and legal education.

Meanwhile, we should also be aware that, although China has made splendid achievements in the construction of the rule of law, there is still a gap between the current level of the rule of law and the new expectations of the Chinese people and China's continuously rising status as a big power in the world: although the strategy of ruling the country by law has been implemented for many years, the development of the rule of law in different places, different links, and different fields is still very unbalanced; although general requirements on the exercise of the ruling power have already been put forward, no concrete institutions and procedures have been adopted to ensure their implementation; although a socialist legal system with Chinese characteristics have already taken shape, this system still needs further improvement and development; although remarkable achievements have already been made in the legislative work and the problem of having no law to go by has been basically solved, situations of enforcement of law, administration of justice, observance of law and legal supervision are still not satisfactory; and although huge results have been achieved in legal publicity and education, there is still no fundament improvement in the environment of the rule of law in China.

On December 4, 2012, Party Secretary General Xi Jinping pointed out in a speech given at the Conference Commemorating the 30th Anniversary of the Promulgation and Implementation of the Current Constitution that: "While fully confirming the achievements, we must also see the existing problems, which include the followings: the supervision mechanisms and concrete institutions that ensure the implementation of the Constitution are still incomplete and imperfect; the phenomena that laws exist but are not followed, law enforcement is not strict and law-breakers aren't punished still exist in some areas and sectors; there are still some prominent problems in law enforcement and judicial practices that affect the immediate interests of the people;

the behaviors of some public officials, such as abuse of power, dereliction of duty, breaking laws while in charge of their enforcement, and even bending the law for the benefit of relatives or friends, are seriously undermining the authority of the legal system; and the consciousness of the constitution among citizens, including some leading cadres, still needs to be further enhanced. China must pay high attention to the above problems and take effective measures to solve them."[1] The key to the effective resolution of the institutional problems in the process of construction of the rule of law and ruling the country by law is to comprehensively deepen the legal reform in such fields and links as legislation, law enforcement, administration of justice, observance of law and legal supervision under the leadership and support of the CPC and in accordance with the strategic arrangement of ruling the country by law. Deepening the legal reform is in itself a political reform and strengthening the construction of the rule of law is in itself the advancement of the development of socialist democratic politics with Chinese characteristics.

7.3.2 The Rule of Law Is an Important Guarantee of Comprehensive Deepening of the Reform

The nation-wide effort of comprehensively deepening the reform cannot succeed without the guidance, regulation and guarantee by the rule of law, the comprehensive planning and overall arrangements by the relevant laws, the adoption, revision, abolition of the relevant laws, the strict enforcement and fair administration of law, the observance of law by the whole people, and the effective implementation of the Constitution and laws. Therefore, comprehensively advancing ruling the country by law and applying the rule of law thinking and method to deepen various reforms, adjusting social relations in an orderly way, reasonably allocating social resources, effective regulating social behaviors, and realizing social justice is a necessary requirement of comprehensive deepening of the reform under the new situation as well as a historical mission of the development of the rule of law in China. It is been proved in practice that, with the deepening of the reform, various conflicts of interest will become increasingly intense and more and more uncertain factors and unpredictable risks will emerge. Therefore, it has become increasingly important to give full play to the dominant role of the rule of law, continuously strengthen the construction of the rule of law, and bring all aspects of the work of comprehensive deepening of the reform, such as public opinions, interest game playing, adjustment of relations, allocation of resources, choice of plans, top-level design, path arrangement, implementation process and supervisory safeguards, into the framework and the legal order of comprehensively ruling the country by law and constructing the rule of law and realize the objectives of comprehensively deepening the reform in the practice and process of construction of the rule of law in China.

---

[1] Xi (2012).

In December 1978, Deng Xiaoping pointed out that: "We should continue to develop socialist democracy and improve the socialist legal system. This is a basic, consistent policy that has been carried out by the Central Committee ever since its Third Plenary Session, and there must be no wavering in its enforcement in future."[2] In February 1996, former Party Secretary General Jiang Zemin pointed out in a lecture on the legal system given at the CPC Central Committee that: "Strengthening the construction of socialist legal system and ruling the country by law are an important parts of Deng Xiaoping's theory of socialism with Chinese characteristics and an important policy by which the CPC and the Chinese government administer state and social affairs."[3] At its Fifteenth National Congress in 1997, the CPC established ruling the country by law as its basic strategy of leading the people to administer state affairs and the construction of a socialist state under the rule of law as its objective of political development in China. In 2002, the CPC clearly stated at its Sixteenth National Congress that in implementing the strategy of ruling the country by law, China must adhere to the Party's leadership and the principle of the people being masters of the country and realize the "organic unity of the three". In 2004, the NPC adopted an amendment to the Constitution, which enshrines in the Constitution the basic strategy of ruling the country by law and constructing a socialist state under the rule of law, thereby making ruling the country by law a constitutional principle with highest legal effect. At its Seventeenth National Congress in 2007, the CPC put forward the task of comprehensively implementing the basic strategy of ruling the country by law and speeding up the construction of a socialist state under the rule of law. And at its Eighteenth National Congress in 2012, the CPC further stressed that it would "comprehensively advance ruling the country by law and speed up the construction of a socialist state under the rule of law". All these show that speeding up the construction of socialist rule of law, comprehensively advancing ruling the country by law, and building China into a country under the rule of law have been a long held basic policy of the CPC and the Chinese government and the construction of a socialist state under the rule of law is an important strategic objective of the modernization drive in China.

The strategic reform objective of building China into a state under the rule of law is not something that comes from thin air, but is compatible with the overall development strategy of the country and supplementary to the strategic objectives of the Chinese dream and the "two centenary goals". In accordance with the state development strategy of "two centenary goals", against the background that remarkable results have already achieved in the construction of the rule of law and obvious progresses already made in ruling the country by law, and on the basis of the formation on schedule of a socialist legal system with Chinese characteristics, China should further strengthen the construction of the rule of law, comprehensively advance ruling the country by law, continuously deepen legal reform, transform its legal system into a system of the rule of law, and turn the country from a big power with a complete

---

[2] Deng (1993).
[3] Jiang (1996).

legal system into a big power under the rule of law. To do so, it should establish the following "two-step" strategic objectives:

The first step is to basically complete the construction of China into a state under the rule of law by 2020, when China becomes a moderately well-off society in all respects. The CPC stated at its Eighteenth National Congress that: "An examination of both the current international and domestic environments shows that China remains in an important period of strategic opportunities for its development, a period in which much can be achieved. We need to have a correct understanding of the changing nature and conditions of this period, seize all opportunities, respond with cool-headedness to challenges, and gain initiative and advantages to win the future and attain the goal of completing the building of a moderately prosperous society in all respects by 2020." The strategic objective of completing the building of a moderately prosperous society in all respects by 2020 naturally includes the strategic objective of building China into a country under the rule of law (a country with a moderately high standard of the rule of law), namely the goal of "basically completing the construction of China into a state under the rule of law".

The second step is to complete the overall construction of China into a country under the rule of law by 2049, the 100th anniversary of founding of the PRC. The report of the 15th National Congress of the Communist Party of China stated that: "By the middle of the next century when the People's Republic celebrates its centenary, the modernization program will have been accomplished by and large and China will have become a prosperous, strong, democratic and culturally advanced socialist country." The Report of the Eighteenth CPC National Congress further stressed that: "As long as we remain true to our ideal, are firm in our conviction, never vacillate in or relax our efforts or act recklessly, and forge ahead with tenacity and resolve, we will surely complete the building of a moderately prosperous society in all respects when the Communist Party of China celebrates its centenary and turn China into a modern socialist country that is prosperous, strong, democratic, culturally advanced and harmonious when the People's Republic of China marks its centennial. The whole Party should have every confidence in our path, in our theories and in our system." Party Secretary General Xi Jinping pointed out at the Third Collective Study Session of the Political Bureau of the Eighteenth CPC Central Committee that: "The CPC clearly put forward the "two centenary goals" at its Eighteenth National Congress and China has also put forward the objective of realizing the "Chinese dream" of the great rejuvenation of the Chinese nation". The Chinese dream is the dream of the Chinese people and the Chinese nation. Undoubtedly, it also includes the "dream of building China into a socialist state under the rule of law", namely China should complete the task of building itself into a state under the rule of law by the middle of the 21st Century when the People's Republic of China marks its centennial. By then China will become a modern socialist country that is prosperous, strong, democratic, culturally advanced and harmonious, and the great rejuvenation of the Chinese nation will become a reality.

7.4   Overall Thinking and Basic Requirements of Comprehensively Advancing Ruling the Country by Law and Building China into a Country Under the Rule of Law

7.4.1   The Overall Thinking of Comprehensively Advancing Ruling the Country by Law and Building China into a Country Under the Rule of Law

The overall thinking of comprehensive advancement of ruling the country by law and building China into a country under the rule of law is: to proceed from the strategic objective of building China into a country under the rule of law and the overall needs of economic, political, social, cultural and ecological development, to adhere to the organic unity of upholding the Party's leadership, the people being masters of the country, and ruling the country by law, actively and prudently deepen the legal reform, focus on the solution of such problems as wrongful legislation, slack enforcement of law, unfair administration of justice, disorderly observance of law, and weakness of the rule of law, advance in a comprehensive and orderly way ruling the country by law, exercise the ruling power by law and administration by law, strive to construction a law-based state, a law-based government and a law-based society, so as to build China into a modern state under the rule of law as soon as possible.

Comprehensively deepening the reform inevitably includes comprehensively deepening the reform of the legal system. The legal system is a general term for laws and legal institutions and it covers such systems as the legislative system, the law enforcement system, the judicial system, the legal supervision system, the system of implementation of laws, the legal service system, the constitutional law system, the administrative law system, the economic law system, the civil and commercial law system, the criminal law system, the social law, the litigious and non-litigious procedure law system, and the international law system. Comprehensively deepening the legal reform means to further increase the breadth, the depth and the strength of the comprehensive reform of the legal system in accordance with the "two centenary strategic objectives and general tasks", and, on the basis of the legal reform carried out in the thirty years since the reform and opening up, to continuously improve, innovate and develop the legal system, so as to enable it to better satisfy the need of socialist modernization with Chinese characteristics and of the great rejuvenation of the Chinese nation, the need of comprehensive deepening the reform, further opening up, and promoting development, the people's increasing need for the safeguarding of human rights and fundamental freedoms, for the realization of fairness and justice, and for a safe, stable and happy life, the need of ruling the country by law, realizing scientific legislation, strict enforcement of law, fair administration of justice, observance of law by the whole people, and building China into a country under the rule of law.

In comprehensive deepening the legal reform, which is an important component of the political reform and the self-improvement and development of the socialist legal system, China must adhere to the organic unity of upholding Party's leadership, the people being masters of the country and ruling the country by law, uphold the authority of the Constitution and the principle of the rule of law, proceed from its own national conditions, carry forward the fine tradition of Chinese legal culture while at the same time drawing on all beneficial results of the development of political and legal civilization of mankind, and follow the road of development of socialist rule of law with Chinese characteristics.

In comprehensively deepening the legal reform, China must make special efforts to solve the various problems in the legislative system, legislative procedure and legislative process that lead to wrongful legislation, various problems in the law enforcement institutions, mechanisms and procedures that lead to slack law enforcement, such as the problems of duplicate law enforcement, multi-level law enforcement, non-enforcement of law, arbitrary law enforcement, entrapment law enforcement, uncivilized law enforcement, rent-seeking law enforcement, restrictive law enforcement, selective law enforcement, campaign-style law enforcement, weak law enforcement, and lagging law enforcement, problems in judicial institutions, mechanisms and procedures that lead to judicial tyranny and miscarriage of justice, such as the problems of difficulties in accessing to justice, high litigation cost, judicial corruption, abuse of discretional power, seeking private gains through the handling of judicial cases, backlog of cases, delay in closing a case, difficulties in the execution of judgments, extorting a confession by torture, presumption of guilt, and arbitrary application of laws, problems resulting from the ideas, habits and institutions of disorderly observance of law, such as relying on power, connections, money, and complaint by visit and letters, rather than law, to solve disputes, the situation in which those who create a big disturbance get a total solution of their problems, those who create a small disturbance get a partial solution of their problems, and those who create no disturbance get no solution of their problems, widespread violation of law, Chinese-style violation of law, and selective application of law, and problems relating to the weakness of the rule of law, such as the situation in which the constitution has become an "idle law" and laws and regulations exist only in name, the superiority of policies, politics, privileges, and state leaders over law, violations of law by leaders of government organs, violations of law by those in charge of enforcement of law, the practice of bullying the weak and fearing the strong, etc.

7.4.2 Basic Requirements of Comprehensively Advancing Ruling the Country by Law and Building China into a Country Under the Rule of Law

China should scientifically understand and accurately grasp the basic meaning of the strategy of comprehensive advancement of ruling the country by law and construction of the rule of law. The so-called "comprehensive" advancement of ruling the country by law means to treat ruling the country by law as a huge system engineering project and to take into overall consideration various links and elements of construction of the rule of law, so as to ensure the comprehensive and effective implementation of the basic strategy of ruling the country by law; to integrate the spirit, value, consciousness, idea and culture of the rule of law, unify ruling the country by the Constitution, ruling the country by law, exercising the ruling power by law, administration by law, and handling public affairs by law, to ensure that there are laws to go by, the laws are observed and strictly enforced, and lawbreakers are prosecuted, to unify scientific legislation, strict enforcement of law, fair administration of justice, observance of law by the whole people, and effective upholding the authority of laws, and to closely combine legal research, legal education, publicity of law and the practice of the rule of law, so as to systematically integrate the various elements of ruling the country by law, comprehensively unblock various links in and develop a system engineering project on the construction of the rule of law, and ensure the concrete implementation of the basic strategy of ruling the country by law in practice.

The so-called comprehensive "advancement" of ruling the country by law means that China should make progress, rather than retrogression, actively promote, rather than passively idle around, carry out the work in a down to earth way, rather than engage in empty talk, and proceed without hesitation, rather than give up half way, in implementing the strategy of ruling the country by law. In comprehensively advancing ruling the country by law, China should unswervingly take the road of socialist rule of law with Chinese characteristics and to the rule of law orientation of development, resolutely oppose and resist various forms of rule of man and autocracy, prevent stagnation, retrogression, deviation, and alienation of ruling the country by law. If, at any time, China abandons the basic strategy of ruling the country by law and the road of socialist rule of law, there will be no comprehensive advancement of ruling the country by law or the great rejuvenation of the Chinese nation to talk about.

The so-called "speeding up" the construction of the rule of law in China, means to speed up both the process of ruling the country by law and the realization of the objective of construction of the rule of law in China. Without the acceleration of the process, it would be impossible to accelerate the realization of the goal; and without the steady speed of advancement, it would be impossible to realize the goal of speeding up the construction of the rule of law in China. Therefore, "speeding up" is seemingly a requirement on the goal and the speed of the construction of the rule of law in China, but in essence a requirement on the process of construction of the rule of law and ruling the country by law, which sets an arduous task for China. "Speeding up" means that, firstly, China must have a development strategy and goal pursuit for the construction of the rule of law, including the objectives and tasks for different time periods and at different stages; secondly, China must has a concrete and operable index system for the assessment of ruling the country by law and construction of the rule of law in the country; thirdly, China must have concrete roadmap, timetable and assignment book that set out various target tasks of construction of the rule of law. And fourthly, China must increase the speed of advancement of ruling the country by law and construction of the rule of law as much as possible whenever conditions permit, so as to "speed up" the realization of the goal of construction of rule of law. The proposition of speeding up the advancement of ruling the country by law and construction of the rule of law in China is undoubtedly conditional and relative. Here, "speeding up" should not be divorced or deviate from the levels of economic, social, political, and cultural developments at the current stage, from the main path and basic law of self-improvement and development of the rule of law, or from the understanding, approval, respect and observance of the rule of law by the whole people. Compared to economic and social development during the period of reform, which is characterized by constant change, the rule of law has the characteristics of lagging behind economic and social development and being conservative. Therefore, in speeding up the advancement of ruling the country by law and construction of the rule of law, China must master the speed and the strength of the development of the rule of law from a strategic height. Otherwise, the more haste, the less speed.

On the basis of the timetable, the roadmap and the assignment book of comprehensive advancement of ruling the country by law and speeding up the construction of the rule of law, China should strive to meet the basic reform requirements of the strategic goal of the "two-step process" of construction of the rule of law.

As the first step, China should realized scientific legislation, strict enforcement of law, fair administration of justice, and observance of law by the whole people, achieve full implementation of the basic strategy of ruling the country by law, further improve the legal system with Chinese characteristics, basically complete the construction of a law-based government, continuously enhance judicial credibility, effectively respect and safeguard human rights, bring all aspects of the state work under the rule of law and basically complete the construction of a state under the rule of law by the year 2020, when it becomes a moderately prosperous society in all respects. Here, "a moderately high standard of the rule of law" is an organic component as well as an important guarantee for the successful construction of a moderately prosperous society in all respects. At the value level, it pursues freedom, equality, democracy, the rule of law, fairness, justice, happiness, fraternity, harmony, order and full realization of human rights and human dignity; at the institutional level, it pursues popular sovereignty, the supremacy of law, ruling the country by the constitution, exercising the ruling power by law, administration by law, judicial fairness, regulation of power in accordance with law, and construction of a state under the rule of law; and at the practical level, it pursues the universal observance of law, strict enforcement of law, and the realization of good law and good governance. Meanwhile, through the institutional arrangements, regulatory means and educational and coercive functions that are unique to ruling the country by law, "a moderately high standard of the rule of law" creates a good legal environment and provides effective legal safeguards for the construction of a moderately prosperous society in all respects.

As the second step, China should complete various tasks of simultaneous advancement of ruling the country by law, exercising the ruling power by law, and administration by law, reach various targets of integrative construction of a law-based state, a law-based government and a law-based society, meet various requirements of the spirit, authority and order of the rule of law, and complete the construction of China into a harmonious and civilized country under the rule of law, with the full realization of freedom, equality, democracy, human rights, fairness and justice, by the year 2049, when it celebrates the 100th anniversary of the founding of the PRC.

7.5 Several Issues to Be Dealt with in the Comprehensive Advancement of Ruling the Country by Law and Construction of the Rule of Law in China

7.5.1 Strengthening and Improving the Ruling Party's Leadership Over Ruling the Country by Law

The leadership of the ruling party is the key to the advancement of ruling the country by law, the construction of the rule of law and the deepening of legal reform in China. Therefore it is necessary to give full play to the role of the ruling party as the leading core in various aspects of the work of ruling the country by law. The CPC is the ruling party in China. Adhering to the exercise of the ruling power by law is of great significance to comprehensive advancement of ruling the country by law. China should adhere to the organic unity of upholding the Party's leadership, the people being the masters of the country and ruling the country by law and implement the Party's leadership in the whole process of ruling the country by law. Party organizations at all levels must act within the scope of the Constitution and laws, leading cadres at various levels must take the lead in observing the law and acting by law, and organizational departments of the CPC at various levels should take the capacity for observing the law and acting by law as one of the important criteria for the assessment of cadres.[4]

Strengthening and improving the ruling party's leadership over the work of ruling the country by law is the basic political guarantee for the construction of rule of law in China. In order to give full play to the Party's role as the leading core in ruling the country by law, the following measures should be taken to improve the relevant policies, institutions and mechanisms: firstly, to adhere to the constitutional principle that the Party must act within the scope of the Constitution and laws and to the principle of exercising the ruling power in accordance with the Constitution and laws and administration by law, apply the rule of law thinking and method to lead the legislation, take the lead in abiding by the law, and guarantee the enforcement of law, and continuously strengthen the Party's leadership authority, its position as the ruling party in the country, and its ruling basis through comprehensive advancement of ruling the country by law; secondly, to establish a leading group under the CPC Central Committee to be responsible for the unified leadership over and organization and coordination of ruling the country by law, for carrying out study and formulating mid- and long-term reform and development plans and near-term basic tasks of comprehensive advancement of ruling the country by law and construction of the

---

[4]Xi (2013).

rule of law in China in accordance with the "two-centenary national strategies", and for carrying out study on and formulating the Party's programs on exercising the ruling power in accordance with the Constitution and laws and on leading and guiding all Party members and Party organizations to exercise the ruling power by law; thirdly, to carry out in-depth research on some of the important relations under the new situation, such as the relations between the Party and the law, between the Party and the government, and between the Party and the people, implement through the relevant institutions and procedures "the organic unity of upholding the Party's leadership, people being masters of the country, and ruling the country by law", guarantee through leadership structure and administrative mechanisms the comprehensive implementation of the strategies of "simultaneous advancement of ruling the country by law, exercising the ruling power by law and administration by law" and "integrated construction of a law-based state, a law-based government and a law-based society"; and fourthly, to carry out in-depth research on the reform of the system of political and legal affairs commissions in light of the new situation of construction of the rule of law in China, adhere to the ideological, political and organizational leadership of the commissions, give full play to the commissions' political advantages and their role as organizational safeguard in eliminating all kinds of interference in judicial work and ensuring the lawful and independent performance of functions and exercise of powers by courts and procuratorates.

7.5.2 Advancing Democratic and Scientific Legislation, Improving the Quality of Legislation, and Perfecting the Legal System

The current legislative reform in China should be focused on making the legislation more democratic and scientific, improving the quality of legislation, perfecting the legal system, strengthening the legislation in key fields, and preventing legislative corruption.

In strengthening the legislative work and promoting the legislative reform, attention should be paid to the following aspects of work: firstly, to change the situation of passive legislation, and coordinate the relationship between legislation and reform, so as to provide legal basis and legal safeguard for the comprehensive deepening of the reform through the adoption, revision and abolition of laws; secondly, to advance by various means democratic and scientific legislation, guarantee the extensive and effective public participation in legislation, increase the standardization and operability of laws, ensure that legislation truly embodies the will and the interest demand of the people, rather than the interest of certain administrative departments or certain special interest groups, so as to realize the "distributive justice" of legislation; thirdly, to promote reform, innovation, and solution of tough problems in legislative work; to have the courage to tackle the difficult problems encountered in the comprehensive deepening of the reform and be good at solving them, rather than avoiding the important and dwelling on the trivial, mutually making excuses, engaging in endless haggling and shifting of responsibility, and holding on to departmental interests; fourthly, to actively design and construct "a legal system with Chinese characteristics" under the guidance of the policy of "one country, two systems" and in light of the national situation of "one country, two political systems, three legal systems, and four jurisdictions", so as to lay a sound legal foundation for the unification, prosperity and great rejuvenation of the Chinese nation; and fifth, to give full play to the role of the rule of law in creating favorable international and regional environments, in safeguarding national interest and promoting China's peaceful development, and clearly provide for in the Constitution the relationship between international law and Chinese domestic law, so as to create more favorable international law condition for the reform and opening up in China.

7.5.3 Comprehensively Deepening Administrative Reform and Speeding up the Construction of a Law-Based Government

Administration by law is the key to ruling the country by law and the construction of a law-based government is the emphasis of the construction of a law-based state in China. In advancing administration by law and speeding up the construction of the rule of law, China must comprehensive deepen of the reform of the administrative system. Otherwise, unreasonable administrative institutions will be "legalized" and, as a result, the difficulties of administrative reform will increase. This is because, compared to substantive administration, such as administrative power, administrative institutions, administrative functions, administrative organs, administrative relations, administrative behavior, and administrative interest, laws, administrative regulations, administration by law, and law-based government are all a kind of package of legalization or confirmation by laws and administration regulations. If the functions of administrative organs are not transformed, the reform on administrative institutions not carried out, departmental interest not abolished, and monopolization of administrative power not broken up, then strengthening the construction of a law-based government and the bringing administrative power under the law will only legalize unreasonable administrative functions and institutions and departmental interests through the confirmation by laws and administrative regulations and further impede the reform of the administrative system. Therefore, China must deepen the reform of the administrative system before the construction of a law-based government.

To deepen the reform of the administrative system and speed up the construction of a law-based government, China must, firstly, comprehensively deepen the reform of the administrative approval system through extensive democratic participation and supervision by people's congresses, so as to minimize the number of items subjected to administrative approval; secondly, to ensure that the government do what is required by law and refrain from doing what it is prohibited to do by law, namely ensure that the government does a good job and provides good service in the fields of public security, environment protection, food safety, social security, public transportation, education, medical treatment and public health, while at the same time minimize its intervention in and control of the market, society and enterprises, give back to the market what belong to the market, give back to society what belong to society and give back to enterprises what belong to enterprises; thirdly, to comprehensively advance ministerial-level reform, streamline government organs, reduce layers of administration, weed out superfluous personnel, raise efficiency, and construct an efficient government; fourthly, to comprehensively advance administration by law on the basis of the unity of the rule of law, reduce administrative legislation, strengthen administrative law enforcement, improve administrative procedure, intensify administrative supervision, and construction a law-based government; and fifthly, to effectively control administrative power, make administrative behavior more transparent, severely punish administrative corruption, and make special efforts to fight corruption in such fields and links as supervision over state-owned enterprises, government procurement, and bidding and tendering, so as to construct a transparent, clean and honest government.

7.5.4 Comprehensively Deepening the Reform of the Judicial System

Judicial reform is an important component of political reform in China, a major measure for the comprehensive advancement of ruling the country by law, and an important basis of comprehensive implementation of the Constitution and laws. China should, in accordance with the spirit of the Eighteenth CPC National Congress and the strategic arrangement for comprehensively deepening the reform, and in light of the new situation and new demands of political reform and comprehensive advancement of ruling the country by law, make top-level design and scientific planning for the new round of judicial reform, so as to enable the reform to embody the principles and the spirit of the Constitution, the thinking and the method of rule of law, and the respect for the objective law and the nature of administration of justice. Currently, the key to deepening the judicial reform is to work hard to solve the problems of politicization, administrativation, localization, and bureaucratization of administration of justice, enhance judicial authority and judicial credibility, and truly ensure that people's courts and people's procuratorates independently and fairly exercise their functions and powers in accordance with law.

In comprehensively deepening the judicial reform, China must: firstly, make decisive decision to get out of the dilemma of whether to ensure the "independence" or the "fairness" of judicial organs first. Currently there are two opposing opinions with respect to this dilemma: one is that miscarriage of justice is caused by the inability of courts and procuratorates to independently exercise their functions and powers; the other is that courts and procuratorates are unable to independently exercise the adjudicative and procuratorial powers because of judicial corruption. This is a very difficult question that has been bothering China since the beginning of the reform and opening up. If this question is not answered in a satisfactory way, it would be impossible for China to make substantive progress in judicial reform; secondly, apply the rule of law thinking and method to adjust in accordance with the Constitution and laws the external relations of administration of justice, such as relations between administration of justice and the Party committee, between administration of justice and the political and legal affairs commission, between administration of justice and the people's congress, between administration of justice and the government, between administration of justice and the new media, and between administration of justice and social organizations, so as to guarantee through the division of jurisdiction, establishment of political and legal institutions and mechanisms, and allocation of human, financial and material resources the independent exercise of judicial powers by courts and procuratorates free from the interferences by various other powers, as well as interference by such factors as money, personal favor, and connections; thirdly, comprehensively reform internal judicial institutions, including those relating to the selection, appointment, assessment, reward and punishment of judges and procurators and the regulation, assessment, supervision and accountability of judicial activities, in accordance with the relevant provisions of the Constitution, organic laws of courts and procuratorates and litigation laws, so as to ensure that judges and procurators independently exercise their powers, independently perform their functions and duties, and independently bear their legal responsibilities in accordance with law; and fourthly, bring the whole system of the handling of litigation- and law-related complaints by letters and visits on the track of the rule of law, so as to change the people's habit of "relying on complaint by letters and visits or creating a disturbance, rather than law, to solve their problems", give full play to the role of administration of justice as the last resort of dispute resolution, reconstruct a virtuous-cycle mechanism for the judicial resolution of litigation- and law-related disputes, and strive to establish a rule of law order that can ensure lasting political stability.

7.5.5 Continuously Strengthening the Respect for and Safeguarding of Human Rights

Human rights are the rights every individual is entitled to by virtue of his or her natural and social attributes as a human being. Legally prescribed human rights are the embodiment of the legalization of people's interest and needs. In a society, the higher the level of legalization of human rights, the more sufficient the judicial remedies and safeguards for human rights, and the more thorough the realization of human rights, the easier for the society to realize stability, harmony, fairness, justice, good faith and order. Therefore, full respect for, safeguarding and realization of human rights is an important content of ruling the country by law and constructing the rule of law in China.

China plans to realize the objective of "effective respect for and safeguarding of human rights" by 2020, when it completes the construction of a moderately prosperous society in all respects. This objective of struggle and strategic task is very difficult to achieve but of great significance. To realize this objective, China should take the following steps of strengthening the construction of human rights: firstly, to implement in an all-round way the basic principle of "respecting and safeguarding human rights" enshrined both in the Constitution of the PRC and the Constitution of the CPC, truly ensure that citizens and Party members enjoy extensive rights and freedoms, and comprehensively improve various legal provisions and legal systems relating to the safeguarding of human rights; secondly, to continue to bring various basic constitutional rights into the scope of protection of law by carrying out study on and formulating such laws as the Press Law, the Law on Association, the Law on the Freedom of Religious Belief, the State Compensation Law, the Law on the Declaration of Property by Civil Servants, and the Law on the Protection of Personal Information, abolishing the Regulations on Reeducation through Labor, and reforming the household registration system; thirdly, to further revise the Criminal Law to drastically reduce the number of crimes punishable by death (at the current stage, it is advisable for China to abolish the death penalty for various economic crimes), so as to prepare for the ultimate abolition of the death penalty in the future, and eliminate death penalty cases in which people are unjustly, falsely or erroneously charged; fourthly, to further strengthen the protection of citizens' economic, social and cultural rights, work hard to solve such long-standing problems as "difficulties in school enrollment", "difficulties in getting medical service", "housing problems", "pension problems", "unfair distribution of social wealth", and "the gap between the rich and the poor", which have caused general public concern, to put more efforts on the safeguarding of the rights of disadvantaged groups, and realize social justice and common prosperity through the rule of law; and fifthly, to conscientiously implement the National Human Rights Action Plan (2012–2015), strengthen the research on International Covenant on Civil and Political Rights, which should be ratified by the NPC at an appropriate time.

7.5.6 Strengthening the Implementation of the Constitution and Laws

As Zhang Juzheng, a politician in the Ming Dynasty, pointed out: "The difficulty lies not in the making of laws, but in the strict implementation of laws."[5] The life and the authority the Constitution and laws lie in their implementation. After the formation of the socialist legal system with Chinese characteristics and the basic

---

[5]See The Memorial Submitted by Zhang Juzheng to the Emperor in 1573 Requesting the Establishment of a System for the Evaluation of Government Officials.

solution of the problem of there being no law to go by, China must pay high attention to solving the problems in the institutions and mechanisms for the implementation of the Constitution and law, so as to transform laws on paper into laws in action, and turn legal provisions into people's belief.

In light of the current situation of the low authority, the weak role and the poor implementation of the Constitution and laws, China should take the following reform measures: firstly, to shift the emphasis of the work of constructing the rule of law and ruling the country by law from legislation to the implementation of the Constitution and laws, in accordance with the overall objectives of the strategy of speeding up the construction of the rule of law in China and comprehensively deepening the reform, so as to give fuller play to the role of the Constitution and laws in the reform, opening up, and modernization in China; second, to establish and improve a complete system of review of constitutionality and legality, to establish a Constitutional Supervision Committee under the NPC, which should, under the leadership of NPC Standing Committee, be responsible for the review of constitutionality and legality in the process of implementation of the Constitution and laws, and to find institutionalized solutions to such problems as "conflicts of laws", "fighting each other by law", and "laws existing only in name"; third, to promote ministerial-level reform in the judicial field. China may consider merging the Legislative Affairs Office under the State Council with the Ministry of Justice and let judicial administration departments exercise the power of execution of judgments, which is currently exercised by people's courts; judicial organs should reduce as much as possible their economic, civil, administrative and social activities, so as to prevent themselves from becoming the defendant in a lawsuit and minimize through institutional design and procedural arrangement the possibility of judicial corruption. Detention houses, which are current under the administration of pubic security organs, should be put under the administration of judicial administrative organs; fourth, to draw on the practice of the rule of law index of World Justice Project and that of Hong Kong and summarize the successful experience of the pilot projects on the evaluation of rule of law index in some localities in the Mainland,[6] adopt national index of the rule of law, take the rule of law index as the key link in the implementation of the strategy of ruling the country by law in various localities, departments and industries, and popularize "projects on the assessment of rule of law index" in the whole country, so as to enable the construction of the rule of law in China to be quantitatively evaluated; fifthly, to continue to deepen the publicity of and education on the rule of law, innovate the methods of and mechanisms for publicity and education, carry forward the spirit of the rule of law, cultivate the culture of the rule of law, establish the idea of the rule of law, and take the rule of law capacity as the basic capacity of state governance and as a content of the system of evaluation and rigid assessment of leading cadres at various levels.

---

[6]Pilot programs on "the rule of law index" have been implemented in the Yuhang District of Hangzhou City, Zhejiang Province, Kunming City of Yunnan Province, Nanjing City and Wuxi City of Jiangsu Province, and Chengdu City of Sichuan Province.

7.5.7 Advancing "The Fight Against Corruption and Regulation of Power" Through the Application of the Rule of Law Thinking and Method

The corruption of power is the mortal enemy of democracy and the rule of law and the biggest obstacle to the construction of a socialist state under the rule of law. In order to advance ruling the country by law, construct the rule of law in China, and deepen the reform, China must put power into the cage of laws and institutions, and advance the "fight against corruption and regulation of power" through the application of the rule of law thinking and method. Firstly, we must acknowledge the "evil human nature" in the faced of public power, namely, faced with the huge temptation of public power, no one is a saint, every one has weaknesses, defects and limitations, and all can make mistakes or abuse power: "Even great revolutionists and Marxists like Mao Zedong could make mistakes and did make mistakes". Acknowledging the "evil human nature" means that we should not blindly trust or give free rein to holders of public power, but should establish effective legal systems and rule of law mechanisms to put all public powers into the cage of laws and institutions, supervise and control all public powers and every holder of public power. Secondly, we should control power with law, regulate power with institutions, supervise power with democracy, check and balance power with rights, and restrain power with ethics, so as to minimize the opportunity and maximize the cost of corruption of public power. A top priority in the fight against corruption and regulation of power under the rule of law is to answer such questions as "Who will supervise the supervisors?" "Who will supervise top leaders?" and "Who will supervise the holders of powers over personnel, financial and material resources?" at the institutional and legal levels as soon as possible. For this purpose, we should carefully study the reasonableness of the mechanism of "separation of and check and balance between the legislative, administrative and judicial powers", which has been widely accepted by the international community, and actively introduce "rock, paper and scissors" cyclic check and balance mechanism. Thirdly, attention should be paid not only to the top-level design of the fight against corruption and regulation of power, but also to proceeding from the concrete institutions, links, procedures and mechanisms, not only to educating, keeping watch against, and punishing holders of public power, but also to being on guard against and controlling such channels and conditions of corruption as market behaviors, economic behaviors, and social behaviors, so as to effectively plug up the institutional loopholes that lead to corruption and remove the soil and the hotbed that produce corruption. China should integrate state anti-corruption resources, merge various Party and state anti-corruption organs to form a unified National Anti-Corruption Committee and apply the rule of law thinking and method to solve the legality problem of the system whereby a Party official suspected of corruption is require to report his or her problems within a prescribed time and in a prescribed place (*shuanggui*). Fourthly, we must give full play to the role of administration of justice in the fight against the corruption of power, eliminate various interferences, and truly ensure the independent exercise of functions and powers by judicial organs. Judicial organs should take facts as the basis and the law as the criterion, deal with cases in an impartial way, and severely punish various crimes of corruption in accordance with law. They should adhere to the principle of equality of everyone before the law, and make sure that "anyone who violates Party disciplines or state laws must be severely punished, no matter who he is, how big his power is, and how high his position is".

7.5.8   Comprehensively Deepening the Reform on the Track of the Rule of Law

Comprehensively deepening the reform is the only road to the realization of the "two centenary objectives of struggle" as well as the top priority of our current work. How to comprehensively deepen the reform? Party Secretary General Xi Jinping points out that, in the whole process of reform, high attention should be paid to the application of the rule of law thinking and method: all the major reforms must be based on law. This fully underscores the important role played by the rule of law in comprehensively deepening the reform.

7.5.8.1   Grasping the Relationship Between Reform and the Rule of Law at the New Historical Starting Point

Since the reform and opening up, the CPC and the Chinese government, in order to appropriately deal with the relationship between reform and the rule of law and on the basis of national condition, have adopted some targeted and effective measures for appropriately solving the conflicts between the stability of law and the changeability of practice and ensuring the compatibility between the legislative process and the process of reform, opening up, and socialist modernization. For example, the NPC and its Standing Committee have speeded up the work of adoption, revision and abolition of laws and revised the 1982 Constitution several times in the past 30 years with a view to providing important legal basis to many major reforms.

It can be said that, during the 30 years since the reform and opening up, China has made huge achievements and accumulated many successful experiences in and reached many consensuses on combining theoretical innovation with practical exploration and the correct handling of the relationship between reform and the rule of law, and thus created favorable conditions and laid a solid foundation for the comprehensive deepening of the reform and speeding up the construction of the rule of law in the country. One of the important legislative experiences gained by China is to correctly handle the relationship between reform, development and stability, appropriately solve the conflicts between the stability of law and the changeability of practice, and ensure the compatibility between the legislative process and the process of reform, opening up, and socialist modernization. With respect to experiences that are relatively mature and on which consensus has already been reached, more detailed legal provisions can be adopted, so as to increase the operability of the law; with respect to experiences that are not yet mature, but need to be regulated in practice, some general legal provisions can be adopted, so as to provide some guidance and safeguards for the practices, while at the same time leave space for the deepening of the reform and for the revision or supplementation of the relevant laws when conditions are ripe; and with respect to new situations and new problems encountered in the process of reform and opening up that are not yet ready to be regulated by law, administrative regulations or local regulations can be adopted first in accordance with legally prescribed competences, and laws can be adopted later when the necessary experiences have been gained and conditions are ripe.

After the efforts made by China in the 60 years since the founding of the PRC, especially in the 30 years since the reform and opening up, a socialist system of law with Chinese characteristics has already taken shape, which provides legal basis for the economic, political, cultural, social and ecological constructions in the country, and created the social condition and laid the legal foundation for the advancement of all kinds of reform on the track of the rule of law. Since the Eighteenth CPC National Congress, the CPC Central Committee headed by Party Secretary General Xi Jinping has attached high importance to comprehensive advancement of ruling the country by law and construction of the rule of law in China, stressed that ruling the country by law is the basic strategy by which the Party leads the people to administer state affairs, that the rule of law is the basic method of state governance, and that all major reforms must be based on law. Currently, China has a relatively complete socialist legal system with Chinese characteristics to be taken as the legal basis of reform. Meanwhile cadres and the masses of people have a higher legal rationality and rule of law consciousness, enabling them to pay more attention to deepening the reform through the application of the rule of law thinking and method. These are the most important objective and subjective conditions for the correct handling of the relationship between the reform and the rule of law under the framework of the Constitution and on the track of the rule of law.

Reform liberates and develops productive forces, invigorates society, and is an inexhaustible driving force of innovative development of the state and society. At the current stage of construction of the rule of law in China and in the great practice of construction and development of socialism with Chinese characteristics, reform and the rule of law are means, methods, measures and processes for the completion of the strategic task of "five-in-one" economic, political, cultural, social and ecological construction, for the construction of China into a moderately prosperous society in all respects and for the realization of Chinese dream of great rejuvenation of the Chinese nation. The two are consistent with each other in terms of value characteristics, essential attributes and objectives, and there is no inherent fundamental contradiction or conflict between them. Ideas such as "the reform and the rule of law are oppose to each other and mutually exclusive", "the rule of law should not be stressed in order to carry out reform and innovation", "law should give way to reform", and "in order to develop, we must not be constrained by the rule of law" are all against the rule of law thinking and principle, and harmful to the deepening of reform and advancement of the rule of law.

Under the current internally harmonious and unified system of the Constitution and laws in China, the relationship between reform and the rule of law is one of intrinsic unity and mutual complementarity. The comprehensive advancement of ruling the country by law, the realization of scientific legislation, strict enforcement of law, fair administration of justice, and the observance of law by the whole people, the integrated advancement of ruling the country by law, the exercise of the ruling power by law and administration by law, and the simultaneous construction of a law-based state, a law-based government, and a law-based society are important components and main path dependences of various reforms that guide, promote, regulate and safeguard the deepening of the reform. On the one hand, reform cannot succeed, but will lead to chaos without the guidance and the guarantee by the rule of law; on the other hand, the rule of law would be abandoned if it does not keep up with the pace of reform.

Needless to say, reform and the rule of law, as the ways and means of operating and developing the state and society, are bound to have distinctions, differences, even conflicts between them. The most important distinction between the two is that the rule of law, as an important means of state governance, takes the upholding and maintenance of the existing order as its task and, as such, is relatively stable and standardized, whereas reform, as a means of innovative development, is more changeable and challenging. Therefore, there exist certain tension, and under certain circumstances even resistance, contradiction, and conflicts, between the "breaking up" by reform and "maintenance" by the rule of law. In a certain sense, the directions of the operation and the inherent tension between reform and the rule of law have determined that the "engagement" between the two is an inevitable objective reality. We should not deny, ignore or do nothing about this reality, but should adopt a positive attitude towards and a correct method to understand, grasp and appropriately deal with this problem. Comrade Xi Jinping emphasizes that "all major reforms must be based on law" and this should be taken as the guiding ideology and basic principle for handling the relationship between reform and the rule of law. It is an outlook on reform that is based on socialist rule of law and requires comprehensive deepening of reform through the application of the rule of law thinking and method.

7.5.8.2   Correctly Handling the Relationship Between Reform and the Rule of Law in the Process of Building China into a Country Under the Rule of Law

China should strengthen the coordination between various kinds of legislative work to ensure that the reform is carried out on the track of the rule of law. Looking from the strategic height of advancement of ruling the country by law, the relationship between reform and the rule of law involves not only legislation and reform, but also such links of the rule of law as strict enforcement of law, fair administration of justice, and observance of law by the whole people, although scientific legislation is the key link and main aspect of the relationship.

Adhering to scientific legislation means to closely combine the state's legislative decision-making, legislative planning, legislative projects, and legislative drafts with the Party's reform decision-making, so as to transform in a reasonable and timely manner through legislation the Party's major decisions into laws, legal standards, and the will of the state. China should, in accordance with the requirement that the CPC exercises the ruling power and the leadership over legislation in accordance with law, closely combine the Party's reform decisions with legislative decisions and bring the reform decisions onto the track of the rule of law in the process and at the stage of decision-making.

In handling the relationship between reform and the rule of law, China should follow the following lines of thinking: first, adhering to the unity of reform decision-making and legislative decision-making and giving full play to the guiding, promotional, regulatory and safeguarding role of legislation; second, all major reforms must have legal basis. Before a reform is carried out, the necessary laws must be first adopted; if problems in the reform can be solved through the interpretation of law, the reform should be carried out after the interpretation; and laws that are incompatible with a reform should be resolutely abolished before the reform is carried out, so as to ensure various reforms can be carried out in an orderly and lawful way; third, carrying out the reform under the current Constitutional and legal framework, fully utilizing the institutional conditions created and spaces left for reform by the Constitution and laws, and being bold in exploration and innovation. The Constitution is the fundamental law of the state and the general rules on administering state affairs and ensuring national security. As such, it has the highest legal status, authority and effect and is of fundamental, global, stable and long-term nature; and fourth, if a pilot reform really needs to break the limits set by the current Constitution and laws, and the problem cannot be solved through the interpretation of the Constitution or the adoption, revision, abolition or interpretation of laws, the method of legislative authorization can adopted to provide basis of legitimacy to the pilot reform.

The NPC and its Standing Committee are responsible for the supervision over the implementation of the Constitution and local people's congresses and their standing committees have the responsibility of ensuring the implementation of laws, administrative regulations and local regulations. Therefore, people's congresses at various levels and their standing committees should bring into the scope of their supervision such questions as whether reform decision-making is closely combined with legislative decision-making, whether reform is in unity with the rule of law, and whether a reform measure is contradictory to legal provisions. Once a problem is discovered, they should put forward opinions or suggestions on countermeasures or adopt relevant measures in accordance with law.

China also needs to correctly understand and appropriately handle the relationship between reform and the rule of law in such links as strict enforcement of law, fair administration of justice and observance of law by the whole people. The life of law lies in its implementation. Law enforcement, administration of justice, and observance of law are important methods of implementation of law. Legal norms that embody the will of the state are implemented through the advancement of administration by law and strict enforcement of law by state administrative organs, through the correct application of law and fair administration of justice by judicial organs, and through the conscientious study of law, respect for the law, observance of law and the use of law by all citizens and other social subjects. In the process of implementing the law in accordance with the principle of socialist rule of law, all subjects of legal relations must adhere to the principle of acting by law and the principle of equality of everyone before the law. They may not refuse to implement, apply or abide by law, or even violate the law, under any excuse or on any ground.

Against the background of comprehensively deepening the reform, it is normal to have disharmony and conflicts between the reform and the rule of law. We should adhere to the principle of seeking truth from fact, carry out concrete analysis of concrete conditions, and appropriately deal with relationship between reform and the rule of law. Firstly, in cases where a conflict between a reform decision or measure and a provision of law has become inevitable, the procedure for the revision or interpretation of law should be initiated as soon as possible to solve the conflict. Secondly, if it is found out in the process of concrete enforcement of law, administration of justice and observance of law that a reform measure conflicts with the law, the relevant subjects should, in accordance with the provisions of the Legislation Law and other relevant law, report the conflict and submit related suggestions to the competent organs in a timely manner so that the conflict can be dealt with in a timely manner in accordance with law. Thirdly, in accordance with the principle of "no touching the legal red line and no crossing the legal bottom line", China should resolutely put to a stop and rectify any act of deliberately evading or violating the law or practicing departmental or local protectionism in the name carrying out the reform.

References

Deng X (1993) Selected works of Deng Xiaoping, vol 3. People's Publishing House, Beijing, p 359

Jiang Z (1996) Implementing and adhering to the strategy of ruling the Country by Law and guaranteeing long-term political stability. People's Daily, 9 Feb 1996

Xi J (2012) Speech given at the conference of representatives of all circles in Beijing in commemoration of the thirtieth anniversary of the implementation of the current constitution. People's Publishing House, Beijing, 5 Dec 2012

Xi J (2013) Chairs the fourth collective study session of the political Bureau of the CPC central committee. People's Daily, 24 Feb 2013

Chapter 8
High-Degree Unity of the Party and the Law: The Fundamental Characteristic of the Chinese Road of the Rule of Law

In the process of developing socialist democracy and rule of law since the founding of the PRC, especially since the reform and opening up, the debate on the relationship between the Party (mainly referring to the CPC and the leadership of the CPC) and law (mainly referring to the Constitution, laws, socialist rule of law, ruling the country by law, and the construction of the rule of law) has never ceased. In China, the relationship between the Party and the law, or the question of whether the Party is higher than the law or the law is higher than the Party, is not only a legal question, but also a political question, and not only a theoretical question, but also a practical question. Party Secretary General Xi Jinping points out that the relationship between the Party and the law is a fundamental question which, if dealt with correctly, can bring about prosperity of the rule of law, the Party and the state, but if dealt with incorrectly, can lead to the failure of the rule of law, the Party and the state. The Party's leadership is the soul of the socialist rule of law with Chinese characteristics. Xi Jinping points out that the relationship between the Party and the rule of law is the core of the construction of the rule of law in China. The key to comprehensive advancement of ruling the country by law is the correctness of direction and the strength of the political guarantee, more specially, the adherence to the Party's leadership, to the socialist system with Chinese Characteristics, and to the theory of socialist rule of law with Chinese characteristics. The Party's leadership is the most essential characteristic of socialism with Chinese characteristics and the most fundamental guarantee of socialist rule of law. The system of socialism with Chinese characteristics is the basic institutional foundation of the system of socialist rule of law with Chinese characteristics and the fundamental institutional guarantee for the comprehensive advancement of ruling the country by law. The theory of socialist rule of law with Chinese characteristics is the theoretical guidance and support for the system of socialist rule of law with Chinese characteristics and a guide to action for the comprehensive advancement of ruling the country by law. The above three aspects are in essence the core of the road of socialist rule of law with Chinese characteristics that determine and guarantee the institutional attributes and orientation of the system of socialist rule of law with Chinese characteristics.

© China Social Sciences Press and Springer Nature Singapore Pte Ltd. 2018
L. Li, *The Chinese Road of the Rule of Law*, China Insights,
https://doi.org/10.1007/978-981-10-8965-7_8

Adhering to the Party's leadership is a basic requirement of socialist rule of law, the foundation and the lifeline of the Party and the state, the guarantee of the people's interest and welfare, and an inherent component part of comprehensive advancement of ruling the country by law. The Party's leadership is consistent with socialist rule of law: the latter must adhere to the former whereas the former must rely on the latter.

In order to comprehensively advance ruling the country by law, construct the system of socialist rule of law with Chinese characteristics, and build a socialist state under the rule of law, China must give a straight answer to the question of the relationship between the Party and the law by combining theory with practice and history with reality. Only in this way can we more conscientiously adhere to and realize the high degree of unity of the Party and the law.

8.1   The Conceptual Categories of "the Party" and "the Law"

In discussing the relationship between the Party and the law and answering the question of "whether the Party is higher than the law or the law is higher than the Party" in the context of China, we must first have a clear understanding of conceptual categories of "the Party" and "the law" and the main relationships they involve.

8.1.1   The Conceptual Categories of "the Party"

Firstly, from the point of view of full name concept, "the Party" here refers to the Communist Party of China, rather than any other political party or social organization. The Constitution of Communist Party of China provides that: "The Communist Party of China is the vanguard both of the Chinese working class and of the Chinese people and the Chinese nation. It is the core of leadership for the cause of socialism with Chinese characteristics" and that "the Party has no special interests of its own apart from the interests of the working class and the broadest masses of the people." And according to the Constitution of the People's Republic of China, "the Party" is the leadership party of the state political power of the People's Republic of China. It is the ruling party that must take the Constitution as it basic standard of conduct, and has the duty to uphold the dignity of the Constitution and ensure its implementation. Secondly, from the point of view of the subject, "the Party" here is a collective concept that covers all Party members, leading Party cadres, as well as Party organizations and Party organs at various levels. This means that individual Party members, leading Party cadres, Party organizations, even Party secretaries and Party leaders are all components of "the Party", and should not be equated with "the Party". Their statements and acts may represent the image, the authority and the will of "the Party" in a limited sense, but should not be equated with "the Party". Thirdly, from the point of view of the leadership and ruling behaviors, "the Party" here sometimes also has such extended meanings as the Party's leadership, the Party's exercise of the ruling power, the Party's policies, the Party's decision-making, the Party's documents, the Party's decisions, the opinion of a Party organization, the speech of a Party leader, the instruction from a secretary of Party committee, or an order from a high-level Party organization. All these are important ways and means by which the CPC, Party organizations at various levels, and leading Party cadres at various levels implement the Party's plans, exercise the Party's leadership, carry out ruling activities, and lead the people to govern the state and administer state affairs. However, such individual acts should not be equated with the collective will or acts of the CPC.

8.1.2   The Conceptual Category of "the Law"

"The law" here refers to the system of code of conduct that is adopted by the state and implemented with the guarantee of state coercive force, provides for citizens' rights and obligations, and adjusts social relations. In China, it refers to the socialist system of law with Chinese characteristics. The Chinese legal system mainly consists of: firstly, the Constitution, basic laws, laws, administrative regulations, local regulations, regulations on the exercise of autonomy, and separate regulations; secondly, such concepts and activities as the legal system, the rule of law, ruling the country by law, exercising the ruling power by law, administration by law, handling public affairs by law, scientific legislation, strict enforcement of law, fair administration of justice, and observance of law by the whole people; and lastly, such extended meanings as the legislative activities of the legislators, the law enforcement activities of law enforcers, the judicial activities of judges and procurators, and observance of law by all citizens and social organizations.

8.1.3   The Relationship Between "the Party" and "the Law"

In the Chinese context, the relationship between "the Party" and "the law" can be understood as the followings: firstly, it refers to the relationship between the CPC and state laws; secondly, it refers to the relationships between the Party's leadership and the rule of law and ruling the country by law, and between the Party's leadership and scientific legislation, strict enforcement of law, fair administration of justice, and observance of law by the whole people; thirdly, it refers to the relationship between the Party's lines, strategies and policies and state constitution, laws, and regulations; fourthly, it refers to the relationship between the Party's leadership and ruling styles and the rule of law and ruling the country by law; fifthly, it refers to the relationships between concrete powers and behaviors of leading Party cadres, civil servants, law enforcement officials, and judicial officials and such principles as the rule of law, administration by law, and handling public affairs in accordance with law; and sixthly, it refers to such questions as whether there is any privilege above the law, or whether everyone can be equal before the law in the treatment of concrete persons, matters and cases by "the Party" and "the law"; etc.

In real life, as a result of the people's different understandings of the concepts of "the Party" and "the law" and different combinations of various relationships between "the Party" and "the law", the question of the relationship between "the Party and the law" often evolves into such questions as "whether to apply Party document or state law?", "whether to follow the instruction of the Party leader or the state law?", "whether the court should deal with a case in accordance with law or in accordance with the instruction of a leading Party cadre?", "whether the matter should be determined by the leader or by the law?", or "whether the secretary of a Party committee is above the law?" People often take the instruction of Party leaders as the law, the statements and acts of a Party official, a Party leader, even the secretary of a Party committee as "the Party", and the concrete acts of legislative, administrative, and judicial organs as Party activities, and hence the question of "whether is the Party superior to the law?"

Party Secretary General Xi Jinping points out that the question of "whether the Party is higher than the law or the law is higher than the Party" is a political trap, a pseudo-proposition, because it will lead us into a dilemma whatever answer we give to it: if our answer is yes, then we will be attacked for putting the Party above the law, for substituting the law with the Party and for ruling the country by the Party; but if our answer is no, then people will say: "If so, why do you still adhere to the Party's leadership?" Theoretically speaking, the question "whether the Party is superior to the law or is law superior to the Party" is indeed a pseudo-proposition. This question and the question about the relationship between the Party and the law have already been answered in a satisfactory way from the perspective of the combination of legal theory with institutions and the combination of Party constitution with state constitution. However, from the perspective of various inadequacies and defects in the construction of the rule of law in China[1] that are observed and felt by the people and from the

---

[1] The CPC Central Committee Decision on Several Major Issues concerning Comprehensively Advancing Ruling the Country by Law points out that, while fully confirming the historical achievements made by China in the construction of the rule of law, "we must be soberly aware that the construction of the rule of law still have many problems that are incompatible with the development needs of the undertakings of the Party and the State, with the expectations of the masses of people, and with advancement of ruling the country by the law and modernization of governing capacity. The main manifestations of these problems are: some laws and regulations have failed to completely reflect objective laws and the will of the people and lack focus and operability; the tendencies of departmentalization, turf battles and shifting of responsibility are still relatively prominent in legislative work; the phenomena that laws exist but are not followed, law enforcement is not strict and law-breakers aren't punished remain serious; the problems of separation of powers and responsibilities in the law enforcement, multi-headed law enforcement and selective law enforcement, irregular, non-strict, non-transparent, and uncivilized law enforcement and administration of justice, miscarriage of justice and judicial corruption have cause strong concern among the general public; some members of society have weak consciousness of respecting the law, trusting the law, abiding by the law, using the law, and upholding their rights in accordance with the law; and some state personnel, especially some leading cadres, lack the consciousness of and capacity for handling affairs according to the law, knowingly violate the law, substitute their own views for the law,

perspective of the people's high expectation of the realization of good governance, under which "laws are abided by, lawbreakers are prosecuted, the enforcement of law is strict, the administration of justice is fair, the power is controlled in accordance with law, and everyone is equal before the law", the question of "whether the Party is higher than the law or the law is higher than the Party" the question of "what should relationship between the Party and the law be" is not merely a theoretical or cognitive question, but also a practical question. In other words, if the theory of socialist rule of law with Chinese characteristics cannot effectively solve the problems that still exist in some local governments, government departments, and among some leading cadres, such as power being superior to law, suppressing law with power, putting personal views above the law, non-observance of law, slack law enforcement, miscarriage of justice, and perverting justice for a bribe, and the failure to solve the law enforcement and judicial problems that touch upon the personal interest of the people, then the violations of law by some local governments, government organs, or individual Party or government officials will be imputed to the political system, the Party's leadership and the socialist rule of law, and the question of "whether the Party has supremacy over law or the law is superior to the Party" would never fade out from the real life in China. Therefore, on the basis of expounding the high-degree unity of the Party and the law from the perspective of the combination of theory and institutions and answering the question of "whether the Party is higher than the law or the law is higher than the Party", China needs to make more efforts to answer a series of institutional and practical questions, such as how to regulate public power and public officials in accordance with law and put power into the cage of laws and institutions, in the practice of comprehensively deepening the reform, comprehensively advancing the rule of law, and comprehensively strengthening Party discipline.

8.2 The Unity of the Rule of Law and Politics

The high-degree unity of the Party and the law is ultimately determined by the close correlation between law science and political science and the unity of the rule of law (the law) and politics. As far as its source is concerned, in early western societies (for example, the ancient Greece), law science was part of political science,

---

suppress the law by power, and bend the law for personal gains or for the interest of their relatives and friends. These problems are against the principles of socialist rule of law, harm the interests of the people, impede the development of the undertakings of the Party and the country, and therefore must be resolved at any cost. Party Secretary General Xi Jinping further points out in Explanation of the "CPC Central Committee Decision concerning Several Major Issues in Comprehensively Advancing Ruling the country by Law" that at present, "the main problems existing in the judicial field include judicial unfairness and low level of public trust in the judiciary, which are extremely serious. Some judicial personnel have improper work styles, do not handle cases cleanly, bend the law for personal gains or for the benefit of relatives and friends, and accept bribes from both the plaintiff and the defendant, etc."

or it can be said that for a long period of time the law science and the political science had been integrated. Today, political science and law science are often inseparably combined to form a discipline called "politics and law". Law and politics have become interdependent, inseparable and highly unified components of the art of ruling the country (governance). Therefore, the rule of law and politics are highly unified in core value and substantive functions. Law science and political science intersect with each other and scientifically integrate with each other to form a discipline called politics of law, which takes social phenomena with the dual political and legal attribute as its objects of study and applies methodologies of both political science and law science to study these phenomena.[2] The Oxford Companion to Law points out that: "Just as theoretical research on jurisprudence is closely related to political theories, the more practical legal rules are always closely related to real politics. Legal rules are adopted or abolished by politicians and political organizations to realize certain political theories, political beliefs and political objectives… The whole field of public administration is filled with interactive influences between legal needs and political needs, between legal means and political means, and between legal effects and political effects."[3] Lenin penetratingly pointed out that "Laws are political measures, politics."[4] Therefore, the constitution and laws sometimes are called codified politics and politics under the regulation of the constitution sometimes called "constitutionalism". The justifiability, legitimacy and legalization of political power, political system, and political behavior, and the political orientation, the political attribute and the will-of-the-state characteristic of the legal system, the process of the rule of law, and judicial power are undoubtedly major issues that cannot be avoided in both law science and political science and in both the rule of law and politics. In the sense of politics of law, state law and legislation are inseparable from party politics, political party election, and the theories, objectives and policies of the ruling party; state law is inseparable from the people's democracy, popular sovereignty, the people's interest, and the people's rights; state constitution is inseparable from legislative power, administrative power, judicial power and civil rights; state politics is inseparable from judicial power; politics is inseparable from judicial independence; political principles are inseparable from judicial activities; political system is inseparable from judicial system; and political reform is inseparable from judicial reform. From a more macro perspective, politics, the rule of law, and the rule of virtue are in essence all the ways, means and institutional arrangements by which mankind governs the state and society. They are all different theories and methods of "heteronomy, autonomy, and shared governance" and their ultimate objective is to make governance more scientific and democratic and to bring it under the rule of law.

At the value level, the rule of law involves not only such abstract values as rationality, justice, fairness, will, good and evil, happiness, equality and freedom, but also such concretized values as interest, rights, democracy, order, efficiency, safety, peace,

---

[2]Zhuo (2005, p. 5).
[3]Walker (1989, pp. 520–521).
[4]Lenin (1990, p. 140).

and development. "The relationships between these values can be basically divided into the following four types: consistency, antagonism, principal and subordinate, and mutual-independence."[5] The values of law are attached to legal norms and realized in the process of implementation of law. The values of law themselves have strong political color and so does administration of justice, which pursues fairness and justice. "Compared to legislative and administrative functions, judicial activities have been a rather strong political function since the ancient times", "a state can exist without a parliament...and its administrative organs can be reduced to a minimum level. However, its judicial organs cannot be abolished or weakened. Judicial function is one of the state's most basic political functions, without which the state cannot exist."[6] The political nature of law and administration of justice is obvious. Under the condition of party politics, legal values and administration of justice will inevitably and strongly manifest the political orientation and policy inclination of the ruling party. In other words, the ruling party will inevitably transform through various means and channels its basic ruling ideas and policy demands into provisions of law and implement them in the concrete judicial process.

The US is a country that attaches great importance to judicial independence, even believes that there is no connection between administration of justice and politics. However, in the judicial life of the US, "judicial independence, as a principle, is inevitably subjected to certain degree of distortion in real political life."[7] In the US, the selection of judges is a process with strong political color. "The Supreme Court itself, however upright and irreproachable its members, has generally had and will undoubtedly continue to have a distinct political complexion, taken from the color of the times during which its majority was chosen."[8] Among the 211 federal judges appointed by Democratic President Franklin Roosevelt, 203 were members of the Democratic Party and eight were members of the Republican Party; among the 187 federal judges appointed by Republican President Dwight Eisenhower, 176 were members of the Republican Party and 11 were members of the Democratic Party; among the 180 federal judges appointed by Democratic President J. F. Kennedy, 169 were members of the Democratic Party and 11 were members of the Republican Party; among the 213 federal judges appointed by Republican President Richard Nixon, 198 were members of the Republican Party and 15 were members of the Democratic Party; and among the 64 federal judges appointed by Republican President Gerald Ford, 52 were members of the Republican Party and 12 were members of the Democratic Party.[9] "Almost without exception, the style of all the judges who have been rated as "great" or "near great" has always been more 'political' than 'judicial'. From John Marshall to Earl Warren, the majority of the most influential judges in the US Supreme Court had taken up elected or appointed political posts before they become a judge, and they have been often political figures with strong partisanship. Once

---

[5] See Zhuo (2006).

[6] Hu (1994, p. 34).

[7] Ibid., p. 63.

[8] Wilson (1986, p. 24).

[9] Hu (1994, p. 63). See also Abraham (1990, pp. 39–61).

they entered into the Supreme Court, their political experience would have an impact on their case handling style."[10] In fact, the US Supreme Court is not an independent organ transcendent of politics. Rather, it often plays an important role in American political life. "The US Supreme Court has indeed participated in the political process of the country" and "some major decisions in US political history have been made not by the President or the Congress, but by the Supreme Court."[11] Meanwhile, the US Supreme Court, "as an organ with legal, political and human characteristics, has various advantages and weaknesses along with these characteristics."[12] Tocqueville described the relationship between politics and administration of justice in the US from another angle in his book *On Democracy in America*: of all the problems in the US, very few are not converted into judicial problems, and most of them will ultimately boiled down to judicial problems. Therefore, in the US, "the authority of a judge is invoked in the political occurrences of every day."[13] Therefore, it is not difficult to understand why President Franklin Roosevelt implemented the "court-packing" plan in the 1930s to reconstruct the Supreme Court in terms of party composition.

In a society based on autonomous law, as advocated by Nonet and Selznick, the separation of law and politics is also relative. The law is the guarantee of the loyalty to the current political order. By performing political functions in close coordination with the state, and committing themselves to order, control and submission, legal institutions (including courts) give their substantive compliance in exchange for pro-cedural autonomy, and maintain substantive consistency with politics in exchange for relative procedural independence, rather than real separation of law from politics.[14]

Carl Marx pointed out that "All those which people struggle for are related to their interest."[15] Interest is a social principle. Jurisprudence of interests, as a branch of western sociology of law, takes the balance of various interests by the judge as its theoretical basis, and maintains that laws are the principles adopted by legisla-tors to resolve the conflicts of various interests. Therefore, to ensure the fairness of judgment, judges must determine the interests the legislators' intend to protect in a law before applying it. They should never act like a law-selling machine that oper-ates mechanically according to the logic of law, but should be independent-thinking assistants of legislators. They should not only pay attention to the provisions of law, but also try to understand the intention of the legislators through the examination of the relevant interests. Western jurisprudence of interests advocates "social benefit" as the important objective of adjudication by judges, and "stresses the political function of application of law, namely the relationship between the law science, the court's practice, and politics".[16] An epoch-making achievement of Western jurisprudence

---

[10]Woll (1992, p. 355).

[11]Vile (1981, p. 211).

[12]Abraham (1990, p. 270).

[13]de Tocqueville (1988, p. 109).

[14]Nonet and Selznick (1994, pp. 63–66).

[15]Marx and Engels (1956, p. 82).

[16]Rüthers (2003, p. 241).

of interest is "to take into consideration of social and political reality and policy objectives of legal norms."[17] Regardless of whether it is recognized by the people, it is impossible for the court to make judgment only on the basis of provisions of law, and one-sidedly emphasize the principle of "supremacy of the Constitution and laws", without taking into consideration such complicated factors as politics, society, ethics, interest, people's condition, and culture.

Even some western jurists have been forced to acknowledge the value of Marxist jurisprudence as a school of legal theory and accept the following viewpoints of Marxist jurisprudence: "All laws are in favor of the political party of the ruling class...they form, cultivate, and shape consciousness, and protect the existing ruling relations from the attack by hostile forces", "socialist law is a tool of the working class that has seized state power under the leadership of a Marxist political party". Its primary task is to protect socialist society and the unitary rule of the Marxist party from the sabotage by foreign and domestic hostile forces; and its secondary task is to promote the construction of socialism and guide the construction of a communist society.[18] "Administration of justice is in essence the tool of state activity. It realizes various judicial functions through the effective supplementation of the legitimacy, ideology and morality of the ruling class."[19]

According to the Marxist outlook on the rule of law, the rule of law (the legal system) in all class societies have political color, class color and legal color. The political color or nature of the rule of law (legal system) is determined by and manifested in the programs, lines, principles and polices of the ruling party or the ruling group; the class color or nature of the rule of law (legal system) is determined by and manifested in the interests, will and fundamental requirement of the ruling class and its allies; and the legal color or nature of the rule of law (legal system) refers to all the technical and cultural attributes the rule of law ought to possess. Just as Xie Juezai, the first President of the Supreme People's Court of the PRC frankly pointed out in the article "The Marxist Outlook on Law: "Our laws are subjected to politics. No law is independent of politics. Our judicial workers must understand politics. Otherwise they would not know how to apply the law." The most important work of people's courts is trial, which is not only highly professional, but also highly political. "A trial consists of two steps: the first step is to clarify the facts of the case, which must be objective facts, rather than the subjective imagination of the judge; the second step is to make a ruling or judgment on the basis of clarifying the facts of the case, namely to determine the sentencing in accordance with the Party's principles and policies and within the scope of the law."

In China, under the system of socialism with Chinese characteristics, the political nature of socialist rule of law is embodied in a concentrated way the nature, purposes, basic tasks and objectives of struggle of the CPC, as well as the institutionalization, standardization and legalization of the CPC's lines, principles and policies. The class nature of socialist rule of law is embodied in a concentrated way in its popular and

---

[17] Ibid., p. 247.

[18] Ibid., pp. 226–228.

[19] Kaufmann and Hassemer (2002, p. 443).

democratic nature, because at the current stage of development, class contradiction is no longer the main contradiction in Chinese society. The absolute majority of members of society are citizens, who belong to the category of the people. The people, as masters of the country, are in control of the state political power. The class nature of the rule of law is replaced by the popular nature of the rule of law. The legal nature of socialist rule of law is embodied in a concentrated way in the following two aspects: first, the inherent objectivity, normativity, coerciveness, foreseeability, definitiveness, procedural natures and technicality of law and the rule of law; second, the Chinese legal cultural tradition and its modern characteristic and its capacity for learning from, drawing on and absorbing all beneficial elements of the rule of law civilization of mankind.

Of course, while demonstrating the close correlation between law science and political science and the inherent unity of the rule of law (the law) and politics, we must also acknowledge the obvious distinctions and major differences between them. Their distinctions and differences in disciplinary division, research objects, conceptual category, practical operation, and institutional mechanism are exactly the premises and the bases of the discussion of their correlation and unity.

8.3 High-Degree Unity of the Party and the Law

Under the western political philosophy and constitutional mode of separation of three powers and multi-party system, different political parties represent different interests, and the ruling party, the party out of power and the opposition party each plays a different role in politics. As a result, political parties and the rule of law in western countries are often in a relationship of pluralism, dislocation, even disconnection. Western political parties represent different classes, different social strata and different interest groups whereas the western rule of law claims to be the embodiment of the will of the state, which in turn represents the common will of the whole people. As a result, contradictions and conflicts are inevitable between the multi-interest orientation of the western political party system and the neutrality, equality and fairness flaunted by the western rule of law and it is very difficult to achieve the unity of western political parties and the rule of law.

In China, the socialist system, the system of one-party leadership by the CPC, the economic system based on public ownership and the political system of popular sovereignty are confirmed and guaranteed by the Constitution and laws; the CPC represents the common interest of the people and has no special interest of its own; and the socialist law embodies the unity and consistency between the Party's propositions and the will of the people. All these have determined that the relationships between the CPC and the people and between the state and the rule of law are not that of contradiction and opposition, but that of harmony, consistency and high-degree unity.

8.3.1   The High-Degree Unity of the Party and the Law from the Perspective of the Party's Leadership and the Essence of Socialist Rule of Law

In a certain sense, adhering to and improving the Party's leadership, implementing socialist rule of law, and advancing ruling the country by law are all ways, means, measures and processes. Their essence is to serve the people whole-heartedly and their objective is to achieve the "Chinese dream" of national prosperity, the people's happiness and the rejuvenation of the Chinese nation, and realize socialist modernization. The CPC represents the fundamental interest of the broadest masses of people and has no special interests of its own apart from the interests of the working class and the broadest masses of the people. It always puts the people's interest first, shares the comforts and hardships with the people, maintains the closest connection with the people, functions by the mandate of the people, empathizes with the feelings of the people, works for the well-being of the people, and does not allow any Party member to divorce himself/herself from the people and put himself/herself above the people. The socialist rule of law is the rule of law that is for the people, depends on the people, benefits the people, and protects the people; it takes the people as the subjects, the regulation of power and Party and government officials by law as the means, and the promotion of the people's fundamental interest as the starting point and ultimate goal, ensures that the people enjoy extensive rights and freedoms in accordance with law, upholds social fairness and justice, and promotes common prosperity. In the final analysis, both the Party and the law and both the Party's leadership and the socialist rule of law take the people's happiness as their ultimate pursuit, the people's satisfaction as their highest appraisal, the people's support as their political basis, and the people's democracy as their source of life. Ultimately, the high-degree of unity of the Party and the law and of the Party's leadership and socialist rule of law is embodied in the essential attribute and the inherent requirement of serving the people wholeheartedly.

8.3.2   The High-Degree Unity of the Party and the Law from the Perspective of the Chinese Constitution

The Constitution, as the fundamental law of the country, is of highest legal effect and authority in China. It contains the general rules by which the CPC leads the Chinese people to administer state affairs and ensure national security. The Chinese Constitution confirms in the form of basic law the CPC leadership position and the role it has played in the historical process of leading the Chinese people in carrying out the revolution, construction and reform and it will continue to play in the process of building China into a prosperous, powerful, democratic and culturally advanced socialist country. The Constitution also provides for the principles of ruling the country by law and upholding the unity and the dignity of the socialist rule of law. It requires that various political parties, including the CPC, take the Constitution as the basic guidelines and perform their duty of upholding the dignity and ensuring the implementation of the Constitution, that everyone abide by the Constitution and laws, that any act of violation of the Constitution and laws must be investigated and punished, and that no organization or individual has the privilege above the Constitution and laws. The above provisions of the Constitution provided constitutional basis for the high-degree unity of the Party and the law and created a new type of relationship between political party and the law with characteristics completely different from those of the system of separation of three powers and the multi-party system in western countries.

8.3.3 The High-Degree Unity of the Party and the Law from the Perspective of the Constitution of the CPC

The Constitution of the CPC is the highest norms on Party institutions and conducts, the fundamental rules on strengthening Party self-discipline and running the Party in accordance with regulations, and the fundament intra-Party regulations that guarantee the high-degree unity of the Party and the law. It clearly provides that the CPC is the core of leadership for the cause of socialism with Chinese characteristics, and demands the Party to adhere to the organic unity the leadership of the CPC, the people being the masters of the country, and ruling the country by law, take the road of development of socialist political system with Chinese characteristics, expand socialist democracy, perfect the socialist legal system, build a socialist country under the rule of law, improve the socialist legal system with Chinese characteristics, and strengthen the implementation of laws, so as to bring all aspects of the work of the state under the rule of law. To ensure the high-degree unity of the Party and the law and of the Party's leadership and the rule of law, the Party Constitution especially provides that the leadership by the Party means mainly political, ideological and organizational leadership, that the Party must act within the scope of the Constitution and laws, persist in scientific, democratic and law-based governance, and ensure that the legislative, judicial and administrative organs of the state and the economic and cultural organizations and people's organizations work with initiative and independent responsibility and in unison, and that apart from the individual interest and job-related powers provided for by laws and policies, Party members may not seek any private interest or privilege and must abide by state laws and regulations in an exemplary way. The above provisions of the Party Constitution are more specific, stricter, and more targeted than the relevant provisions in the Constitution, and therefore play the very important role as the fundamental normative and institutional safeguard for the realization of a relationship of harmony and unity between the Party and the law.

8.3.4   The High-Degree Unity of the Party and the Law from the Perspective of Documents of CPC Party Congresses

How to correctly handle the relationship between the Party and the law and construct a new type of relationship of high-degree unity between the CPC and the rule of law and between the Party's leadership and ruling the country by law has been a major theoretical and practical question that the CPC has been attaching high importance to and making great efforts to answer in the process of leading the Chinese people in carrying out the construction of socialist democratic political system with Chinese characteristics and in advancing governance by law. The Report of the Fifteenth Party Congress, while establishing ruling the country by law as the basic strategy by which the CPC leads the Chinese people to govern the country, especially stresses that: "The Party has led the people in drawing up the Constitution and other laws, to which it confines its activities. The strategy of ruling the country by law unifies the principles of upholding the Party's leadership, developing people's democracy and acting in strict accordance with law, provides institutional and legal guarantees for the implementation of the Party's basic lines and policies, and ensures that the Party plays the role of the core of leadership at all times, commanding the whole situation and coordinating the efforts of all quarters." The report has, for the first time in history and in the form of the political document of the Party Congress, put forward the proposition and the demand of unifying "the Party's leadership, people's democracy and acting in accordance with law", thereby clearly answering the question of how to construct the relationship between the Party and the law against the background of ruling the country by law. The Report of the Sixteenth Party Congress expounds the essential characteristics and inherent requirements of the democratic politics with Chinese characteristics by pointing out that "The key to developing socialist democracy is to combine the need to uphold the Party's leadership and to ensure that the people are the masters of the country with the need to rule the country by law", thus establishing for the first time the basic political principle of "organic unity of the three". The Report of the Seventeenth Party Congress, on the basis of adhering to the principle of "organic unity of the three", clearly raises the demand of "adhering to the Party's core leadership role of commanding the overall situation and coordinating the efforts of all quarters, enhancing the Party's capacity for scientific, democratic, and law-based governance, and ensuring that the Party leads the people in effectively ruling the country."

The Report of the Eighteenth Party Congress further emphasizes the importance of ruling the country by law and the rule of law in the relationship between the Party and the law, reiterates that ruling the country by law is the basic strategy of state governance, points out for the first time that the rule of law is the CPC's basic mode of state governance, stresses the need to give better play to the important role of the rule of law in state and social governance, and emphasizes that no organization or individual should be allowed to have any privilege above the Constitution and law, to substitute the law with their own views, to suppress the law with power, or to bend the law for personal gains. At the Fourth Plenary Session of its Eighteenth Central

Committee, the CPC gave a systematic answer to the question of how to correctly understand in theory the relationship between "the Party and the law" and unify "the Party's leadership and ruling the country by law" through top-level design and institutional arrangement. The Decision of the Fourth Plenary Session of Eighteenth CPC Central Committee explains the new relationship between "the Party and the law" under the socialist system with Chinese characteristics from the following six perspectives: First, essential characteristic. The Chinese Constitution establishes the leadership position of the CPC, which is the most essential characteristic of socialism with Chinese characteristics and the most fundamental guarantee of the socialist rule of law. Second, basic experience. One of the basic experiences of the construction of the socialist rule of law with Chinese characteristics is to adhere to the CPC's leadership in the whole process and all aspects of ruling the country by law. Third, basic requirement. Adhering to the CPC's leadership is the basic requirement of socialist rule of law and the essence of comprehensive advancement of ruling the country by law. Fourth, interrelationship. On the one hand, the CPC's leadership is consistent with socialist rule of law and must be adhered to in building the socialist rule of law. On the other hand, the CPC must rely on the socialist rule of law in exercising its leadership. Fifth, exercising the ruling power by law. The CPC rules the country in accordance with Constitution and laws, administers Party affairs in accordance with intra-Party regulations, leads the state legislation, guarantees the enforcement of law, supports administration of justice, and takes the lead in abiding by law. Sixth, highly unified top-level design, which includes "ensuring three unities" and "being good at four things". Namely, the Party must ensure the unity of the basic strategy of ruling the country by law and the basic mode of exercising the ruling power by law, the unity of the CPC's work of commanding the overall situation and coordinating the efforts of all quarters and the performance of functions by people's congresses, governments, people's consultative conferences, trial bodies and prosecutorial bodies in accordance with laws and regulations, and the unity of the Party's work of leading the people in adopting and implementing the Constitution and laws and the Party's obligation to act within the scope of the Constitution and laws, and be good at transforming the Party's propositions into the will of the state through statutory procedures, being good at ensuring that the candidates recommended by Party organizations become leaders of state political bodies through statutory procedures, being good at implementing Party leadership over the country and society through state political bodies, and being good at applying the principle of democratic centralism to uphold the authority of the CPC Central Committee and the unity of the entire Party and the entire country.

8.3.5 The High-Degree Unity of the Party and the Law from the Perspective of the Legalization of the CPC's Lines, Principles and Policies

In China, the Constitution and laws are the embodiment of the legalization of CPC's lines, principles and policies. They guarantee to the maximum extent the unity of and coordination between state legislation and the CPC's major decisions on reform, development and stability—which are the sources of laws and regulations, thereby organically unifying the Party and the law in the state legal system. On the one hand, legislation uses legal method to transform the mature lines, principles and policies of the CPC into institutions and laws of the state, and use state laws to guide, promote and guarantee the comprehensive implementation of the CPC's lines, principles and policies. On the other hand, the successful practice of the implementation of the CPC's lines, principles and policies provides the guidance and motive force for the continuous improvement of state laws.

8.3.6 The High-Degree Unity of the Party and the Law from the Perspective of Democratic State Legislation

Legislation is in essence the product of the process in which the propositions of the CPC and the will of the people are combined and transformed into the will of the state. State legislative organs, on the basis of fully developing democracy, transform in a timely way the CPC's propositions that reflect the will and the fundamental interests of the whole people into the will of the state through democratic and scientific legislative procedure, give it legal effect, guarantee its implementation with state coercive force, and require all members of society to abide by it, thereby realizing through legislation the transformation and elevation the CPC's propositions into the will of the people and the will of the state, the combination of the Party and the law, and the organic unity of the CPC's leadership and ruling the country by law.

8.3.7 The High-Degree Unity of the Party and the Law from the Perspective of Adhering to the CPC's Leadership and to the Independent Exercise of Powers by Judicial Organs in Accordance with Law

In China, the relationship between adhering to the CPC's leadership and the independent exercise of judicial powers by courts and procuratorates in accordance with law is that of unity and consistency. Firstly, the Constitution and laws, which are the concentrated manifestations of the unity of the CPC's propositions and the will of the people and the legalization of the CPC's lines, principles and policies, achieve at the legislative level the organic unity of the CPC's leadership and ruling the country by law and guarantee the unity of and the consistency between the CPC's policies and state laws. On this basis, judicial organs, by independently exercising adjudicative and procuratorial powers in strict accordance with the principle of the rule of law and relevant provisions of law, perform the judicial functions in accordance with the CPC's proposition and the will of the people and embody the unity of the CPC's leadership and the independent exercise of judicial power in accordance with law. The former President of China, Mr. Liu Shaoqi, gave the following explanation to the independent exercise of judicial powers by people's courts and people's procuratorates on basis of the reality in China: "Courts should try cases independently. This is required by the Constitution. Neither Party committees nor the government may interfere with the trial of cases. Procuratorates should fight against violations of laws and disciplines by any organ or individual. Judicial organs should not be required to unconditionally obey the orders of Party committees at various levels. They should not obey any order which is against the law. What should they do if the decision of a local Party committee is inconsistent with state laws or the policies of the Central Party Committee? They should obey state laws and the policies of the Central Party Committee."[20] As far as the judicial organs are concerned, "obeying state laws and decisions of the CPC Central Committee and decisions of organs of highest state power is obeying the will of the whole people."[21] Secondly, against the background that the construction of the system of law in China has already been completed on schedule, that most of the content of the CPC's lines, principles and policies as well as the CPC's political and organizational leadership have already been brought under the rule of law, and that most of the strategic arrangements made by the CPC for the promotion of economic, political, cultural, social and ecological constructions have already been embodied in laws, judicial organs should adhere to the Party's leadership, implement the Party's will and uphold the Party's authority mainly by way of exercising the judicial power in an independent and fair way and handling cases in strict accordance with law. Moreover, the best way judicial organs, judges and procurators embody the Party's purposes, implement the Party's principles and policies, and uphold the Party's leadership is to independently exercise judicial power, and enable the people to feel the justice and fairness of the rule of law in each case, "take facts as the basis and the law as the criterion, be upright and incorruptible, and impartially enforce the law." Finally the best way for the CPC to effectively strengthen the legal basis of its leadership and its position as the ruling party is to support and safeguard the independent exercise of judicial power by judicial organs. The independent exercise of adjudicative and procuratorial powers provided for in the Chinese Constitution and laws and the adherence to the CPC's leadership are organically unified in theoretical logic and completely consistent with each other in institutional design, and develop interactively in judicial practice.

---

[20]Document Editing Commission of the CPC Central Committee (1985, p. 452).
[21]Peng (1992, p. 178).

Here, it should be especially pointed out that adhering to the high-degree unity of the Party and the law is by no means "no separation of the Party and the law", "substituting the law with the Party", "substituting the state with the Party", or even "ruling the country by the Party". As early as in 1941, Deng Xiaoping pointed out in the article The Party and the Anti-Japanese Democratic Government that: "We must ensure the Party's leadership over the government."[22] However, "The Party exercises leadership by providing political principles, not by monopolizing everything, interfering in everything or placing Party power above everything else. This is diametrically opposite to the policy of 'ruling the country by the party', which is an abominable tradition of the Kuomintang, the easiest way to paralyse and corrupt the Party and alienate the masses."[23] "Some leading comrades have held to this mistaken idea for a long time, bringing about the following disastrous consequences: they misunderstand the leading role played by the Party, believing that to play such a role, Party members should monopolize everything; they interfere in government work, change at will decrees promulgated by the government at a higher level, and transfer cadres who work in organs of political power without going through administrative procedures… the authorities in some places have refused to carry out government decrees without Party notification…" "Some Party members have gone a step further, taking 'Party leadership is above everything else' to mean 'Party members are above everything else' and believing that Party members can do evil and that the ones who have violated the law can be forgiven. This has given the masses the impression that the government is incompetent and that it is the Communist Party that has the final say in everything…and is responsible for all the mistakes made by the government. Hence, the government is not respected by the masses and the Party has alienated itself from them. What stupidity!"[24] "No separation between the Party and the government", "substituting the law with the Party" and "ruling the country by the Party" are in essence the denial of the rule of law and people's democracy, which completely deviate from the principle of adhering the high-degree unity of the Party and the law.

8.4 Adhering to the High-Degree Unity of the Party and the Law Is a Basic Experience of the Construction of the Rule of Law in China

Adhering to the leading position of the CPC and giving full play to the role of the CPC as the leading core has always been the key to the success and a basic experience of revolution, construction and reform in China. The high-degree unity of the Party and the law has been achieved by adhering to the socialist rule of law and taking it as the basic mode of state governance, adhering to ruling the country by law and taking

---

[22]Deng (1994, p. 16).

[23]Ibid., p. 12.

[24]Ibid., pp. 10–11.

it as the basic strategy by which the CPC leads the people in administering state and social affairs, and adhering to the exercise of ruling power by law, and taking it as the CPC's basic ruling mode. In the pursuit of this goal, China has undergone a process of transition from a society under the rule of law, to a society with a legal system, and to a society under the rule of law. In this historical process, with the continuous strengthening of the construction the socialist rule of law, the continuous advancement of ruling the country by law, and the continuous enhancement the people's consciousness of the rule of law, the relationships between the Party and the law and between the Party's leadership and the rule of law have been in a condition of dynamic coordination and development towards high-degree unity.

During the period of New Democratic Revolution, the CPC, as a revolutionary party taking the seizure of state political power as its mission, organized and led the revolution mainly by relying on policies, orders, decisions and resolutions. The process in which the CPC led the people to seize political power was a process of breaking the old laws and abolishing the old legal system. In the revolution, the working class did not recognize the constitution and laws of the Kuomintang Regime. "Back then, if we obeyed the laws, we would not be able to make the revolution, but instead would be upholding the ruling order of imperialism, feudalism and bureaucrat-capitalism. To fight reactionaries, we must break their laws. And we mainly relied on policies to mobilize the people and solve the conflicts and disputes among the people."[25] The CPC "had overthrown the 'three big mountains' (imperialism, feudalism and bureaucrat-capitalism) by relying on policies. At that time, we could only rely on policies."[26] Revolutionary laws were only an auxiliary means used by the CPC in leading mass movements and carrying out armed struggles.

On the eve of the founding of the New China, the CPC Central Committee issued the Instruction on Abolishing the Six Codes of the Kuomintang Regime and Establishing the Judicial Principles in Liberated Areas (hereinafter referred to as the Instruction), which clearly pointed out that: "Under the political power of people's democratic dictatorship led by the proletariat and with the worker-peasant alliance as its main body, the Six Codes of the Kuomintang regime should be abolished. The people's judicial work should no longer take the Six Codes as its basis. Instead, it should take the people's new laws as the basis of its work." Meanwhile, it required people's judicial organs "to educate and reform judicial cadres to always show contempt for and denounce the Six Codes and all the other reactionary laws and decrees issued by the Kuomintang as well as all the laws and decrees of the US, Japan, Europe and all other capitalist countries and to study and master the Marxist-Leninist-Maoist outlook on state and law, and new democratic policies, programs, laws, orders, regulations, and resolutions." The Instruction clearly required judicial organs to enable judicial cadres to realize that our laws belong to the people and our courts are the tools of the people. Our laws are subjected to politics… They should provide for what are needed in politics. Therefore, "judicial workers must understand politics. Those who do not understand politics can never understand law." They must carry

---

[25] Document Editing Commission of the CPC Central Committee (1991, p. 491).
[26] Writing Group for Biography of Peng Zhen (2012, p. 1570).

out judicial work in a political way", handle cases by taking into consideration of various political factors. This requires them to have political awareness.

In 1949, the CPC led the people in establishing a national political power, thereby opening a new chapter in the history of people's legal system. The adoption of the Common Program of the Chinese People's Political Consultative Conference and the Constitution of the PRC (1954) and the promulgation of a number of important laws and decrees had laid the legal foundation of the construction of political power of the New China. The CPC began a gradual transition of its ruling mode from one that relies on policies to one that relies not only on policies, but also on the laws. "After the founding of the PRC, the CPC, as the ruling party, changed its leadership mode from one that had been formed during war times to one that relies not only on policies, but also on laws. The Party should not only make decisions on important matters that concern the state and the people, but also transform such decisions into state laws. The Party's leadership is consistent with the principle of acting by law."[27]

However, since the start of the "Anti-Rightist Movement" in the second half of 1957, abnormal phenomena began to emerge in the political, economic, and social lives of the country. "The main Party leaders began to change their views on the question of 'whether to implement the rule of man or the rule of law'. Mao Zedong said that 'Although we should not discard the law altogether, we have our own way of doing things. We rely mainly on resolutions and meetings, rather than the civil law or the criminal law, to maintain social order. The people's congresses and the State Council have their ways of doing thing, but we would rather rely on our own way.' 'Should we implement the rule of man or the rule of law? It seems that in reality we still rely on the rule of man. Laws can only be taken as reference in our work.'"[28] During the "Cultural Revolution", "class struggle was taken as the key link and the so-called "big-democracy"-style mass movements had become main mode of state governance. Local people's congresses and local governments were replaced by "revolutionary committees", public security organs, procuratorates and courts were smashed, democratic and legal institutions were almost completely destroyed, and socialist legal system was serious undermined.

One of the fundamental causes of the tragedy of "the Cultural Revolution" was that the state legal system was severely damaged, leading to a chaotic situation of lawlessness in life of the Party and the state. During the period of "taking class struggle as the key link" and practicing "big democracy", a handful of people had placed themselves above the CPC and the state leadership system, substituted law with their personal views, suppressed the law with power, and acted without regard for any authority. Under this abnormal historical condition, some cadres and ordinary citizens raised the question of "whether the Party is higher than the law or the law is higher than the Party" to expressed their dissatisfaction with the acts of Lin Biao and the "Gang of Four" of undermining the system of intra-Party regulations, trumping up the Constitution, violating human rights, and sabotaging the legal system in the name of the CPC, and to fight against such retroactions. Their real intention was to

---

[27] Jiang (2002, pp. 307–308).

[28] Writing Group for Biography of Peng Zhen (2012, p. 1572).

adhere to the collective leadership of the CPC and uphold people's democracy and the state legal order.

Deng Xiaoping pointed out in an article entitled On the Reform of the System of Party and State Leadership that: "It is true that the errors we made in the past were partly attributable to the way of thinking and style of work of some leaders. But they were even more attributable to the problems in our organizational and working systems. If these systems are sound, they can place restraints on the actions of bad people; if they are unsound, they may hamper the efforts of good people or indeed, in certain cases, may push them in the wrong direction…the problems in the leadership and organizational systems are more fundamental, widespread and long-lasting."[29] It has been proven in practice that, in a socialist country led and ruled by the CPC, the implementation of the governance mode of the rule of man would inevitably lead to the dual damage to the CPC's leadership and to the state legal system: It would damage the collective leadership and weaken the political authority of the CPC, while at the same time trample upon people's democracy, sabotage socialist legal system and bring disaster to the CPC, the state, the people and society. After the downfall of the "Gang of Four" and the end of the "Cultural Revolution", the CPC made a profound summarization of the painful lesson of the destruction of democracy and the legal system in the "Cultural Revolution", analyzed the fundamental institutional defects in the governance mode of the rule of man, and decisively chose the political road of developing socialist democracy and improving socialist legal system. Just as the Decision of the Fourth Plenary Session of the Eighteenth CPC Central Committee points out: "Since the Third Plenary Session of the Eleventh CPC Central Committee, our Party has summarized the successful experiences and profound lessons of the construction of socialist rule of law in the country, and has come to the conclusion that, in order to safeguard people's democracy, China must strengthen the rule of law and institutionalize and legalize democracy." Unswervingly adhering to the road of socialist rule of law under the leadership of the CPC and to the high-degree unity of the Party and the law is the inevitable choice made by New China in the practice of socialist construction as well as a necessary requirement of reform and opening up in the new historical period.

During the 30 years since the reform and opening up, the CPC, in the practice of leading Chinese people in strengthening the construction of the rule of law and advancing ruling the country by law, has always attached high importance to the correct understanding of "the relationship between the Party and the law", which is the core issue in the construction of socialist rule of law. In December 1978, Deng Xiaoping pointed out in the article Emancipate the Mind, Seek Truth from Facts and Unite as One in Looking to the Future that: "To ensure people's democracy, we must strengthen our legal system. Democracy has to be institutionalized and written into law, so as to make sure that institutions and laws do not change whenever the leadership changes, or whenever the leaders change their views or shift the focus of their attention." He said that: "The trouble now is that our legal system is incomplete, with many laws yet to be enacted. Very often, what leaders say is taken as the law and

---

[29]Deng (1994, p. 293).

anyone who disagrees is called a law-breaker. That kind of law changes whenever a leader's views change." With respect to the abnormal phenomenon of taking what leaders say as the law and thinking leaders as representing the Party,[30] some citizens raise the question of "whether the Party is higher than the law or the law is higher than the Party", which is in essence a criticism of the rule of man practice whereby only one person or a few persons have the final say in the political life of the Party and the state and a denunciation of the bureaucratic phenomenon of power overshadowing law. With respect to the phenomenon of power overshadowing law and replacing the law with personal views, Deng Xiaoping pointed out as early as in the beginning of the reform and opening up that: "We should put to an end to the situation in which what leaders say is taken as the law and anyone who disagrees is called a law-breaker."[31]

In July 1979, Peng Zhen gave a very clear answer to the question of "whether the Party is higher than the law or the law is higher than the Party" when he discussed the leadership of the CPC and the duty of people's courts and people's procuratorates to independently exercise their functions and obey only the law. He said that: "Some comrades raised the question of whether the law, a certain leader or a Party committee at certain level has higher authority. In my opinion, the law has the higher authority…anyone must obey the law, no matter who he is. No one has any privilege before the law. Obeying the law is obeying the decisions of the leaders of the Central Party Committee, of the highest organs of state power, and of the people in the whole country."[32] In March 1984, Peng Zhen further explained the relationship between the Party and the law in an article entitled We Should not Rely only on Party Policies, but also Act in accordance with Law in Our Work: "The relationship between the Party's leadership and the principle of acting by law is that of consistency and unity. The Party leads the Chinese people in adopting the Constitution and laws and it leads the people in observing and implementing the Constitution and laws. The Constitution of the CPC clearly provides that Party organizations and Party members must act within the scope of the Constitution and laws. This provision is the summarization of the bitter lesson of a decade of domestic turmoil." "Is it OK for the Party to act outside the scope of law? No! Absolutely not! This has already been proved by the decade of domestic turmoil and provided for in the Party Constitution and state

---

[30]Deng Xiaoping pointed out that: "Because democratic centralism was undermined, the Party was afflicted with bureaucratism resulting from, among other things, over-concentration of power. This kind of bureaucratism often masquerades as 'Party leadership', 'Party directives', 'Party interests' and 'Party discipline'" Deng Xiaoping, "Emancipate the Mind, Seek Truth from Facts and Unite as One in Looking to the Future", in Deng (1994). Deng Xiaoping also said that: "'Centralized Party leadership' often turns into leadership by individuals… Over-concentration of power in the hands of an individual or of a few people means that most functionaries have no decision-making power at all, while the few who do are overburdened. This inevitably leads to bureaucratism and various mistakes, and it inevitably impairs the democratic life, collective leadership, democratic centralism and division of labour with individual responsibility in the Party and government organizations at all levels." Deng (1994)

[31]Literature Research Office of the CPC Central Committee (1998, p. 84).

[32]Peng (1992, pp. 176–177).

Constitution."[33] We can draw the following conclusions from Peng Zhen's classic explanations of the relationship between the Party and the law: (1) "The law" here, whether as an abstract concept or as a concrete concept, is the embodiment of the authority and the will of the state and therefore must be obeyed by all organizations and individuals; (2) "The Party" here refers not to the abstract concept of "the Communist Party of China", but to such concrete persons and entities as "a Party leader" or "the Party committee at certain local level". We should not confuse an individual Party leader, a Party organization or a Party organ at certain level with the CPC; (3) everyone is equal before the state law. All leading Party cadres (even those in high positions) and Party organizations and Party organs at all levels must obey the state law and act within the scope of the Constitution and laws; (4) state law always has supremacy over leading Party cadres or Party organizations or Party organs at any level; (5) as far as leading Party cadres and Party organizations or Party organs are concerned, obeying the state law is obeying the leadership of CPC Central Committee, the decisions of the highest organ of state power and the will of the people in the whole country. The Party and the law, the Party's leadership and the state legal system are completely unified.

Former Party Secretary General Jiang Zemin has expressed his view on the relationship between the Party and the law on many different occasions. In an interview by a reporter of New York Times on September 26, 1989, he said that: "We should never replace the government or the law with the Party. This is a question of whether to practice the rule of man or the rule of law, which is often discussed in new media. I think we must follow the principle of the rule of law." In a working conference on Deng Xiaoping's Theory in 1998, he stressed that, in the process of constructing socialist democratic politics, China must correctly handle the relationships between the Party's leadership, the development of democracy, and acting by law: the Party's leadership is the key, the development of democracy is the basis, and acting by law is the guarantee. The three should never be separated from or antagonized against each other. He pointed out that adhering to the CPC's leadership is completely consistent with ruling the country by law. Both the propositions of the CPC and the laws of the state represent and embody the will and the interest of the people. The CPC leads the people to adopt Constitutions and laws through organs of state power, thereby transforming the Party's propositions into the will of the state. At the same time, the Party acts within the scope of the Constitution and laws, and governments at various levels administer public affairs in accordance with law, thereby unifying the Party's leadership and ruling the country by law.

Former Party Secretary General Hu Jintao also clearly pointed out that the key to developing socialist democracy is to organically unify adhering to the CPC's leadership, the people being masters of the country, and ruling the country by law. The CPC's leadership is the fundamental guarantee of people being masters of the country and ruling the country by law; people being the masters of the country is an essential requirement of socialist democracy; and ruling the country by law is the basic strategy by which the CPC leads the people in administering state affairs.

---

[33] Peng (1989, pp. 220–221).

Only by correctly understanding and handling the relationships between the three can China further mobilize the will and the strength of all Party members and Chinese people of all nationalities.

At the historical new starting point of advancing ruling the country by law and speeding up the construction of a socialist state under the rule of law after the Eighteenth Party Congress, Party Secretary General Xi Jinping attaches more importance to the correct handling of the relationship between the Party and the law at the overall strategic situation of the work of the Party and the state. In an important speech given at the working conference on political and legal affairs work of the CPC Central Committee in January 2014, Xi Jinping demanded that political-legal organs "adhere to the supremacy of the Party's undertakings, the supremacy of the people's interest, and the supremacy of the Constitution and laws, and correctly handle the relationship between Party policies and state laws. The CPC's policies and state laws are consistent with each other in essence because they both embody the fundamental will of the people. The Party leads the people in adopting the Constitution and laws and it leads the people in implementing the Constitution and laws." In October 2014, Xi Jinping further pointed out in the Explanation of the Decision of the Fourth Plenary Session of the Eighteenth CPC Central Committee that the relationship between the Party and the rule of law is a core question in the construction of the rule of law in China. The organic unity of the CPC's leadership, the people being masters of the country, and ruling the country by law is one of the basic experiences of construction of socialist rule of law in China. The key to ensuring the success of the advancement of ruling the country by law is to adhere to the correct orientation and to provide strong political guarantee—more specially, to adhere to the Party's leadership and to the system of socialism with Chinese characteristics, and to implement the theory of socialist rule of law with Chinese characteristics. In February 2015, he once again stressed in the opening ceremony of a training course for provincial-level leading cadres that adhering to the CPC's leadership is the most important characteristic of the road of socialist rule of law with Chinese characteristics and the most fundamental guarantee for the construction of the system of socialist rule of law with Chinese characteristics. Therefore, the key to the advancement of ruling the country by law is the correct orientation and strong political guarantee. The socialist rule of law can be implemented only if it adheres to the leadership of the CPC and the leadership of the CPC can be adhered to only if it relies on the socialist rule of law. The law is the unified embodiment of the propositions of the CPC and the will of the people. The Party leads the people in adopting the Constitution and laws and it leads the people in implementing the Constitution and laws. The Party itself must act within the scope of the Constitution and laws. China should implement the Party's leadership in the whole process and all aspects of ruling the country by law. Firstly, the Party must lead the legislation and, in light of the overall situation of the Party and the state and in accordance with the will of the people, adopt good laws that conform to the Party's proposition, respect the will of the people, and satisfy their practical needs. Secondly, the Party should ensure the enforcement of law, construct a law-based government that has scientific functions and legally prescribed powers and responsibilities, strictly enforces the law, abides by the law, and is open, just, clean, honest and effective. And it should adhere to the principle of doing what it is required by law to do and refraining from doing what it is not authorized by law to do. Thirdly, the Party should support administration of justice, provide solid safeguard for the independent and fair performance of functions by judicial organs, improve the institutional mechanism for supervising and restraining judicial activities, and ensure that judicial power operate in a standardized way within the cage of institutions. Fourth, the CPC should take the lead in observing the law. Every leading cadre must obey and abide by the Constitution and laws, and may not take the CPC's leadership as the excuse for engaging in such practices as substituting the law with personal views, suppressing law with power, and bending the law for personal gains, but should play an exemplary role in respecting, studying, abiding by and applying the law.

In conclusion, from the perspective of the theory of socialist rule of law with Chinese characteristics, the CPC has since its Sixteenth National Congress always put the emphasis of the road of socialist rule of law with Chinese characteristics on the organic unity of adhering the Party's leadership, the people being masters of the country and ruling the country by law, applied this political philosophy to understand and grasp the relationship of high-degree unity between the Party and the law, and maintained that the Party's leadership is the basic guarantee of ruling the country by law whereas ruling the country by law is the basic strategy by which the Party leads the people to administer state affairs and the basic mode by which the Party rules the country. In the practice of constructing the socialist rule of law with Chinese characteristics, the relationship between the Party and the law has undergone a process of long-term exploration, a process of continuous transformation and development from one dominance by polices to one dominance by law, from one characterized by the rule of man to one characterized by the legal system, and to characterized by the rule of law, and an process in which the Party and the law, politics and the rule of law, and the Party's leadership and ruling the country by law complement each other and integrate with each other to realize high-degree unity. In the process of developing socialist rule of law with Chinese characteristics, with the continuous implementation and comprehensive advancement of the basic strategy of ruling the country by law, the so-called "question" of "whether the Party is higher than the law or the law is higher than the Party" has become a historical concept of the past and the high-degree unity of the Party and the law is increasingly becoming a consensus among all Party members and all the people of the country, as well as a basic characteristic and political advantage of socialist rule of law with Chinese characteristics.

References

Abraham HJ (1990) Justices and presidents: a political history of appointments to the Supreme Court. Chinese edition (trans: Liu T). The Commercial Press, Beijing
Deng X (1994) Selected works of Deng Xiaoping, vol 1. People's Publishing House, Beijing

de Tocqueville A (1988) De la démocratie en Amérique, Part One. Chinese edition (trans: Dong G). The Commercial Press, Beijing

Document Editing Commission of the CPC Central Committee (1985) Selected works of Liu Shaoqi, Part II. People's Publishing House, Beijing

Document Editing Commission of the CPC Central Committee (1991) Selected works of Peng Zhen. People's Publishing House, Beijing

Hu W (1994) Judicial politics. Joint Publishing (H.K.), Hong Kong

Jiang J (2002) Jiang Zemin on socialism with Chinese characteristics (excerpts). Central Party Literature Press, Beijing

Kaufmann A, Hassemer W (eds) (2002) Einfithrung in Rechtsphilosophie und Rechtstheorie der Gegenwart. Chinese edition (trans: Zheng Y). Law Press China, Beijing

Lenin VI (1990) Complete works of Lenin, vol 28, Chinese edition. People's Publishing House, Beijing

Literature Research Office of the CPC Central Committee (1998) A chronicle of Deng Xiaoping's thought. Central Party Literature Press, Beijing

Marx C, Engels F (1956) Complete works of Marx and Engels, Chinese edition, vol. 1. People's Publishing House, Beijing

Nonet P, Selznick P (1994) Law and society in transition: toward responsive law. Chinese edition (trans: Zhang Z et al). China University of Political Science and Law Press, Beijing

Peng Z (1989) On the construction of socialist democracy and legal system in the new period of time. Central Party Literature Press, Beijing

Peng Z (1992) On the political and legal work in the new period of time. Central Party Literature Press, Beijing

Rüthers B (2003) Rechtstheorie. Chinese edition (trans: Ding X et al). Law Press China, Beijing

Vile MJC (1981) Politics in the USA. Chinese edition (trans: Wang H et al). The Commercial Press, Beijing

Walker DM (ed) (1989) Oxford companion to law. Chinese edition (trans: Deng Z et al). Guangming Daily Press, Beijing

Wilson W (1986) Congressional government. Chinese edition (trans: Xiong X, Lu D). The Commercial Press, Beijing

Woll P (1992) Behind the scenes in American Government: personalities and politics. Chinese edition (trans: Li H et al). Social Sciences Academic Press, Beijing

Writing Group for Biography of Peng Zhen (2012) A biography of Peng Zhen, vol 4. Central Party Literature Press, Beijing

Zhuo Z (2005) Politics of law. Law Press China, Beijing

Zhuo Z (2006) On the value of law. Law Press China, Beijing

Printed by Printforce, the Netherlands